THE *EXAGOGE* OF EZEKIEL

The *Exagoge* of Ezekiel

HOWARD JACOBSON
Professor of the Classics
University of Illinois, Urbana

CAMBRIDGE UNIVERSITY PRESS
CAMBRIDGE
LONDON   NEW YORK   NEW ROCHELLE
MELBOURNE   SYDNEY

CAMBRIDGE UNIVERSITY PRESS
Cambridge, New York, Melbourne, Madrid, Cape Town, Singapore,
São Paulo, Delhi, Dubai, Tokyo

Cambridge University Press
The Edinburgh Building, Cambridge CB2 8RU, UK

Published in the United States of America by Cambridge University Press, New York

www.cambridge.org
Information on this title: www.cambridge.org/9780521122436

© Cambridge University Press 1983

First published 1983
This digitally printed version 2009

A catalogue record for this publication is available from the British Library

Library of Congress Catalogue Card Number: 82–4410

ISBN 978-0-521-24580-7 Hardback
ISBN 978-0-521-12243-6 Paperback

CONTENTS

To the memory of my father, אבא מת: אב בתורה אב בחכמה :זצ״ל

     and

For my wife Elaine: אין ברכה מצויה בתוך ביתו של אדם אלא בשביל אשתו

PREFACE

In studying a work like the *Exagoge*, so important yet so little understood, my goal has been not merely to illuminate the poem within its literary, historical and cultural contexts but also to open a path for others who will elucidate where I have not been able and will correct me where I have gone wrong. What Paul Friedländer said in another context seems to me applicable here: 'There may be a danger of hearing the grass grow, and I am not quite sure whether this danger has been avoided throughout. But the danger of seeing too little is much greater.'

Economic considerations prevent me from reprinting here several of my studies on the *Exagoge* which complement the present volume. They are referred to at the appropriate places.

I have the happy duty of expressing my gratitude to many scholars. An early version of this book was read by Professors William M. Calder III and Shaye J. D. Cohen, both of whom offered helpful comments and criticisms. Professor G. M. Browne read several sections to my benefit and Professors David Sansone and John Vaio helpfully discussed with me some difficult points. Professor Gene Gragg kindly answered two questions on Ethiopic texts. I am also indebted to Professor Arnaldo Momigliano who discussed with me a number of pertinent problems and throughout encouraged me in my work.

Many other friends and colleagues took an active interest in my work and in particular often loaned me books and journals from their personal libraries, for which I am very grateful. I am also indebted to several scholars who read the typescript anonymously and gave helpful advice.

I am grateful to the Research Board of the University of Illinois for providing a publication subvention.

My father died shortly before the Cambridge University Press accepted this book for publication and it is to his memory that I dedicate it:

מתלמידיו של אברהם אבינו: עין טובה ורוח נמוכה ונפש שפלה.

Illinois, 1981   H. J.

INTRODUCTION

1. The *Exagoge*

Ezekiel the tragedian is a writer of major importance. The fragments of his *Exagoge* represent the most extensive remains of any Hellenistic tragedy – or indeed tragedian. Consequently, Ezekiel is our most significant source of evidence for Hellenistic tragedy, though it is not possible to determine whether the *Exagoge* is representative of Hellenistic tragedy or in what particular ways it may be.[1] Further, for the student of Jewish literary history and thought Ezekiel is one of our most important sources for the Hellenistic period in the diaspora and may even be of importance for students of the New Testament and early Christianity. The *Exagoge* is the solitary surviving example of Jewish drama in Greek and the largest extant example of ancient Greco-Jewish poetry. Yet, Ezekiel has never been given his due by scholars of Judaism and early Christianity and even less by Classicists. 'Comprehensive' works often skim over or completely ignore Ezekiel. Thus, for instance, both the first edition of A. Körte's fundamental *Die Hellenistische Dichtung* (Leipzig 1925) and its revision by P. Händel (Stuttgart 1960) fail to mention Ezekiel. A. E. Haigh's *The Tragic Drama of the Greeks* (Oxford 1925) lists the Greek tragic poets, including tragedians not from Greece (pp. 463–72), but ignores Ezekiel. P. Wendland, in his famous study *Die hellenistisch-römische Kultur in ihren Beziehungen zur Judentum und Christentum* (Tübingen 1912[3]) does not, as far as I can tell, ever mention Ezekiel by name (cf. p. 197). In his monumental study *Die griechischen Tragödien* (Bonn 1841) F. G. Welcker allotted two and one half lines to Ezekiel (p. 1270). Perhaps most grievous, in his great collection of Greek tragic fragments August Nauck excluded Ezekiel, on the grounds that the contemporary state of scholarship on the manuscripts of Eusebius' *Praeparatio Evangelica* did not allow for a satisfactory edition.[2] True as this was, serviceable editions of the *Exagoge* had already been prepared by several scholars (e.g. Dübner and Philippson). It was undoubtedly the absence of Ezekiel from Nauck's *TGF* which kept him in obscurity for so long. Schramm's exclusion of Ezekiel from his collection of Hellenistic tragic fragments scarcely helped the matter.[3] For some years now the interested reader has had to have recourse to Wieneke's edition,[4] a fine piece of work but little known and not readily accessible. Only in the last decade has Nauck's omission been redressed with Snell's publication of the fragments of the *Exagoge* in his *Tragicorum Graecorum Fragmenta*.[5] Students of the Greek theatre and of Greek literature will no longer have an excuse for ignoring – or being ignorant of – the *Exagoge*. Similarly, the publication of these fragments in A. M. Denis' recent *Fragmenta Pseudepigraphorum Quae Supersunt Graeca* (Leiden 1970; pp. 207-16) should reawaken scholars of Judaica and early Christianity to the importance of Ezekiel.

The tendency to ignore Ezekiel was till recently matched by (and perhaps caused by) the outright scorn with which he was treated by those scholars who deigned to mention him. Often the intensity of the hostility is hard to imagine and understand: 'Alexandria produced many bad poets. Among the worst is Ezekiel.'[6] But perhaps no one has gone as far as J. L. Klein[7] who believes that the only virtue of the *Exagoge* is that it was the starting point for the Christian mystery plays.

Till recently, Schumann's estimate was virtually unique:[8] the play 'ob versuum elegantiam nos delectavit.' Dübner had limited praise: 'Arte loquitur aliquoties felici, nec spiritus poetici prorsus expertem dixerim' (p. vii). Of late, Ezekiel has been winning admirers. Snell's appreciation of his acquaintance with fifth-century tragedy and his modest ability to work securely within its stylistic framework is a reasoned and restrained position.[9] Some have waxed enthusiastic. 'From a literary point of view, the great achievement of the Greco-Jewish writers was in the field of poetry and drama ... Hellenistic Jewish literature attained its zenith in the drama *Exagoge*;' Ezekiel's 'great drama called ''The Exodus''.'[10] Others have not hesitated to praise him.[11] It is clear that scholars are now ready for a balanced treatment and evaluation of Ezekiel and his work.

Snell has published two essays on the *Exagoge* in addition to his text of the fragments.[12] All this is valuable, but only marks a beginning. In particular, Snell fails to place Ezekiel adequately within his Jewish context. Though he comments on the 'Jewish' aspects of

the play in a rather broad and sweeping fashion, he never deals with
the Jewish details that play so important a role both within the play
and as background to it. More recently Peter Fraser, in his *Ptolemaic
Alexandria*,[13] has devoted several pages to the *Exagoge* but – as
inevitably happens in monumental works that strive to embrace an
entire civilization – he has occasionally been compelled to read and
judge cursorily. Thus, his treatment of Ezekiel is occasionally marred
by neglect of important secondary sources (as is also the case with
Snell) and by some misunderstanding – or misreading - of the text.
The most useful discussion of the *Exagoge* – inadequate as it is – remains that of Yehoshua Gutman in his *The Beginnings of Jewish-
Hellenistic Literature*,[14] a rather large book written in Hebrew which,
to my knowledge, has never been mentioned in *L'Année Philologique*
and is unknown to Snell, Fraser and virtually all those European
scholars who have written on Ezekiel.[15] Gutman was familiar with
both Greek and Jewish sources and his discussion is the only well-
balanced treatment of Ezekiel. Unfortunately, Gutman was often
ignorant of the work of his predecessors and his judgement is frequently not sound.

Nonetheless, I do wish to give Gutman's book the prominence that
it deserves and especially to emphasize that any attempt at discussing
Ezekiel which fails to consider his roots in both the Jewish and Greek
traditions cannot come to terms with the nature of his work nor with
the complex problems it poses for us. Ezekiel must be understood in
the broad context of what being both Jewish and Alexandrian[16]
would have meant, which entails *inter alia* those Jewish and Greek
elements that were intrinsically a part of his culture, a culture infused
with the sense of Jewish-Biblical history and law and their elaborations, both legal and exegetical.

Aeschylus' *Persae* is the only extant 'historical' tragedy of the fifth
century, though it is not the sole example known to us. The genre
was perhaps more in favor in the fourth century and Hellenistic
period;[17] Moschion, Philicus, Lycophron and probably others wrote
such plays.[18] The problems of definition and categorization are difficult. A Hellenistic play on Themistocles would scarcely have the
same impact on its audience as a play on the fall of Miletus or the
battle of Salamis on an early fifth-century audience. Are we justified

in putting them all into one category? Further, how sharply would the Greeks themselves have distinguished between the 'historical' and the 'mythological', between the wars of the fifth century between Greeks and non-Greeks and the wars of the Trojan era between Greeks and non-Greeks? Are we justified in thinking that the Jews of Alexandria, seeing on stage the events of the Exodus of centuries before, would have responded and reacted to them in a substantially and qualitatively different manner from that of fifth-century Greeks viewing episodes about Greek heroes and peoples from eras gone by? Perhaps we are, but it is probably not so clear-cut an issue as it may *prima facie* seem. At all events, the *Exagoge* is a non-Greek national play. We may well have Hellenistic parallels. Dymas of Iasos, a tragedian of probably the early second century B.C., wrote a play about Dardanus.[19] The Gyges papyrus may also come from a non-Greek nationalistic play.[20] What sort of tragedies the first-century B.C. Armenian king Artavasdes wrote we can only conjecture (Plutarch, *Crassus* 33). The *Exagoge* is a drama about the Jewish people and as such it does not have a 'tragic hero' in the familiar sense.

As for plays on Biblical – or at least Jewish – subjects the only other possible example from antiquity seems to be a play about Susanna by Nicolaus of Damascus. The only evidence is Eustathius' comment *ad* verse 984 of Dionysius Periegetes:[21] ὁ γράψας τὸ δρᾶμα τῆς Σωσάννης, οἶμαι ὁ Δαμασκηνός. Since Nicolaus' Jewish connections and interests were many and he did write (at least according to the Suda s.v.) tragedies and comedies, it is generally believed that this is a reference to him. But this is by no means certain and some scholars dissent, including Jacoby *ad FGrHist* 90 F132 (p. 290) who thinks *Damaskenos* surely not Nicolaus and perhaps John of Damascus.[22] In this connection the existence of a 'Christian Ezekiel' seems not to have been noticed. When in the fourth century Julian prohibited the use of pagan classics by the Christians, the Bishop Apollinarius proceeded to write epic in the fashion of Homer, comedy in the fashion of Menander, tragedy in the fashion of Euripides, lyric in the fashion of Pindar, all on subjects of Biblical history.[23] Finally, I note what seems to me the most striking overall parallel to Ezekiel's *Exagoge* (though not a drama), the Persian poem called *The Moses Book* by the fourteenth-century Jew Shahin. This is an epic poem on Moses in the tradition of classical Persian poetry, making use of both Biblical and post-Biblical traditions about Moses and his life.[24]

2. The date of the *Exagoge*

We know very little about Ezekiel. In referring to him Alexander Polyhistor and Clemens respectively call him ὁ τῶν τραγῳδιῶν ποιητής (*PE* 9.436d) and ὁ τῶν Ἰουδαικῶν τραγῳδιῶν ποιητής (*Strom.* 1.23.155). Aside from the fragments of the *Exagoge* there survive no remnants from nor allusions to other tragedies by Ezekiel, but the access that Polyhistor had to libraries justifies our willingness to trust his testimony.[1] And if Clemens' added adjective is more than guesswork and inference on his part we may perhaps suppose that Ezekiel's other plays also treated 'Jewish' topics.[2] A few scholars once believed him Christian,[3] but his *terminus ante quem* makes this impossible. If there were some pressing reason we might imagine a pagan writing drama on Jewish subject matter; but there is none. His name Ezekiel (יחזקאל) guarantees his Jewishness.[4] Delitzsch raised a serious question that is hardly ever noticed. Eusebius sets forth his programme for *PE* book nine clearly and explicitly (403c–d): his purpose now is to show that famous Greeks themselves (i.e. pagans) were familiar with Jewish matters and testified to the truth of Jewish history. Delitzsch reasonably argued that this means that the writers quoted in book nine like Philo epicus, Theodotus, etc., who are routinely assumed to be Jews, were in fact pagans.[5] As for Ezekiel, since his name is clearly Jewish, Delitzsch thought he might have been a proselyte and consequently Eusebius was confused. But Delitzsch has misunderstood Eusebius' purpose. The latter is not using Philo epicus, Artapanus, Demetrius or Ezekiel as evidence, but rather is showing that the famous pagan historian, Polyhistor, testifies to the validity of Jewish history and traditions. As it turns out, Polyhistor does so by himself using Jewish sources (as well as non-Jewish ones). Conversely Eusebius cites Josephus in *PE* 9 for the pagan sources the latter quotes! In sum, then, Eusebius' programme does not argue against Ezekiel's being Jewish.

When did Ezekiel live?[6] Several scholars argued that Ezekiel is later than Josephus.[7] The essential – or rather single – argument is that Josephus would have mentioned him had he already lived. Philippson's

refutation (though he was not the first to notice the essential fact)
should have deterred anyone from returning to this view: Polyhistor,
over a century earlier than Josephus, quotes extensively from
Ezekiel.[8] Nonetheless, Magnin revived the old theory by arguing
futilely that Eusebius was citing Ezekiel first hand.[9] This too was
thoroughly refuted.[10]

Caution should be exercised, but Denniston goes too far when he
can say of Ezekiel only 'date unknown.'[11] We do have *termini*. At
one end stands the Septuagint which he used extensively, at the other
Polyhistor who knows the *Exagoge*. The latter seems to have been
born around 100 or 110 B.C. and to have been active in Rome till the
forties or thirties.[12] It is therefore *prima facie* possible that Ezekiel
may have been writing in the middle of the first century and that
Polyhistor was citing the work of a contemporary, as he did in the
case of Apollonius Molon. Indeed, a few early scholars did date
Ezekiel to c. 40 B.C.[13] As will become clear, I think this rather
unlikely.

Within this range of some two centuries virtually every possibility
has been suggested. I offer here a brief spectrum.

(1) Ezekiel was one of the translators of the Septuagint;[14] (2) he
wrote in the third century;[15] (3) middle or late third century;[16] (4)
end of the third century;[17] (5) third or second century;[18] (6) second
century;[19] (7) c. 200;[20] (8) c. 150;[21] (9) middle or end of second
century;[22] (10) before the first century;[23] (11) after 217;[24] (12) c.
100;[25] (13) not later than the second century;[26] (14) first century;[27]
(15) c. 90;[28] (16) 87;[29] (17) c. 40;[30] (18) between 200 and the mid-
first century;[31] (19) before the Christian era.[32]

Amidst this plethora of hypotheses, what can we discern of argumentation? Surprisingly little. Many scholars, one suspects, have
been guided by intuition. Most of the hypotheses are brief unsup-
ported statements. The trend seems to have been set by A. Possevinus
(= Possevino) who was, to my knowledge, the first to attempt to date
Ezekiel: 'qui anno ab c.v. 667 vixit,' i.e. 87 B.C., with no further
comment.[33]

The theory that Ezekiel was one of the translators of Scripture
into Greek rests totally on the occurrence of the name Ezekiel in
Aristeas' list of the 72 translators, and is quite unlikely. First, we
have no guarantee as to the genuineness and reliability of the list.

Second, it would make Ezekiel Palestinian which, as we shall see in the next chapter, is not likely. Finally, as Magnin notes,[34] a member of this special group probably would not have committed the 'sacrilege' of putting Scripture on the stage, especially when *Aristeas* itself, it seems, describes such a venture as sacrilege (316).

Those who believe that Ezekiel wrote in the mid- or late third century rely on the argument of Kuiper (*Mnemosyne* 274f) who observed that, according to Tacitus *Ann.* 6.28, the Phoenix appeared in Egypt in the reign of Ptolemy III (Euergetes, 246–222). He hypothesized that this appearance was the very cause for Ezekiel's introduction of the (non-Biblical) episode of the Phoenix. Consequently, Ezekiel would have written the *Exagoge* either in or shortly after the reign of Euergetes. Fraser has added one further argument to support the mid- or late third century date, that Ezekiel's familiarity with the classical tragedians is most natural in this period.[35] While neither argument can be rejected, neither is cogent. Ezekiel could readily have known Phoenix-traditions from Egyptian, Greek or Jewish circles at other times in our two-century span.[36] As for his familiarity with the classical Greek tragedians, the fact is that by the middle and late third century tragedy in Alexandria had already passed its peak, and though we can feel certain that Ezekiel would have seen dramas of the old playwrights performed, it is highly probable that he gained much of his familiarity from reading and for this the second or first centuries are no less likely than the third.

Huet's view that Ezekiel is earlier than Demetrius is based on the erroneous belief that some of the fragments of the *Exagoge* in Eusebius are cited via Demetrius.[37]

Trencsényi-Waldapfel's opinion (161f) that the date is c. 90 is based on a tissue of unlikely hypotheses: that Ezekiel is the Theodectes of *Aristeas*,[38] that *Aristeas* is engaged in polemic with Ezekiel, that the date of *Aristeas* can be fairly well fixed, and that Polyhistor probably knew the work of Ezekiel before his arrival in Rome.

A few other arguments have been made. Dalbert (55) noted that Ezekiel is cited in the company of Demetrius, Eupolemus and Artapanus and thus may be their contemporary.[39] Philippson (11) argued that Ezekiel would not be before c. 200 since it would have taken approximately a century for the Septuagint to have become sufficiently influential for Ezekiel to take it as his source.[40] This is not unreasonable but certainly not necessary. Finally, we have Müller's interesting argument that the battle formation described in the *Exagoge* involves strategy not utilized till 217 and therefore provides a *terminus post quem*.[41]

To my knowledge this brief survey exhausts all the arguments and evidence that have been adduced for dating Ezekiel. Unfortunately, there is not a significantly cogent argument among the lot. I am here concerned to suggest that there are several facets of the play that may be relevant to the problem of dating and should at least be noticed. Some may be deemed insignificant or irrelevant, others as pertinent, but perhaps in ways different from those I remark.

The *Exagoge* was written for non-Jews as well as Jews. Further, the very nature of the play's theme as well as some details indicates that the non-Jews expected and intended as audience were Greeks, not native Egyptians.[42] There may even be attempts to 'identify' the Jews with the Greeks as opposed to the Egyptians. Further, there is evidence of polemic engaged in by Jews and Egyptians to gain favor with the Greeks. On the other hand, there is nothing in the fragments to suggest hostility toward Greeks or any other pagans aside from the Egyptians or toward paganism in general.[43] This suggests a variety of things, but essentially that (1) relations between Jews and Greeks were probably fairly good; (2) relations between Greeks and Egyptians were probably not so good; (3) Jews were evidently sufficiently influential in Egypt to find themselves in this situation of conflict; (4) there was probably some deterioration taking place – or at least foreseen – in the Jews' situation vis-à-vis the Greeks, such as to motivate Ezekiel's engaging in this kind of propaganda/public relations endeavor. If this be reasonable, some broad conclusions might be drawn. The first century would seem too late for the *Exagoge*. The Jewish position vis-à-vis the Greeks had greatly deteriorated while the bonds between the Greeks and the natives had grown tighter. Anti-semitism among the Greeks was evident. A book like *3 Maccabees* suits the first century. The third century might well seem too early. It was not till the end of that century that the Jewish community in Alexandria began to flourish and so it is less likely that there was much competition then between Jews and Egyptians for the favor of the Greeks.[44] Moreover, there is no evidence that Alexandrian Jews of the third century were yet significantly involved in adopting and imitating the literary forms of the Greeks.

Let us turn to another, but complementary, aspect of the play. I remark in advance the danger of arguing *ex silentio* when dealing with a fragmentary work like the *Exagoge.* It is interesting that Ezekiel never mentions the land of Israel (Judaea). It is not as if our extant fragments do not allow for the possibility. Ezekiel twice speaks of the future destination: ἄλλην χθόνα (154), ἴδιον χῶρον (167), with no mention of Israel. It is also curious and perhaps noteworthy that instead of speaking, as the Bible does, of the land which God has promised to the Jews, he speaks of it as the land to which God promised to bring them (154). Whereas the Bible constantly describes the promised land in glorious and laudatory terms, Ezekiel has nothing of the sort. Indeed, his emphasis is not so much on coming to the promised land as on the escape from the place of persecution. When Ezekiel tells of Jacob's descent from Palestine to Egypt, he speaks of γῆν Χαναναίαν (1). This name would undoubtedly have meant nothing to the Greeks in the audience. It is true that such a designation was historically accurate since in Jacob's time it was Canaan, but Ezekiel could have readily called it Israel (Judaea). If he did not do so, it is probably because he did not want his Greek audience to understand. What then could have motivated him to eliminate from his version of the Exodus all references to the land of Israel? I would guess because Judaea was at the time of his writing not under Ptolemaic rule. Had Palestine been part of the Ptolemaic Egyptian empire, I can see no reason why he would have avoided mentioning it. If true, this suggests that the play was not written before 200, a period in which Judaea was under the Ptolemies. Two other subsidiary facts also support the theory that Ezekiel was deliberately shunning all mention of Israel. The first is the total absence of Jerusalem and the Temple, the spiritual centers of Judaism.[45] Here too he could have incorporated references had he desired. In the instructions on the Passover, he gives explicit directions about the procedures the Jews will follow when they reach their land (167ff).[46] *Exodus* itself speaks of bringing the first fruits to the house of God (23.19). Second, throughout the play Ezekiel calls the Jews only Ἑβραῖοι. In the Hellenistic period the most common 'Greek' designation of the Jews was Ἰουδαῖοι. Ἰσραηλ is less frequent and ʽΕβραῖοι probably least used. In the chapters of *Exodus* which served as Ezekiel's source for the play ⟨υἱοὶ⟩ Ἰσραηλ is routinely used for the Jews, while ʽΕβραῖοι occurs a few times. It is conceivable that Ezekiel felt ʽΕβραῖοι had a more solemn tone or was particularly appropriate to the Jews of ancient times (cf. Jos. *AJ* 1.146).[47] But there may be another reason. If Ezekiel is deliberately avoiding allusions to the land of Israel, then he would not want to use Ἰουδαῖοι of the Jews, for Ἰουδαῖοι is the 'national-geographical' designation of the Jews, the people of Judaea.[48]

Thus, both the position of the Jews in Alexandria vis-à-vis Greeks and natives that can be inferred from the play and Ezekiel's desire to avoid mentioning the land of Israel suggest that the *Exagoge* was written between 200 and c. 100. Can we delimit this further? An obvious breaking point would be the Maccabean revolt. Does this play date from the period of Judaea's subjugation to the Seleucids or to the era of independence? That Ezekiel abstains from mentioning the land of Israel would probably suit either. To speak of the happy escape of the Jews from Egypt and Egyptian rule to the land of Israel when the latter had recently been wrenched from Egyptian (Ptolemaic) rule and passed to that of their arch-rivals would scarcely have been diplomatic. As Bickerman writes, 'the fact that Jerusalem, the spiritual center of the diaspora, belonged to one of the rival powers cast suspicion on the loyalty of the Jews under the dominion of the other.'[49]

Unfortunately, detailed information about the vicissitudes of Jewish life in second-century Alexandria is lacking. But there seems to be nothing that would argue against the *Exagoge* coming out of the first four decades of the century.

What then of the following half-century or so, with the struggle and attainment of independence for Judaea? If Ezekiel wrote in this period one can also understand his reluctance to mention Judaea. The Maccabean wars were characterized by intense antipathy to the Greeks which culminated in hostilities against Greek cities of Palestine. This in turn stimulated feelings of hostility in Greeks throughout the world toward Jews. Sympathetic allusions to Judaea at such a time would not have produced feelings of good will in the Greeks of Alexandria. As for the internal status of the Jews in Alexandria, there are a few potentially relevant facts. It was during the reign of

Philometor that Jewish population, accomplishments and influence grew by leaps and bounds (181–145). At the same time there was increased intercourse between Greeks and native Egyptians. Finally, in these years anti-Hellenism among Palestinian Jews was manifesting itself. These three factors may have contributed to the beginnings of a rift between Jews and Greeks in Alexandria, or at least to fear on the part of the Jews that such might be imminent. There may have been an increased attempt on the part of the natives to gain favor for themselves and stir hostility against the Jews by spreading anti-semitic propaganda that revolved around the Exodus.[50] The indisputably polemical explanation Ezekiel gives of the 'payment' the Jews took out of Egypt occurs in one other early text, *Jubilees*, which may well date from this very period. In sum, while all this does not mean that the *Exagoge* must have been or even probably was written during the second half of the second century, it does suggest that it may well have been.[51]

I conclude with a few small points that may add support to the second century dating. In general, this was a century of widespread and significant writing in Greek by the Jews. It is generally held that the following works were all written during this century: Sirach (translation into Greek), the Septuagint *Daniel*, the Greek additions to *Esther*, the Jewish Sibyl, Jason of Cyrene, Eupolemus, Artapanus. Other possibilities are *Aristeas*, *Joseph and Asenath*,[52] *Wisdom* and pseudo-Phocylides.

The Egyptian messenger refers to God as ὕψιστος (239). One should not build much upon this,[53] especially since it might be an ethopoeic touch in the mouth of the non-Jew. Yet, the Septuagint here gives φύγωμεν ἀπὸ προσώπου Ἰσραηλ· ὁ γὰρ κύριος πολεμεῖ περὶ αὐτῶν. So ὕψιστος could well refer here to the 'God of Israel.' Thus, we should note that it is during the second century that the Jewish use of ὕψιστος for God seems to have burgeoned and been most popular.[54]

A word about the Phoenix. Broek has shown that extant references to the Phoenix in the pre-Christian period are very few and most of them extremely brief.[55] He calculates that in the first century A.D. there are more than twice as many references to the Phoenix as in the preceding eight centuries together. Of the several pre-Christian references to the Phoenix, three belong to the first

century. Further, of all these references only two are in any way
detailed and extensive, Ezekiel's and Manilius'. The latter was writing at the very beginning of the first century B.C. Furthermore,
Manilius (Pliny, *NH* 10.4–5) may be the first extant source explicitly
to connect the Phoenix to the *magnus annus* and to tie its appearance
to great historical events. I shall argue that the latter and possibly the
former features are present in the *Exagoge*. In short, this may indicate that at the beginning of the first century B.C. there was a
heightened interest in the Phoenix and his symbolic value for momen-
tous events. A date for Ezekiel in the late second century might fit
this trend.[56]

Ezekiel's description of Raguel is interesting and I believe without
parallel.[57] He is ruler of the country (ἄρχων, τύραννος, ἄρχει, κρίνει),
military leader (στρατηλάτης) and also priest. In addition, he can
foretell the future (85ff, interpretation of Moses' dream). This con-
glomeration of offices and abilities may make us recall Philo's description of Moses (see especially *Moses* 2.3f, 187, 251f). The notion
of priest-ruler seems to become popular in Jewish circles in the
second half of the second century when the Maccabean leaders take
on this role. Furthermore, the addition of prophetic ability to the
role of priest-ruler was evidently made in the case of John Hyrcanus.[58]
But we should not press this too far since the concept of priest-ruler
existed in ancient Egyptian and Mesopotamian cultures and could
be argued for the state of Judaea in the Persian period.

Is it possible to infer anything about the date of the play from the
style and language? Unfortunately, I think, very little that would
help us delimit the *termini* beyond their obvious range. Stylistically,
the play has two layers. First, there is the 'archaizing' element, that
is, much of the language and idiom of the play is frankly imitative of
classical Greek poetry. Second, there is a general stylistic level which
may simply be called 'post-classical,' 'Hellenistic' or 'late,' but which
cannot be temporally fixed within a short span of time like a decade
or even a century.[59] In this category one may note the diminished
frequency of the optative (twice in 269 lines), the increased use of
the perfect at the expense of the aorist, ὥστε + infinitive denot-
ing purpose, etc. Two additional items are of interest. The verb
ἐπιγεννάω, not that unusual in later Greek (see Lampe s.v.), seems
to occur for the first times in Ezekiel (*Exag.* 3) and two first-century

B.C. texts (see LSJ s.v.). This may support a date for Ezekiel closer to the first century B.C. The phrase ἐν χειρῶν νομαῖς occurs but twice in Greek, at *Exag.* 42 and in a second-century B.C. inscription (*Syll.*³ 700.29).

To sum up, there are quite a few considerations that point to a second century date for Ezekiel, and some to a date in the latter part of the century.

3. The provenance of the *Exagoge*

Where did Ezekiel live and write? There is no external evidence. Nearly all scholars believe Alexandria was his home.[1] As with a work like *Joseph and Asenath*, the general scholarly attitude amounts to, 'Where else could such a work have been written?' As Fraser puts it,[2] 'There is a certain general probability that a purely dramatic work . . . is most likely . . . in a major literary centre . . . Alexandria is (in spite of the limited activity there in the dramatic field) the most likely.'[3] It is reasonable to ask whether any other city in the Hellenistic world would really have suited a Greek *play* on a *Jewish* subject. Further support for Egyptian provenance may be found in those elements of the play that suggest hostility between Jews and native Egyptians.[4] Very few scholars have dissented,[5] but their views must be noted.

The impetus for seeking places other than Alexandria has come primarily from two arguments which (their proponents believe) indicate that Ezekiel could not have written in Egypt. Thus, Kuiper has argued that Ezekiel's setting of Arabian Midian in Libya is an error that would have been impossible for someone living in Egypt. We discuss this later[6] and observe that (1) there is no reason for assuming any geographical expertise on Ezekiel's part (as Wieneke 125 well pointed out), and (2) there are complicating factors which could have led Ezekiel into such an error. Consequently, Kuiper's argument has little cogency. The other argument against Egypt has been raised by Magnin and Gutman. Magnin (200) argued simply that a play on the Exodus could not have been presented in Egypt, since its contents would not have pleased the inhabitants, while Gutman (66) cannot imagine a representation of the plagues and the drowning of the king in Egypt, especially since the Ptolemies tried to identify themselves with the Pharaohs.[7] But these arguments are not forceful. The pagans to whom Ezekiel was addressing the play were not the natives, but rather the Greeks who would have felt no emotional attachment to the dying Egyptians of remote antiquity.[8] Philo too did not avoid describing (in the *Vita Mosis*) the plagues and the drowning to his non-Jewish audience. Gutman's observation on the identification of the Ptolemies with the Pharaohs misses the point. It was the native Egyptians who made this identification which the Ptolemies were, of course, happy to exploit. The Greeks did not concur in such an identification nor did the Ptolemies expect them to. Consequently, the worship and honors paid to the Ptolemies by the Egyptians were quite distinct from those rendered by the Greeks.[9] There is no reason to believe that the Greeks would have identified Ezekiel's Βασιλεὺς Φαραώ with the Ptolemaic ruler. That the Ptolemies themselves were not scrupulously devoted to this identification may perhaps be seen in the vigorous persistence of the tradition that a Ptolemy was patron of the Greek Pentateuch, a major emphasis of which is the Exodus and the punishment of the Egyptians. Thus, a play on the Exodus would not have offended the Greeks who were in the audience.

What alternatives have been offered? Kuiper argued for Samaria[10] in the belief that the confusion between Libya and Arabian Midian could be attributed to Ezekiel's knowledge of a tradition preserved in the Samaritan writer Cleodemus-Malchus. This may or may not be so, but even if possible there is no reason to believe the tradition a strictly Samaritan one. He also points out that Ezekiel's γεννητόρων at 104 does not match the singular אבי of the Hebrew Bible (*Exod.* 3.6) or the πατρός of the Septuagint, but corresponds to אבותיך of the Samaritan Pentateuch. This is a nice point, but Ezekiel could readily be making the change deliberately to the (more familiar) plural. Further, recent scholarship has suggested that the notion of an independent Samaritan Pentateuch in the Hellenistic age may not be a valid one.[11] The plural found in our Samaritan text may have been present in a Hebrew or Greek text available to Ezekiel. Kuiper also argues that since Ezekiel uses the Greek version of the Bible and not the Hebrew, this shows that he must be from Samaria in Palestine where Hebrew was neglected and the Greek Bible used. I am not at all sure whether this argument can be reconciled with his previous one, but at all events there is no evidence that such was the case in

Samaria anyway.[12] And, of course, the need for such an argument only exists if one has excluded Egypt as a possible place of origin. Finally, Kuiper asserts that Samaria is well suited for such a play since it was Hellenized from the time of Alexander. Wieneke (125) retorted that Samaria was not Hellenized till the time of Herod. The truth is that we simply do not know how early Samaria was sufficiently Hellenized, from a cultural point of view, to have provided a milieu suitable for a Greek drama on a Biblical subject.[13] As against Samaria (or indeed any location in Palestine),[14] one might observe that Ezekiel seems deliberately to avoid mentioning the land of Palestine, which would seem quite inexplicable in a Palestinian author.[15] Further, the portrait of Moses in the *Exagoge* does not appear to tally with the grandiose view of Moses held by the Samaritans (at least as evident in later sources).[16] Finally, since at least by the end of the second century B.C., if not earlier, the Jews and the Samaritans were powerful enemies, it would be surprising to find a tradition that placed Ezekiel, if he were a Samaritan, among the Jews (as 'Ιουδαικῶν τραγῳδιῶν seems to indicate).

In sum, one can conclude that while it is not impossible for Ezekiel to have been Samaritan, there is no good evidence to believe him such. This is now *communis opinio*, though several still remark the Samaritan option.[17] Most strikingly, I. Ben-Zvi, in an unfortunate discussion of Samaritan-Hellenistic literature, puts Ezekiel among the Samaritans.[18]

Gutman has argued for Cyrenaica (67ff). He has little to support this view aside from the role of Libya in the play, the occasionally hostile relations between Egypt and Cyrene and the fact that Jason wrote Jewish history in Greek in Cyrene. Further support he finds in the possible presence of a Jewish amphitheatre in Cyrene.[19] This opinion has little to commend it aside from the fact that it presents us with a Hellenized state that had a Jewish community. But one can think of yet others both inside and outside Egypt (e.g. Antioch).

We return to *Aristeas'* tale (312ff) of one Theodectes who sought to use Biblical material for a tragedy and was smitten in his eyes for the sacrilege. Upon praying to God he was healed. Graetz suggested that this Theodectes might be Ezekiel.[20] He argued that this tragedian could not be the famous Theodectes since the Bible was not yet translated into Greek in the latter's time. He also observed that

Ezekiel, i.e. יחזקאל, = θεοῦ δέκτης.[21] Trencsényi-Waldapfel, while noting the possibility that Ezekiel may have adopted the name Theodectes as the Greek equivalent of his Hebrew name, prefers to take the argument in a slightly different direction (161). He believes that the author of *Aristeas* is engaged in a polemic against his contemporary Ezekiel's use of Biblical material for the profane stage and so, as a kind of attack on and warning to Ezekiel, he invents the story of a poet who has been punished for such activity and gives him the name of the famous Theodectes, especially since the names were virtually equivalent (160f).

Graetz' version of the theory is not likely. *Aristeas* says explicitly of Theodectes παραφέρειν μέλλων and, Graetz' professions notwithstanding, this does not suit a completed Biblical drama. Second, Aristeas' narrative would lose its credibility – one presumes the author would not wish to do so – by having Demetrius anachronistically speak of a tragedian who lived after him. Further, the king's question clearly refers to pagan writers and so Demetrius' response can only be suitable if he alludes to pagans. It is also worth noting that although Jews in Egypt did sometimes adopt Greek names that were the equivalent of Hebrew names, there is no definite extant example of an Egyptian Jew with a double name made up of Greek and Hebrew equivalents.[22] Trencsényi-Waldapfel's hypothesis, insofar as it is less specific and more ambiguous than Graetz', is so much the harder to treat. One wonders why *Aristeas* would have invented an *exemplum* in which the poet is smitten *before* completing the Biblical play when his target has evidently completed his (and perhaps more than one). It would have been a more appropriate and effective warning if Theodectes were represented as having completed his play (though, to be sure, this would not well suit the king's question). It is moreover not clear whether an *exemplum* in which a *pagan* is represented as sacrilegiously using Biblical material for drama would be taken as relevant for a Jewish writer. One may also wonder how readily *Aristeas* would have equated יחזקאל with Theodectes. It is true that Jerome (Migne 23.835) gives *adprehendens deum* as explication for Iezechiel, but it is also true that this is a very unlikely explanation and one found only here. The many other extant explications of the name all revolve around the sense of חזק = strong, strength (e.g. κράτος θεοῦ, *fortitudo domini*).[23] The only use of the verb in the 'Hiphil' *with God as object* in the Bible seems to be *Isa.* 64.6 where the Septuagint has ἀντιλάβεσθαι and the Vulgate *teneat* (though one notes that there are examples of the 'Hiphil' translated by *apprehendere* in the Vulgate, e.g. *Isa.* 42.6, 45.1). If *Aristeas* were interested here in polemic against Ezekiel, he might have done better by using a name (whether or not it matched a real pagan author) that would have been more readily recognizable as the equivalent of Ezekiel, e.g. θεοκράτης (θευκράτης). Finally, if indeed *Aristeas* is identifying the two names as equivalents, then something has gone wrong. For to make Ezekiel θεοῦ δέκτης, he who accepts God, would scarcely make sense if this were meant as an attack on him for sacrilege.[24] In conclusion, one realizes that Trencsényi-Waldapfel's thesis rests on the additional hypothesis that at the heart of this section of *Aristeas* lies a literary-religious polemic – and there is really no evidence for this.

In sum, though one may admit that none of the arguments against this view is decisive, one feels still that Hengel's verdict is justified: Trencsényi-Waldapfel's suggestion is too bold to merit acceptance.[25]

In short, while no hard and fast decision can be made, Alexandria seems to be a most appropriate location for Ezekiel nor are there any cogent objections to this hypothesis. It would be surprising if Ezekiel wrote anywhere else but in Alexandria.

4. Ezekiel's audience, purpose and religious position

For what kind of audience and with what purpose(s) was the *Exagoge* written? Scholars have divided on the former question, some believing Ezekiel wrote for a non-Jewish audience,[1] some for a Jewish audience,[2] and others for both.[3] For the non-Jews the play would have been intended as educational and propagandistic, to teach the Greeks something about Jewish history and to impress upon them the greatness and special qualities of the Jews' heroic leader and the people themselves.[4] For the Jews it was a reminder of their noble history and perhaps an attempt to draw them away from contemporary pagan influences.[5] For the less well educated among the Jews it may have served an educational function. For cultivated Jews and pagans alike it would have provided evidence that Jewish history and tradition could be comfortably and successfully accommodated to

the ancient art forms of the Greek world. I myself argue that there
are clear indications within the text itself that Ezekiel was considering an audience of both Jews and pagans. There is present an element
of polemic against anti-Semitic Exodus-traditions. Further, Ezekiel
leaves out material from the Biblical narrative that would be offensive
to non-Jews or that would put the Jews in a bad light before them.
On the other hand, he occasionally introduces adaptations of the
Biblical account that seem to exploit and take for granted a Jewish
acquaintance with post-Biblical exegetical material.

The question of Ezekiel's religious position is a difficult one and
may be divided into several aspects: first, the matter of devotion and
faithfulness to the Biblical text;[6] second, the presentation of sacred
history in the pagan context of the theatre and (specifically for the
Exagoge) the bringing on stage of God (or at least God's voice).[7]
Unfortunately, it seems nearly impossible to get an unambiguous set
of criteria by which to evaluate any of these aspects. To begin with
the first question: one would at the least expect to be able to determine whether Ezekiel is faithful to the Biblical text. A brief glance at
scholarly opinion should disabuse us of this illusion. Thus, Ziegler
writes that Ezekiel makes free use of the Biblical material and concludes that Ezekiel deals with his Biblical source in much the same
way as the Greek tragedians use their epic-heroic material.[8] Gutman
(16), on the other hand, asserts that Ezekiel's treatment of the
Biblical material shows the sanctity it held for him and comments
on the total absence of all free use of the material such as Euripides,
e.g., practised with regard to his mythological material. Such examples can be multiplied.[9]

That Ezekiel does not literally follow the narrative of the Bible,
that the 'inviolate' authority of the narrative in this sense did not
exist for him, there can be no question. Yet even in ancient Alexandria
we know that literalism and orthodoxy were not necessarily identical.[10] Further, if my association of the *Exagoge* with the ancient
genre of Midrash is correct, then the kind of changes, eliminations
and additions that Ezekiel makes are in the main no different from
those of the Rabbis and need imply no disrespect for Scripture at all.
A work like the Qumranian *Genesis Apocryphon* goes beyond the
Bible in all its 'dramatic' embellishments, while some of the *para-
phrases* 'violate' the Scriptural authority by re-arranging Biblical

passages.[11] In other words, even if we guarantee the sanctity of the Biblical text at that time we are not able to define that 'sanctity' and to ascertain what would have constituted a violation of it. Furthermore, we do not know when the narrative sections of the Bible began to be considered authoritative and beyond questioning.[12]

Ezekiel's use of the pagan theatrical context for presentation of sacred history also raises questions. Feldman has argued that the practice of Alexandrian Jews to attend the theatre is a part of the Alexandrian Jewish community's non-orthodoxy (and *a fortiori* one assumes the same of Ezekiel's presentation of Biblical history in the theatre).[13] This raises a serious and complex problem, as does all the valuable material in Feldman's essay. Can we limit and define the term 'orthodoxy' in any meaningful fashion and in particular for the Hellenistic period when our evidence is so sparse?[14] Do we know enough about Jewish life and beliefs in the fifth to the first centuries B.C. to establish criteria for orthodoxy? Are we to use later Rabbinic attitudes as standards? Is it right to use Palestinian standards as a litmus test for Alexandrian practice? Can we even assume that there was a well-defined Jewish orthodoxy at that time? For the immediate question we may be justified in querying whether in fact for the observant Alexandrian Jewish community attendance at a theatre was considered sacrilegious. I know no evidence for this (though this in itself proves nothing). Philo evidently regularly attended the theatre (but what would *this* prove?). *Aristeas* speaks favorably of proper theatrical performance. The later Rabbinic attitude is clearly hostile, but is it relevant? To what did the Rabbis object? In part, to the associations with idol worship, though exactly what they had in mind is unclear. Would it have been the presence of idols in the theatre? Did they feel the play itself was an act of worship or honor to the pagan deities? This is not clear from the phraseology at Bab. Tal. *Avodah Zarah* 18b, מזבלין שם זיבול לעבודת כוכבים ('they perform idolatrous practices'), but the commentary of the Tosaphot takes this to refer to the offering of sacrifices. Indeed, the Tosephta *Avodah Zarah* 2.5 explicitly refers it to sacrifices (if the reading מזבחין is correct). On the other hand, a major reason was the Rabbis' fear of the ill effects, moral, religious and psychological, on the people of simply going to the theatre (as embodied in the phrase מושב לצים 'place of the wicked'). The question of 'idol worship' may have been in essence a rationalization. Rabban Gamaliel felt free to bathe in the bathhouse of Aphrodite, in the presence of the idol itself, and was readily able to defend himself.[15] In sum, one wonders whether attendance at the theatre – especially in Alexandria – would have been felt as a *religious* trespass.

Finally, Feldman[16] and others have argued that the 'representation' of God on stage in the scene of the burning bush is itself a deviation from orthodoxy on Ezekiel's part. But Ezekiel deliberately avoids bringing God on stage for theologico-religious reasons (101f) and all one hears is a voice. One might, of course, consider even the representation of God's voice in a theatrical performance sacrilegious but again the lack of evidence for the period and the Alexandrian-Jewish milieu leaves us uncertain. In addition, while it does not amount to the same thing, the phenomenon of a human being speaking the words of God in the first person had a routine place in Jewish liturgy and public Bible-reading. In sum, Ezekiel's introduction of God here may have been offensive to some, but we cannot be certain.

In brief, while we might readily state that by later standards, in particular by Palestinian Rabbinic standards, Ezekiel would have been violating certain canons in presenting the *Exagoge* in the Greek theatre, there is no evidence – one way or the other – to allow us to conclude whether this would also have been true in his contemporary Alexandria.[17]

5. Traditional exegesis in the *Exagoge*

At several places in the *Exagoge* I shall suggest that understanding or illumination can be achieved by placing the text within a Midrashic tradition and comparing it to extant Midrashic sources.[1] Thus, to mention a few, the notion of repayment for enforced labor and the direct rescue of Moses by the princess have exact Midrashic parallels. The phrase δοῦλοι ἐμοί (108), the sentence κακῶν γὰρ τῶνδ' ἀπαλλαγήσεται (190), and the difficult clause on the Egyptians encountering night at the Red Sea (231f) will all be explained by recourse to Midrashic material.[2] In brief, then, my belief is that Ezekiel was well-versed in the traditional exegesis of the Biblical text with which we are most familiar from various Rabbinic compilations.[3] In this context three questions arise. First, was there Midrashic exegesis and elaboration of the Bible at so early a date? Second, even if there was, is there any evidence that such existed in Alexandria (i.e. outside Palestine)? Third, is it reasonable to use much later Midrashic compilations as evidence for specific Midrashic traditions centuries earlier?

To the first question it seems beyond doubt that the answer is yes. Kaufmann demonstrated that Halachic Midrash had its beginnings in the period of the Return. Further, there are elements of Midrash already present in the Bible. In general, *Chronicles* is probably the best, but not the only, example. With regard to the Exodus one can argue for Midrashic elaborations of the Pentateuchal account in *Psalms*. Arguments have been proffered for the presence of Midrash in the prophets.[4] At all events, Aggadic exegesis of Biblical accounts that are perhaps nearly contemporary with the *Exagoge* may be found in *Jubilees*, the Dead Sea Scrolls and perhaps pseudo-Philo.

Was there then such in Alexandria? Yes, and not only in Alexandria, but quite demonstrably in Alexandria before Ezekiel. As Lieberman has put it, the Septuagint is 'the oldest of our preserved *Midrashim*.'[5] Bloch may exaggerate, but only a little, when she writes that on nearly every page of the Septuagint there are modifications influenced by oral traditions.[6] We need not go into the vexed problems of the dating of the Septuagint, or the dating of its separate parts, or the role of revision, to believe that this was its character in its earliest stages.[7] Bickerman has noted the remarkable accuracy of the transmission of the Septuagint Pentateuch from an early stage.[8] More than a century ago Z. Frankel brilliantly demonstrated the presence of Midrash in the Septuagint[9] and in recent years D. W. Gooding has been doing much the same, if in a quite different vein. He has argued for a number of Midrashic modifications in the Septuagint *Exodus* and in a few cases considers the evidence sufficient to conclude that the modifications are the original Septuagint.[10] More recently he has argued that Septuagint *3 Kings* displays much Midrashic interpretation introduced into the 'translation.'[11] 'The two miscellanies not only contain individual examples of midrashic exegesis, but they are carefully arranged so that their very arrangement serves the purpose of making some midrashic point.'[12] For my purposes it makes no difference whether Alexandrian Midrash is genuinely Alexandrian or an imported product, that is to say, whether the particular Midrashic exegesis was formulated in Alexandria or merely came there, by whatever avenues, from Palestine.[13] In the case of the Septuagint, the latter is a very distinct possibility. Although no one takes seriously Gaster's view that the Septuagint was produced in Palestine,[14] yet it is a widely held and reasonable view that there was significant Palestinian participation in its creation.[15] Thus, Palestinian exegesis could easily have been introduced. In the succeeding centuries Alexandrian Jews could have developed their own exegetical schools, perhaps in part dependent on their Palestinian counterparts. Freudenthal argued that such Alexandrian schools developed a 'hellenistischer Midrasch.'[16] Hölscher believes that Philo and Josephus drew upon the oral and written traditions of these Alexandrian schools.[17] There are unusual elaborations on the Biblical text in Artapanus, Eupolemus and Demetrius.[18] Gooding has concluded his recent study by observing 'the only certainty which we can claim is that the miscellanies and 3 Reigns as they now stand bear many marks of the studies and debates of a rabbinic school, or schools, in Palestine or Alexandria, or both.'[19] At any rate, what is important for us is not whether there was an indigenous and independent Alexandrian Midrash, but rather the fact that Midrashic exegesis would have been abundant in Ezekiel's Alexandria.

For a later period more evidence is available. Philo's knowledge of the oral tradition, both Halachic and Aggadic in character, is undeniable, even if one remains skeptical of the extent to which Belkin and Wolfson consider it present.[20]

How then would Ezekiel have acquired this knowledge? If there were written Midrashic works, he could have read them.[21] He may have sought help from the learned scholars of the Jewish community who were repositories of oral traditions, as Philo seems to have done (*Moses* 1.4). He may have attended the public Sabbath gatherings at which the Scriptures were explained and expounded.[22] Finally, since the play is after all on the Exodus, he may simply have been familiar with Midrashic interpretation of the Exodus from the annual celebrations of the Passover, at which it was customary to retell the historical events, in accord with the Biblical injunction (*Exod.* 12.25-7, 13.8; cf. perhaps *Deut.* 6.20ff).[23]

The third and last question. Is it fair to use late Midrashic compilations as evidence for much earlier texts? When Wolfson did this in his

Philo, Goodenough attacked him strongly.[24] Bamberger defended
Wolfson and pointed out that the late Midrashim use much older
material preserved through oral tradition.[25] The incredible tenacity
of the conservative Jewish tradition cannot be gainsaid.[26] Aggadic
embellishment of *Genesis* material found in much later Midrashic
texts occurs also in the Hellenistic author pseudo-Eupolemus.[27]
Similarly, much non-Biblical narrative found in *LAB* can be paralleled in later Midrashic sources. As Feldman has observed, if we
could recover more of the lost Midrashim, probably nearly all the
LAB divergences from the Bible would find parallels.[28] But most
significant is the recent work on Midrash done by G. Vermes who
demonstrates, I think beyond any real doubt, that very early Midrashic traditions were carefully transmitted over centuries so that
often late Midrashic collections preserve material that is even over a
millennium old.[29] As he puts it, 'the present inquiry clearly shows
how unwise and unscholarly it is to neglect, in the study of early
Jewish exegesis, the testimony of a midrashic collection merely on
the grounds of its late appearance.'[30] In the light of this conclusion,
what is the most reasonable way of approaching a portion of text
from the *Exagoge* which has a direct parallel in Midrashic literature
or can be illuminated by placing it within a particular Midrashic
tradition? We might call it coincidence – *sometimes* it really will
be – that is, the same exegetical elaboration begotten for a given text
by more than one individual independently. Or we might assume that
the exegesis was invented by Ezekiel and from him filtered into the
body of Midrashic literature. This cannot be dismissed out of hand,
but seems rather unlikely. Finally, we may assume that Ezekiel
derived it from the Midrashic traditions that were already widespread
and for this reason it is also found in our later sources. The last seems
to me easily the most likely probability.

6. The *Exagoge* and fifth-century tragedy

Wieneke established beyond any reasonable doubt that the play is,
both in small points of phraseology and style and in the larger realm
of dramatic technique and structure, much influenced by Euripides.[1]
This is only natural since of the fifth-century tragedians Euripides
was easily the most popular in the Hellenistic age. Occasionally,

scholars have gone further. P. Collart wrote that Ezekiel was 'tout pénétré . . . des drames d'Eschyle, de Sophocle et surtout d'Euripide.'[2] Snell observes that he is well versed in classical Attic tragedy and is secure in fifth-century style.[3] He also discusses the likelihood of influence of the *Persae* on the *Exagoge*.[4] Fraser notes Ezekiel's 'familiarity with the classical tragedians, particularly Euripides' and remarks that 'his vocabulary . . . attests a full knowledge of tragic and particularly Euripidean usage.'[5] I shall argue that there is some evidence for Sophoclean influence on the *Exagoge*[6] and significantly more for Aeschylean. Here I want to attend to one additional aspect of the influence of Aeschylus on Ezekiel.

Throughout I shall point to possible instances of Ezekiel's use of or familiarity with the plays of Aeschylus, with particular emphasis on his use of the *Persae* in the messenger scene. Ezekiel knew well and was greatly influenced by Aeschylus.[7] In the story told in Aeschylus' *Persae* he saw the Hellenic counterpart to the Jews' victory over the Egyptians. In each case the small, seemingly helpless people overcomes the awesome and hybristic enemy with divine aid. For each victorious people the event in a sense marks its birth as a nation. I suspect that Ezekiel was also influenced by Aeschylus' *Supplices*, and for much the same reason, that he saw therein a conceptual analogue to the story of the Exodus. While there are few verbal parallels between the two plays,[8] larger considerations support this view. Further, since the *Supplices* is part of a connected trilogy approximately two thirds of which is lost and the extant *Exagoge* is no more than one fourth of a play, it becomes difficult to establish a connection which might be manifest if all four plays were intact.

Like the *Exagoge* the Danaid trilogy involves a group of young sisters (a rarity in Greek tragedy). Moreover, both groups were evidently negroid.[9] The daughters of Raguel may have been, like the Danaids, a chorus. One girl is singled out for a special role in each. Further, two verses have luckily been preserved from the *Exagoge* (66f) which reveal that there was a dispute in the play over Moses' marriage to Sepphora, and dispute over a marriage is a theme of central importance in the Danaid trilogy. Indeed, it is not improbable that the objections raised against Moses centered on his being an Egyptian, just as the undesired prospective grooms in Aeschylus are Egyptians. There is also dramatic similarity in the initial confrontations between the newcomer Moses and Raguel's daughters in the *Exagoge* and between the newly arrived Danaids and Pelasgus in Aeschylus.

As with the *Persae* I believe that Ezekiel sensed in the Danaid trilogy major parallels between Greek and Jewish history. I can only hazard the guess that this would be substantially clearer if the plays had all survived whole. Ezekiel, I think, saw in the myth of the Danaids the story of the primeval Greeks' escape from Egypt and return to their ancestral homeland. He saw in this myth the depiction of the formation of a national entity and identity, a *Bildungsroman*, so to speak, on a national scale. Here is the story of the beginnings of the Greek people, on its own soil. And so, Ezekiel would have perceived himself as recreating Aeschylus' *Danaides*, as well as *Persae*, in its Jewish guise, quite likely to elicit sympathy and respect for the Jews from his Greek audience, showing that both Greeks and Jews have similar ancestral stories of persecution, escape and return to a homeland.[10] In doing so he would have been cleverly and effectively turning to his advantage Egyptian anti-Semitic propaganda of long standing. By the third century B.C. Egyptian circles had formulated stories of the Exodus which were calculated to belie and discredit the Biblical tale: the enslaved Jews were a mix of lepers and other polluted persons who, in the final analysis, were expelled from Egypt for the benefit of the Egyptian people.[11] Now it seems likely that at least one Egyptian version of the Exodus incorporated anti-Greek as well as anti-Jewish elements. The native Egyptian population was often no more enamored of the Greeks than of the Jews. Thus, among the people banished from Egypt Danaus was included.[12] In other words, Egyptian propagandists took the liberty of conflating and rewriting the Jewish tale of the Exodus and the Greek story of the migration of Danaus. Ezekiel then exploited this association before his Greek audience by presenting the Exodus of the Jews as the Jewish version of the story of Danaus and his daughters. Moreover, in establishing this implicit association, if not quite identification, between Jews and Greeks, Ezekiel was perhaps exploiting a tradition that may go back to the fourth century, that the Jews and Greeks (Spartans) were kin (*1 Macc.* 12.7). The near-identification of Moses with a Greek mythical hero would be in keeping with Jewish propaganda. We know he was sometimes identified with Musaeus.[13]

Since I have argued for the importance of fifth-century tragedy in a study of the *Exagoge*,[14] we must examine Ezekiel's position both within the context of Jewish-Greek Hellenistic literature and within that of the *Nachleben* of the tragedians, particularly Aeschylus.

In the Hellenistic period Jews took to writing works in traditional Greek literary genres. Jason of Cyrene wrote a *History* which was 'a large-scale historical work . . . written according to the rules of Hellenistic historiography and served as a first-rate source.'[15] But Jews also adopted more belletristic genres. The author of *Joseph and Asenath* was writing a Hellenistic Romance.[16] Philo and Theodotus were composing epics, the *Phocylidea* are proverbial wisdom poetry. Caecilius of Calacte was doing literary criticism in the tradition of Aristotle. Even the Septuagint translation of *Proverbs* occasionally breaks into iambic and hexameter verse.[17] Within this literary activity a play on the Exodus should come as no surprise.[18] We might term the *Exagoge* a Midrashic drama.

Ezekiel did not limit himself to contemporary pagan models but sought centuries back for sources from the classical period – and indeed not always for those authors and works which retained the highest popularity in his own day. Yet here too it is not hard to find parallels among Hellenistic Jewish writers.[19] The Samaritan Theodotus clearly imitates Homer, as does the author of *Or. Sib.* 3.[20] The author of *Wisdom* has recourse to words and usages that derive from early Greek poetry.[21] *Sirach* is acquainted with classical Greek literature, especially Theognis.[22] *Aristeas* seems to quote from Greek tragedy (2). Both Eupolemus and pseudo-Eupolemus appear to have been familiar with Herodotus (with whose work I believe Ezekiel was familiar).[23] To move briefly into the Roman period, Josephus seems to have been well read in Herodotus, Thucydides, Homer and the tragedians.[24] Hadas has argued that the author of *4 Macc.* thinks and writes in terms of Greek tragic forms and themes.[25] If Hadas probably goes too far, his words are still worth heeding: 'Every work in the Apocrypha and Pseudepigrapha of the Old Testament has expressions from or allusions to tragedy which the reader was obviously expected to recognize.'[26]

What of Aeschylus in particular? From the fourth century the performance of his plays waned drastically and he was the least popular of the three tragedians.[27] However, there is no reason to believe that revivals of his plays completely stopped.[28] Further, there is the possibility that selections from his works were performed in productions of dramatic excerpts.[29] Vase-paintings depicting what seem to be scenes from Aeschylean tragedy are not few from fourth-century Sicily and Southern Italy and attest to the continuing interest in his plays.[30] At all events, regardless of Aeschylus' popularity on the stage, there is no doubt that, at the least, his plays continued to be read. Pack[2] (pp. 16–19) lists thirty papyri of Aeschylus, of which a few even come from the Hellenistic period.[31] The Gyges play shows Aeschylean influence,[32] as does perhaps a tragic fragment which is probably fourth century.[33] But our best evidence for abiding interest in his plays comes from the Romans. Roman dramatists of the third, second and first centuries used his plays. O. Ribbeck lists seven Latin plays (by Livius, Pacuvius, Ennius, Accius) as possibly or quite probably having Aeschylean tragedies as their model and two more which may have involved contamination using an Aeschylean play.[34] The list inexplicably (I presume a printer's error) leaves out Ennius' *Eumenides* which seems to have been modelled on Aeschylus' play of the same name. References to Aeschylus in Horace and Cicero suggest that they read him. Ovid probably used his plays as a source for his *Heroides*, and Quintilian exercises critical judgment on his tragedies (10.1.66). Seneca's *Agamemnon* may be influenced by Aeschylus' *Agamemnon*.[35]

There is even an occasional piece of evidence for Jewish interest in or knowledge of Aeschylus. Philo quotes or echoes Aeschylus at least three times. In one case (*Moses* 1.279 = frg. 62 N² = Mette 278a), he may, as Heinemann believes, have the phrase from Plato.[36] But at *Aet. Mundi* 49 a quote from the *Myrmidons* is preceded by φησὶ ὁ τραγικός and a quote from Aeschylus' *Argo* is given in Aeschylus' name at *Probus* 143. The latter is particularly interesting since it is preceded by a spirited defense of the educational value of the Greek poets.[37] In Philo epicus there occurs a rare word ἄκτωρ (*PE* 9.430c) which does not occur in Homer, Sophocles or Euripides, but is found twice in Aeschylus (*Pers.* 557, *Eum.* 399). Is there influence here? Hellenistic Jewish writers, in propagandistic attempts to convince non-Jews of the value of Jews and Judaism, occasionally forged works in the names of well-known pagan writers. Such activity – and in particular the ability to do so with some degree of success – means that these writers were familiar with the actual works of the pagan authors involved. As early as Aristobulus and pseudo-Hecataeus we meet forgeries of Homer and Sophocles[38] and the collection of (Jewish) hexameters falsely attributed to Phocylides probably comes from the first or second century B.C. Among these forgeries there are twelve verses attributed to Aeschylus on the nature of God (frg. 464 N^2 = Mette 627) which it seems reasonable to assume were written by a Hellenistic Jew who was quite familiar with Aeschylus' poetry.[39]

In short, if themes and language suggest that Ezekiel may have been influenced by Aeschylus there are no *a priori* grounds on which to disbelieve this. Because Ezekiel could not write like Aeschylus does not mean that he could not – or did not – read him.

7. The dramatic structure of the *Exagoge*

The 269 surviving verses of the *Exagoge* are surely but a small fraction of the entire play. Scholars have struggled to learn about the structure and movement of the play as a whole from the extant fragments. Interest has centered on the *Exagoge* as potential evidence for the 'five act' drama,[1] and on Ezekiel's adherence (or lack of it) to the 'unities' of time and place. Both questions are intimately tied to one's reconstruction of the setting of each scene and the relationship of the scenes to one another. Consequently, opinions differ. It is, however, generally believed that the play did consist of five acts[2] nor does this strain the evidence: (1) Moses' monologue and his meeting with the daughters of Raguel; (2) Moses' dream and its interpretation by Raguel; (3) the burning bush and God's appearance to Moses; (4) the messenger speech recounting the crossing of the Red Sea; (5) the scouting report on the oasis at Elim and the Phoenix. But within this framework there are disagreements. While it is agreed that the first 89 lines belong to the opening two acts, scholars dispute whether there is a change of location from the first act to the second and whether the two acts are temporally continuous or broken by some gap in time. Kappelmacher (82) argued that the two acts were broken neither by any significant lapse of time nor by any change in location:[3] the daughters of Raguel, having gone home at the end of the first act, return immediately with their father who desires to meet their benefactor. Moses relates his dream, Raguel interprets it and then offers Sepphorah in marriage. He leaves, and Chum enters to dispute the matter.[4] Wieneke has argued (60) that Kappelmacher's reconstruction violates the Biblical narrative in two ways, for in the Bible Raguel does not go out to the well to meet Moses (which is true) nor does Raguel give Sepphorah as wife to Moses till he has lived some time with them (which is not so clear). Consequently, Wieneke assumed that the second act, i.e. Moses' dream, the betrothal and the intrusion of Chum, was separated from the first by a substantial period of time and took place at the home of Raguel in Midian. He further suggests that the dialogue between Chum and Sepphorah enabled the latter to fill in the events of the intervening period. Neither the fragments of Ezekiel nor the remarks of Polyhistor offer any real evidence one way or the other. While Wieneke's arguments from Ezekiel's faithfulness to the Biblical text are not terribly persuasive, Kappelmacher's version, entailing the almost immediate betrothal by Raguel of his daughter to a stranger, may strain credulity. But even here one must be careful not to underestimate the power of dramatic illusion and convention.

The third act (the burning bush) presumably takes place some time later. Kappelmacher (81) holds that the scene has not changed from the first two acts. Natural expectation and the Biblical narrative both argue against this. Mount Horeb is clearly not the very place where Moses has met Raguel's daughters at a well. Wieneke (71) has well remarked that the description in Ezekiel ἁγία γὰρ ἧς σὺ γῆς ἐφέστηκας πέλει (98) would scarcely make sense if the location were the very place where the first two acts had already been set. It would seem all but certain that a change of location is demanded. Yet again caution must be exercised. Might a mere movement by Moses to a corner of the stage hitherto not approached have sufficed the playwright and audience?

The fourth act, it is generally agreed, is represented by the messenger's speech beginning at 193. There can be no doubt that the setting has changed. Only those scholars who cling to the ideal of unity of place can affirm that this speech is set in the same place as the earlier scenes.[5] The same is true of the following set of excerpts (243-53, 254-69), which surely demand another change of scene.

The play extends over a lengthy span of time, from the flight of Moses from Egypt through the Exodus itself to the arrival of the

Jews in the desert near Elim.[6] It is beyond reasonable dispute that there are at least three different locales in the play (near Midian, in Egypt, near Elim), probably four (Horeb), and possibly five (Raguel's home).[7] So much then for the 'Aristotelian' unities of time and place. To be sure, as Aristotle might have put it, Ezekiel was trying to turn the epic that is *Exodus* into a drama, a difficult and perhaps inadvisable venture.[8] No ancient tragedy covers so long a period of time as the *Exagoge*. Even those plays which, one might argue, transgress Aristotle's 24 hour limit represent, I think, a qualitatively different kind of temporal movement. Thus, scholars point to the *Eumenides* in particular, also *Agamemnon* and *Andromache*.[9] *Trachiniae* could be added. But each of these plays 'violates' the unity of time in one fell swoop, e.g. Orestes' journey to Athens, Agamemnon's return to Greece, etc. None even approximates what Ezekiel does here:[10] extend the action of the play over a long period in which there are distinct intervals at various points of the drama.[11] Further, the lapses of time in fifth-century tragedy all appear to have allowed for off-stage journeys. This is simply not the case in the *Exagoge* where the sheer number of *distinct* events must have *ipso facto* occupied much time. Indeed, at various points the play itself calls attention to the passage of time: the plague of darkness will occupy three days (144), the Passover preparations and sacrifice occupy five days (175 ff) and the Egyptians, in their pursuit of the Jews, encamp overnight (217f). There was also much 'empty' time, as is common in contemporary drama, that is, points in the play at which one merely posits a lapse of time (as our playbills will note, 'one week later'). Thus, defending Ezekiel by observing that he had precedents for violating the unity of time in fifth-century tragedy really misses the point. For the qualitative differences in the nature of his 'violations' reveal that he is operating under a quite different set of dramatic assumptions than did the fifth-century tragedians.

It is similarly true that discovering instances of shifts of scene will not explain (or explain away) Ezekiel's procedure.[12] It is commonplace to refer to the *Eumenides* (a valuable example in that it demonstrates that the unities of time and place are sometimes intertwined) and the *Ajax*. Snell (175) has mentioned (unfortunately, without elaboration) Aeschylus' *Aitnae*, which is probably closest to the *Exagoge* in this regard. It seems that this play was divided into five parts, each of which had a different setting from the immediately preceding one.[13] It is worth remembering this when we consider how strongly Ezekiel was influenced by Aeschylus. This play aside, there is no evidence for so bold a shifting of scenes in Greek tragedy. Indeed, even Seneca's plays, loosely constructed as they are, show nothing like the alterations in setting present in the *Exagoge*. The *Phoenissae* appears to have three settings, but the preserved play is fragmentary or unfinished. The *Hercules Oetaeus* (whether or not Seneca's) may have two settings, though this is not certain. Otherwise Seneca seems to observe unity of place.

How were these changes in the *Exagoge* executed? We know too little of ancient theatre production to be sure. Conceivably, the decisive factor in each scene could simply have been the express designation by a character of the (new) place. On the other hand, Sifakis has suggested that revolving περίακτοι may have provided changes of scenery.[14]

Was there a chorus in the *Exagoge*? To be sure, there is no solid evidence. Wieneke (30) and others have argued that the complete absence of lyric fragments from our surviving text is an indication that there was no chorus.[15] But Lesky was right when he asserted that this proves nothing since Eusebius (or Polyhistor) would simply not have found choral songs of any use for his purposes.[16] Similarly, objections to a choral presence on the grounds that the chorus would have to absent itself on at least one occasion (the bush scene) and that there would have to be a second chorus in the Egyptian scene(s) are also not persuasive.[17] If such conclusions be necessary, then they may certainly stand.[18] Multiple choruses in a single play did occasionally occur.[19]

Was there a chorus in Hellenistic tragedy and if so what was its function and role? Sifakis has collected the evidence and concluded that (at least sometimes) there was.[20] One piece of positive evidence comes from Egypt during the reign of Ptolemy II (270–246).[21] Evidence from Rome may not be irrelevant for Greek Hellenistic tragedy. Early Roman tragedy used a chorus,[22] as did later imperial tragedy. Lucian's (?) 'tragedy' ποδάγρα also has a chorus, replete with lyric odes. Thus, it is safe to say that there are no historical grounds for denying Ezekiel the use of a chorus.

There is evidence for the familiarity of Egyptian Jews with choruses. Philo's account of the Song of the Sea (*Moses* 1.180, 2.256f) is cast in terms of choral singing (cf. too 1.255). Ezekiel could have presented this episode as a choral ode.[23] The author of *4 Maccabees* uses imagery which reflects his familiarity with choruses (8.4, 13.8, 14.8).[24] To be sure, a number of these passages seem clearly to be thinking in terms of a circular chorus and this may militate against the view that they are thinking of tragic choruses. But there is some evidence for circular choral dance in tragedy.[25]

Who would the chorus have been? The obvious choice is Raguel's daughters.[26] Krauss (170) has noticed that the introduction of the sisters at verse 59 could well be preliminary to a parodos. Whatever we think of the possible role of these maidens in the scenes at the bush and near Elim, there is scarcely any way to place them relevantly in 'act 4,' which takes place at the palace in Egypt. A chorus here would have to be a different group.[27] Gutman has proposed a chorus of Egyptian women who lament (13). A more plausible suggestion lies at hand, especially if (as I will argue below) the setting of the Egyptian court was used for a number of scenes, including confrontations between Moses and Pharaoh. The chorus could well have been the Egyptian wizards who appear often from chapter 7 on in the *Exodus* narrative, in a series of episodes in which their ability to withstand God is progressively diminished. Ezekiel could have used the messenger scene as the ultimate in their decline, perhaps incorporating professions on their part of the total victory of God and the Jews. We have noted in an earlier chapter how this scene was in all probability modelled on the *Persae*. If so, the presence of a group of distinguished and authority-bearing men who act as aides and counselors to the throne would well parallel the setting of the corresponding scene in the *Persae*. Finally, it is a curiosity (in our context) that these wizards are called ἐπαοιδοί in the Septuagint, a name which might have naturally suggested their use as a chorus.

What would the chorus' (or choruses') role have been? If the daughters of Raguel were the chorus in the opening act and the watering of the flocks was depicted, if too the wizards were the chorus in the palace scene, then it would be fairly certain that the chorus played an 'organic' role in the play, at least at times (cf. Arist. *Poet.* 1456a 26ff). What of their odes? Would they have been pointed or irrelevant? Composed for the occasion or mere ἐμβόλιμα? Tied to the dramatic movement or simply interludes to separate the acts?[28] I see no way in which we can even begin to answer these questions.

In sum, while one may posit a chorus for the *Exagoge* and even hypothesize perfectly suitable and potentially effective choruses and choral odes, there is no convincing evidence that there was a chorus in the play.[29]

Why have scholars been so concerned to divide the extant remains of the *Exagoge* into acts? Primarily because in so doing they can produce a large piece of evidence in accord with the so-called Hellenistic rule of five acts (cf. Hor. *AP* 189f).[30] Indeed, we would have here our first real example of a five-act Greek tragedy. Menander's *Dyscolos* provided an instance for Hellenistic comedy and Seneca's plays furnish many examples for Roman tragedy. Yet, there is a striking conceptual uniqueness here. By and large our ability to divide the *Exagoge* into five acts is the result of a close substantive analysis of the text which, to a good degree, revolves around the violation of the unities of time and place. We separate the Elim-scene from the Egyptian's speech because they clearly are set in different places; the bush scene from the messenger scene for the same reason; and the dream scene from the bush scene because they appear to be played in different places at some time interval. We distinguish the dream scene from the opening scene for the same reasons, though here there can be some argument. But nothing that we had known of ancient drama could have prepared us for this. These features tend to be more the marks of act-division in modern drama than in ancient. Time passes, the locale changes, the curtain goes up. Examine the plays of Seneca. The division of these plays into five acts is based on the separations effected by four choral odes.[31] Contrarily, there does appear to be a change of setting after verse 232 of the *HO*, but there is no choral ode here nor, consequently, is there any call for the marking of a new act. In general, if the choruses were removed, one could not tell where the act-divisions are in Seneca's plays. Similarly, without the χοροῦ references in the *Dyscolos*, one could not divide it into its five acts.[32] This leaves us two possibilities. Either Ezekiel's construction of act-divisions in the *Exagoge* was based on a radically different (and personal?) conception from what was customary, or else we may have to ponder the possibility that act division in Hellenistic tragedy was very different from act division in Hellenistic comedy and Roman (or at least Senecan) tragedy.

I offer a reconstruction of the play that goes beyond the extant fragments, because I think some new and reasonable suggestions can be made. Of course, it is easy enough to hypothesize scenes on the basis of *Exodus* 2–20 (and conceivably beyond). Further, Ezekiel was capable of introducing material that had no foundation in the Biblical text, e.g. the conflict with Chum and the appearance of the Phoenix. Here I suggest additional episodes either because the extant evidence seems to point to their existence or because dramatic requirements appear to make their presence necessary.

The play opens with Moses alone on the stage. There is evidently a well nearby. Moses makes his opening speech. The seven daughters of Raguel enter and a conversation ensues in which they and the location are identified. Some shepherds appear and seek to drive the maidens away from the well, but Moses comes to their rescue. Polyhistor's brief remarks indicate that Ezekiel depicted this episode from *Exod.* 2. Exactly what happened then we cannot determine. The Biblical narrative would suggest that Moses returns with Raguel's daughters to their home. Some time passes and Raguel decides to marry Sepphorah to Moses. Chum appears and apparently protests; Raguel was evidently not present, but Moses was, though perhaps at some distance from Chum and Sepphorah.[33] I suggest below that this may have been followed by a scene in which Moses defended himself by pointing out the kinship between Raguel's family and himself. This would have been followed (immediately?) by the dialogue between Moses and Raguel concerning his dream.

The setting changes and Moses appears alone on the stage. He is evidently tending sheep, as in *Exodus* (cf. ῥάβδον τετραπόδων ... κολάστριον, 121). He sees the burning bush and God speaks to him. The dialogue continued at some length, passing through the signs God performs for Moses to the account of the plagues and the Passover regulations. I argue later that line 174 is the last line (extant) from this scene. Shortly thereafter Ezekiel probably brought Aaron on stage to meet and speak with Moses (cf. 116ff), in the very setting as depicted in *Exodus* (4.27f). Moses would have told him briefly of his mission.

The setting changes to Egypt. I argue below that Ezekiel presented a scene in which Moses (and Aaron?) confers with the elders of the people and verses 175–92 are part of it (cf. *Exod.* 4.29f). Our next fragment is the survivor's report at 193ff. Clearly, much must have taken place between these two episodes. Kappelmacher proposed the appearance of Moses and Aaron before Pharaoh, then followed by the survivor's monologue (81). Wieneke (93) thought this implied too long a time interval between the two successive scenes of the act and assumed a scene depicting the queen and attendants lamenting the results of the plagues before the messenger arrives. These two views can, of course, be readily reconciled. Trencsényi-Waldapfel's account is not completely clear to me, but he seems to conceive 175ff as a speech of God opening the act (148, 155); he does not specify in what context. Pharaoh then learns of his son's death and releases the Jews. But he changes his mind and leaves to pursue them. Then follows the survivor's speech.

What seems to me undeniable is that Ezekiel must have presented a scene in which Moses directly confronts Pharaoh. Everything calls for this, logically and dramatically, not to mention the demands of the Biblical narrative. Further, if verses 109f are an anticipation of the later scene in which Moses meets with the elders of the people, then 111f can readily be taken as anticipating what immediately follows, the meeting with Pharaoh. Thus, after Moses and Aaron speak with the elders, we can assume that they were presented going to see Pharaoh. Instead of the repeated confrontations of *Exodus* which would have necessitated multiple exits and entrances, Ezekiel may have compressed it all into one scene. Moses asks Pharaoh to free the people; he refuses. Moses performs a few signs which perhaps the wizards duplicate. Moses then calls down upon Egypt the plagues, whether one at a time or in groups. Perhaps they are each described by Moses or Aaron, perhaps by Pharaoh, the wizards or someone else. The scene probably followed a pattern: invocation by Moses (Aaron), description of the plague, reaction of the Egyptians present, ultimate refusal by Pharaoh to yield. The rapid-fire introduction of the plagues one after another would be compatible with the description at 133ff.[34] At the death of the firstborn Pharaoh gives in and Moses and Aaron depart. Some conversation ensues between Pharaoh and his attendants and the decision is made to pursue. Pharaoh leaves.

Those remaining continue to speak and shortly thereafter the messenger enters with his tale of woe.

The setting again changes. We are in the desert on the other side of the Red Sea. It is impossible to tell what Ezekiel may have presented. He could have shown the Jews rejoicing over their salvation, perhaps with something like the Biblical Song of the Sea. All we can safely guess is that Moses was probably portrayed sending out scouts to investigate the area and shortly thereafter they return with their reports of 243-69. We shall discuss later possible ways the play might have ended.

One final question. Did Ezekiel adhere to the 'law' of three actors? It is risky to attempt an answer on the basis of 269 lines, but the available evidence does not indicate anything to the contrary.[35] But some suggested reconstructions, while not necessitating a fourth actor, might effectively have utilized one. There could have been a scene involving Moses, Sepphorah, Chum and Raguel together. The scenes at the Egyptian court could readily have used someone aside from Moses, Aaron and Pharaoh. But this is speculation.

8. Ezekiel's influence

Mentions of Ezekiel and quotations from his work are found in only three writers. Eusebius (*PE* 9) provides us with all the extant fragments (taken from Alexander Polyhistor). One long section from the prologue speech is quoted by Clemens at *Strom.* 1.23.155. The description of the Phoenix is given by Eustathius at *Comment. in Hexaemeron* (*PG* 18.729) in the midst of a discussion of various animals, within the context of God's creation of the world. Unlike Eusebius (Polyhistor) and Clemens, Eustathius quotes anonymously: ὡς καὶ αὐτοὶ διαγράφοντες φάσκουσιν οὕτως. It seems likely that Eustathius knew neither the text of the *Exagoge* nor the excerpts in Polyhistor (in either of which cases he would have known the author's name), but probably had before him an anthology of Greek writings on animals in which Ezekiel's depiction of the Phoenix had been incorporated. Did Clemens himself have a text of the *Exagoge* or merely the excerpts as recorded in Polyhistor?[1] Unlike Eusebius, he does not say that he is quoting Ezekiel via Polyhistor, but it seems eminently likely that this is what he was doing. Clemens' discussion here of Moses quotes from Eupolemus and Artapanus before Ezekiel, exactly Polyhistor's order in Eusebius. In Clemens' quotations from Eupolemus, Artapanus and Ezekiel there is nothing that does not occur in Polyhistor's excerpts. This could be coincidence, but certainly suggests strongly that Clemens was using Polyhistor here, not the texts of the individual authors themselves.[2] Further, we know that Clemens did use Polyhistor's work. At 1.15.70 he utilizes his *Pythagorean Symbols*, at 3.7.60 his *Indica* and at 1.21.130 his *On the Jews*. In this last selection Clemens notes that Polyhistor transcribed correspondence between Solomon and other kings, a passage which seems (on the basis of Eusebius) to have occurred in Polyhistor very shortly after his excerpts from the *Exagoge*. Thus, it seems highly probable that Clemens knew Ezekiel (and other Hellenistic Jewish writers) only through Polyhistor.

Ezekiel has been preserved by excerpts in the pagan Polyhistor quoted by the Church Fathers. The same is true for most of the other Hellenistic Jewish authors.[3] Indeed, were it not for the Church, Philo himself would be virtually unknown to us. Till the renaissance there is not a reference to him in a Jewish source. This would seem to indicate that at some point a conscious decision was made by Jewish leaders not to preserve the Judaeo-Greek literature. In simplistic terms, one can understand the *Exagoge* falling between two stools and not appealing to later generations of Jews, with traditionalists feeling it too much a paganization of Holy Scriptures, more Greek than Jewish, while assimilated Jews would have had no interest in seeing the 'backward' Jewish culture and history publicly presented to non-Jews from whom they would have preferred to hide nationalistic Jewish traditions.[4]

But are there any indications that Jewish writers were familiar with the *Exagoge*? I have argued[5] that the absence of Ezekiel from Josephus' literary review at *Apion* 1.218 and elsewhere in Josephus is no indication in itself that the latter did not know Ezekiel's work. Indeed, there is substantial evidence that he was familiar with the *Exagoge*.[6] His account of the crossing of the Red Sea was probably influenced by Ezekiel, especially in the ways he uses non-Biblical material that does occur in Ezekiel. In all the following Josephus shows similarities with Ezekiel: the Jews are without weapons

(*AJ* 2.321, 326/*Exag.* 210); Moses strikes the sea with his staff (2.338/*Exag.* 227: the verb is τύπτειν in both); darkness overcomes the Egyptians (2.344/*Exag.* 231); the element of κόπος *(2.321/Exag.* 208); the Egyptians defer battle till the morrow (2.334/*Exag.* 218); the energetic entry into the sea (2.340/*Exag.* 228f). Finally, Josephus emphasizes the absence of any Egyptian survivor to report back to Egypt, a feature hard to explain except as polemic against Ezekiel (2.344).[7] There are other possible traces of the influence of Ezekiel elsewhere in Josephus. I shall argue[8] that Polyhistor's remarks suggest that the *Exagoge* may have included a third miraculous sign in the bush scene; this is exactly what Josephus has (2.273). The latter's account of the oppression of the Jews leaves out the role of the Jewish midwives (2.206f); so too Ezekiel.[9] Josephus uses λανθάνω of Jochebed's secretly hiding the infant Moses (2.218); so too Ezekiel (15). That Josephus could have been familiar with Ezekiel is not hard to believe. We know he used the work of Polyhistor. It is likely that he cites from his *On the Jews* (*AJ* 1.240f).[10] It may be possible that he even had a text of the complete *Exagoge.*[11]

That Philo never mentions Ezekiel is no surprise; he never mentions any Jewish sources aside from Scripture. If, as seems quite likely, Ezekiel was Alexandrian, it would be hard to imagine Philo's not being familiar with his work. Freyhan and Wieneke have suggested that he may have used the *Exagoge.*[12] The former noted the similarity between Ezekiel and Philo in expounding Moses' royal education. The latter observed a number of similarities in language: (first references to *Moses* 1, second to the *Exagoge*): τροφῆς βασιλικῆς (20)/ τροφαῖσι βασιλικαῖσι (37); ἀτραπός in the crossing scene (179/229); προσδραμοῦσα of Miriam in the Nile scene (16/23); Moses' description of himself as οὐκ εὔλογος (83/113), where the Septuagint gives ἄλογος. Expansion of Wieneke's list is possible. Ezekiel's scouts are divinely aided (246f): τόθεν δὲ φέγγος ἐξέλαμψέ νιν κατ' εὐφρόνης σημεῖον ὡς στῦλος πυρός. Compare Philo's description of the cloud that guided the people by day, ἡλιοειδὲς ἐκλάμπουσα φέγγος and was like fire at night, φλογοειδές (166). Concerning the exposure of the infant Moses, there are several similarities: both Ezekiel and Philo leave out the ark. In Philo the baby is found ἐν τῷ δασυτάτῳ τῶν ἑλῶν (14); cf. Ezekiel's λάσιον εἰς ἕλος δασύ (17); παρὰ τὰς ὄχθας τοῦ ποταμοῦ (10) is probably closer to Ezekiel's παρ' ἄκρα ποταμοῦ (or whatever he wrote) than to the Septuagint's παρὰ τὸν ποταμόν. Miriam keeps guard πέλας in the *Exagoge* (18) and μικρὸν ἄποθεν in Philo (12); contrast the Septuagint's μακρόθεν. Pharaoh's daughter descends for λουτροῖς in both (14/20). When she recognizes that the baby is Jewish, both use the verb γιγνώσκω (15/22), which is not here in the Septuagint. Miriam runs up in both (16/23). The naming of the baby appears to take place immediately on finding him (17/30) and the etymology seems to be based on Egyptian *mu* (17/30f).

As is the case in Josephus, Philo too leaves out the Jewish mid-wives (8) and uses λανθάνω in the context of the concealment of the baby (9). He too seems to be engaged in polemic against Ezekiel when he stresses that no messenger survived to report the disaster (179). Finally, as seems to be the case in the *Exagoge*, Philo's account of the Exodus in *Moses* 1 does not depict the revelation at Sinai.

I am not aware of any other substantial possibilities of the influence of the *Exagoge*. There are a few very tenuous similarities between Ezekiel and *Wisdom* but nothing really striking. At any rate, the date of *Wisdom* is also debated.[13]

Scholars have occasionally suggested possible instances of the *Exagoge's* influence. I note them here, though none has any real cogency. Weinreich discussed the possibility of Ezekiel's influence on the book of *Acts*, but reasonably rejected it.[14] Klein thought the *Exagoge* the starting-point for Christian mystery plays, but it is not clear whether he believed the influence direct or indirect.[15] Gutmann (*EJ* 887) suggested that Pliny's account of the Phoenix may reflect indirect influence of Ezekiel, but there are no significant similarities here. The sixth-century Coptic text discussed later[16] records the Phoenix' appearance at the time of the Exodus. Whether this in some fashion reflects influence of the *Exagoge* cannot be determined.[17] Snell (185, n. 14) notes the phrase θάρσησον ὦ παῖ at *POxy* 2746.1 and at *Exag.* 100. This does not seem significant.[18]

In sum, it seems likely that both Philo and Josephus knew and used the *Exagoge*, the former perhaps knowing the whole play, the latter the excerpts in Polyhistor. There is no further indication that the play itself survived. But Polyhistor's selections did and some of them at least have been preserved for us by the Church Fathers.

9. Ezekiel's knowledge of Hebrew and the Hebrew Bible

That Ezekiel made abundant use of the Septuagint is evident even upon superficial and cursory reading. The number of places where there is sameness or similarity of expression far exceeds what one could reasonably expect simply from two authors translating and adapting in Greek from a Hebrew model. Long ago Philippson made the first thorough study of the question and no one has felt the need seriously to revise his work or conclusions. He counted (pp. 50–2) 41 places in the *Exagoge* where he considered the phraseology influenced by the Septuagint.[1] While it is true that many, perhaps most, of these could be explained as the natural product of translation of the same source, it would be straining credulity to so argue for some ten or dozen of them which manifest striking coincidences of language. One notes, for instance, the parallels at verses 13, 17, 19, 21, 24, 108, 114, 185, 251.[2] Writing in 1830, Philippson did not have access to Field's edition of Origen's *Hexapla*. By examining the various other Greek translations made of these opening chapters of *Exodus* we can only be impressed by how often Ezekiel's language jibes with the Septuagint where however the other translations use different expressions.[3] A few illustrations: At 13, τάρσενικά; LXX τὰ ἄρσενα; Aquila and Theodotion τὰ παιδία. 13, ποταμὸν ἐς; LXX εἰς τὸν ποταμόν; Aquila εἰς τὸ ῥεῖθρον. 17, εἰς ἕλος; LXX εἰς τὸ ἕλος; Aquila ἐν τῷ παπυρεῶνι. 19, ἄβραι; LXX ἄβραι; Aquila παιδίσκαι; Symmachus κοράσια. 92, καίεται; LXX καίεται; Aquila ἀναπτόμενος; Symmachus ἐφλέγετο. 97, λῦσαι; LXX λῦσαι· Aquila ἔκσπασον; Symmachus ὑπόλυσαι. 114, ἰσχνόφωνος; LXX ἰσχνόφωνος; Aquila βαρὺς στόματι. 123, δράκων; LXX δράκων; Aquila κῆτος. 182, ἐν σπουδῇ; LXX μετὰ σπουδῆς; Aquila ἐν θάμβῳ; Symmachus ἐν ἐπείξει.

Finally, during the course of my discussions I shall point to a number of places where the Septuagint and the Hebrew Bible differ and Ezekiel's text seems to be following the Septuagint. Thus, the chariot wheels refuse to turn as if bound (232f), as in the Septuagint (14.25, συνέδησεν) and not the Hebrew ויסר. God's command to Moses, ἔρπε καὶ σήμαινε (109), seems a distinct echo of βάδιζε εἰπόν (6.6), where however the Hebrew has no verb other than 'tell.' Ezekiel places locusts among the 'heaven-plagues' (141ff) which particularly well suits the Septuagint's description of Moses stretching his rod toward heaven (10.13), a description not present in the Hebrew which merely has Moses stretch his hand over the land of Egypt. At 4.6 the Hebrew records that Moses' hand became 'leprous, like snow.' The Septuagint has the hand become 'like snow.' So too Ezekiel (130). In his description of the Jews' encampment by the Red Sea, Ezekiel mentions the presence of their 'household goods,' δόμων ἀποσκευή, 209. There is no mention of such in the Biblical account and it is hard to see why Ezekiel would have introduced this. I shall argue that its presence here is the result of his confusing the sense of ἀποσκευή at LXX 12.37, since the word can mean both 'children' and 'equipment.' Had he been using the Hebrew text here such confusion would have been virtually impossible (Hebrew טף).

This brings us to the next question. Is there any evidence that Ezekiel knew Hebrew and utilized the Hebrew Bible?[4] In truth, this embraces quite distinct questions which should be set out one by one. (1) Did Ezekiel know Hebrew? (2) Was Hebrew (or Aramaic) Ezekiel's native language? (3) Did Ezekiel make use of the Hebrew Bible? Let us begin with this last question.

This is methodologically a difficult issue. One must seek out differences between the Septuagintal and Hebrew versions of the Exodus where Ezekiel follows the Hebrew version. Even when we find instances the possibility always remains that Ezekiel himself knew a post-Biblical tradition that agreed with the Hebrew version or indeed that the Greek version of the Bible *that Ezekiel read* did agree with our Hebrew text.[5] Prior to Wieneke, most scholars simply did not broach the issue.[6] Since Wieneke, many have simply followed in his footsteps.[7] Wieneke is the only scholar who has made a substantial attempt to argue that Ezekiel was using the Hebrew Bible: (1) At verse 2 Ezekiel's '70' agrees with the Hebrew, while the Septuagint has 75. (2) At 14, Moses' mother hides him, as in the Hebrew, while the Septuagint uses the plural verb, evidently of both parents. (3) Wieneke emends the text at 17 on the assumption that it should be brought into accord with the Hebrew of 2.3. There is, unfortunately, little here that one can rely on. The change from the Septuagint's plural to Ezekiel's singular is trivial, especially when we consider that Ezekiel seems to have written Amram out of Moses' life. As for the number 70 in verse 2, this is surely the strongest argument for Ezekiel's use of the Hebrew Bible. Yet, as I shall argue at length,[8] it is not difficult to account for his choice of 70 on totally other grounds than his use of the Hebrew Bible. I myself will suggest in a number of places that Ezekiel's version or phraseology could reflect acquaintance with the Hebrew Bible. Thus, for example, τις ἠλάλαξε (238) is closer to Hebrew ויאמר מצרים than to the Septuagint's Αἰγύπτιοι (14.25). Ezekiel's choice of ἄμωμα (177) for the Septuagint's τέλειον may reflect familiarity with Hebrew מום. But these and a few others of the same ilk will not convince anyone that Ezekiel was using the Hebrew Bible. In short, no cogent evidence has been adduced to support the view that Ezekiel knew the Hebrew Bible.

How then are we to treat the question of whether Ezekiel knew Hebrew at all?[9] The common approach to such a problem would be to examine and evaluate the Greek style in the hope of determining whether or not Hebraisms are present.[10] But here too difficulties loom large. Whether or not one is disposed to believe in the existence of a 'Jewish Greek,'[11] Hebraisms may in fact be not the result of the writer's familiarity with Hebrew but rather the product of his acquaintance with the Septuagint. That is to say, the 'Hebraisms' may really be 'Septuagintalisms.'[12] Finally, the very marking of a 'Hebraism' is often in doubt. Scholars have often been able to dig up seeming parallels to 'Hebraisms,' especially in the papyri. Some have gone so far as virtually to deny totally the presence of Hebraisms in any Greek documents, assigning every apparent example to the broad embrace of the *koine*.[13] This surely carries a sensible notion to a perverse extreme. Allowing for a generous interpretation and embrace of the term, we must first ask whether any possible Hebraisms can be found in the *Exagoge*. It is quite remarkable to note how many scholars assert that there are none or very few. Gutmann explicitly declares that there are no Hebraisms in Ezekiel (*EJ* 887) and Fraser comments that his Greek is 'quite uninfluenced by Hebraisms.'[14] Similarly, Christ–Schmid–Stählin (2.1.608) observe that 'alle Hebraismen vermieden werden.' Kuiper appears to note one or two instances (*ad* verses 132 and 239), but concludes that Ezekiel is relatively free of Hebraisms.[15] Snell refers to occasional Hebraisms but points to only one (ἐν ῥάβδῳ, 132).[16] It seems, however, to me that we can discern a number of 'Hebraisms' in Ezekiel, if we are willing to take a relatively generous view of the term and do not, in cavalier fashion, dismiss every example for which some parallel or parallels can be dredged up from the *koine* or even from classical Greek.[17]

1. The use of instrumental ἐν (132). Schwyzer–Debrunner 1.2, p. 458 believe the use of instrumental ἐν only comes in late Greek and then under foreign influence. Blass–Debrunner sect. 195 are a bit more cautious. Cf. KG 1.436, 464–6.

2. The very liberal use of the pronoun αὐτός, often in the nominative where it seems to have no particular emphatic force, and excessively in oblique cases.[18] Blass–Debrunner sect. 278 see this as more a reflection of vernacular Greek than a semiticism. But cf. Norden, *Antike Kunstprosa* 2.484f.

3. Absence of the article with a noun followed by a genitive (construct usage), e.g. 31, 32, 34.

4. Future for imperative (152, 160, 171, 188).

5. Frequent use of comparative ὡς (81, 233, 234, 247, 263, 268).

6. Pleonastic ἄρχεσθαι + infinitive (possibly at 220f).

7. Sentences in which no finite verb is found. These fall into two broad categories: (a) sentences in which no verb form at all is present;[19] (b) sentences in which it appears that the participle is doing the work of a finite verb. Both types can readily be tied to the Biblical Hebrew phenomena of (1) the absence of a copula and consequently the common occurrence of verbless sentences;[20] (2) the apparent use of the participle as a finite verb.[21] Examples of the first may be seen in the *Exagoge* at 209, 261, 198f, possibly 249. Examples of the second may be present at 169 (depending on one's reading and understanding of the text), 180–2 (depending on how one takes the sentence), and possibly 198f (though see above).

8. The use of καί as the equivalent of 'vav' to introduce an apodosis.[22] This seems to me the only reasonable way to make sense of the manuscript reading of verses 1–6 (with reference to καί in line 3). I see no way of taking καί here as 'pleonastic' or 'redundant,' some examples of which (quite unlike the passage in Ezekiel) can be found at KG 2.255. It is, however, more than likely that we should accept Dübner's emendation of κακούμενον to κακούμεθα.

The simple truth is that should we be so inclined we could find some parallel in a non-Jewish (non-Christian) Greek text for each of these phenomena. But would there be any point in so doing? Would it really tell us anything? After all, what can be surprising in the fact that a Jewish author who was steeped in the Septuagint should have been to some degree influenced in his own writing style - especially when writing a Biblical drama based on the Septuagint - by the peculiarities of the Greek of that work? Indeed, we can only be surprised that Ezekiel successfully managed to avoid so many of the common 'Hebraisms' that abound in the Septuagint, e.g. the redundant use of pronoun + relative, εἴς instead of τις, high frequency of καί, Hebrew word order, the phrases καὶ ἐγένετο and εἶναι εἰς + accusative, οὐρανοί = שמים,[23] and many others.

What then can we conclude from the demonstration that there are a decent number of Hebraisms in Ezekiel insofar as the question of his knowledge of Hebrew goes? I think nothing. There is no reason not to believe that he could have had all these Greek Hebraisms from the Septuagint.[24]

Finally, the question of Ezekiel's mother tongue. I raise this simply because so many scholars have not hesitated to assert that it was not Greek. Some have gone so far as to state baldly that it was Hebrew (if in fact some semitic language was his native tongue, then Aramaic would probably be a better choice). Snell (193) proclaims, 'offenbar Hebräisch seine Muttersprache war' and Wieneke's argument on the basis of hiatus in the *Exagoge* clearly assumes the same.[25] Others have pointed in this same direction: Lesky observes that Ezekiel does not write from an inborn Greek feeling for the language[26] and Dübner (p. vii) thinks it clear that Ezekiel had learned Greek late:[27] 'graeca ei non profluunt ex intimis sensibus.' Most of this patently relies on the belief that the scholar can intuitively sense what the Greek of a native-Greek-speaking Jew of the second century B.C. would be like. Argumentation is generally not proffered. Lesky alone is specific, resting his case on the absence of 'Gefühl für die Antithese' in two passages (9ff and 200f) which he believes characterizes the non-Greek writing Greek. It may consequently be of value to look briefly at solecisms and 'barbarisms' in the text of the *Exagoge* to determine whether on the basis of the style it is possible to argue that Greek was not Ezekiel's mother tongue.

We begin with Lesky's observation on the lack of feel for antithesis. I count 17 examples of μέν, most of which are well within the bounds of 'good Greek.' Instances of μέν followed by δέ are at 36,

43, 60, 92, 119, 198, 240, 258, 262. Perfectly defensible examples
of μέν followed by a temporal conjunction occur at 12, 110, 133.[28]
In general, Ezekiel does not seem to have any particular problem in
use of μέν . . . δέ (ἐνταῦθα) and antithesis. But two passages stand
out, as Lesky has noted. The first is 8–11:

> δόλον καθ᾽ ἡμῶν πολὺν ἐμηχανήσατο
> βασιλεὺς Φαραώ, τοὺς μὲν ἐν πλινθεύμασιν
> οἰκοδομίαις τε βαρέσιν αἰκίζων βροτούς
> πόλεις τ᾽ ἐπύργου σφῶν ἔκατι δυσμόρων.

The imbalance is patent: μέν is picked up by τε, τοὺς μέν is never
balanced by a comparable phrase, the participle is 'balanced' by a
finite verb. Yet it would seem rash to take this as evidence that
Greek was not the writer's native language. The passage is probably
anacoluthic. Nor is there any problem in finding parallels in good
Greek texts. Examples of μέν . . . τε can be found at Denniston,
Particles 374–6. Antithetical clauses (μέν . . . δέ and the like) in
which the first clause uses a participle while the second a finite
verb occur in the best of classical authors.[29] This is also found in
Judaeo-Christian Greek texts.[30] A number of interesting examples
are available in Sophocles, e.g. OC 348ff (and see Jebb ad 351) and
Trach. 836f where we may have a μέν . . . τε along with the shift
from participle to finite verb (see Kamerbeek ad loc.). At Exag. 200f
the text reads, ἱππεῖς δ᾽ ἔταξε τοὺς μὲν ἐξ εὐωνύμων,/ἐκ δεξιῶν δὲ
πάντας Αἰγυπτίου στρατοῦ. Again, the text looks anacoluthic, though
I shall argue that it is probably corrupt since it seems to make no
sense as it stands. At all events, the shift from τοὺς μέν would not
justify large conclusions. One further strange usage in μέν clauses
deserves a glance (205–11):[31]

> οἱ μὲν παρ᾽ ἀκτὴν πλησίον βεβλημένοι
> Ἐρυθρᾶς Θαλάσσης ἦσαν ἠθροϊσμένοι·
> οἱ μὲν τέκνοισι νηπίοις δίδουν βοράν
> ὁμοῦ τε καὶ δάμαρσιν ἔμπονοι κόπῳ·
> κτήνη τε πολλὰ καὶ δόμων ἀποσκευή·
> αὐτοὶ δ᾽ ἄνοπλοι πάντες εἰς μάχην χέρας
> ἰδόντες ἡμᾶς ἠλάλαξαν ἔνδακρυν

It is not even clear what the basic skeleton of this passage is. Is the οἱ
μέν . . . οἱ μέν balanced by κτήνη τε or, as seems more likely, by
αὐτοὶ δέ? What exactly does οἱ μέν . . . οἱ μέν mean? I know no example of duplicated μέν that parallels this.[32]

That there are some peculiarities in Ezekiel's use of μέν clauses is clear. That they justify denying him Greek as a native language seems dubious. One last suggestion on this score. I shall argue that Ezekiel was familiar with Herodotus. If so, his affection for imbalance may in some measure be influenced by that author who has a marked propensity for this sort of thing.

Other solecisms or peculiarities are present. Snell has noted τοῦ χάριν for οὕνεκα at 30 and οἴκοι for οἴκαδε at 239, asyndeta at 216 and 231 and occasional strange meanings of words (e.g. παρθένοι at 173).³³ He notes too the occasional δέ in apodosis.³⁴ Kuiper sees peculiarities or barbarisms at several places, most notably perhaps in the strange use of μάλιστα at 49 and 72, in the article for relative at 70, 103, and 225, the phrases δεξιᾷ . . . ἔνευσε (72f), τῇ ἐπαύριον (48) and the use of ἀπογυμνῶσαι (47). Examples could be added. The relative used for the demonstrative (45, 240, possibly 43), a somewhat free use of the dative case (see 37, 109, 257, 260), occasional strange uses of τε . . . καί (27, 165 (text problematic or disputed in both), 208).

But all this is little enough. Relative for demonstrative and article for relative are common enough.³⁵ Brief glances at Wieneke's commentary or LSJ quickly reveal that the usages in question here for οἴκοι, τῇ ἐπαύριον, ἀπογυμνόω really offer no problems. The free use of the dative case is probably no more than a reflection of the general trend to use the dative more loosely in *koine* Greek.³⁶ The three (at most) examples of unusual τε . . . καί all seem in some degree to point to an otiosity of expression. Peculiar use of τε and of τε . . . καί are very frequent in the *koine*.³⁷ As for the phenomenon of 'otiose τε' there are several examples in the papyri.³⁸ But even in the earlier classical period strange uses of τε and τε . . . καί crop up.³⁹ As for the unusual meanings of μάλιστα, παρθένοι, and τοῦ χάριν,⁴⁰ I know no good parallels but we should probably attribute the odd meanings to semantic developments within the *koine*. There is a lesson to be learned from the phrase ἐν χειρῶν νομαῖς at *Exag.* 42. Kuiper took this as another instance of Ezekiel's barbaric Greek. Most students and editors of the *Exagoge* have simply followed Stephanus in emending to νόμῳ. But we now know that the use of νομαῖς in this expression is indeed a development of the *koine*, for the identical phrase occurs in a second-century inscription from Macedonia (*Syll.*³ 700.29).

Does all this demonstrate that Greek was Ezekiel's native language? Surely not.[41] But I think it does show how rash it is to draw conclusions from what amounts to very insubstantial evidence. When we consider that Ezekiel is after all writing in a hodge-podge of styles,[42] a mix of elevated Greek tragic diction, contemporary *koine* Greek, and Septuagintalisms derived from the Bible, and is additionally subject to metrical constraints which at times probably result in arrangement of words dictated *metri causa*, it should scarcely surprise us to find occasional usages which are strange or solecistic. At all events, it goes far beyond the available evidence to conclude that Greek was not Ezekiel's native tongue.

THE EXAGOGE

ΜΩΣΗΣ   ἀφ᾽ οὗ δ᾽ Ἰακὼβ γῆν λιπὼν Χαναναίαν
κατῆλθ᾽ ἔχων Αἴγυπτον ἑπτάκις δέκα
ψυχὰς σὺν αὑτῷ καὶ ἐπεγέννησεν πολύν
λαὸν κακῶς πράσσοντα καὶ τεθλιμμένον,
ἐσάχρι τούτων τῶν χρόνων κακούμεθα   5
κακῶν ὑπ᾽ ἀνδρῶν καὶ δυναστείας χερός.
ἰδὼν γὰρ ἡμῶν γένναν ἅλις ηὐξημένην

δόλον καθ᾽ ἡμῶν πολὺν ἐμηχανήσατο
βασιλεὺς Φαραώ, τοὺς μὲν ἐν πλινθεύμασιν
οἰκοδομίαις τε βαρέσιν αἰκίζων βροτούς   10
πόλεις τ᾽ ἐπύργου σφῶν ἕκατι δυσμόρων.
ἔπειτα κηρύσσει μὲν Ἑβραίων γένει
τἀρσενικὰ ῥίπτειν ποταμὸν ἐς βαθύρροον.
ἐνταῦθα μήτηρ ἡ τεκοῦσ᾽ ἔκρυπτέ με
τρεῖς μῆνας, ὡς ἔφασκεν. οὐ λαθοῦσα δέ   15

ὑπεξέθηκε, κόσμον ἀμφιθεῖσά μοι,
παρ᾽ ἄκρα ποταμοῦ λάσιον εἰς ἕλος δασύ·

Μαριὰμ δ᾽ ἀδελφή μου κατώπτευεν πέλας.
κἄπειτα θυγάτηρ βασιλέως ἅβραις ὁμοῦ
κατῆλθε λουτροῖς χρῶτα φαιδρῦναι νέον·   20
ἰδοῦσα δ᾽ εὐθὺς καὶ λαβοῦσ᾽ ἀνείλετο,
ἔγνω δ᾽ Ἑβραῖον ὄντα· καὶ λέγει τάδε
Μαριὰμ ἀδελφὴ προσδραμοῦσα βασιλίδι·
'θέλεις τροφόν σοι παιδὶ τῷδ᾽ εὕρω ταχύ
ἐκ τῶν Ἑβραίων;' ἡ δ᾽ ἐπέσπευσεν κόρην.   25
μολοῦσα δ᾽ εἶπε μητρὶ καὶ παρῆν ταχύ

αὐτή τε μήτηρ καὶ ἔλαβέν μ᾽ ἐς ἀγκάλας.
εἶπεν δὲ θυγάτηρ βασιλέως· 'τοῦτον, γύναι,
τρόφευε, κἀγὼ μισθὸν ἀποδώσω σέθεν.'
ὄνομα δὲ Μωσῆν ὠνόμαζε, τοῦ χάριν   30
ὑγρᾶς ἀνεῖλε ποταμίας ἀπ᾽ ἠόνος.

*   *   *

Moses:*   When Jacob left Canaan
            he came to Egypt with seventy
            souls and fathered a great
            people that has suffered and been oppressed.
            Till this day we have been ill-treated   5
            by evil men and a powerful regime.
            For king Pharaoh, when he saw our people increas-
                               ing in number,
            devised many plans against us.
            He afflicted us with brickwork
            and the hard labor of construction   10
            and he had turreted cities built by our ill-fated men.
            Then he ordered that the Hebrew
            male children be cast into the deep-flowing river.
            My mother hid me for three months
            (so she has told me). But when she could no longer
                         escape detection,   15
            she dressed me and exposed me
            by the bank of the river in the thick and overgrown
                               marsh.
            My sister Mariam stood guard nearby.
            Then the princess with her maidservants
            came down to bathe.   20
            When she saw me, she took me up and
            recognized that I was a Hebrew.
            My sister Mariam then ran up to her and spoke,
            'Shall I get a nursemaid for this child
            from the Hebrews?' The princess urged her on.   25
            Mariam went to fetch our mother who presently
                               appeared
            and took me in her arms.
            The princess said to her, 'Woman, nurse this child
            and I shall pay your wages.'
            She then named me Moses, because   30
            she had taken me from the watery river-bank.

* * *

*This translation is intended solely as an aid to readers with little or no Greek.

ἐπεὶ δὲ καιρὸς νηπίων παρῆλθέ μοι,
ἦγέν με μήτηρ βασιλίδος πρὸς δώματα,
ἄπαντα μυθεύσασα καὶ λέξασά μοι
γένος πατρῷον καὶ θεοῦ δωρήματα.   35
ἕως μὲν οὖν τὸν παιδὸς εἴχομεν χρόνον,
τροφαῖσι βασιλικαῖσι καὶ παιδεύμασιν
ἄπανθ᾽ ὑπισχνεῖθ᾽, ὡς ἀπὸ σπλάγχνων ἐῶν·
ἐπεὶ δὲ πλήρης †κόλπος ἡμερῶν παρῆν,
ἐξῆλθον οἴκων βασιλικῶν (πρὸς ἔργα γὰρ   40
θυμός μ᾽ ἄνωγε καὶ τέχνασμα βασιλέως).

ὁρῶ δὲ πρῶτον ἄνδρας ἐν χειρῶν νομαῖς
τὸν μὲν ⟨τὸ⟩ γένος Ἑβραῖον, ὃν δ᾽ Αἰγύπτιον.
ἰδὼν δ᾽ ἐρήμους καὶ παρόντα μηδένα
ἐρρυσάμην ἀδελφόν, ὃν δ᾽ ἔκτειν᾽ ἐγώ,   45
ἔκρυψα δ᾽ ἄμμῳ τοῦτον, ὥστε μὴ εἰσιδεῖν
ἕτερόν τιν᾽ ἡμᾶς κἀπογυμνῶσαι φόνον.
τῇ 'παύριον δὲ πάλιν ἰδὼν ἄνδρας δύο,
μάλιστα δ᾽ αὐτοὺς συγγενεῖς, πατουμένους
λέγω· ᾽τί τύπτεις ἀσθενέστερον σέθεν;᾽   50

ὁ δ᾽ εἶπεν· ἡμῖν τίς σ᾽ ἀπέστειλεν κριτὴν
ἢ 'πιστάτην ἐνταῦθα; μὴ κτενεῖς σύ με,
ὥσπερ τὸν ἐχθὲς ἄνδρα;᾽ καὶ δείσας ἐγώ
ἔλεξα· ᾽πῶς ἐγένετο συμφανὲς τόδε;᾽
καὶ πάντα βασιλεῖ ταῦτ᾽ ἀπήγγειλεν ταχύ·   55
ζητεῖ δὲ Φαραὼ τὴν ἐμὴν ψυχὴν λαβεῖν·
ἐγὼ δ᾽ ἀκούσας ἐκποδὼν μεθίσταμαι
καὶ νῦν πλανῶμαι γῆν ἐπ᾽ ἀλλοτέρμονα.

* * *

ὁρῶ δὲ ταύτας ἑπτὰ παρθένους τινάς.   59

* * *

ΣΕΠΦΩΡΑ Λιβύη μὲν ἡ γῆ πᾶσα κλῄζεται, ξένε,
οἰκοῦσι δ᾽ αὐτὴν φῦλα παντοίων γενῶν,

When my infancy had passed,   32
my mother brought me to the princess' palace,
after telling me all about
my lineage and God's gifts.   35
Accordingly, for the period of my youth, the princess
gave me a royal upbringing and education,
as if I were her own son.
But when I grew into an adult,
I went forth from the royal palace   40
at my spirit's urging, to see the deeds and devices
                              wrought by the king.
First, I saw two men fighting,
one a Hebrew, the other an Egyptian.
I saw that we were alone, no one else was present.
So I rescued my kinsman and slew the other.   45
Then I buried him in the sand so that
no one else should notice and disclose the killing.
On the morrow I again saw two men
fighting, this time men of the same race.
I addressed one, 'Why are you striking a weaker
                                        man?'   50
He answered, 'Who made you our judge
and overseer? Or are you going to kill me,
as you killed the man yesterday?' In fear
I thought, 'How has this become known?'
The news quickly reached the king   55
and he sought to take my life.
When I heard this I left the country
and have now in my wandering come to this
                              foreign land.

*   *   *

Here are seven maidens coming.   59

*   *   *

Sepphora: Stranger, this land is called Libya.   60
             It is inhabited by tribes of various peoples,

Αἰθίοπες ἄνδρες μέλανες· ἄρχων δ᾽ ἐστὶ γῆς

εἷς καὶ τύραννος καὶ στρατηλάτης μόνος.
ἄρχει δὲ πόλεως τῆσδε καὶ κρίνει βροτούς
ἱερεύς, ὅς ἐστ᾽ ἐμοῦ τε καὶ τούτων πατήρ.   65

* * *

ΧΟΥΜ   ὅμως κατειπεῖν χρή σε, Σεπφώρα, τάδε.
ΣΕΠΦ.   ξένῳ πατήρ με τῷδ᾽ ἔδωκεν εὐνέτιν.

* * *

ΜΩΣΗΣ   ἔ⟨δο⟩ξ᾽ ὄρους κατ᾽ ἄκρα Σιν⟨αί⟩ου θρόνον

μέγαν τιν᾽ εἶναι μέχρι 'ς οὐρανοῦ πτύχας,
ἐν τῷ καθῆσθαι φῶτα γενναῖόν τινα   70
διάδημ᾽ ἔχοντα καὶ μέγα σκῆπτρον χερί
εὐωνύμῳ μάλιστα. δεξιᾷ δέ μοι
ἔνευσε, κἀγὼ πρόσθεν ἐστάθην θρόνου.
σκῆπτρον δέ μοι πάρδωκε καὶ εἰς θρόνον μέγαν
εἶπεν καθῆσθαι· βασιλικὸν δ᾽ ἔδωκέ μοι   75

διάδημα καὶ αὐτὸς ἐκ θρόνων χωρίζεται.
ἐγὼ δ᾽ ἐσεῖδον γῆν ἅπασαν ἔγκυκλον
καὶ ἔνερθε γαίας καὶ ἐξύπερθεν οὐρανοῦ,
καί μοί τι πλῆθος ἀστέρων πρὸς γούνατα
ἔπιπτ᾽, ἐγὼ δὲ πάντας ἠριθμησάμην,   80
κἀμοῦ παρῆγεν ὡς παρεμβολὴ βροτῶν.
εἶτ᾽ ἐμφοβηθεὶς ἐξανίσταμ᾽ ἐξ ὕπνου.

* * *

⟨ΡΑΓΟΥΗΛ⟩ ὦ ξένε, καλόν σοι τοῦτ᾽ ἐσήμηνε⟨ν⟩ θεός·
ζώην δ᾽, ὅταν σοι ταῦτα συμβαί⟨ν⟩ῃ ποτέ.
ἆρά γε μέγαν τιν᾽ ἐξαναστήσεις θρόνον   85
καὶ αὐτὸς βραβεύσεις καὶ καθηγήσῃ βροτῶν;
τὸ δ᾽ εἰσθεᾶσθαι γῆν ὅλην τ᾽ οἰκουμένην
καὶ τὰ ὑπένερθε καὶ ὑπὲρ οὐρανὸν θεοῦ·
ὄψει τά τ᾽ ὄντα τά τε πρὸ τοῦ τά θ᾽ ὕστερον.

* * *

Ethiopians, black men. One man is the ruler of
                                        the land:
he is both king and general.
He rules the state, judges the people,
and is priest. This man is my father and theirs.   65

* * *

Chum: Sepphora, you must reveal this.   66
Sepphora: My father has given me as spouse to this stranger.

* * *

Moses: I had a vision of a great throne on the top of
                                        mount Sinai   68
            and it reached till the folds of heaven.
            A noble man was sitting on it,   70
            with a crown and a large sceptre in his
            left hand. He beckoned to me with his right hand,
            so I approached and stood before the throne.
            He gave me the sceptre and instructed me to sit
            on the great throne. Then he gave me the royal
                                        crown   75
            and got up from the throne.
            I beheld the whole earth all around and saw
            beneath the earth and above the heavens.
            A multitude of stars fell before my knees
            and I counted them all.   80
            They paraded past me like a battalion of men.
            Then I awoke from my sleep in fear.

* * *

Raguel: My friend, this is a good sign from God.   83
            May I live to see the day when these things are fulfilled.
            You will establish a great throne,   85
            become a judge and leader of men.
            As for your vision of the whole earth,
            the world below and that above the heavens –
            this signifies that you will see what is, what has been
                                        and what shall be.

* * *

ΜΩΣ.   ἔα· τί μοι σημεῖον ἐκ βάτου τόδε,   90
          τεράστιόν τε καὶ βροτοῖς ἀπιστία;
          ἄφνω βάτος μὲν καίεται πολλῷ πυρί,
          αὐτοῦ δὲ χλωρὸν πᾶν μένει τὸ βλαστάνον.
          τί δή; προελθὼν ὄψομαι τεράστιον
          μέγιστον· οὐ γὰρ πίστιν ἀνθρώποις φέρει.   95
ΘΕΟΣ   ἐπίσχες, ὦ φέριστε, μὴ προσεγγίσῃς,
          Μωσῆ, πρὶν ἢ τῶν σῶν ποδῶν λῦσαι δέσιν·
          ἁγία γὰρ ἧς σὺ γῆς ἐφέστηκας πέλει,
          ὁ δ᾿ ἐκ βάτου σοι θεῖος ἐκλάμπει λόγος.
          θάρσησον, ὦ παῖ, καὶ λόγων ἄκου᾿ ἐμῶν·   100
          ἰδεῖν γὰρ ὄψιν τὴν ἐμὴν ἀμήχανον
          θνητὸν γεγῶτα, τῶν λόγων δ᾿ ἔξεστί σοι
          ἐμῶν ἀκούειν, τῶν ἔκατ᾿ ἐλήλυθα.
          ἐγὼ θεὸς σῶν, ὧν λέγεις, γεννητόρων,
          Ἀβραάμ τε καὶ Ἰσαὰκ καὶ Ἰακώβου τρίτου.   105
          μνησθεὶς δ᾿ ἐκείνων καὶ ἔτ᾿ ἐμῶν δωρημάτων
          πάρειμι σῶσαι λαὸν Ἑβραίων ἐμόν,
          ἰδὼν κάκωσιν καὶ πόνον δούλων ἐμῶν.
          ἀλλ᾿ ἕρπε καὶ σήμαινε τοῖς ἐμοῖς λόγοις
          πρῶτον μὲν αὐτοῖς πᾶσιν Ἑβραίοις ὁμοῦ,   110
          ἔπειτα βασιλεῖ τὰ ὑπ᾿ ἐμοῦ τεταγμένα,
          ὅπως σὺ λαὸν τὸν ἐμὸν ἐξάγοις χθονός.
ΜΩΣ.   οὐκ εὔλογος πέφυκα, γλῶσσα δ᾿ ἐστί μοι
          δύσφραστος, ἰσχνόφωνος, ὥστε μὴ λόγους
          ἐμοὺς γενέσθαι βασιλέως ἐναντίον.   115
ΘΕΟΣ   Ἀάρωνα πέμψω σὸν κασίγνητον ταχύ,
          ᾧ πάντα λέξεις τἀξ ἐμοῦ λελεγμένα,
          καὶ αὐτὸς λαλήσει βασιλέως ἐναντίον,
          σὺ μὲν πρὸς ἡμᾶς, ὁ δὲ λαβὼν σέθεν πάρα.

                              *   *   *

⟨Θ.⟩   τί δ᾿ ἐν χεροῖν σοῖν τοῦτ᾿ ἔχεις; λέξον τάχος.   120
⟨Μ.⟩   ῥάβδον τετραπόδων καὶ βροτῶν κολάστριαν.
⟨Θ.⟩   ῥῖψον πρὸς οὖδας καὶ ἀποχώρησον ταχύ.
          δράκων γὰρ ἔσται φοβερός, ὥστε θαυμάσαι.

Moses:	Ha, what is this portent from the bush,	90
	miraculous and hard for a man to believe?	
	The bush has suddenly burst into furious flame,	
	yet all its foliage stays green and fresh.	
	What is going on? I shall approach and examine this	
	great miracle. For it is hard to believe.	95
God:	Halt, great sir. Moses, do not come near,	
	until you have removed your shoes from your feet.	
	For the ground on which you are standing is holy.	
	The voice of God rings out to you from the bush.	
	Have courage, my child, and hear my words –	100
	for that you, a mortal, should see my face is impossible.	
	But you may hear those words of mine	
	that I have come to speak to you.	
	I am the God of your 'patriarchs' (as you call them),	
	Abraham and Isaac and Jacob.	105
	I have called them to mind, them and my gifts,	
	and so I have come to save my people, the Hebrews.	
	For I have seen my servants' suffering and distress.	
	Now go, and report in my words	
	to all the Hebrews and	110
	then to the king my instructions to you,	
	that you lead my people from the land.	
Moses:	I am not articulate. My tongue is	
	neither skilled at speech nor fluent. I cannot	
	address the king.	115
God:	I shall soon send your brother Aaron	
	and you will tell him everything I have spoken.	
	He will speak before the king.	
	You shall converse with me, Aaron will receive my	
	instructions from you.	

* * *

God:	What is that in your hands? Speak quickly.	120
Moses:	A rod wherewith to chastise beasts and men.	
God:	Throw it on the ground and withdraw quickly.	
	For it shall turn into a fearsome snake and you will	
	marvel at it.	

⟨Μ.⟩   ἰδοὺ βέβληται· δέσποϑ᾽, ἵλεως γενοῦ·

                ὡς φοβερός, ὡς πέλωρος· οἴκτειρον σύ με·   125
                πέφρικ᾽ ἰδών, μέλη δὲ σώματος τρέμει.
⟨Θ.⟩   μηδὲν φοβηϑῇς, χεῖρα δ᾽ ἐκτείνας λαβέ
                οὐράν, πάλιν δὲ ῥάβδος ἔσσεϑ᾽ ὥσπερ ἦν.
                ἔνϑες δὲ χεῖρ᾽ εἰς κόλπον ἐξένεγκέ τε.

⟨Μ.⟩   ἰδοὺ τὸ ταχϑέν· γέγονεν ὡσπερεὶ χιών.   130
⟨Θ.⟩   ἔνϑες πάλιν δ᾽ εἰς κόλπον, ἔσται δ᾽ ὥσπερ ἦν.

                            *   *   *

ΘΕΟΣ   ἐν τῇδε ῥάβδῳ πάντα ποιήσεις κακά·
                πρῶτον μὲν αἷμα ποτάμιον ῥυήσεται
                πηγαί τε πᾶσαι καὶ ὑδάτων συστήματα·
                βατράχων τε πλῆϑος καὶ σκνῖπας ἐμβαλῶ χϑονί.   135

                ἔπειτα τέφραν οἷς καμιναίαν πάσω,

                ἀναβρυήσει δ᾽ ἐν βροτοῖς ἕλκη πικρά.
                κυνόμυια δ᾽ ἥξει καὶ βροτοὺς Αἰγυπτίων
                πολλοὺς κακώσει. μετὰ δὲ ταῦτ᾽ ἔσται πάλιν

                λοιμός, ϑανοῦνται δ᾽ οἷς ἔνεστι καρδία   140
                σκληρά. πικράνω δ᾽ οὐρανόν· χάλαζα νῦν
                σὺν πυρὶ πεσεῖται καὶ νεκροὺς ϑήσει βροτούς.
                καρποί τ᾽ ὀλοῦνται τετραπόδων τε σώματα·
                σκότος τε ϑήσω τρεῖς ἐφ᾽ ἡμέρας ὅλας
                ἀκρίδας τε πέμψω, καὶ περισσὰ βρώματα   145
                ἅπαντ᾽ ἀναλώσουσι καὶ καρποῦ χλόην.
                ἐπὶ πᾶσι τούτοις τέκν᾽ ἀποκτενῶ βροτῶν
                πρωτόγονα. παύσω δ᾽ ὕβριν ἀνϑρώπων κακῶν.

                Φαραὼ δὲ βασιλεὺς πείσετ᾽ οὐδὲν ὧν λέγω,

                πλὴν τέκνον αὐτοῦ πρωτόγονον ἕξει νεκρόν·   150
                καὶ τότε φοβηϑεὶς λαὸν ἐκπέμψει ταχύ·

Moses: There, I have thrown it down. Oh Master, be
                                                                merciful.
            How dreadful, how monstrous. Have pity on me.   125
            I shudder at the sight, my limbs tremble.
God: Have no fear. Reach out your hand and seize its
            tail. It shall turn back into a rod.
            Now put your hand into your bosom and with-
                                                                draw it.
Moses: There, I've done it. It's become like snow.   130
God: Put it back into your bosom and it shall be as it
                                                                was before.

                        *   *   *

God: With this rod you shall work all kinds of plagues.   132
            First, the river, all the springs
            and pools will flow blood.
            I shall bring a multitude of frogs and lice upon the
                                                                land.   135
            Thereafter, I will sprinkle on them ashes from a
                                                                furnace
            and fierce sores will erupt on their bodies.
            Flies will come and torment many
            of the Egyptians. Afterwards there will come in
                                                                its turn
            a pestilence and all who possess hard hearts will die.   140
            Then I will make the heavens violent: hail mixed
            with fire will descend and lay men dead.
            Crops and animals will be destroyed.
            I will bring darkness for three whole days
            and will send locusts which will destroy   145
            all the remaining crops and the young shoots.
            And after all this I shall slay the firstborn children.
            Thus, I shall bring to an end the arrogance of this
                                                                evil people.
            King Pharaoh shall suffer none of the plagues I have
                                                                described,
            until he sees his firstborn son a corpse.   150
            Then in fear he will quickly send forth the people.

πρὸς τοῖσδε λέξεις πᾶσιν Ἑβραίοις ὁμοῦ·

'ὁ μεὶς ὅδ' ὑμῖν πρῶτος ἐνιαυτῶν πέλει·
ἐν τῷδ' ἀπάξω λαὸν εἰς ἄλλην χθόνα,

εἰς ἣν ὑπέστην πατράσιν Ἑβραίων γένους.'   155
λέξεις δὲ λαῷ παντί, μηνὸς οὗ λέγω
διχομηνίᾳ τὸ πάσχα θύσαντας θεῷ

τῆς πρόσθε νυκτὸς αἵματι ψαῦσαι θύρας,

ὅπως παρέλθῃ σῆμα δεινὸς ἄγγελος.
ὑμεῖς δὲ νυκτὸς ὀπτὰ δαίσεσθε κρέα.   160
σπουδῇ δὲ βασιλεὺς ἐκβαλεῖ πρόπαντ' ὄχλον.
ὅταν δὲ μέλλητ' ἀποτρέχειν, δώσω χάριν

λαῷ, γυνή τε παρὰ γυναικὸς λήψεται

σκεύη †κόσμον τε πάνθ', ὃν ἄνθρωπος φέρει,
χρυσόν τε καὶ ἄργυρόν τε καὶ στολάς, ἵνα   165
⟨ἀνθ'⟩ ὧν ἔπραξαν μισθὸν ἀποδῶσιν βροτοῖς.

ὅταν δ' ἐς ἴδιον χῶρον εἰσέλθηθ', ὅπως
ἀφ' ἧσπερ ἠοῦς ἐφύγετ', Αἰγύπτου δ' ἄπο
ἕπτ' ⟨ἦτ'⟩ ὁδοιποροῦντες ἡμέρας ὁδόν,
πάντες τοσαύτας ἡμέρας ἔτος κάτα   170
ἄζυμ' ἔδεσθε καὶ θεῷ λατρεύσετε,
τὰ πρωτότευκτα ζῷα θύοντες θεῷ,
ὅσ' ἂν τέκωσι παρθένοι πρώτως τέκνα
τἀρσενικὰ διανοίγοντα μήτρας μητέρων.

*   *   *

ἀνδρῶν Ἑβραίων τοῦδε τοῦ μηνὸς λαβών   175

κατὰ συγγενείας πρόβατα καὶ μόσχους βοῶν
ἄμωμα δεκάτῃ· καὶ φυλαχθήτω μέχρι
τετρὰς ἐπιλάμψει δεκάδι, καὶ πρὸς ἑσπέραν
θύσαντες ὀπτὰ πάντα σὺν τοῖς ἔνδοθεν

Further, you will speak the following to the whole
                Hebrew people:
'This month is for you the beginning of your years.
In this month I shall bring the people into another
                land,
as I promised the patriarchs of the Hebrew race.'   155
Tell the whole people that they should
sacrifice the Pesach to God this month on the day
                of the full moon,
before nightfall, and should daub the door with
                the blood,
so that my dread messenger will pass them by.
During the night you shall eat the roasted meat.   160
Then the king will drive the whole people out in haste.
But when you are about to leave, I will make the
                Egyptians
well-disposed to you and each of your women will
                receive from
her neighbor vessels and raiment of all kinds,
gold, silver and garments, so that   165
the Egyptians shall render payment for all the work
                the Jews have done.
When you reach your own land,
since you will have had a journey of seven days
from that morning on which you left Egypt,
you shall all, for seven days each year,   170
eat unleavened bread, and you shall worship God,
sacrificing to Him the firstborn male animals,
the offspring that the young mothers first bear and
that open first their mothers' wombs.

           *   *   *

On the tenth day of this month let the Hebrew
                men take 175
for their families unblemished lambs or calves
and keep them until the
fourteenth day. Then at evening
you shall make the sacrifice and eat it all, including
                the innards, roasted.

οὕτως φάγεσθε ταῦτα· περιεζωσμένοι   180
καὶ κοῖλα ποσσὶν ὑποδέδεσθε καὶ χερί
βακτηρίαν ἔχοντες. ἐν σπουδῇ τε γὰρ
βασιλεὺς κελεύσει πάντας ἐκβαλεῖν χθονός·
κεκλήσεται δὲ πᾶς. καὶ ὅταν θύσητε δέ,

δέσμην λαβόντες χερσὶν ὑσσώπου κόμης   185
εἰς αἷμα βάψαι καὶ θιγεῖν σταθμῶν δυοῖν,
ὅπως παρέλθῃ θάνατος Ἑβραίων ἄπο.
ταύτην δ᾽ ἑορτὴν δεσπότῃ τηρήσετε,
ἔφθ᾽ ἡμέρας ἄζυμα· καὶ οὐ βρωθήσεται

ζύμη. κακῶν γὰρ τῶνδ᾽ ἀπαλλαγήσεται,   190
καὶ τοῦδε μηνὸς ἔξοδον διδοῖ θεός·
ἀρχὴ δὲ μηνῶν καὶ χρόνων οὗτος πέλει.

                        *   *   *

ΑΓΓΕΛ.   ὡς γὰρ σὺν ὄχλῳ τῷδ᾽ ἀφώρμησεν δόμων

ΑΙΓΥΠΤ.   βασιλεὺς Φαραὼ μυρίων ὅπλων μέτα
ἵππου τε πάσης καὶ ἁρμάτων τετραόρων   195
καὶ προστάταισι καὶ παραστάταις ὁμοῦ,
ἦν φρικτὸς ἀνδρῶν ἐκτεταγμένων ὄχλος.

πεζοὶ μὲν ἐν μέσοισι καὶ φαλαγγικοί
διεκδρομὰς ἔχοντες ἄρμασιν τόπους·
ἱππεῖς δ᾽ ἔταξε τοὺς μὲν ἐξ εὐωνύμων,   200
ἐκ δεξιῶν δὲ πάντας Αἰγυπτίου στρατοῦ.
τὸν πάντα δ᾽ αὐτῶν ἀριθμὸν ἠρόμην ἐγώ {στρατοῦ}·
μυριάδες ⟨ἦσαν⟩ ἑκατὸν εὐάνδρου λεώ⟨ς⟩.
ἐπεὶ δ᾽ Ἑβραίων οὑμὸς ἤντησε στρατός,
οἱ μὲν παρ᾽ ἀκτὴν πλησίον βεβλημένοι   205
Ἐρυθρᾶς Θαλάσσης ἦσαν ἠθροϊσμένοι·
οἱ μὲν τέκνοισι νηπίοις δίδουν βοράν
ὁμοῦ τε καὶ δάμαρσιν, ἔμπονοι κόπῳ·
κτήνη τε πολλὰ καὶ δόμων ἀποσκευή·
αὐτοὶ δ᾽ ἄνοπλοι πάντες εἰς μάχην χέρας   210
ἰδόντες ἡμᾶς ἠλάλαξαν ἔνδακρυν

In this fashion you should eat it, all girded up,   180
with your shoes on your feet and your
walking sticks in your hands. For the king will order
that you be banished from the land in haste.
But every man shall be summoned. And after you
                          have sacrificed,
take a handful of hyssop,   185
dip it in the blood and touch it to the two doorposts,
so that death will pass the Hebrews by.
This festival you shall keep for the Lord,
seven days of unleavened bread. No leaven shall
                              be eaten.
For you shall receive release from these evils   190
and God grants you this month departure from Egypt.
This month is the beginning of months and eras.

*   *   *

Egyptian   For when king Pharaoh went forth with this multi-
                                  tude of men

Messenger: from his palace, with armed soldiers,
all his cavalry, four-horsed chariots,   195
soldiers on the flank and soldiers in the front ranks,
there was an awesome host of men drawn up in
                            battle formation.
There were infantry in the middle and phalangists,
but space was left for the chariots to pass through.
On the left the horsemen were stationed,   200
on the right were other Egyptians.
I inquired as to the total number of the army:
it came to one million men.
When my army overtook the Hebrews,
they were lying in groups by   205
the shore of the Red Sea.
The men, worn out, were giving food to
their children and wives.
Flocks and household utensils were all around.
They themselves were all unarmed   210
and on seeing us cried out tearfully

†φωνὴν πρὸς αἰθέρα τ᾽ ἐστάθησαν† ἀθρόοι,
θεὸν πατρῷον. ἦν πολὺς δ᾽ ἀνδρῶν ὄχλος.

ἡμᾶς δὲ χάρμα πάντας εἶχεν ἐν μέρει.
ἔπειθ᾽ ὑπ᾽ αὐτοὺς θήκαμεν παρεμβολήν   215
(Βεελζεφών τις κλήζεται πόλις βροτοῖς).
ἐπεὶ δὲ Τιτὰν ἥλιος δυσμαῖς προσῆν,
ἐπέσχομεν, θέλοντες ὄρθριον μάχην,
πεποιθότες λαοῖσι καὶ φρικτοῖς ὅπλοις.

ἔπειτα θείων ἄρχεται τεραστίων   220
θαυμάστ᾽ ἰδέσθαι. καί τις ἐξαίφνης μέγας
στῦλος νεφώδης ἐστάθη πρὸ γῆς, μέγας,

παρεμβολῆς ἡμῶν τε καὶ Ἑβραίων μέσος.
κἄπειθ᾽ ὁ κείνων ἡγεμὼν Μωσῆς, λαβὼν
ῥάβδον θεοῦ, τῇ δὴ πρὶν Αἰγύπτῳ κακά   225

σημεῖα καὶ τερ⟨ά⟩ατ᾽ ἐξεμήσατο,
ἔτυψ᾽ Ἐρυθρᾶς νῶτα καὶ ἔσχισεν μέσον
βάθος Θαλάσσης· οἱ δὲ σύμπαντες σθένει
ὤρουσαν ὠκεῖς ἁλμυρᾶς δι᾽ ἀτραποῦ.
ἡμεῖς δ᾽ ἐπ᾽ αὐτῆς ᾠχόμεσθα συντόμως   230
κατ᾽ ἴχνος αὐτῶν· νυκτὸς εἰσεκύρσαμεν

βοηδρομοῦντες· ἁρμάτων δ᾽ ἄφνω τροχοὶ
οὐκ ἐστρέφοντο, δέσμιοι δ᾽ ὡς ἥρμοσαν.
ἀπ᾽ οὐρανοῦ δὲ φέγγος ὡς πυρὸς μέγα
ὤφθη τι ἡμῖν· ὡς μὲν εἰκάζειν, παρῆν   235
αὐτοῖς ἀρωγὸς ὁ θεός. ὡς δ᾽ ἤδη πέραν
ἦσαν θαλάσσης, κῦμα δ᾽ ἐρροίβδει μέγα
σύνεγγυς ἡμῶν. καί τις ἠλάλαξ᾽ ἰδών·
᾽φεύγωμεν οἴκοι πρόσθεν Ὑψίστου χέρας·

οἷς μὲν γὰρ ἔστ᾽ ἀρωγός, ἡμῖν δ᾽ ἀθλίοις   240
ὄλεθρον ἔρδει.᾽ καὶ συνεκλύσθη πόρος
Ἐρυθρᾶς Θαλάσσης καὶ στρατὸν διώλεσε.

* * *

toward the heaven and their
ancestral God. There was great turmoil among
                                        the men.
We in contrast were delighted.
We pitched our camp opposite them –   215
the place is called Beelzephon.
Since the sun was on the verge of setting,
we waited, desiring a morning battle:
we were confident in our numbers and our fear-
                              some weapons.
Then, divine wonders and portents began   220
to occur. A large pillar,
looking like a cloud, suddenly appeared and took
                                        up a
position between our camp and that of the Hebrews.
Then their leader Moses took
the staff of God with which he had previously
                              wrought the 225
prodigies and plagues against Egypt and
striking the surface of the Red Sea he split it
in two. All of them rushed energetically and
swiftly through the sea's pathway.
We entered the path quickly,   230
on their track. We hastened forward, but en-
                              countered night.
Suddenly, the wheels of the chariots
would not turn, as if they were bound fast.
From the heavens came a great flash, as if
of a fire. It seemed that   235
God was helping them. When they had reached
the other side, a large wave surged
around us. One man, on seeing this, cried out:
'Let us run back home and flee the power of the
                              Supreme One.
For He is helping them, but is wreaking   240
our destruction.' Then the path was washed away
and the army perished.

* * *

66   The Exagoge

⟨ΣΚΟΠΟΣ⟩κράτιστε Μωσῆ, πρό⟨σ⟩σχες, οἷον εὕρομεν
τόπον πρὸς αὐτῇ τῇδέ γ᾽ εὐαεῖ νάπῃ.
ἔστιν γάρ, ὥς που καὶ σὺ τυγχάνεις ὁρῶν,   245
ἐκεῖ· τόθεν δὲ φέγγος ἐξέλαμψέ νιν
κατ᾽ εὐφρόνης σημεῖον ὡς στῦλος πυρός.
ἐνταῦθα λειμῶν᾽ εὕρομεν κατάσκιον
ὑγράς τε λιβάδας· δαψιλὴς χῶρος βαθύς,
πηγὰς ἀφύσσων δώδεκ᾽ ἐκ μιᾶς πέτρας,   250
στελέχη δ᾽ ἐρυμνὰ πολλὰ φοινίκων πέλει
ἔγκαρπα, δεκάκις ἑπτά, καὶ περίρρυτος

πέφυκε χλο⟨ί⟩η θρέμμασιν χορτάσματα.

*   *   *

ἕτερον δὲ πρὸς τοῖσδ᾽ εἴδομεν ζῷον ξένον,

θαυμαστόν, οἷον οὐδέπω †ὥρακέ τις.   255
διπλοῦν γὰρ ἦν τὸ μῆκος ἀετοῦ σχεδόν,
πτεροῖσι ποικίλοισιν ἠδὲ χρώμασι.
στῆθος μὲν αὐτοῦ πορφυροῦν ἐφαίνετο,
σκέλη δὲ μιλτόχρωτα, καὶ κατ᾽ αὐχένων
κροκωτίνοις μαλλοῖσιν εὐτρεπίζετο.   260
κάρα δὲ κοττοῖς ἡμέροις παρεμφερές,
καὶ μηλίνῃ μὲν τῇ κόρῃ προσέβλεπε
κύκλῳ· κόρη δὲ κόκκος ὣς ἐφαίνετο.
φωνὴν δὲ πάντων εἶχεν ἐκπρεπεστάτην.
βασιλεὺς δὲ πάντων ὀρνέων ἐφαίνετο,   265

ὡς ἦν νοῆσαι· πάντα γὰρ τὰ πτήν᾽ ὁμοῦ
ὄπισθεν αὐτοῦ δειλιῶντ᾽ ἐπέσσυτο,
αὐτὸς δὲ πρόσθεν, ταῦρος ὣς γαυρούμενος,
ἔβαινε κραιπνὸν βῆμα βαστάζων ποδός.

Scout: Great Moses, take note of the
place we have discovered, by that airy valley.
It is over there, as, I think, you can see.   245
From there a light flashed out
at night, some sort of sign, a pillar of fire.
There we discovered a shady meadow
and springs of water. The spot is lush and abundant.
Twelve springs issue forth from one rock,   250
there are many strong and fruitful palm trees,
seventy in all. And there is grassland with water
                              round about,
forage for our animals.

*   *   *

We saw something else too, a strange and remark-
                              able creature,
such as no man has ever seen before.   255
He was about twice the size of an eagle
and had multi-colored wings.
His breast was purplish
and his legs red. From his neck
saffron tresses hung beautifully.   260
His head was like that of a cock.
He gazed all around with his yellow eye
which looked like a seed.
He had the most wonderful voice.
Indeed, it seemed that he was the king of all the
                              birds. 265
For all of them
followed behind him in fear.
He strode in front, like an exultant bull,
lifting his foot in swift step.

COMMENTARY

1. The prologue (1–59)

The Euripidean nature of the prologue is evident and reflects a broad acquaintance on Ezekiel's part with Euripides' plays. That the prologue is cast in the form of a monologue which is, for all intents and purposes, addressed to the audience is itself Euripidean.[1] Sophocles tends to begin his plays with the appearance of two characters who speak to each other, though sometimes in lengthy speeches. Aeschylus is much closer to Euripides, for he sometimes presents a character on stage alone reciting an opening monologue (as in *Agamemnon* and *Eumenides*). But it is particularly Euripidean to have a speaker open the play with a sweeping historical account directed to the audience. The geographical element is typically (though not exclusively; compare Aeschylus' *Eumenides* and *Supplices*) Euripidean. In his prologues we often read that someone left one place and travelled to another (*Troades, Phoenissae, Bacchae, Heracles, Hecuba, Archelaus, Phrixus B*). Often the account is characterized by a participle of λείπω followed by a finite form of ἥκω or ἔρχομαι. Sometimes the speaker is talking of his own journey, sometimes of another's (e.g. *Heracles, Phoenissae*; Aeschylus' *Eumenides*). Again, completely (if not exclusively) Euripidean is the delay in identifying the prologue-speaker (*Electra, Phoenissae, Helen, Orestes*; Sophocles' *Philoctetes*). Recounting one's own birth, as Moses does, may be strictly Euripidean (*Ion, Bacchae, Orestes, Helen*). Ezekiel has exploited another prologue element that may be exclusively Euripidean by capitalizing on its coincidental occurrence in the Biblical narrative, namely the use of etymology. Thus, Moses' name is significantly explicated (30–1) just as are the names of Ion and Oedipus in the *Ion* and *Phoenissae*. Of the major tragedians only Euripides seems to have introduced quotations into prologue speeches (*Ion, Phoenissae, IT, Stheneboia*). So too Ezekiel (24–5, 28–9). Finally, the transitional 'here comes someone' (59) is particularly common in Euripides

(*Alcestis*, *Medea*, *Hippolytus*, *Hecuba*, *Ion*, etc; Aeschylus, *Choephoroi*, *Persae*; Sophocles, *OC*). If any single prologue is to be deemed closest to that of the *Exagoge*, it is probably the *Ion*'s which not merely has many of those elements enumerated above but also has many similar thematic elements: a secret pregnancy followed by exposure of the child; the subsequent rescue of the infant, with his discovery by a priestess who rears him; the maturing of the child into a young man of importance at the temple. With the change of temple to palace and priestess to princess we have much the same story as of Moses in Ezekiel's prologue. There is at least one slight verbal similarity here: τρέφει δέ νιν λαβοῦσα (*Ion* 41)/λαβοῦσ᾽ ἀνείλετο; τρόφευε (Ezekiel 21, 29). But in truth all this does not amount to much. There is no substantial evidence that Ezekiel had the *Ion* specially in mind.[2]

We turn to the text:

> ἀφ᾽ οὗ δ᾽ Ἰακὼβ γῆν λιπὼν Χαναναίαν
> κατῆλθ᾽ ἔχων Αἴγυπτον ἐπτάκις δέκα
> ψυχὰς σὺν αὐτῷ καὶ ἐπεγέννησεν πολύν
> λαὸν κακῶς πράσσοντα καὶ τεθλιμμένον,
> ἐσάχρι τούτων τῶν χρόνων κακούμεθα
> κακῶν ὑπ᾽ ἀνδρῶν καὶ δυναστείας χερός.   (1-6)

Did the *Exagoge* begin with the words ἀφ᾽ οὗ δ᾽ Ἰακώβ? In terms of sense there is no objection. The obstacle is δέ (which is omitted by one late manuscript, leaving a hiatus). No Greek tragedy opens with a δέ, but we should remember that we are dealing with Hellenistic tragedy here, for which we have no substantial evidence.[3] Many works of prose and poetry do begin with a δέ,[4] which is a weakened form of δή.[5] Instances occur in poems by Mimnermus, Solon, Archilochus, Callimachus (*AP* 7.519) and Theocritus (?) (25).[6] Verdenius has recognized the same phenomenon at work in a speech in Aeschylus' *Persae* (480).[7] I observe further that Josephus' *Life* begins with a δέ,[8] as does *3 Maccabees*.[9] Whether one can categorically dismiss all these parallels by asserting that tragedy is different from all these genres may be open to doubt.

Indeed, there may be good arguments to support verses 1ff as the opening of the drama, even if ἀφ᾽ οὗ is an unusual way to begin. In the first place, it is good Euripidean practice to open a play with the name of an important personage (often from the past) in the first line (*Ion, IT, Archelaus, Peliades, Phrixus B*, perhaps *Hypsipyle*). Second, for centuries it had been more or less traditional to begin accounts of the Exodus with Jacob's descent to Egypt.[10] We see this already at *Deuteronomy* 26.5ff and at *1 Samuel* 12.7ff. In the latter passage the prophet recounts God's favors to the Jewish people, beginning with the salvation from Egypt. The account starts, 'when Jacob came to Egypt' (12.8). There was also a tradition that the time from Abraham's coming to Canaan until the departure from Egypt was 430 years, 215 until Jacob's arrival in Egypt and 215 until the Exodus, thus reflecting a feeling that the events which conclude with the deliverance from Egypt begin with Jacob's descent thereto.[11] In fact, the verses at *Deut.* 26.5ff were recited at the first-fruits ritual by pilgrims to Jerusalem and would have been familiar to many Jews if only from this annual occasion (cf. *Bikkurim* 3.6–7; Philo, *Spec. Leg.* 2.215ff) – verses which are almost a capsule statement of what Ezekiel declares in the opening verses of the prologue. Moreover, in the family celebration of the Passover festival the father's narrative elaboration of the events of the Exodus began with this verse from *Deuteronomy* (*Pesachim* 10.4). As we shall see later, there is evidence that Ezekiel was influenced by elements of the familiar Passover celebration.[12]

Immediately preceding the verses of Ezekiel in Eusebius (*PE* 436d) is Artapanus' account of Moses and the Exodus, taken from Alexander Polyhistor. Polyhistor writes:

> περὶ δὲ τοῦ τὸν Μώυσον ἐκτεθῆναι ὑπὸ τῆς μητρὸς εἰς τὸ ἕλος καὶ ὑπὸ τῆς τοῦ βασιλέως θυγατρὸς ἀναιρεθῆναι καὶ τραφῆναι ἱστορεῖ καὶ Ἐζεκιῆλος ὁ τῶν τραγῳδιῶν ποιητής, ἄνωθεν ἀναλαβὼν τὴν ἱστορίαν ἀπὸ τῶν σὺν Ἰακὼβ παραγενομένων εἰς Αἴγυπτον πρὸς Ἰωσήφ. λέγει δὲ οὕτως, τὸν Μώυσον παρεισάγων λέγοντα·

As Polyhistor is here interested in Moses one might reasonably wonder why he begins his excerpt with Jacob. Clemens quite naturally begins his excerpt from Ezekiel with verse 7. Polyhistor could have done the same, or even begun with verse 12.[13] Polyhistor must have seen some natural reason for beginning with ἀφ' οὗ and perhaps the most natural would have been that it is the opening of the play. His terminology may support this. ἄνωθεν ἀναλαβών probably means, 'taking up from the beginning' (cf. Eusebius' use at *PE* 18d, 69b, 208c, 215c). ἱστορίαν merely picks up ἱστορεῖ. One might argue that 'from the beginning' signals where Polyhistor understands Moses' tale to begin. But it is hard to see why, if there were a few further introductory lines, he would not have cited them too. The large difference between Polyhistor's introduction here and his introductions elsewhere to quotations from Ezekiel after citations from other authors is striking and suggestive. Thus, before 68:

> Λέγει δὲ περὶ τούτων καὶ Ἐζεκιῆλος ἐν τῇ Ἐξαγωγῇ, προσπαρειληφὼς τὸν ὄνειρον τὸν ὑπὸ Μωσέως μὲν ἑωραμένον, ὑπὸ δὲ πενθεροῦ διακεκριμένον. λέγει δὲ αὐτὸς ὁ Μωσῆς δι᾿ ἀμοιβαίων πρὸς τὸν πενθερὸν οὕτως πως.

Before 193 (presumably after citations from other writers):

> Φησὶ δὲ καὶ Ἐζεκιῆλος ἐν τῷ δράματι τῷ ἐπιγραφομένῳ Ἐξαγωγή, παρεισάγων ἄγγελον λέγοντα τήν τε τῶν Ἑβραίων διάθεσιν καὶ τὴν τῶν Αἰγυπτίων φθορὰν οὕτως.

Before 243:

> Ἐκεῖθεν ἦλθον ἡμέρας τρεῖς, ὡς αὐτός τε ὁ Δημήτριος λέγει καὶ συμφώνως τούτῳ ἡ ἱερὰ βίβλος. μὴ ἔχοντα δὲ ὕδωρ ἐκεῖ γλυκύ, ἀλλὰ πικρόν, τοῦ θεοῦ εἰπόντος ξύλον τι ἐμβαλεῖν εἰς τὴν πηγὴν καὶ γενέσθαι γλυκὺ τὸ ὕδωρ. ἐκεῖθεν δὲ εἰς Ἐλεὶμ ἐλθεῖν καὶ εὑρεῖν ἐκεῖ δώδεκα μὲν πηγὰς ὑδάτων, ἑβδομήκοντα δὲ στελέχη φοινίκων. περὶ τούτων καὶ τοῦ φανέντος ὀρνέου Ἐζεκιῆλος ἐν τῇ Ἐξαγωγῇ παρεισάγει τινὰ λέγοντα τῷ Μωσεῖ περὶ μὲν τῶν φοινίκων καὶ τῶν δώδεκα πηγῶν οὕτως.

If ἀφ᾿ οὗ is not the initial verse, how would the play have begun? It is usually held that the opening lines would have dealt in some way with the patriarchs Abraham and Isaac,[14] though whether this was in the form of a mere genealogy (Wieneke 34) or an account of their happy residence in Israel (Dübner vii)[15] is debated. The latter seems unlikely given the way Ezekiel constantly plays down the role of Palestine;[16] the former would seem a reasonable portion of a genealogy extending from Abraham to Moses as in *Exodus* (6.3–27) or in Demetrius (Eus. *PE* 422d–426a). Since it seems evident there was no second half (Jacob to Moses), we may wonder whether there was a first half. After all, Ezekiel is writing a play on the Exodus, on the salvation from Egypt. Continuous Jewish history in Egypt begins with Jacob. His concern is not a History of the Jews. Such would have reasonably begun with Abraham.

The opening lines state that from the time Jacob settled in Egypt with his family and begat a large people, they were maltreated by the evil government.[17] It is impossible to determine what Ezekiel conceived to be the temporal span between κατῆλθε and ἐπεγέννησεν, but it seems probable that the rather rare word ἐπιγεννάω means 'became the forefather of,' or, to reverse the matter, that the Jewish people were the ἐπίγονοι of Jacob. The text then leads the reader to one conclusion, that virtually from the time of Jacob's arrival in Egypt the Egyptians mistreated the Jews. Ezekiel fails to mention that according to the Biblical narrative Jacob and his family were well received and flourished on coming to Egypt and – what is inextricably tied to this – that Joseph was nearly the ruler of Egypt. This is all the more puzzling since the introduction of Joseph would potentially be an avenue for magnifying the crime of the Egyptians. Both the Bible and Josephus exploit this possibility. Joseph was the savior of the Egyptians. But after a lapse of time the Egyptians forgot him and all the benefits he had bestowed upon them and proceeded to persecute his descendants (Jos. *AJ* 2.202). When Ezekiel leaves this out, he is ignoring material which *prima facie* could have been used for very effective dramatic and tendentious purpose. Surely then he must have seen something potentially distasteful or detrimental in the prosperity of the Jews and the position of Joseph. What this was can, I think, be discovered in the anti-Semitic elements preserved in Manetho (*apud* Jos. *Contra Apionem* 1.75–90, 103, 224, 228).[18] There was evidently an Egyptian tradition that identified the Jews with the hated Hyksos, the shepherd-kings who invaded Egypt, burned the cities, set up a king and persecuted the people. After more than two centuries of rule, they are driven out and proceed to march to Judaea where they build Jerusalem. That such an identification should have been made is scarcely surprising when one recalls that Jacob and his sons come to Egypt as shepherds and Joseph is in fact virtually the ruler of the country (*Genesis* 41.41ff, 42.6, 30, 45.8–9). To call him a shepherd-king of Egypt would not have been far from the truth. Indeed, when Manetho elsewhere refers to the conspiracy of the shepherds and the lepers against Egypt, he remarks that their leader was a priest of Heliopolis, Osarsiph by name, who later took the name Moses (1.238, 250). It has been suggested that Osarsiph is merely the Egyptian theophoric equivalent of Joseph.[19] The designation of Osarsiph as priest of Heliopolis would then probably be related to the fact that Joseph's father-in-law was priest of Heliopolis (*Gen.* 41.45; *Joseph and Asenath* 1.5). Confused variations on this theme can be seen in Chaeremon's version that the leaders of the polluted exiles were the scribes Moses and Joseph, also called Peteseph (1.290), and in the versions of Apollonius Molon (*apud* Eus. *PE* 421a) and Pompeius Trogus (Justin 36.2) who make Moses respectively the grandson and son of Joseph. What is clear from all this is that the Egyptians had a tradition that the Hyksos invaders who ruled Egypt were the Jews and that their king was Joseph, who was associated with – sometimes identified with – Moses.[20] Remnants of this Egyptian version can, I suspect, be discerned in the Midrash where we read, for instance (*Siphre Deut.* 301 *ad Deut.* 26.5): 'The text says "He sojourned there" so that no one would say that he descended to Egypt with the intent of gaining the crown,' which appears to be deliberate polemic against the view that the Jews did in fact rule over the Egyptians. Similarly, Philo writes that Pharaoh began to murder the Jews because, in part, he feared that they would contest his rule (*Moses* 1.8). Such an attitude on Ezekiel's part may also explain why he avoids mention of and allusion to Moses as heir to the Egyptian throne, a theme common in Rabbinic and Greco-Jewish sources.[21] In sum, Ezekiel decided that to mention the prosperity of the Jews in Egypt and Joseph's lordly position there would have the effect of undercutting the picture of the Jews as the oppressed and enslaved and too readily call to mind the Egyptian version of the Jews in Egypt in which the latter were not the oppressed, but the oppressors.[22] So he portrayed the Jewish experience in Egypt as one continuous period of persecution.

The narrative moves ahead:

ἰδὼν γὰρ ἡμῶν γένναν ἅλις ηὐξημένην
δόλον καθ' ἡμῶν πολὺν ἐμηχανήσατο
βασιλεὺς Φαραώ, τοὺς μὲν ἐν πλινθεύμασιν
οἰκοδομίαις τε βαρέσιν αἰκίζων βροτοὺς
πόλεις τ' ἐπύργου σφῶν ἕκατι δυσμόρων.

As in the Bible, Pharaoh in fear of the increasing number of Jews seeks various ways of controlling them. First, he puts them to forced labor and compels them to build his cities. Then, he tries to murder them outright:[23]

ἔπειτα κηρύσσει μὲν Ἑβραίων γένει
τἀρσενικὰ ῥίπτειν ποταμὸν ἐς βαθύρροον.

Ezekiel leaves out the episode of the midwives (perhaps subsuming it under δόλον πολύν of 8), as do other narratives of these Biblical events, e.g., *Jubilees* (ch. 46), the version at *Jerahmeel* ch. 42, perchance Philo at *Moses* 1.5–8, Josephus, *AJ* 2.205–7 (though with a strange twist involving *Egyptian* midwives), and *LAB* (ch. 9).

We move on to the fate of Moses:

ἐνταῦθα μήτηρ ἡ τεκοῦσ᾽ ἔκρυπτέ με
τρεῖς μῆνας, ὡς ἔφασκεν. οὐ λαθοῦσα δὲ
ὑπεξέθηκε, κόσμον ἀμφιθεῖσά μοι,
παρ᾽ ἄκρα ποταμοῦ λάσιον εἰς ἕλος δασύ.

Exodus 2.3 has merely ἐπεὶ δὲ οὐκ ἡδύναντο αὐτὸ ἔτι κρύπτειν. Ezekiel's explanation, an easy expansion on the Biblical text, matches other 'midrashic' elaborations. Thus, *Jubilees* 47.3 reports that she hid the infant three months and then [informers] told on her. Similar is Philo, *Moses* 1.9–10.[24] Targum Jonathan[25] translates 2.3 by expanding it: she could no longer hide him for the Egyptians were tracing her, were on her trail.

The Bible reports that Moses' parents built an ark and sealed it with pitch (presumably to keep water out) and then placed it in the marsh by the water, εἰς τὸ ἕλος παρὰ τὸν ποταμόν. The ark is absent in Ezekiel. On the other hand, *Exodus* simply states that she placed Moses in the ark; there is no mention of her clothing him first. Both these deviations are in tune with the earlier elaboration οὐ λαθοῦσα. The Biblical narrative, with its ark sealed by tar, clearly suggests that when Moses is placed in the marsh he is indeed in the water. This is made explicit when Pharaoh's daughter names the child (*Exod.* 2.10), ἐκ τοῦ ὕδατος αὐτὸν ἀνειλόμην. Josephus even has the ark sail down the river (*AJ* 2.221). Ezekiel is then in the tradition of the Jochebed-defenders. There was, it seems, a debate among post-Biblical exegetes whether Jochebed (the name commonly given to Moses' mother) had done wrong in exposing Moses and risking his death. Ezekiel, by adding οὐ λαθοῦσα, justifies her decision to expose the infant. By having Jochebed place the baby by the water and not in it (contrast παρὰ τὸν ποταμόν with Ezekiel's παρ᾽ ἄκρα ποταμοῦ) and by removing the ark, thus indicating that there was no danger of the baby's drowning, he absolves the mother of the charge of endangering her child's life. When the Biblical ἕλος becomes λάσιον εἰς ἕλος δασύ, the exaggerated emphasis on the vegetative overgrowth is designed to suggest a relatively warm and protected area.[26] When Pharaoh's daughter later names the baby, the difference between the Bible and Ezekiel is exactly to the point. In the former she says she drew him ἐκ τοῦ ὕδατος. In contrast, Ezekiel's princess merely drew him from the moist bank of the river, ὑγρᾶς . . . ποταμίας ἀπ' ἠόνος (31: the notion of wetness could not be completely avoided since the etymology depended upon it). It is possible that some of the Targumim are doing much the same as Ezekiel. Thus, Jerusalem Targum and Neofiti write באפרה,'in a meadow' while Onqelos' בירא seems to mean 'in the woods.' At all events, neither of these words seems to be used to translate סוף elsewhere. The regular term is גומא. Similarly, when Ezekiel's Jochebed dresses the baby it is clearly an attempt to indicate her concern for his welfare. He will be kept neat, warm, dry and comfortable in this fashion.[27]

Sister Miriam then takes up guard to see what will happen. *Exodus* is clear: she watches μακρόθεν, from afar (2.4). In Ezekiel, however, she is πέλας (18). Once again we detect the honor of the family being defended. Miriam did not watch fearfully from afar, but stood close by and alert.[28]

The princess comes to the Nile to bathe:

> κἄπειτα θυγάτηρ βασιλέως ἅβραις ὁμοῦ
> κατῆλθε λουτροῖς χρῶτα φαιδρῦναι νέον·
> ἰδοῦσα δ' εὐθὺς καὶ λαβοῦσ' ἀνείλετο.

It is perfectly conceivable that this is no more than an abbreviated form of the Biblical exposition:

> καὶ ἰδοῦσα τὴν θῖβιν ἐν τῷ ἕλει ἀποστείλασα τὴν ἅβραν ἀνείλατο αὐτήν.

But midrashic exegesis eliminated the maidservant who fetches the baby and gave the deed to the princess herself, by reinterpreting the Hebrew text. In the Hebrew ותשלח את אמתה (= ἀποστείλασα τὴν ἅβραν) the word אמה seems to have had – or was supposed to have had – a sense 'forearm.' Thus, the phrase could be understood 'she put forth her forearm.' Some exegetes worked this into a miracle, claiming that the princess' arm was supernaturally lengthened to reach the ark.[29] Whether Ezekiel is then our earliest evidence for some such tradition must remain speculation.[30]

The princess takes up the baby and recognizes it as a Jew:

ἔγνω δ' Ἑβραῖον ὄντα· καὶ λέγει τάδε
Μαριὰμ ἀδελφὴ προσδραμοῦσα βασιλίδι·
'θέλεις τροφόν σοι παιδὶ τῷδ' εὕρω ταχύ
ἐκ τῶν Ἑβραίων;' ἡ δ' ἐπέσπευσεν κόρην.
μολοῦσα δ' εἶπε μητρὶ καὶ παρῆν ταχύ
αὐτή τε μήτηρ καὶ ἔλαβέν μ' ἐς ἀγκάλας.
εἶπεν δὲ θυγάτηρ βασιλέως· 'τοῦτον, γύναι,
τρόφευε, κἀγὼ μισθὸν ἀποδώσω σέθεν.'
ὄνομα δὲ Μωσῆν ὠνόμαζε, τοῦ χάρω
ὑγρᾶς ἀνεῖλε ποταμίας ἀπ' ἠόνος.

Ezekiel, like the Bible, does not explain how she knows this (in contrast to much Midrashic literature). Miriam runs up[31] and inquires whether the princess might have an interest in a wet-nurse (ταχύ is an attempt at achieving a sense of dramatic urgency).[32] She assents and the mother is summoned. Again, Ezekiel strives to enhance her character: she arrives quickly and takes the child (affectionately) in her arms (26-7; none of this in the Bible). The princess' instructions are much what they are in *Exodus*, but one wonders whether the twofold μοι of 2.9 is deliberately left out, to diminish the proprietary connection between the princess and the baby. She then names the baby 'Moses,' because she took him from the watery riverbank. The Bible reports that the princess named the child only after it tells us that he has grown and returned to the palace. Perhaps Ezekiel felt it more natural for her to name the baby at the very moment rather than leave it nameless. Philo also reverses the sequence (*Moses* 1.17-18). It is manifest that Ezekiel assumes his audience will make the connection between 'Moses' and Egyptian μῶυ (cf. Philo, *Moses* 1.17; Jos. *AJ* 2.228, *Ap.* 1.286).

After verse 31 Polyhistor interrupts (*PE* 438a): τούτοις μεθ' ἕτερα ἐπιλέγει καὶ περὶ τούτων ὁ Ἐζεκιῆλος ἐν τῇ τραγῳδίᾳ, τὸν Μωυσῆν παρεισάγων λέγοντα. This is, as Kuiper observes,[33] rather surprising since 32 follows quite naturally on 31, so much so that one manuscript of Eusebius and, more significantly, the text as quoted in Clemens moves from 31 to 32 as if it were a continuous passage. One can guess that any lacking verses may have explicitly recorded the mother's taking her child back into her own home. Given Ezekiel's interest in putting Jochebed in a positive light, Kuiper's suggestion that he may have dwelled a bit on the mother's devotion to her son is reasonable.[34]

Infancy passes. Moses is brought by his mother to the royal palace:

> ἐπεὶ δὲ καιρὸς νηπίων παρῆλθέ μοι,
> ἦγέν με μήτηρ βασιλίδος πρὸς δώματα,
> ἅπαντα μυθεύσασα καὶ λέξασά μοι
> γένος πατρῷον καὶ θεοῦ δωρήματα.

But before so doing she instructs him in the history of his race. This has no parallel in the Bible and appears to be Ezekiel's attempt to resolve a problem that the Biblical account raises but never answers, namely, how does Moses become aware that he is Jewish?

The princess raises and educates the boy in royal fashion, as if he were her actual son:[35]

> ἕως μὲν οὖν τὸν παιδὸς εἴχομεν χρόνον,
> τραφαῖσι βασιλικαῖσι καὶ παιδεύμασιν
> ἅπανθ' ὑπισχνεῖθ', ὡς ἀπὸ σπλάγχνων ἐῶν·

Here we have, be it in ever so brief form, the earliest mention of Moses' royal Egyptian education, a theme which is treated expansively by Philo (*Moses* 1.20ff) and occurs briefly but emphatically at *Acts* 7.22. This is the reverse of the theme, found for example in Artapanus (*PE* 432a–c),[36] that Moses was the founder and discoverer of civilization, and seems a more tactful way to approach a non-Jewish audience and win its good will. A passage in *Jubilees* (47.9) may reflect a Palestinian, non-Hellenizing attempt to combat the view that Moses' education was in the hands of the Egyptians. On the contrary, we are told that after he was delivered to the princess his father taught him writing.[37]

Moses grows up. He leaves the palace and goes forth into the world:

> ἐπεὶ δὲ πλήρης †κόλπος ἡμερῶν παρῆν,
> ἐξῆλθον οἴκων βασιλικῶν (πρὸς ἔργα γὰρ
> θυμός μ' ἄνωγε καὶ τέχνασμα βασιλέως).
> ὁρῶ δὲ πρῶτον ἄνδρας ἐν χειρῶν νομαῖς
> τὸν μὲν ⟨τὸ⟩ γένος Ἑβραῖον, ὃν δ' Αἰγύπτιον.
> ἰδὼν δ' ἐρήμους καὶ παρόντα μηδένα[38]
> ἐρρυσάμην ἀδελφόν, ὃν δ' ἔκτειν' ἐγώ,
> ἔκρυψα δ' ἄμμῳ τοῦτον, ὥστε μὴ εἰσιδεῖν
> ἕτερόν τιν' ἡμᾶς κἀπογυμνῶσαι φόνον.

He sees two men fighting,[39] the one a Jew, the other an Egyptian. In these lines there occurs one of the most perplexing deviations that Ezekiel makes from the Biblical account, a change so surprising that, I think, no scholar has even noticed it, so strange that I have not the slightest notion why Ezekiel made it. In the Bible the Egyptian is (quite naturally) beating the Jew (*Exod.* 2.11): ὁρᾷ ἄνθρωπον Αἰγύπτιον τύπτοντά τινα Ἑβραῖον τῶν ἑαυτοῦ ἀδελφῶν τῶν υἱῶν Ἰσραηλ. Why should Ezekiel have turned the Biblical episode, which is a conspicuous manifestation of the persecution wrought by the Egyptians on the Jews, into a simple altercation in which neither man is seen as the villain?[40] In fact, this particular Biblical passage raised problems for the Rabbis and other exegetes who were somewhat dismayed by Moses' killing of the Egyptian here. Consequently, post-Biblical writers approach this event in one of two ways. Josephus (and perhaps Artapanus)[41] ignores it. Others attempted to justify the slaying by magnifying the villainy of the Egyptian.[42] Indeed, the book of *Acts* (7.24) clearly, if not expansively, seeks to justify Moses' act: the Jew is ἀδικούμενον and Moses ἠμύνατο καὶ ἐποίησεν ἐκδίκησιν τῷ καταπονουμένῳ. In short, whereas many Jewish readers of Scripture were in some degree bothered by this deed of Moses and sought to pass it over or whitewash it, Ezekiel did not merely forgo this path, but seems to have gone in precisely the opposite direction. For whereas the Bible makes it undeniably clear that the Egyptian is the aggressor, the Jew the victim, Ezekiel so revises this that it is in no way clear who is villain and who victim. Why? To me this remains a puzzle.[43]

On the following day Moses is again witness to a fight. *Exodus* so reads (2.13-14):

ἐξελθὼν δὲ τῇ ἡμέρᾳ τῇ δευτέρᾳ ὁρᾷ δύο ἄνδρας Ἑβραίους διαπληκτιζομένους καὶ λέγει τῷ ἀδικοῦντι Διὰ τί σὺ τύπτεις τὸν πλησίον; ὁ δὲ εἶπεν Τίς σε κατέστησεν ἄρχοντα καὶ δικαστὴν ἐφ' ἡμῶν; μὴ ἀνελεῖν με σὺ θέλεις, ὃν τρόπον ἀνεῖλες ἐχθὲς τὸν Αἰγύπτιον; ἐφοβήθη δὲ Μωυσῆς καὶ εἶπεν Εἰ οὕτως ἐμφανὲς γέγονεν τὸ ῥῆμα τοῦτο·

On the surface, Ezekiel appears to follow this closely, with the interesting addition of ἀσθενέστερον. But he introduces a significant deviation which, to my knowledge, has not been noticed by scholars:

τῇ 'παύριον δὲ πάλιν ἰδὼν ἄνδρας δύο,
μάλιστα δ' αὐτοὺς συγγενεῖς, πατουμένους
λέγω· 'τί τύπτεις ἀσθενέστερον σέθεν;'

ὁ δ᾽ εἶπεν· ἡμῖν τίς σ᾽ ἀπέστειλεν κριτὴν
ἢ ᾽πιστάτην ἐνταῦθα; μὴ κτενεῖς σύ με,
ὥσπερ τὸν ἐχθὲς ἄνδρα;᾽

δύο ἄνδρας ῾Εβραίους of the Bible becomes ἄνδρας δύο . . . αὐτοὺς συγγενεῖς. Gifford, Gutman and Dalbert are typical here in their forcing (apparently unintentional) of Ezekiel's text into the Biblical mold.[44] The first translates, 'two of our kin,' the second refers to the speaker of lines 51-3 as Moses' fellow-Jew, the third speaks of the strong Jew and the weak one. The truth is simple, Ezekiel gives no indication whatsoever that the two men are Jewish, only that, in contrast to the earlier pair, these two are members of the same people.[45] Whether the two are Jews or Egyptians we are never told. His desire to do this may also explain why he has changed the combatant's remark ἐχθὲς τὸν Αἰγύπτιον to ὥσπερ τὸν ἐχθὲς ἄνδρα. The designation of the slain man as Αἰγύπτιον in the Bible makes sense and is effective since the three men present are all Jews. Here, with the possibility left open that the two men are Egyptians, Ezekiel leaves out the designation of the dead man as 'Egyptian' since that would be less than natural in the mouth of an Egyptian. Similarly, τί τύπτεις ἀσθενέστερον σέθεν rather than the Biblical τί σὺ τύπτεις τὸν πλησίον has the effect of removing the Jewish element here, for such a complaint on Moses' part (τὸν πλησίον) is natural when directed to fellow-Jews, less so when addressed to Egyptians. Here then we are witness to a phenomenon that occurs a number of times in the *Exagoge*. Ezekiel constructs his narrative in such a fashion that it can be taken in one way by the Jews in the audience, in another by the non-Jews. Thus, the Jewish spectator (at least the one familiar with the Bible) will know that αὐτοὺς συγγενεῖς refers to two Jews. The non-Jewish spectator will most likely, if not necessarily, assume that the two men are both Egyptians.[46] Here, as elsewhere, Ezekiel is doing his best to put the Jewish people in as favorable a light as he can for his non-Jewish audience. This episode, as presented in the Bible, offers two difficulties. First, it represents Jews as fighting among themselves. Second, it implies that one of Moses' fellow Jews informs against him to Pharaoh. By leaving his audience with the vague impression that the two men are both Egyptian, he succeeds in totally circumventing these potential embarrassments. Probably motivated by these same reasons Philo left the episode out com-

pletely and then introduced advisors to the king who slander Moses, thus precipitating his flight (*Moses* 1.46–7).[47]
Moses flees:

καὶ πάντα βασιλεῖ ταῦτ' ἀπήγγειλεν ταχύ.
ζητεῖ δὲ Φαραὼ τὴν ἐμὴν ψυχὴν λαβεῖν·
ἐγὼ δ' ἀκούσας ἐκποδὼν μεθίσταμαι
καὶ νῦν πλανῶμαι γῆν ἐπ' ἀλλοτέρμονα.

This is much the Biblical version, slightly elaborated. Thus, Ezekiel has successfully brought his prologue (speech) to a conclusion, leaving us a scene familiar from classical Greek tragedy: the arrival in a foreign land of a hero-killer in flight. One recalls especially Orestes in *Eumenides*, Oedipus in *Oedipus at Colonus*.

Some 40 lines cover Moses' birth and youth, a subject that received considerable play in post-Biblical elaboration. One thing stands out, the almost total lack of miraculous and supernatural elements. For whether we scan Hellenistic expansions or Rabbinic ones, there is scarcely a single facet of the career of Moses from conception to maturity that is not lent some miraculous character.[48] Thus, for example, Amram (Jos. *AJ* 2.212ff) and Miriam (*LAB* 9.10) have dreams before Moses' birth foretelling his greatness. Jochebed delivers after only six months so as to forestall the Egyptian spies.[49] The baby is born circumcised and the house is filled with light at his birth.[50] The princess' trip to the river is divinely wrought.[51] There is a miraculous and ominous encounter between the baby Moses and Pharaoh, revolving around the latter's crown (Jos. *AJ* 2.233–6). Philo, though modest in details, sums it all up well when he states that these events were the result of divine providence (*Moses* 1.12, 17). In Ezekiel there is not an inkling of any of this, not even a hint of the divine or supernatural.[52] Thus, he sets the tone for what proves to be characteristic of the entire drama, the playing-down of anything supernatural or divine in Moses' role and nature.

One last matter. The question of whether Ezekiel knew Hebrew and utilized the Hebrew Bible as well as the Septuagint is a difficult one. But for those who believe that he did use the Hebrew Scriptures, no part of the play offers as much support as does the prologue. The most impressive piece of evidence is at the very beginning. *Exodus* opens with a list of Jacob's sons who came to Egypt with him. The summation is, ἦσαν δὲ πᾶσαι ψυχαὶ ἐξ Ἰακωβ πέντε καὶ

ἐβδομήκοντα. The Hebrew is strikingly different: ויהי כל נפש יצאי ירך
יעקב שבעים נפש. That is, the Septuagint gives 75 as the number of
Jacob's descendants, the Hebrew 70. Once again the opening lines
of the *Exagoge*:

> ἀφ' οὗ δ' Ἰακὼβ γῆν λιπὼν Χαναναίαν
> κατῆλθ' ἔχων Αἴγυπτον ἐπτάκις δέκα
> ψυχὰς σὺν αὐτῷ

Thus, we have a sharp difference between the Hebrew and Greek
Bibles and Ezekiel follows the Hebrew. *Quod erat demonstrandum* –
or so it would seem. But this conclusion is not as airtight as many
scholars seem to think.[53]

In the first place, one must at least grant the possibility that a
degree of coincidence is at work here, that Ezekiel was using only
the Septuagint but rounded off 75 to 70, especially since 70 was so
traditional a number. In several texts manuscripts reflect a confusion between 70 and some less 'round' number in the seventies, e.g.
Vita Adae 34.1, Luke 10.1 and in particular the puzzling passage in
Josephus (*AJ* 12.56-7) where he first speaks of six members from
each of the twelve tribes, but then refers to them as the seventy! So
it is not beyond all possibility that Ezekiel was simply substituting
the 'traditional' 70 for the 75 of the Septuagint.[54]

It is also possible that the numerical divergences do not reflect the
choice of one source or another but rather differences in the definition of the group's composition. Here we find ourselves in a laby-
rinthine confusion which can scarcely be navigated, a confusion
which begins with the Bible itself. The Hebrew text at *Exodus* 1.5
does not tell us who are included in the 70; indeed, it is not even
explicit as to whether Jacob and Joseph (and his children) are part
of the 70. But *Genesis* 46.8ff are more informative, providing long
lists of Jacob's descendants. Here too the Septuagint has expanded
on the Hebrew account, adding Joseph's grandchildren and great-
grandchildren to come up again with the sum of 75 rather than the
Hebrew's 70. The problems here are so great as to seem insoluble.
Now, if Ezekiel knew the Septuagint texts at both *Genesis* 46 and
Exodus 1 (which he almost certainly did), he would have recognized
the confusion. And when he declares that Jacob went down to Egypt
with 70 souls, he is not, strictly speaking, agreeing with either the
Septuagint or the Hebrew text, since both agree that Jacob went

down with 66. Further, we note that the Septuagint does not merely change the Hebrew 70 to 75 at *Exodus* 1.5, but also transposes the last words of the sentence, 'Joseph was in Egypt,' to the beginning:

ויהי כל נפש יצאי ירך יעקב שבעים נפש ויוסף היה במצרים

'Ιωσηφ δὲ ἦν ἐν Αἰγύπτῳ. ἦσαν δὲ πᾶσαι ψυχαὶ ἐξ 'Ιακωβ πέντε καὶ ἑβδομήκοντα.

This seems an attempt to clarify and justify the change from 70 to 75, as if suggesting that Joseph (and family) was not included in the Hebrew but is being included here with all the other brothers (and families) with whom his name is now joined, thus raising the total to 75. If Ezekiel had only the Septuagint in front of him, he would have been reading a text which asserted that Jacob's descendants (but not only those who travelled with him) were 75. If his intent was to calculate only those who travelled with Jacob, he might have subtracted a small number from 75, e.g. Jacob, two sons and three grandsons, giving 69 which would then be readily rounded off to 70. In other words, the very notion that Ezekiel is here in accord with the Hebrew text may itself be problematic, since the Hebrew does not refer to 70 as the number of those who descended with Jacob, as Ezekiel has it, but rather of 'all the offspring of Jacob' who presumably at some time or another reached (or resided in) Egypt.

The number of Jacob's descendants in Egypt and the constitution of any given number was a matter of interest and debate beyond the limited arena of the differing Biblical texts. Thus, *Jubilees* (44.33) presents Jacob and his descendants as 70, but its list of the 70 individuals differs from that of the Hebrew Bible. *LAB* (8.11) puts the offspring at 72.[55] The Targumim at *Exodus* 1.5 seem to differ in their translations depending on whether they believe Joseph and his family are or are not to be considered as part of the 70. After setting forth a precise and detailed list of the 70, Josephus feels the need to remark that Jacob has not been included in the count (*AJ* 2.183). In brief, it is highly possible that the question of the number of Jacob's descendants was debated in exegetical circles and that Ezekiel knew the number 70 through this avenue, without any need for direct familiarity with the Hebrew Bible.

A last possibility. At *Deut.* 10.22 the Septuagint reads ἐν ἑβδομήκοντα ψυχαῖς κατέβησαν οἱ πατέρες σου εἰς Αἴγυπτον. The Greek text here affirms the number 70.[56] Ezekiel may have chosen to use the 70 of *Deuteronomy* rather than the 75 of *Exodus*. That the difference in number between the Greek *Exodus* and *Deuteronomy* texts was familiar to and a subject of discussion in Hellenistic Jewish circles is evident from Philo's interpretation at *Migr. Abr.* 199ff. One interesting fact may give support to this hypothesis. The passages in *Genesis* and *Exodus* that number Jacob's descendants speak of them as 'coming' to Egypt (εἰσέρχεσθαι, εἰσπορεύεσθαι). Only the passage in *Deuteronomy* speaks of their 'descent' to Egypt, as does Ezekiel.[57] Further, as mentioned above, the Midrashic section of the Passover 'Haggadah' began with *Deut.* 26.5 (a verse which, by the way, also uses 'descent' of Jacob's move to Egypt). This verse is then explicated and expanded in a piecemeal fashion. The section 'he sojourned there with a few' is explicated as follows: 'As it is written, "your forefathers went down to Egypt with seventy people and now the Lord your God has made you like the stars of heaven in numbers",' that is to say, with a verbatim quotation of *Deut.* 10.22 testifying to the number 70.[58] We do not know how foreigners conducted their Passover recitation, be it at home or in Palestine, but whether they handled it in Hebrew (transliterated?) or Aramaic or in their native tongue, or in some mixture of the two, the fact remains. Whether Ezekiel would have recited the verse in the Septuagint version or in the Hebrew one, the crucial words would have been identical: 70 was the number of Jacob's family.

In sum, there are several ways in which Ezekiel could have known the figure 70 without any direct knowledge of the Hebrew Bible.

Other possible traces of the Hebrew Bible have been noticed in the prologue. Kuiper and Wieneke observed that in treating the concealment of Moses (*Exodus* 2.2) the Hebrew mentions merely the mother as agent, while the Septuagint includes both parents. Ezekiel gives only the mother (14). But this is a very small change, readily made by the poet himself, especially when one considers that Ezekiel seems deliberately to have written Amram out of his version.[59] Perhaps this was part of his endeavor to increase the mother's role and honor. Gutman (32) has noted additionally that Ezekiel's ἔκρυπτε is a more precise translation of the Hebrew ותצפנהו than is the Septuagint's ἐσκέπασαν. This is true, but in the very next verse (2.3) the

Septuagint uses κρύπτειν to translate the same Hebrew verb, so Ezekiel could well have the Greek verb from here.[60]

Exodus 2.3 reads על שפת היאר. The Septuagint translates, παρὰ τὸν ποταμόν. Wieneke has suggested that Ezekiel was using the Hebrew and wrote παρ' ἄρθρα ποταμοῦ. In fact, the manuscripts all read ἄκρα, not ἄρθρα, which seems to have nothing to do with שפה. Anyway, this reading has (as argued above) tendentious goals.[61]

In his zeal to find Hebraisms here, Wieneke argues that the strange phrase ἐπεὶ δὲ πλήρης κόλπος ἡμερῶν παρῆν (39) is a Hebraism. His argument will convince no one. Snell obelizes. Müller's καιρός may be the best and easiest way out of the difficulties.[62]

2. Sepphora: meeting and marriage (60-7)

The daughters of Raguel approach and Moses asks them who they are: ἐρωτήσαντός τε αὐτὰς τίνες εἴησαν αἱ παρθένοι (Polyhistor at *PE* 438d). We may think of Odysseus' arrival at Phaeacia and his request of Nausicaa, ἄστυ δέ μοι δεῖξον (*Od.* 6.178) and her response

> ἄστυ δέ τοι δείξω, ἐρέω δέ τοι οὔνομα λαῶν.
> Φαίηκες μὲν τήνδε πόλιν καὶ γαῖαν ἔχουσιν,
> εἰμὶ δ' ἐγὼ θυγάτηρ μεγαλήτορος Ἀλκινόοιο,
> τοῦ δ', ἐκ Φαιήκων ἔχεται κάρτος τε βίη τε. (194-7)

a passage which precisely parallels the words of Sepphora in first setting out the name of the people who inhabit the place and then reporting the speaker's identity as daughter of the ruler. Or we may recall the arrival of Oedipus and Antigone in Colonus. They decide to inquire where they are (Soph. *OC* 23, 26) and Oedipus asks, τίς ἔσθ' ὁ χῶρος (52). Whatever Moses' exact question, the response we do have (60-5):[1]

> Λιβύη μὲν ἡ γῆ πᾶσα κλήζεται, ξένε,
> οἰκοῦσι δ' αὐτὴν φῦλα παντοίων γενῶν,
> Αἰθίοπες ἄνδρες μέλανες· ἄρχων δ' ἐστὶ γῆς
> εἷς καὶ τύραννος καὶ στρατηλάτης μόνος.
> ἄρχει δὲ πόλεως τῆσδε καὶ κρίνει βροτοὺς
> ἱερεύς, ὅς ἐστ' ἐμοῦ τε καὶ τούτων πατήρ.

We are in the land of Libya, inhabited by black Ethiopians.[2] What is Moses doing here? In the Bible he flees to Midian. This discrepancy led Kuiper to argue that Ezekiel could not have been Alexandrian, for no one living in Egypt would have placed Midian in Africa.[3] Wieneke correctly opposed Kuiper by observing[4] that geographical knowledge among the Greeks was so limited that such a blunder can be understood.[5] And yet, it is not geography that is the issue here but rather 'tradition.' For once again we see Ezekiel operating within the framework of post-Biblical Jewish exegesis. In the Bible Moses goes to Midian and marries Sepphora the daughter of Raguel. But at *Numbers* 12.1 we read of האשה הכושית אשר לקח (γυνὴ Αἰθι-όπισσα), Moses' Ethiopian wife. כוש is routinely taken to be Ethiopia and the Septuagint so regularly translates it and its adjectival forms. Thus, readers of the Bible were confronted with a problematic text that ultimately led to several kinds of resolution. The question is simple: how is one to reconcile Moses' marriage to Sepphora the Midianite with the statement that he had an Ethiopian wife? In brief, the 'solutions' are as follows: (1) 'Ethiopian wife' is not to be taken literally. Rather, it is a metaphor of sorts. Ethiopians are strikingly different from other people; so Sepphora was strikingly different from (i.e. superior to) other women.[6] (2) Moses did at some point contract another marriage and this wife was Ethiopian.[7] It appears that from this view of the verse the whole Moses–Ethiopia romance that is attested in Josephus, Jerahmeel and other aggadic texts, arose.[8] (3) The version present in Ezekiel. Sepphora is simply identified with the wife of *Numbers* 12.1 and the reasonable conclusion is drawn that she was Ethiopian. For Ezekiel this would have required nothing more on his part than ignorance as to where Midian was, an ignorance we can readily grant, or at worst if by unlikely chance he happened to know of a Midian in Arabia, the inference that there was another Midian in Ethiopia. That such is the case is strongly supported by Demetrius' exposition of the same business (at *PE* 439b–d): Sepphora turns out to be a descendant of Abraham, an opinion apparently supported by the Septuagint which in the section on the descendants of Abraham and Keturah (*Genesis* 25.1–4) adds the name Raguel (not present in the Hebrew) to the children of Dedan.[9] Demetrius concludes by asserting *both* that Sepphora lived in Midian *and* that she was the Ethiopian woman. There is the further perplexing statement that Abraham sent his children to the East to settle and *therefore* Aaron and Miriam spoke of the 'Ethiopian woman.' What is central here is the potential that exists for confusion between Africa and Arabia[10] and secondly the location of Midian. Thus, the reader of the Bible may well come away bewildered when he reads that Shewa and Dedan are listed among the descendants of both Abraham-Keturah and Cush whose subjects (according to Jos. *AJ* 1.131) were the Ethiopians. Yet, the sons of Cush at *Gen.* 10.7 appear to be Arabian tribes. Indeed, Targum Jon. *ad Gen.* 10.6 designates the eparchy of Cush as ערביא. The traditions preserved in Cleodemus-Malchus and Josephus only add to the sense of confusion.[11] Both point to a tradition in which a son (or descendant) of Abraham and Keturah (Ephren or Apher) settles in Africa and proves to be its eponymous ancestor.[12] Placing the city Midian in Africa merely entails the locating of another of Abraham and Keturah's sons in that continent. We ought perhaps to remember how the apparently Arabian Queen of Sheba is identified with the queen of the Ethiopians.[13] Then there is the question of Midian itself. It is pretty well established that Midian is in Arabia[14] by the Red Sea (though some modern scholars believe that in the story of Moses and Raguel it is conceived of as being in the Sinai peninsula). Aside from considerations already proffered, we might wonder whether Ezekiel thought of Ethiopia rather than Arabia because Moses' journey to Midian is so easy. Recall that Manetho[15] has the Pharaoh in his story flee from Egypt to Ethiopia. Also, in the Hellenistic period Ethiopia was virtually identified with the desert lands that bordered Egypt. It has even been suggested[16] that the Septuagint derives the word ציים from ציה, i.e. those of the desert, and then proceeds to translate it Αἰθίοπες (*Psalms* 72.9).[17]

(4) Finally, we may mention what many scholars today hold to be the genuine solution, namely, that האשה הכושית is indeed an allusion to Sepphora, but כוש here does not mean Ethiopia but rather means Midian, an argument supported *inter alia* by the parallelism of *Habakkuk* 3.7.

We can conclude that in Hellenistic Jewish circles there were probably at least two views of the Moses–Sepphora–Ethiopian woman question circulating (nos. (2) and (3)) and that Ezekiel adopted (3), as did Demetrius.[18] Further discussion may lead us to conclude that he was also familiar with the other view (2).

Polyhistor then informs us that Ezekiel went on to recount the episode of the watering of the sheep (but gives us absolutely no details so we do not know to what degree and in what ways Ezekiel limited himself to the Biblical account[19]) and moved from there to the marriage of Sepphora. In this connection (Polyhistor tells us) Ezekiel brought on stage Sepphora and Chum in conversation. Two lines of dialogue follow:[20]

ὅμως κατειπεῖν χρή σε, Σεπφώρα, τάδε.
ξένῳ πατήρ με τῷδ᾽ ἔδωκεν εὐνέτιν. (66–7)

Chum, a character who is nowhere attested in the Bible, is apparently a suitor of Sepphora who is disturbed to learn that she has been betrothed to Moses by Raguel.[21]

There is no substantial evidence as to whether there was a chorus (or choruses) in the *Exagoge*.[22] The most obvious choice in the extant fragments are the daughters of Raguel. If they can be conceived of as a chorus in this play, whether integral and active or merely residual and unimportant, then we may be able to say a few words about possible sources of influence here.

We would then have a play in which one member of a very well and precisely defined choral group was not part of the chorus but an independent character within the drama. We might see a hint of this separation in line 65, ἱερεὺς ὅς ἐστ᾽ ἐμοῦ τε καὶ τούτων πατήρ. This is very rare in Greek tragedy. One can find loose parallels but they are loose indeed. For instance, in Euripides' *Troades* and *Hecuba* both the chorus and several of the characters are captive Trojan women. But only one substantial parallel exists, namely, the final play of Aeschylus' Danaid trilogy in which Hypermestra may well have been isolated from the chorus of Danaid sisters and have had a role in her own right. The fundamental issue of the trilogy and its final play was a conflict over marriage, which seems to be the issue in this scene of the *Exagoge*.[23]

In the Bible Raguel is priest of Midian (*Exod.* 3.1). Ezekiel turns him into a potentate who combines the privileges of king (including general), judge and priest. Yet, all this is well within the limits of the Biblical text and post-Biblical exegesis. That Raguel was ruler of his land is reported in Hellenistic-Jewish texts, e.g. Artapanus, τῷ τῶν τόπων ἄρχοντι (*PE* 434a) and in Rabbinic ones.[24] That he is a judge here seems to reflect two things. In the Bible it is Raguel who gives advice to Moses on how to construct a judicial system for the people

(*Exod.* 18.13ff). Further, there seems to have been a fanciful etymology associating Midian with the verb דין and so connecting Midian to 'judgment.' Philo (*Mut. Nom.* 110ff) describes the 'Midian-type' of character as κριτικὸν καὶ δικαστικόν, as of the priest Raguel.

The scene that follows in our fragments is that of Moses' dream and Raguel's interpretation. Kappelmacher argued that ξένε (83) indicates that Moses is not yet betrothed to Sepphora. Consequently, he places the dream scene before the dialogue of Sepphora and Chum. This sequence, he suggests, provides a rationale for Raguel's decision to marry his daughter to Moses, since he now realizes that the stranger is destined for great things. Wieneke (60) raised a number of good objections to the peripheral aspects of Kappelmacher's argument but concluded that the transposition is desirable.[25] One might add that in a Rabbinic version of this story Raguel seems to be influenced into marrying Sepphora to Moses because of his feeling that the latter will have a distinguished future.[26] But on balance there does not seem to be any good reason to reverse the scenes. The fact that Moses is now his son-in-law does not render it impossible for Raguel to call him ξένε, which he still is. Strong evidence lies (as Wieneke casually notes, 59) in Polyhistor's introduction to this scene. Before verses 68ff and 83ff he explicitly states that Moses speaks to (and is addressed by) his father-in-law. Moreover, Polyhistor's remarks after 65,

> εἶτα περὶ τοῦ ποτισμοῦ τῶν θρεμμάτων διελθὼν περὶ τοῦ Σεπφώρας ἐπιβάλλει γάμου, δι᾽ ἀμοιβαίων παρεισάγων τόν τε Χοὺμ καὶ τὴν Σεπφώραν λέγοντας·

suggest a close connection between the ensuing events. If indeed there was an episode as important as the dream-scene between the well-scene and the marriage, there seems to be no reason why Polyhistor would not have introduced it right here where it belongs.[27]

3. Moses' dream (68–89)

Moses reports to Raguel a clearly significant dream and the latter interprets it. Nothing like this exists in the *Exodus* narrative. But the presence of a dream with symbolic character will strike neither the reader of Scripture nor the devotee of Greek literature as odd. On the contrary, it is a rather familiar literary phenomenon both among Greeks and Jews.[1]

> ἔ⟨δ⟩οξ' ὅρους κατ' ἄκρα Σιν⟨αί⟩ου θρόνον
> μέγαν τιν' εἶναι μέχρι 'ς οὐρανοῦ πτύχας,
> ἐν τῷ καθῆσθαι φῶτα γενναῖόν τινα
> διάδημ' ἔχοντα καὶ μέγα σκῆπτρον χερί
> εὐωνύμῳ μάλιστα. δεξιᾷ δέ μοι
> ἔνευσε, κἀγὼ πρόσθεν ἐστάθην θρόνου.
> σκῆπτρον δέ μοι πάρδωκε καὶ εἰς θρόνον μέγαν
> εἶπεν καθῆσθαι· βασιλικὸν δ' ἔδωκέ μοι
> διάδημα καὶ αὐτὸς ἐκ θρόνων χωρίζεται.
> ἐγὼ δ' ἐσεῖδον γῆν ἅπασαν ἔγκυκλον
> καὶ ἔνερθε γαίας καὶ ἐξύπερθεν οὐρανοῦ,
> καί μοί τι πλῆθος ἀστέρων πρὸς γούνατα
> ἔπιπτ', ἐγὼ δὲ πάντας ἠριθμησάμην,
> κἀμοῦ παρῆγεν ὡς παρεμβολὴ βροτῶν.
> εἶτ' ἐμφοβηθεὶς ἐξανίσταμ' ἐξ ὕπνου.[2]

Moses' dream here seems to be unique. It is, nevertheless, clear that Ezekiel did not simply concoct it *ex nihilo* but was influenced by many and widespread dream- (and other) traditions. Although one can never be certain whether a given dream-version influenced him, one can reach a general awareness of the sort of versions which may well have had an impact upon him.[3] Let us begin with the Jewish traditions as they relate to the various single aspects of the dream.

The divine throne in the heavens is commonplace in Jewish texts. The association with a mountaintop can probably be paralleled, as perhaps at *Test. Levi* 2.5ff, 5.1, *1 Enoch* 18.8, 25.3, and most relevant for us in the paraphrase by the Aramaic Targumim (Onqelos and Jonathan) of *Exod.* 24.10 'under His feet' in the account of Moses' ascent of Sinai. The phrase is taken to refer to God's throne. Here, in other words, we find evidence for a tradition of Moses' ascent of Sinai which included the divine throne.[4] As for the seating of Moses on the throne, Gutman (43) has remarked Jewish legends in which Moses, when turning over authority to Joshua, places the latter next to him on his seat. But both passages cited by Gutman seem to me to emphasize the *elevation* of Joshua to *Moses' level*, not the *seating* of Joshua on Moses' *seat*.[5] If there is a Jewish tradition here, I suspect it is based on *Psalms* 110.1, 'The Lord said to my lord, "sit at my right hand,"' a passage which continues (as does Ezekiel) with the transmission of the sceptre and the prophecy of future domination.[6]

In addition to the throne, the figure turns over to Moses his sceptre and crown.[7] The sceptre in association with the throne as symbols of rule is frequent in the ancient Near East (in, e.g., the oldest Phoenician inscription), including the Bible, e.g. *Psalms* 45.7.[8] The simple transmission of objects in dreams is not rare,[9] but we must also remember that Moses' ascent of Sinai entails his receipt of the tablets of the Law. The royal figure who sits on his throne and beckons his visitor to approach may recall *Esther* 5.1-2 where the sceptre plays an important role.[10] At *Daniel* 7.9ff the divine being sits on his throne in great splendour and then 'one like a man comes with the clouds of heaven.' Like Moses in Ezekiel, the man approaches the throne and is given sovereignty, glory and kingly power. As for the transmission of the sceptre itself, one recalls *Gen.* 49.10, the angel who comes to transport Abraham heavenward in *Apoc. Abr.* 11ff and the reference to the Messiah (apparently) into whose hand God gives the sceptre at *Or. Sib.* 5.414f.[11] Ezekiel may also be adapting material from the Joseph-story. After Joseph successfully interprets Pharaoh's dreams, the latter makes him vice-regent, turns over to him his ring and also gives him a neck-band and royal garb. He declares that only the *throne* (i.e. Pharaoh) shall be greater than Joseph. This association of the dream-theme with the transmission of the emblems of royalty could have had some influence on the peculiar nature of Ezekiel's dream.[12] As for the transfer of the crown, one cannot but think of the famous legend in which the infant Moses seizes the crown from Pharaoh and places it on his own head.[13] Thus, though we cannot cite any definite text which could have been sufficient source for Ezekiel's version, the components of his account were undoubtedly readily available to him from Jewish Biblical and post-Biblical traditions.[14]

Moses' miraculous observation of the cosmos has many parallels in Jewish literature which derive ultimately from *Genesis* 15 where God takes Abraham 'outside,' directs his gaze heavenward and instructs him to count the stars. Midrashic elaborations take various shapes. In its simplest form God is said to raise Abraham above the heavens and to show him the stars below.[15] More expansively, sometimes Abraham is raised aloft and amidst sights of angels, the divine throne, etc., he looks down and beholds the stars, then Paradise, Hell and other wonders. Indeed Abraham is said to stand on a mountain and look down (*Apoc. Abr.* 15ff).[16] There are such visions not associated with Abraham, e.g. a highly elaborate one at *1 Enoch* 33.3, 72–82.[17] A significant example in the Samaritan 'Death of Moses'[18] bears some resemblance to Ezekiel. It is hard to tell whether it is drawing on the *Exagoge* or is influenced by a legendary tradition which Ezekiel also used. Moses, on the verge of death, ascends a mountain, is raised up by God who reveals to him the four corners of the world. But all in all this passage may be said to shed more light by its differences from the scene in the *Exagoge* than by its similarities to it.

When Ezekiel's Moses counts the stars, the playwright may be elevating Moses above Abraham who, both in the Bible and in the legendary material, refuses to count the stars. Moses in contrast can do it (though if $\pi\lambda\tilde{\eta}\theta o\varsigma$ is a delimitation, then Moses does not count *all* the stars). But when the stars fall before Moses one can scarcely not think of Joseph's dream in *Genesis* (37.9).[19] When the stars march in procession past Moses,[20] we are also dealing with material that has Jewish roots, beginning with *Ps.* 147.4, מונה מספר לכוכבים ('he tells the count of the stars'). The interpreters brought to bear *Job* 25.3 היש מספר לגדודיו ('is there a number to his troops?') and *Isa.* 40.26 'He takes out their host by number' and raised the question of contradiction. But the association of גדוד, which virtually is the equivalent of $\pi\alpha\rho\epsilon\mu\beta o\lambda\acute{\eta}$ (cf. 81), with the stars led to a Rabbinical portrait of a quasi-military roll-call by God of the stars.[21]

At length Moses awakes with a start. To awake in fear from a significant dream is such a commonplace among the ancients, found in Akkadian texts,[22] the Bible (e.g. *Gen.* 28.16–17, 41.7–8), and frequently in Greek literature, that it is not possible to claim the particular influence of one text or one literature.

Raguel then interprets Moses' dream. But in the Bible nowhere does a non-Jew interpret a symbolic dream for a Jew. The opposite is common, e.g. the dreams of Pharaoh and Nebukhadnezzar.[23] Such dreams when dreamt by Jews are usually assumed to be understood by the dreamer (e.g. Joseph's dreams) or else are interpreted by some divine authority (e.g. *Daniel* 8). But no Jewish dreamer in the Bible seems to have active need of a human interpreter, certainly not a non-Jewish one. Further, interpreters of dreams in the Bible (Joseph, Daniel) consciously and explicitly deny their own powers and attribute any interpretation that may come to them as God's work (*Gen.* 40.8, 41.16; *Dan.* 2.18, 28). Such an assertion is conspicuously absent from Raguel's words (unless we conjecture some such remark left out by Polyhistor). Both these deviations reflect, I suspect, either Ezekiel's accommodation of the genre to Greek models and conventions or, more simply, just the influence of the latter. By and large Raguel's explication lacks the close point-by-point exegesis common in the Bible and is closer to the vaguely general dream interpretation of Greek literature.

Text and meaning of verse 85 are debated. The manuscripts read ἀρά γε μέγαν τιν' ἐξαναστήσεις θρόνον. Several scholars take this to mean, 'you will establish a great throne (i.e. kingship).'[24] The majority interpret, 'you will overthrow a great throne.'[25] Stählin emended to θρόνου and is followed by Snell.[26] As Wieneke has noted, the majority view does not quite give an accurate statement of what will occur. In addition, neither it nor Stählin's text is easy to justify by the contents of the dream. It is hard to see in the royal figure's willing transmission of throne and sceptre to Moses a symbolic representation of Moses' overthrowing of Pharaoh's rule. This would seem to leave us with ἐξαναστήσεις θρόνον, in the sense, 'you will establish a throne.'[27] ἐξανίστημι is hard to parallel in the sense 'set up, erect, establish,' but the use of ἀνίστημι with this meaning may provide ample support. The Hellenistic penchant for accumulating prefixes is here in evidence. It is true, as Stählin notes, that on this view καὶ αὐτὸς βραβεύσεις is difficult, but perhaps less of a difficulty than those raised by the other explanations. At all events, Ezekiel is not (classically) exact in his use of αὐτός. On any interpretation there is a peculiar lack of fitness between dream and explication at one point. The figure turns over his throne, crown and sceptre to Moses. Raguel affirms this to signify Moses' future coming to power. But what of the figure on the throne? Surely the appropriate interpretation should be that the rule passes from the first figure to the second (Moses). I shall shortly discuss the possibility of Herodotean influence here. If I am right, then I would suggest that Ezekiel has been trapped into maintaining the scheme of Herodotean dreams which so often involve transfer of power, but at the same time must in interpreting the dream abide by the Jewish tradition in which Moses represents the very beginning of the 'dynasty.' It is important to remember that this is a totally unBiblical conception. Not only is Moses nowhere portrayed as a king in the Bible, but in fact to regard him as such goes against the whole Biblical tradition that the institution of King of Israel is a later development (cf. *Deut.* 17.14ff; *Judges* 17.6; 1 *Sam.* 8.4ff).[28] Nonetheless, in the Hellenistic period the notion of Moses as king did develop. Thus, Philo tells how Moses received τὴν ἀρχὴν καὶ βασιλείαν, not through arms and force but as a gift of God, precisely the picture one gets in Ezekiel (*Moses* 1.148–9). There is also a Rabbinic tradition of Moses receiving a crown (at least metaphorically), but I am unsure whether to see this as part of the tradition or, quite the contrary, as polemic against it. For we are told that there were three crowns (bestowed by God), that of Priesthood to Aaron, of Kingship to David, and of the Law to Moses.[29]

As for Raguel's envisioning of Moses as seer, we are again out of the Biblical realm and in that of the pseudepigrapha and Midrash where we occasionally read that God revealed to Moses the whole course of history.[30] Still, we are closer to the Bible than in the case of 'Moses the king.' For it is possible to take the last chapters of *Deuteronomy* as indications of Moses' prophetic abilities. He relates the future of Israel (contingent on the conduct of the people; see 28; 29.21ff; 30). Later he reiterates God's prophecies (31.16ff, 29). Finally, chapters 32 and 33 are fundamentally a poetic vision of Israel's future.[31]

Raguel's interpretation amounts to a prophecy of Moses' future deeds and greatness. I know no exact parallel in Jewish literature to this episode in the *Exagoge*. But for the basic theme we can bring illumination. Manetho's narrative of the 'Exodus' contains a seer's prophecy of the victory of the persecuted Jews (= lepers) over the Egyptians (Jos. *Ap.* 1.236). More relevant is the tradition of a prophecy by an Egyptian priest that an Israelite child would be born (Moses), who would prove great and humble the Egyptian rule (Jos. *AJ* 2.205). Moreover, in Midrashic texts this forecast is in fact a dream-interpretation for Pharaoh.[32] While most of the dream bears little resemblance to Ezekiel's it does (at least in one version) center around a man sitting upon a throne.[33] Further, when Pharaoh seeks advice from his advisors about the Jews, the one man who acts properly, either by fleeing so as not to have any part in the plot, or by praising the Jewish slaves, counseling the king to free them and perceiving the divine favor that will protect them is indeed Raguel (*Jerahmeel* 46). In the *Asatir*'s version˙ of this prophecy (8.24ff) the seer's name is Palti. Might this be a (Samaritan?) corruption or variation on Putiel, one of the names of Raguel? There is also a Midrashic report that Raguel, after meeting Moses, foretells that he will be a prophet and will overthrow Egypt.[34] Of further interest are the prophetic dreams of Miriam (*LAB* 9.10) and Amram (Jos. *AJ* 2.212ff) on the birth of Israel's savior, Moses.[35] In other words, there seem to have been widespread versions of a tradition in which the salvation of Israel, the destruction of Egyptian rule and the greatness of Moses are foretold in a prophecy or dream (usually before his birth).[36] If the dream-episode as depicted in the *Exagoge* is Ezekiel's invention, it is at all events reasonable to assume that he was adapting and revising traditional material. In his own form of the episode he may have seen a better opportunity to utilize the apocalyptic Moses-material after his own fashion. Or he may have seen in it particularly effective dramatic possibilities.[37]

The attribution to an important Biblical figure of a significant dream not attested in the Bible is not rare in extra-Biblical and Midrashic literature. *Testaments of the Twelve Patriarchs* and *2 Esdras* indulge this license quite a bit.[38] One finds it elsewhere: Abram's dream at *Gen. Apoc.* col. 19; the famous dream of Mordecai at LXX *Esther* 1.1d ff, with interpretation at 10.3a ff;[39] Isaac's at *Test. Abraham* 7; Eve's at *Vita Adae et Evae* 22.4. *Jubilees* refers briefly to a prophetic dream of Rebecca's (35.6).[40]

It is obvious from all this how strongly Ezekiel is fixed in the Jewish tradition of the Hellenistic-Roman period. But his roots are also deep in the Greek world. Aeschylus' *Persae* is a major source of influence. One of the elements common to the *Persae* and the *Exagoge* is a dream of symbolic import. The contents of the dreams are not similar, but the purport is. In the one, the destruction of the Great King's high position; in the other, the ascent to power and domination of the simple shepherd. Moses' dream is the converse of Atossa's. There are a number of possible verbal echoes of Atossa's dream in the *Exagoge*: ἐκπρεπεστάτα (*Pers.* 184; cf. *Exag.* 264), ἀμώμω (*Pers.* 185; cf. *Exag.* 177), ἐπυργοῦτο (*Pers.* 192; cf. *Exag.* 11), ἐστάθην (*Pers.* 206; cf. *Exag.* 73). But I wish to suggest here that there is another Greek 'ancestor' and source of influence, namely Herodotus.⁴¹ Dreams involving the fall of one man (or regime) and the rise of another are commonplace in the *Histories*. Twice figures who appear in Herodotean dreams are μέγας καὶ εὐειδής (5.56; 7.12), much like Ezekiel's γενναῖος φώς on his μέγας θρόνος. The use of δοκέω + accusative + infinitive in the narration of a dream, while not in general rare, is particularly characteristic of Herodotus.⁴² For the Herodotean type of dream that resembles Ezekiel's we might consider Astyages' two dreams (1.107-8) in which his daughter urinates over all Asia and a vine springs from her and spreads over Asia, dreams which his interpreters understand to mean that his daughter's offspring would rule in his stead. Or Cyrus' dream (1.209) in which Hystaspes's son is seen with wings overshadowing all Europe and Asia and which is taken to foretell a plot by Hystaspes against Cyrus' rule. Here we should note, in addition to the introduction of the dream by ἐδόκεε, the use of participial ἔχοντα to describe the paraphernalia of the dream-figure. But of the dreams in Herodotus which symbolize the rise to power and rule perhaps the most relevant to the *Exagoge* is Cambyses' at 3.30. It begins with ἐδόκεε. In the dream Cambyses receives a report that Smerdis has sat on the royal throne and his head has reached the heavens, themes virtually identical to those in Moses' dream. Finally, two dreams of Xerxes. At 7.19 (beginning again with ἐδόκεε) Xerxes sees himself crowned with an olive branch which proceeds to envelop the whole earth. Here are two themes, the 'control' of the whole earth (γῆν πᾶσαν) and the coronation, that recur in Ezekiel. At 7.12 a μέγας καὶ εὐειδής ἀνήρ warns Xerxes not to change his plans. This dream is not like the others since it is not symbolic but merely an explicit warning from the powers above. But within its context it proves to be relevant to Ezekiel. For when Xerxes decides to test the dream's validity he does so by dressing Artabanus in his royal garb (which undoubtedly includes sceptre and crown) and seating him on his throne. This symbolic transfer of royal status by transmission of the royal gear and throne could have influenced the precise form of Ezekiel's dream-account.

We noted earlier that the procession and the counting of the stars were Jewish traditions. But when Moses sits upon a throne on a mountain top, surveying the scene below him and counting the stars as they pass in review before him, we may think of Herodotus' Xerxes who mounts a white throne built upon a hill and looks down on all his forces (7.44). Shortly thereafter he has a census of them taken (7.60).[43]

Why should Herodotus have made an impression upon the *Exagoge*? Although it is hard to distinguish cause and result, an answer seems at hand. When Ezekiel realized that he could turn the tale of the Exodus into a Greek drama after the fashion of the *Persae*, he may have decided to make further study of the Persian Wars. It was consequently natural that he turn to Herodotus for a comprehensive record.[44] Elsewhere I discuss further instances of Herodotean influence on the play.

Lastly, the Hellenized *Egyptian* environment also utilized significant dreams in similar ways. In the dream of Nectanebus the goddess Isis appears sitting on her throne in a boat, a dream which has verbal similarities to Moses', ἔδοξεν . . . ἦν θρόνος μέγας.[45]

In the dream episode we can see Ezekiel for what he was, a remarkable man steeped in both the Biblical and post-Biblical Jewish traditions and in the classical Greek tradition. He has taken legendary material that is thoroughly Jewish, the genre of the symbolic dream, the theme of Moses' ascension and vision of the divine throne, and has transmuted them into nearly perfect Greek substance told in quite routine Greek language and terminology in the guise of acceptable Greek motifs. I have cited numerous parallels and potential sources for the dream-episode from both Jewish and Greek texts. Let it be clear that I did not intend to claim all these as known to and influences on Ezekiel. This was rather an attempt to show the sort of material that was available to Ezekiel in both Greek and Jewish circles, from which a good deal must have been familiar to him. We must remember that the final product which we find in Ezekiel is undoubtedly 'overdetermined.'

4. The burning bush (90–131)

We are, as Gutman has noted (47), thrown into this scene *in medias res*, for Eusebius (or Polyhistor) has not preserved it from the beginning. Moses' opening word in our text is ἔα, that common expletive 'gasp of astonishment,' which regularly expresses surprise,[1] as he suddenly notices the spectacle of the burning bush. He comments on the unbelievable nature of the phenomenon, and decides to approach and examine it. All this is quite in keeping with the brief Biblical account at *Exodus* 3.2–3, though the effectively direct, terse and unadorned style of the Bible vanishes in Ezekiel's attempt to enhance the dramatic quality of the scene, beginning with Moses' exclamation of surprise (nothing of the sort in *Exodus*) and continuing with the explicit and repeated emphasis on the miraculous nature of the event: σημεῖον, τεράστιον, ἀπιστία, τεράστιον μέγιστον, οὐ πίστιν φέρει; all in contrast to the Septuagint's τὸ ὅραμα τὸ μέγα τοῦτο. Verses 96–112 are manifestly based on God's speech at *Exod.* 3.5ff and in most ways are an accurate reflection of the Biblical text, though Ezekiel both expands and contracts it, to some degree simply by incorporating narrative elements of the Biblical account into the speech, but also by utilizing Scriptural material that is not present in this immediate *Exodus* passage. Thus, God declares that Moses may not behold Him, whereas God says no such thing in the Biblical bush scene. This is merely implied in the narrative wherein it is written ἀπέστρεψεν δὲ Μωυσῆς τὸ πρόσωπον αὐτοῦ.[2] It seems not unlikely that after 99 Moses would shrink or turn away, especially since θάρσησον ὦ παῖ at 100 seems well suited to some such demonstration of fear or hesitation on his part. It would also come at precisely the same point as in the Biblical narrative where Moses turns aside immediately after God announces that it is indeed He who addresses Moses. On the other hand, when God declares that His recollection of the patriarchs has impelled Him to free the Jews from bondage (104–7), Ezekiel is introducing here Biblical material which both precedes and follows the bush-scene but is never a part of it. For in the narrative at the end of *Exod.* 2 we read that ἐμνήσθη ὁ Θεὸς τῆς διαθήκης αὐτοῦ τῆς πρὸς Ἀβραὰμ καὶ Ἰσαὰκ καὶ Ἰακώβ (24); again, when Moses has been scorned by Pharaoh and rejected by his fellow Jews God reassures him by telling of His covenant with the patriarchs which He has now called to mind (6.3–5). Thus, as we have seen elsewhere, Ezekiel feels free to use material from one episode in another when it suits his needs and purposes.

Two questions of stagecraft:[3] first, does the presence of a bush on fire – indeed a bush on fire which is not consumed – preclude the possibility that this scene was meant for the stage?[4] It does not. We have ample evidence that Greek plays included representations of phenomena that would have demanded a sophisticated and highly developed stagecraft to be depicted in a naturalistic fashion. Thus, the chorus at *Bacchae* 596ff beholds a fire around the tomb of Semele, just as Moses sees the fire of the bush. Whether Euripides managed this in some realistic way or simply relied upon a convention signalled by the chorus' outburst we cannot say. And of course more elaborate events occur, most notably the earthquakes that 'take place' in the *Bacchae, Prometheus Bound* and *Heracles.* Again, how — or if — these were realistically achieved we do not know.[5] But surely there is no problem in assuming that Ezekiel could achieve the relatively simple phenomenon of a burning bush, even a miraculously burning bush.[6]

The second question is the voice of God. The theological implications are discussed elsewhere; for the moment it suffices to say that Ezekiel had no qualms about representing God speaking in a play – and even 'on stage' (if we assume a staged performance). Even from the Greek perspective the presence of a divine voice with no body visible would not have presented any problem. While the gods did routinely appear in concrete form on the Greek stage, there are occasional instances of a disembodied divine voice, as at *Bacchae* 576ff when the voice of Dionysus is heard but he is not seen.[7] The actor would have spoken from off stage. We can assume that here too the actor speaking the words of God would have done so from off stage. A Greek audience might not have been surprised at the failure of God to appear since Greek tragedy itself rarely (if ever) puts Zeus on stage.[8] In the prologue scene of Aeschylus' *Psychostasia* Zeus apparently appeared weighing out the souls; whether he spoke is disputed.[9]

At verse 99 God reveals to Moses the divine nature of the speaker, ὁ δ' ἐκ βάτου σοι Θεῖος ἐκλάμπει λόγος: the 'word of God' rings out from the bush.[10] Wieneke accurately observed that (ἐκ)λάμπω is used in standard Greek writers of sound as well as of sight, noting *inter alia* Aeschylus' φωνὴν . . . ὄψει (*PV* 21).[11] The verb ἐκλάμπει, as Gutman has noted (50), is also suitable because of the context of the burning bush.

The association of a verb of primarily visual significance with the voice or speech of God in an event intimately tied to the *Exodus* is found both in Philo and Rabbinic tradition. Its foundation, to be sure, is the Bible itself. We read that at the revelation at Sinai וכל העם ראים את הקולת (*Exod.* 20.18), 'The people saw the voices.' The Septuagint translates, ἑώρα τὴν φωνήν. This peculiarity of expression is seized upon by both the Rabbis and Philo for significant explication. One Midrash reads:[12] בנוהג שבעולם אי אפשר לראות את הקל אבל כן ... ראו את הקולות 'Normally it is impossible to see sound but here the people did.' In more sophisticated fashion Philo observes on three occasions the import of this phrase, e.g. at *Moses* 2.213:[13] ἐθέσπισεν . . . ὁ Θεὸς διὰ φωνῆς – τὸ παραδοξότατον – ὁρατῆς ἢ . . . ὀφθαλμοὺς ὤτων ἐπήγειρε μᾶλλον. The oddity of expression in the Biblical text evidently produced a widespread interpretation along the lines indicated in Philo and the Midrash which would have been familiar to the Jewish educated. If so, Ezekiel made deliberate use of an acceptable, if a bit unusual, Greek idiom because he saw that it corresponded to traditional Jewish exegesis. This may then be another case when Ezekiel's text would have had one sense for the pagan audience, another for the Jewish.

A comparison of Ezekiel's description of the burning bush with the Biblical and other versions is instructive: ἄφνω βάτος μὲν καίεται πολλῷ πυρί,/αὐτοῦ δὲ χλωρὸν πᾶν μένει τὸ βλαστάνον. The Septuagint reads ὁ βάτος καίεται πυρί, ὁ δὲ βάτος οὐ κατεκαίετο (3.2). Ezekiel's πολλῷ is mere dramatic or rhetorical flair. But what of the peculiar elaboration in 93? Is this too 'mere' poetic technique? Artapanus (*PE* 9.434c) and Philo (*Moses* 1.55) are primarily impressed by the miracle of the fire persisting without any fuel being consumed, while Ezekiel stresses the continuing greenness of the bush. Τὸ βλαστάνον is a strange phrase and I know no other use of the participle of βλαστάνω in the sense, 'bud, foliage' or the like. *Exodus* 3.2 reports that the angel appeared to Moses בלבת אש מתוך הסנה וירא והנה הסנה בער באש והסנה איננו אכל. The Septuagint translates accurately ὤφθη δὲ αὐτῷ ἄγγελος κυρίου ἐν φλογὶ πυρὸς ἐκ τοῦ βάτου, καὶ ὁρᾷ ὅτι ὁ βάτος καίεται πυρί, ὁ δὲ βάτος οὐ κατεκαίετο. But the Jerusalem Targum goes beyond the text, והא סניא בעיר באשא וסניא מרטיב ולא יקיד, the bush was burning with fire, but it thrived (was green with foliage) and was not consumed.[14] מרטיב is for all intents and purposes the Aramaic equivalent of χλωρός. The Midrash preserves the tradition: (הסנה) מלבלב ועולה מתוך האש the bush flowered and grew from out of the fire.[15] Josephus may be following the same tradition (*AJ* 2.266),

> ... πῦρ γὰρ θάμνου βάτον νεμόμενον τὴν περὶ αὐτὸν χλόην τό τε ἄνθος αὐτοῦ παρῆλθεν ἀβλαβὲς καὶ τῶν ἐγκάρπων κλάδων οὐδὲν ἠφάνισε καὶ ταῦτα τῆς φλογὸς πολλῆς καὶ ὀξυτάτης ὑπαρχούσης.

Ezekiel is here probably preserving a Palestinian exegetical tradition, not merely because we find it in the Jerusalem Targum and Josephus, but also because it appears that the exegesis arose from the association of the Hebrew לבת(ב) (Septuagint correctly ἐν φλογί), with the root לבלב = 'to flower.'

The complicated interaction between Moses and God in *Exod.* 3ff, as God commissions and instructs His prophet while Moses wavers and hesitates, agrees and backs down, is apparently rendered rather briefly and differently by Ezekiel. In the Bible God initially tells Moses to go to Pharaoh (3.10) and lead the Jews from Egypt, whereupon Moses reasonably responds, 'Who am I to go before Pharaoh?' All this Ezekiel ignores. Shortly thereafter God orders Moses to approach the elders of the people and expound God's plan and then to ask Pharaoh's leave to take the people into the desert for three days (3.16ff. This is essentially the point at which Ezekiel begins: God tells Moses to go *first* to the people and thereafter to Pharaoh, telling them all of God's plan that he lead the Jews from the country (109–12).[16] Ezekiel ignores the 'three day' qualification probably for economy's sake, since in terms of the development of the action it has no important role, certainly not for dramatic purposes. It is, however, possible that he avoided it so as not to risk becoming involved in the question of deceit on Moses' part here.[17]

The remainder of the bush-scene, both in Ezekiel and the Bible, deals with Moses' reluctance to accept God's commission and the latter's attempt(s) to persuade him. But quite differently. In *Exodus* Moses claims that the Jews will not believe him, so God displays various wonders that Moses can use to convince the people. Moses then declares himself too inept at speaking for such a mission, so God points out His power to endow anyone with speech. Moses tries once more and asks God to send someone else. The episode ends as God partially acquiesces by saying that Aaron will go as the speaker to the people.

Ezekiel's version is not merely abbreviated but distinctly and deliberately altered. The central focus of the confrontation between God and Moses has shifted. In *Exodus* 4 Moses seeks to avoid his mission to the Jewish people; in the *Exagoge* there is nothing about this. Rather, Moses is reluctant to appear before the king, about which there is in fact nothing in *Exodus* 4. In the Bible God decides to send Aaron to accompany Moses before the people; in Ezekiel he will go to speak before the king.[18] Now Ezekiel is not freely inventing here. Rather, he is bringing together two scenes into one with the concomitant production of some striking and important changes. In *Exodus*, after Moses has met with the Jews and with Pharaoh with disastrous and discouraging results, God instructs him to return to Pharaoh. Moses replies dejectedly, 'The Jews don't listen to me; how will Pharaoh? Anyhow, I'm a poor speaker' (6.12).[19] This is clearly the 'source' for Moses' assertion at *Exagoge* 114–15, ὥστε μὴ λόγους ἐμοὺς γενέσθαι βασιλέως ἐναντίον. It is reasonable to believe that dramatic economy was one reason for Ezekiel's conflating the two scenes into one, but it was not his main motivation. For this we can turn to a characteristic that is manifest at a number of places in the play. The Biblical account is less than complimentary here to Moses who argues and fights with God to the point of arousing His anger. We can discern in Josephus' and Philo's accounts of the bush-scene clear-cut attempts to tone down or do away with the belligerence and obstinacy Moses displays in the Bible. To some degree this may be a factor in Ezekiel. We might contrast Moses' brief objection and God's single answer at 113–19 to the argument at *Exod.* 4.10–16. But something else looms much larger. Ezekiel is chiefly interested, here and elsewhere, in not rendering the Jewish people in a bad light.[20] For Moses' fears (correct, as it turns out) are that the Jews will simply not believe him when he comes bearing God's message, that in their skepticism they will reject him and God's words. Ezekiel completely eliminates this element of the scriptural narrative but manages to retain the important dialogue between God and Moses by introducing into the bush-scene the later (in terms of the Biblical account) objection of Moses with respect to Pharaoh.[21] The relationship between Moses and the Jews in this regard was evidently a point of concern in Jewish tradition, for the Midrash also shows a tendency to exonerate the people from Moses' pejorative aspersions. Thus, we

read that God, on hearing Moses' declaration that the Jews would
not believe, severely rebuked and chastised him (*Exod. Rab.* 3.12).
The other side of the polemical coin is in evidence at *Acts* 7.30ff
where great emphasis is laid upon what Ezekiel seeks to avoid completely, the stubborn rejection of Moses by the Jews when he comes
to them.

What then is the purpose of the scene at 120ff wherein God performs the two miracles for Moses? The Biblical narrative is unambiguous. To Moses' protest that the Jews will not believe him God
offers two miraculous signs by which he will be able to convince
them. But, insofar as the fragments of the *Exagoge* allow us to say,
there seems to be no room for a similar motivation here. We must
then have recourse to speculation, but I think it can be speculation
with some reasonable foundation if we recall how Ezekiel has in this
scene taken to conflating two Biblical episodes, the bush and the
events of *Exodus* 6. If the Biblical motivation, Moses' anxiety over
convincing the Jews, was of no use to Ezekiel,[22] what might have
been? Ezekiel, we have noted, has changed Moses' qualms about the
Jews to doubts about approaching Pharaoh. It then seems reasonable
that Moses may have said, 'What if Pharaoh refuses to listen to us?'
or 'Perhaps Pharaoh will demand proof that we come from God,' to
which God responds by performing the signs of 120ff. This is not
merely a hypothesis of internal consistency and reasonableness, but
one for which we can claim support in the Biblical narrative and the
manner in which we have come to see that Ezekiel utilizes it. At
Exod. 7.8ff, as Moses and Aaron prepare to go to Pharaoh, God
instructs them:

> Καὶ ἐὰν λαλήσῃ πρὸς ὑμᾶς Φαραὼ λέγων Δότε ἡμῖν σημεῖον ἢ τέρας,
> καὶ ἐρεῖς Ἀαρὼν τῷ ἀδελφῷ σου Λαβὲ τὴν ῥάβδον καὶ ῥῖψον αὐτὴν
> ἐπὶ τὴν γῆν ἐναντίον Φαραὼ καὶ ἐναντίον τῶν θεραπόντων αὐτοῦ, καὶ
> ἔσται δράκων.

God's instruction as to what Moses and Aaron should do 'in case
Pharaoh should request a sign' is just the sort of handle Ezekiel was
wont to seize in order to fashion a scene in which *Moses asks God*
what he should do 'if Pharaoh requests a sign.' Further, the vocabulary is revealing. In the Biblical scene at the bush, Moses throws
down his rod and it turns into an ὄφις (4.3). But in the scene at 7.9
the rod, they are told, will turn into a δράκων. So in Ezekiel, the rod

becomes δράκων, not ὄφις. Moreover, at both *Exagoge* 123 and *Exodus* 7.9, since in each God is foretelling what will happen, the verb is in the future, in contrast to the past at *Exod.* 4.3. The phraseology is virtually identical: ἔσται δράκων in the Septuagint, δράκων . . . ἔσται in Ezekiel,[23] whereas *Exod.* 4.3 (and 7.10) has ἐγένετο.

In his introductory remarks to verses 120–31 Polyhistor comments, περὶ δὲ τῆς ῥάβδου καὶ τῶν ἄλλων τεράτων οὕτω δι᾽ ἀμοιβαίων εἴρηκε. That is, in the course of the dialogue Ezekiel tells about 'the rod and the other wonders.' But all we have are the transformation of rod into serpent and the change of skin-color. Polyhistor's remarks suggest that there must have been at least one more. It would be futile to argue that Polyhistor is referring to the following account of the ten plagues since (1) they are preserved in a monologue, not in dialogue and (2) they receive a separate introduction, which indicates that they are not the subject of Polyhistor's comments before 120. A glance at the Septuagint will show us the way. After God has demonstrated to Moses the two signs, he then *tells him* that should these two prove ineffectual he will have a third to perform (4.9):

> καὶ ἔσται ἐὰν μὴ πιστεύσωσίν σοι τοῖς δυσὶ σημείοις τούτοις μηδὲ εἰσακούσωσιν τῆς φωνῆς σου, λήμψῃ ἀπὸ τοῦ ὕδατος τοῦ ποταμοῦ καὶ ἐκχεεῖς ἐπὶ τὸ ξηρόν, καὶ ἔσται τὸ ὕδωρ, ὃ ἐὰν λάβῃς ἀπὸ τοῦ ποταμοῦ, αἷμα ἐπὶ τοῦ ξηροῦ.

It seems reasonable that this is the third sign set out in this scene of the *Exagoge*.[24] Perhaps, as in the Bible, God merely told Moses of this miracle. But it is conceivable that it was actually acted out, that Moses was represented throwing water on the ground which turned to blood. This is, strange to say, exactly what Josephus has (*AJ* 2.273). If Ezekiel did this, we can readily surmise dramatic effect as his motivation. Why Josephus went this route is harder to say, unless there was some Midrashic tradition to this effect (or unless he was influenced here by the *Exagoge*).

Lines 120ff are remarkable for the abundance of apparent 'fillers.' Thus, 120 could do without the last two words, 121 the last four, 122 the final three and 123 the last two without impairing or diminishing the sequence of thought at all. If we examine the Septuagint text on which these verses are based, we note that without these fillers the Biblical text is well represented, while the fillers (with one exception) provide nothing additional. In part we might attribute this to Ezekiel's desire for rhetorical flourish and elaboration; in part, to the exigencies of turning the narrative portions of the Biblical text into dialogue, as at ἀποχώρησον ταχύ (122) representing ἔφυγεν Μωυσῆς. Finally, I suspect that Ezekiel is unwilling to divide a verse between two speakers. At virtually every line in this dialogue the Biblical text could be represented accurately and tersely by dividing verses between God and Moses, e.g. (120) Τί δ' ἐν χεροῖν σοῖν τοῦτ' ἔχεις; ῥάβδον νέμω, which would almost duplicate *Exod.* 4.2. But such ἀντιλαβή was primarily a comic phenomenon, though it does occasionally occur in tragic trimeter dialogue.[25] Aeschylus, so strong an influence on Ezekiel, seems to have used it but once.[26] Perhaps Ezekiel felt it would lend too light a tone to a dialogue that he wanted solemn and august.

Still, it is a peculiar dialogue with its inelegant fullness through which, one imagines, acts which do not happen on the stage are described in words. Some of this is, of course, inevitable. The audience must be told that the rod has changed (twice) and similarly with the condition of Moses' hand. Just so the audience in Greco-Roman drama often must be informed of things 'taking place' on stage, e.g. remarks like 'he is crying.'

If the manuscripts' ἐστι is right at 123, then 123-4 would have to be reversed and both given to Moses. But the fact that God's words at 127-8 also embrace both order and result makes it more likely that the same is true at 122-3. At 129 we move from the first sign to the second. One is surprised not to find some verbal response from Moses after 128. But rather than assuming that something is amiss or missing here, we can again derive help from the parallel at 131, for here too it appears (unless Polyhistor or Eusebius has perversely left out an integral verse or verses) that when the miracle is concluded Moses again makes no response. Peculiar as this seems, the Biblical narrative also gives Moses no verbal reactions at the conclusion of the two miracles (though in the Bible Moses has no words whatsoever during this episode, 4.3-7). At all events, the actor would have indicated appropriate reactions through his movements, gestures and perhaps expressions.

In the Bible Moses responds to God's question 'What is that in your hand?' with one word, 'a rod.' Here is Ezekiel (121): ῥάβδον τετραπόδων καὶ βροτῶν κολάστριαν. Is this a mere rhetorical flourish? Perhaps. But Midrashic texts report that Moses' rod was no simple staff, but rather a magical one given by God to Adam and transmitted to special people over the generations, finally reaching Moses.[27] If this view was already in existence in Ezekiel's day, then his own description may reflect polemic against it and a reaffirmation of the Biblical account: the rod is nothing more than a simple shepherd's staff. That the rod is termed ῥάβδος Θεοῦ at *Exagoge* 225 is not compelling since this is the term occasionally used in the Bible (e.g. 4.20). Further, the phrase is put in the mouth of an Egyptian.

When Moses inserts his hand into his bosom and then withdraws it, he finds that γέγονεν ὡσπερεὶ χιών (130). This is what the Septuagint also has (4.6): ἐγενήθη ἡ χεὶρ αὐτοῦ ὡσεὶ χιών. But the Hebrew text reports that Moses' hand became 'leprous, like the snow.' This is a first-rate and very early example of the tendentious use of translation, for we cannot doubt that the translators knew perfectly well that מצרעת meant 'leprous'; witness their translation at *Numbers* 12.10. They deliberately avoided the element of leprosy here so as not to provide additional fuel for the propaganda-fire of anti-Semites who claimed the Jews in Egypt were a mob of lepers and were banished from the country.[28] Indeed, the Septuagint's implicit defense of Moses here suggests that already at that time there existed the additional slander that Moses himself was a leper and consequently was called ἄλφα (from ἀλφός = leprosy).[29] This anti-Semitic tradition of Jewish lepers may have been widespread: Targumim also render *Exod.* 4.6 in such a way as to conceal Moses' leprosy. Thus, Onqelos and Jonathan, like the Septuagint, translate 'white as snow,' though Neofiti maintains the leprous element. Josephus, too, though familiar with the Hebrew text, skips over the leprosy and makes Moses' hand white in color, like chalk (τιτάνῳ). One particular aspect of Ezekiel's description here may be related to this whole phenomenon. At *Exod. Rab.* 3.13 we are told that Moses' hand did not turn leprous until he had removed it from his bosom. But, in contrary fashion, it was healed as soon as he placed it back in his bosom. This prevented slanderers from claiming that Moses' body had been infected with leprosy.[30] Ezekiel's account duplicates this version precisely. God tells Moses to insert and withdraw his hand, whereupon Moses cries out that his hand has turned white. God then instructs him to reinsert his hand and it will return to normal. There is, to be sure, nothing so strange in

Ezekiel's phraseology as to require subtle explication. But it is at the least a striking coincidence. Perhaps Ezekiel was familiar with this apologetic Midrashic exposition and decided to follow it, even though both he and the Septuagint had removed any need for it by simply eliminating the element of leprosy.

In *Exodus* Moses' protests take the following order: (1) 'The Jews won't believe me.' God responds with the display of signs. (2) 'I cannot speak well.' God asserts that Aaron will be spokesman. In the *Exagoge* this has been reversed. Moses first objects that he is a poor speaker, whereupon God introduces the role of Aaron. Moses evidently continues to argue and God performs the signs.[31] We may guess that Ezekiel has reversed the order for dramatic effect, building to the climax of the miracles rather than to the anti-climax of the introduction of Aaron. It would be hard to go beyond this since we know that there was dialogue between 112 and 113, but do not know what it involved. If the adjectives Moses uses at 113-14 are an indication, we may have further evidence for the conflation here by Ezekiel of episodes at *Exod.* 3-4 and 6-7. When Moses speaks at 4.10, he calls himself ἰσχνόφωνος καὶ βραδύγλωσσος, which appears to be taken up by Ezekiel's γλῶσσα δ᾽ ἐστί μοι δύσφραστος, ἰσχνόφωνος, while ἐγὼ δὲ ἄλογός εἰμι of *Exod.* 6.12 appears to be Ezekiel's οὐκ εὔλογος πέφυκα.[32]

God has come, he declares, to save his people, ἰδὼν κάκωσιν καὶ πόνον δούλων ἐμῶν (108). The source is apparent: κραυγὴ τῶν υἱῶν Ἰσραὴλ ἥκει πρός με, κἀγὼ ἑώρακα τὸν θλιμμόν, ὃν οἱ Αἰγύπτιοι θλίβουσιν αὐτούς (*Exod.* 3.9). But one phrase stands out, δούλων ἐμῶν. The concept of God's slaves has become so familiar within the Judaeo-Christian tradition of the last millennia that commentators on the *Exagoge* routinely pass over this phrase as if it were of no importance.[33] In fact, the story of the Exodus in the Bible contains no reference or allusion to the Jews as God's slaves. Neither δοῦλος nor any related word (δουλεία, δουλεύειν)[34] is used of the status of the Jews vis-à-vis God. On the other hand, the terms are used of the Jews vis-à-vis the Egyptians. The slavery in Egypt is δουλεύειν (14.5, 12); Egypt is οἶκος δουλείας (13.3); God will save the Jewish people from their δουλεία (6.6); the Jews are οἰκέται and παῖδες of Pharaoh (5.16). In other words, the concept of slavery in the Biblical Exodus narrative is limited to the condition of the Jews in Egypt and vis-à-vis the Egyptians. The Hebrew term 'to worship' (לעבד) is consistently translated by the Septuagint in this episode λατρεύειν (e.g. 4.23, 10.8, 24, 3.12, 7.16). It is true that elsewhere in the Bible the Jewish people are designated the slaves of God.[35] But the significance of the term in the *Exagoge* lies in its context. What is relevant here is Rabbinical exegesis with regard to the Exodus from Egypt: Pharaoh is said to declare, 'Go out from among my people. In the past you have been Pharaoh's slaves, henceforth you are God's slaves.' At that point they did say 'Give praise, O you servants of God' – and not servants of Pharaoh.[36] That is, the Rabbis emphasized that the escape from Egypt was in fact a transition from bondage to Pharaoh and the Egyptians to the proper state of being slaves to God. It is in this attitude toward the liberation from Egypt that Ezekiel would have found his source for God's calling the Jews 'my slaves.' The notion that the Jews were God's slaves seems to have been a well accepted one among Jewish exegetes and was utilized as authority for legal exposition as well as Aggadic.[37] Indeed, it was used against the Jews by pagan anti-Semites for whom the very concept of 'slave' was *ipso facto* condemnation.[38] But the specific application of the general concept to the Jews' status on leaving Egypt seems to have grown out of – or at least was regularly connected to – the verse at *Psalms* 113.1, 'Praise, O you servants of the Lord, praise the name of the Lord.'[39] Thus, *Midrash Tehillim Ps.* 113 (469–70) takes this verse as a reference to the night of the tenth plague: 'We were slaves to Pharaoh but You saved us and made us slaves unto You.' The text then brings the story already quoted above.[40] Here now is the text of *Psalm* 113 in its entirety:

> Praise the Lord!
> Praise, O servants of the Lord,
> praise the name of the Lord!
>
> Blessed be the name of the Lord
> from this time forth and for
> evermore!
> From the rising of the sun to its
> setting
> the name of the Lord is to be
> praised!
> The Lord is high above all nations,
> and his glory above the heavens!
>
> Who is like the Lord our God,
> who is seated on high,
> who looks far down
> upon the heavens and the earth?
> He raises the poor from the dust,
> and lifts the needy from the ash
> heap,
> to make them sit with princes,
> with the princes of his people.
> He gives the barren woman a home,
> making her the joyous mother
> of children.
> Praise the Lord!

There is, it would seem, little enough in this Psalm to tie it to the Exodus. But here is the critical point. *Psalm* 113 is the first section of the liturgical Hallel which was so strongly associated with Passover and the Exodus. Thus, we know a tradition that the Jews, on crossing the Red Sea, recited the Hallel.[41] More important, the Hallel was an important portion of the Passover service even in the time of the Temple.[42] In addition, it was also a major part of the ritual Seder.[43] Philo (*Spec. Leg.* 2.148) appears to contain an allusion to the Hallel on Passover and scholars have detected another such allusion at *Wisdom* 18.9. Finkelstein has argued that *Psalms* 113-14 were part of the Passover evening ritual earlier than the middle of the third century B.C.[44] The schools of Shammai and Hillel were even in dispute as to whether *Psalm* 113 alone should be recited at the Seder or more.[45] It is clear that *Psalm* 113 was associated with the Exodus because of its proximity to and recitation with *Psalm* 114 which concerns 'when Israel went out of Egypt, the house of Jacob from a people of strange language' (114.1). Thus, it seems reasonable to assume not merely that the phrase 'slaves (עבדי) of God' was intimately associated with the Passover celebration of the Exodus, but also that the Rabbinic interpretations of the phrase at *Psalm* 113.1 tying it to the salvation from Egypt were formulated and elaborated in the homiletic sermons and exegesis that were so important a part of the Passover holiday.[46] From this milieu Ezekiel would have derived, indeed assimilated, the view that the liberation of the Jews from the bondage of Egypt was also transition to their proper status as slaves of God.[47]

At line 106 there occurs a peculiar expression which is usually explained (when not ignored) by assuming a strange looseness of meaning:

ἐγὼ θεὸς σῶν, ὧν λέγεις, γεννητόρων
Ἀβραάμ τε καὶ Ἰσαὰκ καὶ Ἰακώβου τρίτου.
μνησθεὶς δ' ἐκείνων καὶ ἔτ' ἐμῶν δωρημάτων
πάρειμι σῶσαι λαὸν Ἑβραίων ἐμόν. (104-7)[48]

What can δωρήματα mean here? Kuiper writes reasonably 'promissa dei sunt;' Wieneke (77) and Gutman (150) agree. God recalls the patriarchs of the Jewish people and the promises he made to them. This is well and good, except for one thing. There is no example of δώρημα = promise and it is not particularly desirable to stretch the sense of the word, especially since Ezekiel seems to use it in its normal meaning at 35.[49]

Gifford translates 'my gifts to them.'[50] This suits the Greek, but what could it possibly mean in the present context? We might consider the possibility 'the gifts that I have received.' That is, God recalls the patriarchs and the gifts they made to Him. Now there are several reasons for preferring Gifford's translation. First, the Greek is more naturally taken to mean 'the gifts I bestowed.' For the other translation one might perhaps have expected a dative.[51] Second, the word δώρημα is commonly used of a gift made by a god, rather than to a god.[52] Third, the notion would, I think, be without parallel in Jewish tradition. That God saved the people because of the gifts he received from them would be the sort of rationale one could expect to find in the pagan tradition. Juno's observation at *Aeneid* 1.49 exemplifies it well.

Impressive as these objections are, the phrase may still be susceptible of such an interpretation. For ἐμὰ δωρήματα = 'gifts made to me' there are a number of parallels. Τὰ δ' ἐμὰ δῶρα Κύπριδος (Eur. *Helen* 363), 'Cypris' gifts to me' (though the added genitive certainly makes a difference); ὑπισχνοῦ νερτέρων δωρήματα (Eur. *Orestes* 123), 'offer gifts of the dead' i.e. due to the dead (though the context helps here); ἡ ἐμὴ δωρεά (Xen. *Cyr.* 8.3.32), 'a gift to me.' As for δώρημα of a gift to a god, we might compare Aesch. *Pers.* 523. With regard to the novelty of the thought in a Jewish text, we might posit that Ezekiel is introducing (perhaps for the benefit of the pagans in the audience) a Greek theological concept of the straightforward *do ut des* variety. Yet, if there is some truth to the latter suggestion, we may actually have the subtle deflection of a Rabbinic notion so as to give it the garb and appearance of a pagan one. The Rabbis formulated a concept, which clearly had its roots in the Bible itself, 'the merits of the fathers' (patriarchs; cf. γεννητόρων here in the *Exagoge*). To reduce a complex notion to simplistic terms, this meant that many of the benefits which God bestowed upon the Jews in later generations were due to – or thanks to – the good deeds which the patriarchs of old had performed. The concept clearly seems present at Philo, *Spec. Leg.* 4.180f. Some did not hesitate to assert that all the benefits which had accrued to the Jews were the result of 'the merits of the patriarchs.'[53] The liberation from Egypt

— more narrowly the crossing of the Red Sea – is one of the benefits specifically attributed to the patriarchal merits (especially Abraham and Isaac).[54] The beginnings of this connection may be at *Deut.* 4.37. Granted all this, we might then expect God to say 'I recalled their merits (or their good deeds).' I know no instance in Jewish sources where these 'merits' are called 'gifts' or the like. But it may be precisely in this regard that we can see Ezekiel assimilating his material to non-Jewish conceptions for the benefit of the pagans in his audience, for whom on the one hand the notion of 'remembrance of merit' would have little meaning, while on the other hand the recollection of gifts would be meaningful. To be sure, post-Biblical sources do not equate gift-giving with 'merits.' But Ezekiel could have rationalized and justified this by the fact that the patriarchs do on occasions offer gifts of one sort or another to God.[55] δώρημα may occur at *Sirach* 34.18 in the context of sacrifice and the Talmud writes עולה דורון היא 'The burnt offering is a *doron*' (*Zeb.* 7b).[56] The specific deed of the patriarchs which the Rabbis explicitly suggest as responsible for the sparing of the Jewish first-born in Egypt and the crossing of the sea is the (near-) offering by Abraham of Isaac to God, which might reasonably be called δώρημα.[57]

Finally, I note one interesting expression which is similar to the sentiment that God remembers the 'gifts' of the patriarchs, and occurs in the ancient liturgy. In the prayer known as the עמידה there occurs the phrase זוכר חסדי אבות which is usually taken to mean that God remembers the pious deeds of the patriarchs.[58] It is true that the earliest evidence we have for the Palestinian עמידה does not include this phrase, but there is no good reason to doubt its antiquity and its ancient place in the liturgy.[59] *Sirach* 44.10ff contains similar phrase-ology, with its ἄνδρες ἐλέους, δικαιωσύναι (אנשי חסד, צדקתם?), and 'have not been forgotten,' in regard to the ancestors of the Jewish people. Ezekiel's μνησθείς δ᾽ ἐκείνων καὶ ἔτ᾽ ἐμῶν δωρημάτων may be an adaptation of this particular version of the concept of 'merits of the patriarchs.'

Such an interpretation is offered since the traditional one seems quite unacceptable. If the present view does not convince, I see only one other way to make sense of this sentence, emendation. It is not hard to hazard a guess which with only a slight change of the manu-scripts' reading offers good and appropriate meaning. For ἐμῶν

δωρημάτων read ἐμῶν δὴ ῥημάτων. For examples of δή following
the possessive adjective see Denniston, *Particles* 210. It is striking –
if nothing more than coincidental – that two of Denniston's examples
read Τἀμὰ δή ... ῥήματα (Aristoph. *Pax* 603; Cratinus frg. 198).
The verse may now violate Porson's Law, but since Ezekiel blatantly
violates it on a number of occasions this is not a cogent objection.
Indeed, Ezekiel likes verse-end in a monosyllable followed by a tri-
syllable (e.g. 79, 93, 143, 233). The Bible – including the Exodus
narrative (2.24) – constantly reiterates that God remembers his
covenant with the patriarchs and so saves his people. The theme is
continued into Hellenistic literature (*1 Macc.* 4.10, *2 Macc.* 1.2) and
the New Testament (*Luke* 1.72ff). It is precisely the commonness of
this theme that leads scholars to translate δωρημάτων here 'promises.' With the slight emendation suggested, the three desired elements are now present: (1) God remembers (2) the patriarchs (3) a
word that can easily stand for the concepts of 'covenant' or 'promises' (unlike δώρημα).[60] ῥῆμα (or ῥήματα) Θεοῦ is not an in-
frequent phrase, found in the Septuagint, Hellenistic Jewish texts
and Christian texts. ῥῆμα Κυρίου is common in the Septuagint.

One further point of interest. In the Bible, when God begins to
speak to Moses, he asserts that he will take the Jews from Egypt to
another land, Canaan (3.8). Similarly, in their reports of the bush-
scene, Artapanus (*PE* 9.434c), Philo (*Moses* 1.71) and Josephus (*AJ*
2.269) all make this point, though not necessarily naming the new
land. Ezekiel avoids this. The implications have already been discussed.

5. The plagues (132–51)

A dramatic presentation of the plagues may have been out of the
question for the stagecraft and theatrical conventions of Ezekiel's
day. He chose to present them in a speech. Whereas the unity and
compactness of the Red Sea episode was naturally suited to a retro-
spective messenger's speech, such was not the case with the plagues.
They entail a number of clearly demarcated events that take place
over an extended period of time and so it would have been difficult
for Ezekiel to introduce a speaker recounting all the plagues only
after their completion. Therefore he resorted to a brief but explicit

prophecy by God. Between lines 192 and 193 there is a large temporal gap and it is a matter of conjecture as to how Ezekiel filled this period in his play. It is not inconceivable that in some fashion he did treat the plagues, e.g. in terms of the reactions of the Egyptians or the repeated confrontations between Moses and Pharaoh. Some place for the episode of the plagues, however brief and cursory, must have been found by the tragedian in the later portion of the drama. The whole coherence and sequential logic of the plot demands it. But the manner and length of the episode we cannot know. We should not, however, hesitate to believe that in some degree Ezekiel repeated material already present in 132–51. Although no such prophecy occurs in the book of *Exodus*, Ezekiel probably felt that he had some support in the Bible, for during the conversation between God and Moses at the bush (to which scene lines 132ff seem to belong[1]) God briefly alludes to the coming plagues, both in general (3.20) and in specific terms (4.9). Later God forecasts to Moses the slaying of the (Pharaoh's) first born (4.23). So Ezekiel had a partial precedent in the Biblical narrative for God's telling Moses of the future plagues on Egypt.

We begin with the passage from the *Exagoge*:

> ἐν τῆδε ῥάβδῳ πάντα ποιήσεις κακά.
> πρῶτον μὲν αἷμα ποτάμιον ῥυήσεται
> πηγαί τε πᾶσαι καὶ ὑδάτων συστήματα·
> βατράχων τε πλῆθος καὶ σκνίπας ἐμβαλῶ χθονί.
> ἔπειτα τέφραν οἷς καμιναίαν πάσω,
> ἀναβρυήσει δ' ἐν βροτοῖς ἕλκη πικρά.
> κυνόμυια δ' ἥξει καὶ βροτοὺς Αἰγυπτίων
> πολλοὺς κακώσει. μετὰ δὲ ταῦτ' ἔσται πάλιν
> λοιμός, θανοῦνται δ' οἷς ἔνεστι καρδία
> σκληρά. πικράνω δ' οὐρανόν· χάλαζα νῦν
> σὺν πυρὶ πεσεῖται καὶ νεκροὺς θήσει βροτούς.
> καρποί τ' ὀλοῦνται τετραπόδων τε σώματα·
> σκότος τε θήσω τρεῖς ἐφ' ἡμέρας ὅλας
> ἀκρίδας τε πέμψω, καὶ περισσὰ βρώματα
> ἅπαντ' ἀναλώσουσι καὶ καρποῦ χλόην.
> ἐπὶ πᾶσι τούτοις τέκν' ἀποκτενῶ βροτῶν
> πρωτόγονα. παύσω δ' ὕβριν ἀνθρώπων κακῶν.
> Φαραὼ δὲ βασιλεὺς πείσετ' οὐδὲν ὧν λέγω,
> πλὴν τέκνον αὐτοῦ πρωτόγονον ἕξει νεκρόν·
> καὶ τότε φοβηθεὶς λαὸν ἐκπέμψει ταχύ.

One perceives immediately the relative sparseness and directness of the account. There is little aside from the statement of the nature of each plague and the victim it attacks. We miss the Bible's graphic depiction of the psychological and emotional effects of the plagues on the Egyptians, the repeated confrontations between Moses and Pharaoh, the decisions and retractions of Pharaoh, the explicit emphasis on the miraculous immunity of the Jews from the plagues. It is, to be sure, conceivable (if not likely) that some of this received attention later on in the play. But here limits are strictly adhered to. There are both discrepancies and differences between the *Exodus* account and Ezekiel's. For instance, *Exodus* reports that when the waters turned to blood the fish died. Ezekiel says no such thing. This may simply be the result of epitomization; or he may have taken for granted the inference that when the rivers flow blood fish will not survive.[2] Certainly the second and third plagues (135) are given the bare minimum of description. The plague of boils is limited by Ezekiel to human victims, while in *Exodus* it affects both man and beast. The same is true of the deaths of the first-born. Indeed, in contrast to *Exodus*, animals suffer in Ezekiel only through the hail. The fifth Biblical plague, pestilence, affects only animals. In contrast Ezekiel appears to limit its effect to men (140–1). There are one or perhaps two instances of Ezekiel's arranging plagues in an order which does not match that of the Pentateuch. Boils is in fourth place, between fleas and flies, rather than in sixth after pestilence. Darkness precedes locusts (144–5); the reverse order is in *Exodus*. Finally, Ezekiel appears to say that Pharaoh suffered none of the plagues till the last (149–50), which is quite out of tune with *Exodus*. Most of the deviations need no explanation. Other post-Biblical plague narratives also show deviations from *Exodus*, for instance *Jubilees*, Philo and Artapanus.[3] But the position of boils (and perhaps that of darkness), the nature of Ezekiel's 'pestilence,' and the condition of Pharaoh are significant enough changes to demand attention and explication.

Ezekiel clearly belongs to that era and/or milieu which had been led by the absence of any strict numerical definition of the plagues in *Exodus* to be relatively unconcerned about the precision of its accounts. A reader or spectator who did not know *Exodus* could never calculate from Ezekiel's verses how many distinct and separate plagues there were because of his erratic use of conjunctions and adverbs between plagues and within different aspects of a single plague. When Ezekiel seems to place darkness (ninth in *Exodus*) before locusts (eighth in *Exodus*), we should not conclude that he knew a tradition – or even a version – in which the Biblical order was here reversed, nor that he was unaware of the Pentateuch's order. Indeed, we ought not even to feel certain that he is presenting a novel order. He ties the two so closely together (τε . . . τε) that to separate them out in exact chronological terms may be undesirable, especially since the three days of darkness may overlap the arrival of locusts. Perhaps he tied darkness to locusts to give the former more substance since in itself darkness causes no damage. If so, he may have placed it before locusts for rhetorical and stylistic reasons, as the lengthy elaboration (145–6) will naturally be part of the ἀκρίς plague. Additionally, he may have wanted σκότος immediately after the hail-storms of 141ff since darkness is a common and natural concomitant of storms. So this may involve a bit of rationalism on Ezekiel's part, perhaps for his audience's sake.[4]

Ezekiel shifted boils from sixth to fourth place. To understand this change we must examine the structure of the plague account in the *Exagoge*, a task which will not only prove of inherent value but will also, I think, demonstrate the folly of believing (as does Loewenstamm) that any other source but the book of *Exodus* was here in Ezekiel's mind. In brief, Ezekiel's conception of the plagues is something like the Philonic/Rabbinic one in which the ten plagues are envisioned as three groups of three and one isolated plague. This is also Ezekiel's pattern, though his groupings are slightly different, both in principle and detail. As with Philo, he sees the first three as one group, though unlike Philo he does not report precisely what it is that leads him to join the three together (e.g. Aaron as agent; earth/water as sources). He probably saw frogs and blood as both plagues of the Nile; that he closely connects frogs and fleas is brought out not only by the τε . . . καί, but by the fact that one verb governs them both (ἐμβαλῶ).[5] ἔπειτα in line 136 indicates that we are moving into another group; these are boils, flies, and pestilence. Ezekiel ties them together as plagues that affect human beings, in contrast to the first group where there is no explicit mention of victims at all. Observe the repetition of βροτοί (137–8), followed by the reference to sinful men (140–1). Thus, when Ezekiel moved boils from position 6 to 4 he was, in his mind, reordering the plagues within a single group but was maintaining the identity and substance of the group and the position of that group within the total sequence of plagues. Why then did he not leave boils as the last of this group?[6] It seems possible that once he conceived this particular group as a set to be defined by the identity of the victims he thought it rhetorically effective to present them in an ascending order of severity: pestilence (ϑάνατος in the Septuagint) then immediately usurped position 6 from boils and evidently Ezekiel held flies to be a more severe affliction than boils.

As τέφραν . . . πάσω earlier introduced a new group, so now does πικράνω οὐρανόν.[7] The very phrase suggests the nature of this group. They are all 'heaven sent' plagues, i.e. plagues which affect or issue from the heavens: darkness, locusts (brought by the wind), hailstorms. Indeed, this is fundamentally the category described also by Philo and the Rabbis.[8] For Ezekiel (as for Philo), who was reading the Bible in Greek, this association would have been strengthened by the explicit mention of οὐρανός in the locust plague (10.13), a reference not present in the Hebrew text. Finally comes the tenth and last plague, deservedly occupying a place by itself.

The way in which each plague is announced is geared to the account in *Exodus.*[9] We recall that certain plagues come about through some action of Moses or Aaron (waving a rod, throwing dust, etc.), while a few occur without such action, seemingly through the will of God alone. Of the latter there are three, flies, pestilence and death of the first-born. A glance at the verbs in this passage reveals essentially two categories, strong verbs that indicate or imply a concrete action, weak verbs that simply suggest the appearance of a plague: ῥυήσεται, ἐμβαλῶ, πάσω-ἀναβρυήσει, ἥξει, ἔσται, πικράνω-ϑήσει, ϑήσω, πέμψω, ἀποκτενῶ. Two verbs stand out, ἥξει and ἔσται. Can it merely be a coincidence that these are two of the plagues in *Exodus* where Moses and Aaron do nothing? Further, it will be noticed that in all the other plagues there occurs a first person verb.[10] These first person verbs are spoken by God but are correlated to the activity of Moses and Aaron (most clearly and indisputably at 136, πάσω). This is, for all intents and purposes, God speaking Moses' speech.[11] The conflation of identities serves to explain the one major exception to this pattern, ἀποκτενῶ. The emphasis is on

the tenth plague as God's direct intervention and action. Consequently, since it is after all God who is speaking, the first person
here was unavoidable.

Probably the most serious and difficult question in this section
of the *Exagoge* is the plague of pestilence which in *Exodus* and
perhaps in all other sources is directed solely against animals. Ezekiel
does not mention animals at all. But he does say that the plague
destroyed human beings (140–1), ϑανοῦνται δ' οἷς ἔνεστι καρδία
σκληρά. Hôw are we to explain this? Loewenstamm turns to his
usual argument – and in truth it is probably nowhere as seductive
as here – that Ezekiel was following an alternative tradition. In fact,
here some evidence seems to exist (*Psalm* 78.50): לא חשך ממות נפשם
וחיתם לדבר הסגיר: pestilence seems directed at human beings.[12] It is
still something of a puzzle why, if this was a *tradition*, it never recurs
in the many other accounts of the plagues. Whereas, on the other
hand, if we seek to argue that Ezekiel was here using the text of
Psalms, we must note that the Septuagint, which he surely would
have been using,[13] translates this verse in such a way that the plague
becomes directed at animals.[14] Loewenstamm could have pointed to
some Midrashic material which may further his view here. The
Rabbis argued that pestilence destroyed not only animals but indirectly men also, e.g. the horse afflicted with the plague would
collapse and his rider would fall and die.[15] This appears to be a
Rabbinic attempt to reconcile two conflicting traditions, the one
which reports that only animals died, the other (as perhaps represented by *Psalm* 78.50) that men died too. The Rabbis sought thereby to maintain the authority of the Pentateuchal account by limiting
the plague itself to animals, but accommodated the other tradition
by having men die as an indireci result of the plague.[16]

But the key here lies in the *Exodus* narrative. It is a simple though
usually ignored fact that of the ten plagues in *Exodus* there are two
– and only two – that *are* death. That is, the essence of the plague is
death. Fish die in the first plague, but this is only as a result of the
plague. When men and animals die in the seventh plague, this is only
a possible (note the option of escape, 9.19–21) outcome of the hail-
storms. But in two plagues, the fifth and tenth, the plague is purely
and simply death (even more so in the Septuagint where דבר is
simply called ϑάνατος).[17] There is then an unavoidable and inextric-

able connection between the plagues of pestilence and death of the
first-born that is built into the *Exodus* account and was interpreted
and exploited by later readers in a variety of ways. This connection
could have led to an approximation of one to the other – not merely
death but human death in both. It is interesting that in *Psalm* 78 דבר
is juxtaposed to the slaying of the first-born (50f).[18] An individual
example of this sort of development may be seen in Philo's account,
for he explicitly takes the plague of pestilence as a foreshadowing of
the slaying of the first-born, a clear sign that he connected the two in
their nature as plagues of θάνατος.[19] The somewhat cryptic account
of Josephus may also be relevant (*AJ* 2.293ff). Thackeray and
Feldman[20] have both observed that he leaves out the fifth plague,
even though he claims to be presenting them all. In fact he does not
omit it but tacks it on casually and briefly to the fourth plague, ערוב.
Whatever survived the wild beasts of the fourth plague (303) was
destroyed by νόσος.[21] The difficult words τῶν ἀνθρώπων ὑπομ-
ενόντων and the later allusion at 307 (which Loewenstamm takes as
an inconsistency in the narrative) may suggest that the νόσος attacks
animals. At any rate, the following point is important for us: Josephus
attaches the name νόσος to one other plague, the death of the first-
born (313). He too discerned a similarity between these two plagues.

Thus, the crux of the diverse דבר versions lies in the association
of this plague with the tenth. Ezekiel's is perhaps the most extreme
extension of this association, namely the attribution of human death
to this plague, as at *Psalm* 78. One further peculiarity reinforces this
view. Ezekiel does not simply report that human beings died in this
plague, but rather θανοῦνται δ' οἷς ἔνεστι καρδία σκληρά (140–1).
Here we have the beginnings of the notion that the punishment of
the Egyptians was penalty for their σκληροκαρδία, a theme found
in the early Church, especially with reference to the drowning in
the sea.[22] In the plagues enumerated by Ezekiel only twice are the
victims so described that we understand the plague to be a moral
instrument designed to punish those who for their actions and
natures merit punishment. The first is here; the second is the tenth
(147–8):

> ἐπὶ πᾶσι τούτοις τέκν' ἀποκτενῶ βροτῶν
> πρωτόγονα. παύσω δ' ὕβρω ἀνθρώπων κακῶν.

Once again we see how these two plagues are seen from the same perspective, with the same vision, perhaps we might say as two sides of the same coin.

Ezekiel writes of the last plague (147–51):

ἐπὶ πᾶσι τούτοις τέκν' ἀποκτενῶ βροτῶν
πρωτόγονα. παύσω δ' ὕβρω ἀνθρώπων κακῶν.
Φαραὼ δὲ βασιλεὺς πείσετ' οὐδὲν ὧν λέγω,
πλὴν τέκνον αὐτοῦ πρωτόγονον ἕξει νεκρόν·
καὶ τότε φοβηθεὶς λαὸν ἐκπέμψει ταχύ.

The meaning of 149 is subject to dispute. Does πείσεται come from πάσχω[23] or from πείθω?[24] Both will yield sense. Either Pharaoh will not pay heed to anything said to him until this ultimate plague, or Pharaoh will not suffer from any of the plagues till the last. In support of πείθω there are two arguments: (1) It makes good sense. Pharaoh does ignore the pleas and demands of Moses until the last plague is inflicted. Indeed, at *Exod.* 11.9 God tells Moses and Aaron explicitly that Pharaoh will not heed them. (2) πείσεται from πάσχω is difficult. That Pharaoh does not suffer till the final plague is not supported by the book of *Exodus*. Earlier ones affect him also (7.28–9; 8.4, 7, 17). Nevertheless, it seems to me most natural to take πείσετ' οὐδέν as 'will not suffer.' While it is true that πλήν sometimes serves as little more than δέ, the close-knit quality of these lines suggests a more intimate connection between lines 149 and 150. As is evident from the Septuagint's use of πλήν, even when it is used as a conjunction to introduce a clause, the sense of exclusion or contradiction of what has preceded (sometimes explicit, sometimes implicit) is usually present.[25] If πείσεται is from πείθω, then it is hard to allow πλήν even a weak adversative sense. Further, the words πείσετ' οὐδὲν ὧν λέγω make considerably better sense if πείσεται is from πάσχω. It means, 'Pharaoh will not suffer any of the plagues I have just mentioned.' If from πείθω, we must render 'he will pay heed to none of the things I have mentioned.' This is not impossible, but since πείθεσθαι usually means 'to obey, to be persuaded (to)' and there has been no prior mention of attempts to persuade Pharaoh, no implication even that any of the plagues is avoidable, this would come rather unexpectedly. A verb meaning 'submit to' (e.g. ὑπείκειν) would do better.[26] Still, 'Pharaoh will not suffer' contradicts the Biblical tale. Nor, to the best of my knowledge, is there such a version elsewhere in post-Biblical writings. But other facts must be considered.

Post-Biblical texts that deal with the plagues tend to treat the question of their effect on Pharaoh with rather casual neglect of the Biblical narrative. In a sense Ezekiel is part of this 'negative' tradition. To go to the opposite extreme there is a version that all the plagues began with Pharaoh.[27] On the other hand, and as out of tune with *Exodus* as Ezekiel, is the Midrashic text which seems to imply that Pharaoh himself did not suffer from the plagues till hail.[28] Remark too Josephus. Insofar as his explicit description goes, Pharaoh never seems to be affected by any of the plagues. He appears throughout as little more than interested and concerned spectator of his people's sufferings. In truth, on reading the relevant chapters in *Exodus* one receives the *impression* that Pharaoh does not suffer till the last punishment. The gap between the relatively minor inconveniences which come on him and the loss of his child is so great as to render the former almost meaningless. Of course, the rhetorical and dramatic power of such a climax would not have been lost on Ezekiel. To conclude, an interesting passage found in the Jerusalem and Neofiti Targumim. At the end of *Exodus* 10 these two Targumim add a sentence which is not found in the Biblical text: מחתא עשירא היא לפרעה/מחתה הדא עשירייה הי לפרעה. These appear to say (especially Jerusalem) that the tenth plague is designated specifically for Pharaoh, an interpretation that is supported by the preceding words, דהוה לך רחמין דהוינא מצלי עלך ומחתא מתכליא, which seem to mean that Moses' prayers kept earlier plagues from Pharaoh, but not so now with the tenth. If this interpretation is correct, we then have a substantially similar version to Ezekiel's, that the tenth plague, unlike the earlier ones, was directed against Pharaoh.

Loewenstamm (60) asserts that Ezekiel and Artapanus reflect an ancient tradition that *Moses* brought the plagues.[29] But a comparison of Artapanus with Ezekiel reveals very different descriptions that could scarcely belong to the same tradition, or attitude. The former scarcely mentions God at all; in contrast he reiterates over and again Moses' actions and the role of his rod. This is clearly a version which stresses Moses' role to the near exclusion of God. In Ezekiel the plagues are enumerated by God Himself in a speech replete with first person verbs. Indeed even an action of Moses is declared to be an act

of God ($\pi\acute{\alpha}\sigma\omega$, 136). In Ezekiel's account there is no explicit mention of Moses at all. The basis of Loewenstamm's view, verse 132, is
a flimsy foundation. Even did it mean what Loewenstamm (and
others) take it to mean, that Moses will perform all the miracles with
his rod, any emphasis one might wish to place on the verse is quickly
undermined by the exclusion of Moses from the following 18 lines.
But, to be sure, verse 132 probably means 'you will perform all
sorts of plagues with your rod.'[30] That is, there is no statement that
the rod will be a part of all the plagues. And indeed the rod is never
mentioned in the ensuing account. In Ezekiel's narrative the rod's
role is tied to the first plague and possibly to the next two which
follow closely (135). The most interesting account of the plagues
may be Josephus', in which Moses and Aaron play no role whatsoever: Josephus rejects the notion that Moses was the real author
of the plagues (2.302).[31] Here we undoubtedly have polemic against
such versions as Artapanus attests.[32]

6. The Passover regulations (152–92)

After concluding his recitation of the plagues, God instructs Moses
to transmit to the Jews the laws of Passover (152ff). While most of
the details are taken from the Biblical narrative, certain elements
are clearly not Biblical and may shed further light on Ezekiel's use
of extra-Biblical Jewish traditions.

Scholars have assumed that verses 132–92 are the words of God
to Moses. Most consider the 61 lines a single speech, with a lacuna
of some length between 174 and 175. Some believe that 175–92
belong to a later speech by God to Moses.[1] Even the most superficial
reading of 152–92 reveals a problem which scholars have by and large
glossed over. This is, simply, the almost intolerable way God repeats
to Moses the very same instructions.[2] It is true, as I hope to show
later, that there are very skillful variations from one set of instructions to the other, but this in itself does not justify the numerous
blatant and seemingly uncalled-for repetitions. Thus, to cite some
examples, we are told that the Jews are to sacrifice the Pesach at
157 and 179; that Pharaoh will banish them in haste at 161 and
182–3; that they should daub the doorposts with blood to escape
death at 158–9 and 185–7;[3] that they shall observe the festival for

seven days without eating leaven at 170f and 188–90. Since these are the major elements of the Exodus and the Holiday, one might say that we have essentially the same set of instructions given twice. Ezekiel is not inept. Why would he have God give the Passover rules to Moses twice in one speech or even twice in two separate speeches? In truth, he did not.

That lines 152–92 are not one speech should be clear from two facts. First, the list of repetitions that I have given above shows one critical and illuminating characteristic. All the repetitions are between 152–74 on the one hand and 175–92 on the other. Within the lines 152–74 there is not a single repetition nor is there any within 175–92. This is a cogent sign that we have two speeches, with repetitions from the first in the second. Second, there are the implications of Eusebius' transitional statement between 174 and 175: Καὶ πάλιν περὶ τῆς αὐτῆς ταύτης ἑορτῆς φησὶν ἐπεξεργαζόμενον ἀκριβέστερον εἰρηκέναι.[4] In transitional statements between citations πάλιν alone seems to be used rather of a clear-cut shift, a distinct break, while εἶτα or ὑποβάς designates a less distinct break or a small gap. Thus, unless we are to assume that πάλιν here signifies no more than repetition, which seems unlikely, we should probably take this as an indication of a different speech, a different scene from the one just broken off. To be sure, this still does not answer the basic question: why does God repeat Himself? But once we have reached the conclusion that there are two speeches here it is easy to see the answer. For there is then no reason whatsoever to attribute lines 175–92 to God. I would suggest that these lines are part of a speech by Moses to the Jews (or the elders)[5] in which he reviewed for them the commands of God concerning the coming Exodus and the festival.[6] Indeed, verses 109–10 suggest the existence of some such scene in the play. σήμαινε τοῖς ἐμοῖς λόγοις virtually means, 'tell them, using my words; tell them in my name.' This is, in fact, precisely the pattern of the Biblical narrative. After God outlines the regulations for Moses at *Exod.* 12.1–20 Moses assembles the elders and reviews the instructions which he has just received (12.21–7). But Ezekiel has executed this repetition skillfully through selectivity and elaboration. Thus, certain elements occur only in either 152–74 (= A) or 175–92 (= B). Others are stated barely in one, expanded in the other.[7] Thus, A enjoins a sacrifice in mid-month, B elaborates that the animal is

to be chosen on the tenth and held till the sacrifice on the fourteenth. A orders that blood be daubed on the door, B adds that it be
done with hyssop and defines the location more precisely. A states
that the sacrifice must be eaten roasted, B adds that the whole be
eaten, including the innards. A states that a fierce messenger (angel)
will pass over the Jewish homes, B straightforwardly calls the angel
death.[8] A reports that Pharaoh will banish the people in haste, B
that he will order (the Egyptians) to chase out the Jews in haste. On
the other hand, the etiology of the seven-day festival is set out in A
but not in B; so too the practice of the first-born sacrifice and the
reference to the spoliation of the Egyptians.

The misunderstanding that has plagued this section of the *Exagoge*
is, I suspect, the result of a Biblical stylistic feature that Ezekiel has
here adopted, i.e. the insertion of a speech within a speech at 153ff.
God does not merely recite his injunctions but tells Moses exactly
what to say to the people. Although the immediate quotation of
what Moses is to say concludes at 155, the remaining instructions are
also given with an eye toward Moses' future recitation of them to the
people. Thus, they begin with λέξεις δὲ λαῷ παντί (156) and proceed with constant references to ὑμεῖς, not to 'they' or 'the Jews,'
not even – and this is strikingly significant – to a second person
singular of Moses. In other words, the whole speech (153–74),
though spoken by God to Moses, is conceived of as a speech by
Moses to the people. That is why scholars have so readily assumed
that 175–92 is also spoken by God, for stylistically it looks much
like the preceding. And why should it not? The first we might
describe as a speech of Moses to the people recited obliquely by God;
the second is a genuine speech of Moses to the people. And yet,
precisely because of the fundamental difference between the two,
there are subtle but critical signs that let us see the truth. It was a
difficult task to write a speech 'for Moses' recited by God; here
and there Ezekiel slips. On occasion we do hear God speaking to
Moses and of the Jews. At 154f ἀπάξω and ὑπέστην both refer to
God, while the Jews have become third person Ἑβραίων, after ὑμῖν
at 153. The same is true at 162, δώσω χάριν λαῷ, while at 166 the
Jews ἔπραξαν. All these are simple slips, easily explained and readily
understandable. But compare 175–92. Here there is not a single such
slip. Every reference to the Jews is followed by a second person

plural verb and reference to God is in the third person. For here
there was no potential confusion. Moses merely addresses the people.
I note one further difference between sections A and B which may
be significant. At 188 the Jews are told, ταύτην δ' ἑορτὴν δεσπότῃ
τηρήσετε. In the *Exagoge* God is regularly called θεός, here and at
124 δεσπότης. If one examines the Septuagint one realizes that
perhaps without exception δεσπότης is used of God only by others,
not by God Himself. It is, in other words, essentially like *Adon(ai)*
in the Hebrew. If this is correct, then we have further evidence that
section B was not spoken by God.

Ezekiel, like the Bible, makes Moses' account of the regulations
an expanded version (in some areas) of God's instructions, without
explaining the genesis of the additional elements. Thus, though God
makes no mention in the *Exagoge* of the need to take the animals
four days prior to the sacrifice or of the use of the hyssop or of the
eating of the innards, Moses includes them all in his prescriptions.
Just so in the Bible God's directions to Moses do not include the
hyssop or the need to stay indoors all night or advice on the education of the children concerning the festival, yet all this is in Moses'
instructions to the elders. (Conversely, God requires the choosing of
the animal four days in advance while Moses says nothing of this.)
Perhaps Ezekiel is just maintaining the difficult elliptical style of his
Biblical model here. But possibly he was taking advantage of this
aspect of the Biblical narrative to enhance in the eyes of his Greek
audience Moses' status as νομοθέτης, a role in which Hellenistic
Jews regularly cast Moses to increase his prestige among the Greeks.[9]
Ezekiel might well have wanted his Greek audience to assume that
Moses expanded and developed the instructions given him by God on
his own initiative.

There now emerges a new insight into the dramatic structure of
the *Exagoge*. Between the scene of the bush and that of the messenger's speech (193ff) there was a scene in which Moses instructed the
Jews (or their elders) on the necessary preparations antecedent to
their departure from Egypt, especially with regard to the newly insti-
tuted feast of Passover.

Several elements here can be better understood by recourse to
extra-Biblical texts. We read at 167–71:

ὅταν δ᾽ ἐς ἴδιον χῶρον εἰσέλθηϑ᾽, ὅπως
ἀφ᾽ ἧσπερ ἠοῦς ἐφυγετ᾽, Αἰγύπτου δ᾽ ἄπο
ἔπτ᾽ ⟨ῆτ᾽⟩ ὁδοιποροῦντες ἡμέρας ὁδόν,
πάντες τοσαύτας ἡμέρας ἔτος κάτα
ἄζυμ᾽ ἔδεσϑε καὶ ϑεῷ λατρεύσετε.

The seven-day duration of the holiday is founded on a seven-day journey of the Jews from Egypt. The Bible has nothing like this, not even a mention of a seven-day trip. It seems unlikely that Ezekiel invented this. It is hard to see what reason he could have had for so doing and, further, if it were his innovation he would have been compelled to supply additional detail so his audience could understand his point. But there are post-Biblical sources which do speak of seven-day journeys on the departure from Egypt. Frankel was the first to explain this text on the basis of Rabbinic sources:[10] 'Die Mechilta zu Exod. 14,1 gibt hierüber Aufschluss. Diese erzählt, dass der nachsetzende Pharao die Kinder Israel am sechsten Tage erreicht, und am siebenten fand der Durchgang durch das Meer statt. Am siebenten Tage also war erst die Befreiung vervollständigt, und daher betrachtet auch Ezekiel die Reise, den Auszug, als in sieben Tagen vollendet.' This is a fair synthesis and summary of two separate passages in the Mekhilta (pp. 83f, 91), though the Mekhilta does not explicitly speak of sixth and seventh days. More recently, Gutman (evidently unfamiliar with Frankel's work) has also suggested that a Rabbinical tradition is involved here and cites *Seder Olam Rabbah* 5 which describes a seven-day journey from Egypt to the sea (52).[11] Nevertheless, though these sources describe a seven-day journey, no connection is made between the journey and the length of the holiday (contrary to Gutman's statement). Gutman also notes that Bab. Tal. *Sotah* 12b reports that the song of Moses upon the drowning of the Egyptian host was sung on 21 Nisan, thus also implying a trip of seven days to the sea.[12] But it too makes no etiological links.[13] One more text can be cited, *Jubilees* 49.22f. The Jews are instructed to celebrate the holiday seven days for they celebrated it on leaving Egypt until they crossed the sea. This seems to be making a connection between the seven-day journey and the seven-day festival, though it is not clear whether the writer means 'celebrate seven days because your journey of liberation was seven days' (like Ezekiel) or merely 'celebrate it now as you celebrated it then.'

It should not surprise us to find in the *Exagoge* an etiology for the holiday which has no precedent in the Bible. This kind of etiology may ultimately go back to the Biblical model where, e.g., God works six days and then rests, so men are enjoined to keep a Sabbath after six days of work; or the Jews are compelled to wander forty years because the slanderous spies spent forty days in the holy land (*Nu.* 14.34). Thus, in the *Dires de Moise* from Qumran[14] the text (somewhat difficult and lacunose) seems to say that Yom Kippur is observed on the tenth of Tishre because the Jewish wanderings lasted till that day.[15] In sum, though no exact parallel-etiology appears to be extant, it is probable that Ezekiel was drawing here on current Jewish tradition.

At 162–6 we read:

> ὅταν δὲ μέλλητ᾽ ἀποτρέχειν, δώσω χάριν
> λαῷ γυνή τε παρὰ γυναικὸς λήψεται
> σκεύη †κόσμον τε πάνθ᾽, ὃν ἄνθρωπος φέρει,
> χρυσόν τε καὶ ἄργυρόν τε καὶ στολάς, ἵνα[16]
> ⟨ἀνθ᾽⟩ ὧν ἔπραξαν μισθὸν ἀποδῶσιν βροτοῖς.

The relevant Biblical texts read (*Exod.* 11.2f., 12.35f)

> λάλησον οὖν κρυφῇ εἰς τὰ ὦτα τοῦ λαοῦ, καὶ αἰτησάτω ἕκαστος παρὰ τοῦ πλησίον καὶ γυνὴ παρὰ τῆς πλησίον σκεύη ἀργυρᾶ καὶ χρυσᾶ καὶ ἱματισμόν. κύριος δὲ ἔδωκεν τὴν χάριν τῷ λαῷ αὐτοῦ ἐναντίον τῶν Αἰγυπτίων, καὶ ἔχρησαν αὐτοῖς.

> ... καὶ ᾔτησαν παρὰ τῶν Αἰγυπτίων σκεύη ἀργυρᾶ καὶ χρυσᾶ καὶ ἱματισμόν. καὶ κύριος ἔδωκεν τὴν χάριν τῷ λαῷ αὐτοῦ ἐναντίον τῶν Αἰγυπτίων, καὶ ἔχρησαν αὐτοῖς. καὶ ἐσκύλευσαν τοὺς Αἰγυπτίους.

The purpose of 166 is transparent. It is an apologetic expansion of the Bible and is a well-attested Rabbinic tradition. Again Frankel was the first to point this out.[17] But more is at issue here than parallel passages. For this section of *Exodus* proved of importance for the history of Jewish-Gentile relations over many years. The Bible intimates that on leaving Egypt the Jews borrow all sorts of objects from the Egyptians and then go off with no intention ever to return them. That this posed an ethical problem is not surprising. *Aboth deRabbi Natan* 41A makes clear that the Rabbis themselves were disturbed: the plundering of the treasures of Jerusalem by the Egyptian king Shishak was the means whereby the Egyptian possessions taken at the time of the Exodus were restored to their proper owners. But more important than the qualms of Jewish readers about their forefathers' behavior was the reaction of non-Jews. For it appears that this passage was a prime element in anti-Semitic propaganda. Pompeius Trogus (Justin 36 *Epit.* 2.13), in a rather distorted rewriting of the Bible, reports that Moses in stealth stole the sacred objects of the Egyptians (evidently a conflation of the Exodus tale with Rachel's theft of Laban's household idols). In addition, Rabbinic literature describes encounters between pagans and Jews in which the former accuse the Jews of being thieves on the basis of the story in *Exodus* (Bab. Tal. *Sanh.* 91a). In response the Jews set forth, at somewhat greater length, the defense offered by Ezekiel. The adjudication arrived at is that the Egyptians are still in debt to the Jews for the 430 years of slave labor by 600,000 men. The frequency with which this apologetic theme is reiterated in Jewish texts is a good indication of how real and significant the issue was. Thus, it is found (implicitly or explicitly) at Bab. Tal. *Sanh.* 91a, Philo (*Moses* 1.141-2), *Jubilees* 48.19, *Esther Rabbah* 7, *Meg. Taanit* 3.[18] Josephus varies the apology by asserting that the items were given to the Jews as outright gifts (*AJ* 2.314). When we consider the nature and context of the accusation, it seems fairly likely that it arose – or at least would have flourished – in Egypt. Indeed, at *Sanh.* 91a the charge occurs in a debate between Jews and Egyptians before Alexander. The text of *Esther Rabbah* 7.13 seems to reflect in other details too the influence of Egyptian anti-Semitic propaganda. Thus, one can readily understand Ezekiel's introduction of this *apologia* since his Greek audience might well have been regularly subjected to this argument by anti-Semitic native Egyptians. This is counter-propaganda on Ezekiel's part.

One further passage seems to need explication in light of extra-Biblical material (167-8): ὅταν δ᾽ ἐς ἴδιον χῶρον εἰσέλθηϑ᾽, ὅπως/ἀφ᾽ ἧσπερ ἠοῦς ἐφύγετ᾽, Αἰγύπτου δ᾽ ἄπο. What does ἠοῦς mean? It appears to signify 'day.' But 'day' is not the routine sense of ἠώς, though of course it is a legitimate one. As there is no good reason not to give the word its usual sense here, let us do so, 'dawn, morning.' Ezekiel reports that the Jews left Egypt in the morning. The Septuagint bears no trace of this. Only at *Nu.* 33.3 is there the slightest suggestion: τῇ ἐπαύριον τοῦ πάσχα ἐξῆλϑον and one would not readily see this brief remark as the source for Ezekiel's peculiar version here. Fundamentally, there are two possible answers. (1) Ezekiel was using the Hebrew Bible (for which there is very little evidence; see my discussion in the Introduction, sect. 9) and interpreted the repeated phrase בעצם היום הזה (*Exod.* 12.17, 41, 51) as meaning 'daytime' rather than merely 'day.' This is however unlikely. The phrase does not mean 'daytime' but 'on this very day', as the Greek translators fully realized ἐν τῇ ἡμέρᾳ ταύτῃ (ἐκείνῃ), and Ezekiel would have also, if he knew Hebrew. Further, at 12.41–2 the Septuagint, which Ezekiel unquestionably was using, translates in such a way that it is hard to tell whether 'night' belongs to the end of 41 or the beginning of 42. Editors of the Septuagint differ and, whichever may be correct, it is beyond doubt that a reader of the Septuagint might well have assumed it to be part of 41. That νυκτός is indeed part of 41 may be supported by the Septuagint's ignoring of בעצם היום הזה in 41, an attempt (presumably) to avoid the appearance of inconsistency between ἡμέρα and νύξ in the same verse. Moreover, placing νυκτός in 42 gives νυκτός προφυλακή for ליל שמרים ('a night of watchfulness'), a strange translation whether we take it as a construct usage (reversing that of the Hebrew!) or as a temporal genitive. In addition, the Samaritan text puts 'night' at the end of 41 rather than the beginning of 42. In other words, Ezekiel may have actually had a Greek text of *Exodus* which put the departure at night (cf. *Deut.* 16.1). It is most probable that Ezekiel was familiar with exegetical traditions that emphasized the departure in the daytime. For some sources a mere sentence suffices, 'this teaches that the Jews left in the daytime.'[19] Others are more elaborate:[20] Pharaoh knocked at the door and said to Moses and Aaron, 'Get up and depart from my people.' They answered 'You fool. Are we thieves that we should leave at night? We shall depart in the morning.' In short, it may be reasonable to suppose that Ezekiel here too was drawing on extra-Biblical Jewish sources.

I suspect that verses 189–90 have not been properly understood.

ἐφθ' ἡμέρας ἄζυμα· καὶ οὐ βρωθήσεται
ζύμη. κακῶν γὰρ τῶνδ' ἀπαλλαγήσεται.

γάρ suggests that there is a significant connection here and it is hard to believe that no more is meant than 'you will have a holiday since you shall be freed of troubles.' The emphasis on ἄζυμα, followed by the independent clause καὶ οὐ βρωθήσεται ζύμη, suggests that the connection has to do with the prohibition of leavened bread. Recourse to Midrashic material provides the requisite background. In Greco-Jewish, Rabbinic and New Testament texts leaven is commonly used allegorically of that which is evil or impure.[21] Ezekiel is here exploiting this metaphor: do not eat leaven, for God is now giving you a release from your troubles. That is, since leaven is a symbol of affliction and evil and you are now celebrating a festival of liberation from adversity, you should refrain from eating it, as a sign of your present deliverance. This is fundamentally the same as, though less explicit than, the declaration at Targum 2 to *Esther* 3.8. There the Jews proclaim on the Passover, 'Just as we remove this leaven, so may the evil rule be removed from us and may we be freed from this foolish king.' A symbolic explication of a specific Passover regulation, in much the same manner as Ezekiel's, can be found at *Jub.* 49.13: 'they shall not break any bone of the Passover sacrifice; for of the children of Israel no bone shall be crushed.' Just as in the sacrifice no bone is to be broken, so among the performers of the ritual will no bone be broken.

As Gutman has well noted (51), ὁ μεὶς ὅδε ὑμῖν πρῶτος ἐνιαυτῶν πέλει (153)[22] shows a significant deviation from the Biblical text: ὁ μὴν οὗτος ὑμῖν ἀρχὴ μηνῶν, πρῶτός ἐστιν ὑμῖν ἐν τοῖς μησὶν τοῦ ἐνιαυτοῦ. Where the Septuagint has μηνῶν, Ezekiel reads ἐνιαυτῶν. Gutman proposes that Ezekiel is here referring to the Rabbinic notion of a new era which begins with the Exodus from Egypt. This is an interesting and attractive suggestion. Although none of the Rabbinic texts cited by Gutman actually attest such an idea, there is a source that does:[23] God promulgates, 'Count an era from the Exodus.'[24]

There is an interesting and difficult question at 175-6:[25]

ἀνδρῶν Ἑβραίων τοῦδε τοῦ μηνὸς λαβών
κατὰ συγγενείας πρόβατα καὶ μόσχους βοῶν.

The laws in *Exodus* limit the Passover sacrifice to a πρόβατον from ἄρνες or ἔριφοι (12.5). But at *Deut.* 16.2 the sacrifice may come from πρόβατα καὶ βόας.[26] Gutman (53) believes that Ezekiel's version is an accurate representation of his contemporary situation before the sage Hillel prohibited the use of cattle. This seems reasonable, but some caution is in order. Our information on the rites of Passover in that period seems insufficient to justify so significant a conclusion, especially when Ezekiel could be merely following the Deuteronomic text.[27] Twice in this scene Ezekiel writes of the haste in which the Jews will be banished, σπουδῇ (161) and ἐν σπουδῇ (182), which are both closer to the ἐν σπουδῇ of *Deut.* 16.3 (the very next verse) than to the μετὰ σπουδῆς of *Exod.* 12.11.

Several problems here merit attention. First, verses 167–74:

> ὅταν δ᾿ ἐς ἴδιον χῶρον εἰσέλθηϑ᾿, ὅπως[28]
> ἀφ᾿ ἧσπερ ἠοῦς ἐφύγετ᾿, Αἰγύπτου δ᾿ ἄπο
> ἕπτ᾿ (ἧπ᾿) ὁδοιποροῦντες ἡμέρας ὁδόν,
> πάντες τοσαύτας ἡμέρας ἔτος κάτα
> ἄζυμ᾿ ἔδεσϑε καὶ ϑεῷ λατρεύσετε,
> τὰ πρωτότευκτα ζῷα ϑύοντες ϑεῷ,
> ὅσ᾿ ἂν τέκωσι παρϑένοι πρώτως τέκνα
> τὰρσενικὰ διανοίγοντα μήτρας μητέρων.

The Jews are enjoined (as it seems) to celebrate the Passover in their new homeland with sacrifices of first-born animals.[29] There was, however, no such custom in Jewish worship.[30] The Bible enjoins the sacrifice of first-born animals but it is not an aspect of the Passover festival nor was it ever so. It is possible that Ezekiel misunderstood the Biblical command and because it was juxtaposed to the laws of Passover believed it to be a part of them (*Exod.* 13.5ff, 11ff).[31] But this is almost inconceivable. The source of the problem, I think, lies in the rather elliptical and inelegant style. Once properly understood, the text is in conformity with – indeed an outgrowth of – the Biblical text.[32]

The key is in the phraseology of the relevant Septuagintal passages. At *Exod.* 13.5 begin the instructions for future Passovers in Israel. When this is completed at 13.10, there commence at 13.11 the laws pertinent to the sacrifice of first-born animals. What is crucial here is that each set of laws starts with the same introductory phrase, καὶ ἔσται ἡνίκα (ὡς) ἐὰν εἰσαγάγῃ . . . γῆν. In adapting the two sets of regulations one after the other Ezekiel has simply used the phrase once at the beginning of the whole section, with the intention that it cover both sets. In other words, the clause ὅπως ἀφ᾿ . . . τοσαύτας ἡμέρας goes only with ἄζυμ᾿ ἔδεσϑε. Thus, the passage should be understood, 'when you enter your land you will eat unleavened bread seven days and you shall also offer first-

born sacrifices.' The crux here resides in the common etiology:
when you reach your land, you will do two things that are the outgrowth of and a memorial to God's deliverance of the Jews from
Egypt. You will eat unleavened bread seven days to recall the seven-
day journey from Egypt to the sea and the final liberation. You
will also sacrifice the first-born animals as a remembrance of God's
sparing of the Jewish first-born when he smote the Egyptians.[33]

Ezekiel does not include the additional Biblical injunctions concerning the substitution of 'clean' animals for 'unclean' ones (lamb
for donkey) or the redemption of human first-born. Perhaps he
thought these too provincial for the tastes of his audience; perhaps
he had no special motive for leaving them out.[34] He was, after all,
not producing a lawcode for his audience. Or indeed perhaps he did
include them in the lines that followed but are now lost.

Lines 156–8 have been routinely misunderstood and mistrans-
lated:

λέξεις δὲ λαῷ παντί, μηνὸς οὗ λέγω
διχομηνίᾳ τὸ πάσχα θύσαντας θεῷ
τῇ πρόσθε νυκτὶ αἵματι ψαῦσαι θύρας.

'At the full moon of the month of which I speak, having sacrificed
the Pesach to God on the preceding night, they will touch the
doors with blood.'[35] 'In the month of which I speak at full moon,
having sacrificed the Passover to God on the preceding night, touch
the doors with blood.'[36] These translations are patently absurd. Each
asserts that the sacrifice of the Pesach and the daubing with blood of
the doors were distinct acts that took place on two successive nights.
Gutman (151) does not make this error, but his translation is far
from the Greek: 'In the night before the moon is full in the month of
which I speak sacrifice to God and put blood on the doors.'[37] To my
knowledge the only scholar to have understood this sentence was
Frankel who took τῇ πρόσθε νυκτί[38] to mean 'before nightfall.'[39]
It is simplest to eliminate the hiatus and read τῆς πρόσθε νυκτός,
as does Snell,[40] assuming that the genitive is governed by πρόσθε. If
one retains the dative, we will have to assume that Ezekiel uses
πρόσθε with the dative case or perhaps, very loosely, adverbially to
qualify a dative of time, 'early in the night.'[41] At any rate, there
seems to be no other way of making sense of Ezekiel's words here,
regardless how the Greek is construed. The repetition of νυκτός at

160 seems deliberate. First, Ezekiel explains what must be done before night (158), then what has to be done during the night (160).[42] Gutman's translation of νυκτός (160) as 'on that very night' is wrong: it suggests that the point of the word is to define the proper night for the eating of the sacrifice. In fact, it is meant to limit the time of eating to the night. Ezekiel is following the Biblical injunction:

> οὐκ ἀπολείψετε ἀπ' αὐτοῦ ἕως πρωὶ καὶ ὀστοῦν οὐ συντρίψετε ἀπ'
> αὐτοῦ· τὰ δὲ καταλειπόμενα ἀπ' αὐτοῦ ἕως πρωὶ ἐν πυρὶ κατακαύσετε.
> (*Exod.* 12.10)

Verse 161, σπουδῇ δὲ βασιλεὺς ἐκβαλεῖ πρόπαντ' ὄχλον may be an explanation of 160: you will eat roast because Pharaoh will drive you out in haste. This would agree with Philo's exposition of the instructions to roast the meat (*QE* 1.14). Thus, the connection between 160 and 161 is real, not haphazard as Strugnell implies.[43]

We turn to lines 182–6 where the text has been a matter of dispute and recently a brilliant emendation has been proposed which fundamentally changes the meaning of the sentence.

> ἐν σπουδῇ τε γὰρ
> βασιλεὺς κελεύσει πάντας ἐκβαλεῖν χθονός·[44]
> κεκλήσεται δὲ πᾶς. καὶ ὅταν θύσητε δέ,
> δεσμὴν λαβόντες χερσὶν ὑσσώπου κόμης
> εἰς αἷμα βάψαι, καὶ θιγεῖν σταθμῶν δυοῖν.

Despite the problems, the sense has always been thought clear. Here are two representative translations: 'Ein jeder wird von euch gerufen werden.' 'Each man will be called.'[45] But Strugnell's conjecture has changed things: κεκλήσεται δὲ πάσχ', ὅταν θύσητε δέ. To Strugnell's text there can be few objections. It makes good sense and parallels the Biblical narrative. One may wonder whether Ezekiel would so assertively call attention to the name of the holiday and then forego explaining the name for those in the audience for whom it would have been unfamiliar.[46] Further, it seems peculiar to say at 184 'it will be called Pascha,' when the name 'Pascha' has already been mentioned at 157. Moreover, if one reads the passage from 175 to 184, one must wonder what the non-Jews in the audience would have taken κεκλήσεται πάσχα to refer to. What is the subject? This is, at the least, hard to determine, especially after ἐν σπουδῇ τε γὰρ βασιλεὺς κελεύσει πάντας ἐκβαλεῖν χϑονός. And why the future when a present tense will do so well; compare the Bible's πάσχα ἐστὶν κυρίῳ (12.11)? On the other hand, κεκλήσεται δὲ πᾶς has very desirable advantages. In reading 175–90 the reader's expectation is better fulfilled here by a statement continuing the description of the ritual than by a parenthetical and seemingly purposeless mention of the name. In addition, virtually every detailed Jewish account of the Passover from antiquity lays stress on its universal application, i.e. that all are solicited to perform the sacrificial rite. This begins with *Exodus*: σφάξουσιν αὐτὸ πᾶν τὸ πλῆθος (12.6). Thus, it is inaccurate for Strugnell (449–50) to say that 'the obligation on every Israelite to keep the Passover ... is only spelled out indirectly in *Exod*. 12.3.' We find it again in the Passover account of *Jubilees* (49.6, 8, 16). In Philo (e.g. *QE* 1.10, *Spec. Leg.* 2.144ff) and Josephus (*AJ* 2.312) 'all the people' is stressed.[47] Ezekiel's account emphasizes in different ways and at different points the all-inclusiveness of the festival and its circumstances (152, 156, 161, 170, 183). The repetition of πᾶς in 184 after πάντας in 183 is virtually a stylistic characteristic of the poet's (e.g. 201–2, 264–6, 171–2). There may even be a point of irony in the repetition here: Pharaoh will order all the Jews immediately banished; but on the contrary they will all be summoned to the sacrifice. A last point. Perhaps the most cogent argument in Strugnell's attack on κεκλήσεται πᾶς is that 'while one may translate κληϑήσεται alternatively "will be summoned" and "will be named", κεκλήσεται can only be translated "will be named."'[48] Though one never knows how hard to press Ezekiel into the mold of regular Greek usage, this is certainly a serious argument – if, indeed, it is true. But to the best of my knowledge there survives in extant Greek literature not a single example of either κληϑήσεται or κεκλήσεται in the sense of 'will be summoned.' In other words, we have no evidence to determine how the Greeks would have said, 'he will be summoned,' using the verb καλέω.[49] Thus, there is no reason to believe that κεκλήσεται could not mean 'be summoned.' If it is of any relevance we might note that perfect passive forms of καλέω in the sense 'be summoned'[50] are common in the Septuagint.[51] Finally, the notion of 'summoning' may be important. *Wisdom* (18.8f) reports, in the context of the Passover sacrifice, that God summons (προσκαλεσάμενος) the Jews. It was a

Rabbinic principle that no one could partake of the Paschal sacrifice unless he had been previously counted or registered, i.e. invited to the particular sacrifice: אין הפסח נשחט אלא למנויי (Bab. Tal. *Pes.* 61a). This could be underlying Ezekiel's κεκλήσεται. Everyone must be summoned prior to the sacrifice so that he may share in it. In sum, though I know no alternative emendation that clears up all the metrical difficulties in verse 184 (real or apparent; it is not always easy to say when dealing with Ezekiel), I would be very hesitant to do away with κεκλήσεται δὲ πᾶς 'everyone shall be summoned', which seems most appropriate here.

In a number of places Ezekiel distorts or strangely compresses the Biblical account. Here are verses 153–5:

> ʽὸ μεὶς ὅδ᾽ ὑμῖν πρῶτος ἐνιαυτῶν πέλει·
> ἐν τῷδ᾽ ἀπάξω λαὸν εἰς ἄλλην χθόνα,
> εἰς ἣν ὑπέστην πατράσιν ʽΕβραίων γένους.'

With no prior knowledge of the Bible one would naturally take this to mean that in this month God would take the Jews from Egypt and bring them to the promised land. One who was familiar could place the emphasis on the prepositional prefix ἀπ-, i.e. God was taking them from Egypt in this month, a liberation that would in the end take them to their destined homeland. But the Greeks in the audience who did not know the story would assume that the journey was accomplished within a month's time. Some lines later we read (167–9):

> ὅταν δ᾽ ἐς ἴδιον χῶρον εἰσέλθηϑ᾽, ὅπως
> ἀφ᾽ ἧσπερ ἠοῦς ἐφύγετ᾽, Αἰγύπτου δ᾽ ἄπο
> ἕπτ᾽ ⟨ἧτ᾽⟩ ὁδοιποροῦντες ἡμέρας ὁδόν.

Here again the knowledgeable and the uninformed will understand in different ways. Following upon ὅταν δ᾽ ἐς ἴδιον χῶρον εἰσέλθητε, the uninitiated is likely to assume that the journey referred to is that from Egypt to the promised land. In other words, in his allusions to the journey of the Jews from Egypt Ezekiel shapes his phrases with calculated ambiguity, so that the Jews in the audience will understand his words to be in tune with Biblical and post-Biblical traditions, while the Greeks will quite spontaneously assume that the trip from Egypt to Israel was a direct and quick one. It is not hard to see the reason. In a work one of whose purposes was to propagandize for the Jews among the Greeks it would not have been productive for the dramatist to include or even mention the wanderings of forty years in the desert. In itself forty years of difficult wanderings might have diminished the sense of God's concern and aid for the Jews which Ezekiel was eager to promote. To include the cause of these wanderings, that is the sinfulness of the Jews which impelled God to so punish them, would scarcely have increased the lustre of these ancient Jews in the eyes of the pagan audience.

Ezekiel ignores the Biblical injunctions that no uncircumcised man may eat of the Passover and that all slaves and resident aliens must be circumcised before they can partake (*Exod.* 12.43–9; cf. *Josh.* 5.2–11).[52] Scholars who have noted the absence believe that Ezekiel did not want to include what might have been offensive to the non-Jews in the audience.[53] This must be true. But there was, I think, another factor. Ezekiel may not have wanted to raise what was a touchy issue for the Jews in antiquity. The practice of circumcision was a focal point in anti-Semitic campaigns of the Greeks and among Jewish hellenizers.[54] In antiquity the Jews and the Egyptians were probably the two peoples best known for the use of circumcision (cf. Hdt. 2.104).[55] Anti-Semites commonly maligned Jews by proclaiming that they had adopted the 'barbaric' custom from the Egyptians.[56] Thus, had Ezekiel mentioned the limitation of the Passover to the circumcised, he would have been associating the Jews with the native Egyptians in an area in which the two peoples were distinct from the Greeks. He would, in other words, have been aligning the Jews with the Egyptians, not with the Greeks. In the serious struggle between the Jews and the Egyptians for the sympathy and good will of the Greeks, this would have been an ill-conceived act. So he wisely decided to ignore the whole issue.

What motivated Ezekiel to expound at length on the Passover? In fact, nothing could be more natural. The paramount importance of the Passover runs through most of Jewish antiquity. One recalls the 'reinstitutions' of the Pesach by Josiah, Hezekiah and later by Ezra, and the famous Passover-letter to the Jews in Elephantine. Both literary texts like *Jubilees* (49) and documentary papyri attest its significance.[57] A play on the Exodus could hardly have done without some mention of the Passover for the Jews in the audience. Ezekiel may have wanted to emphasize the significance of the holiday and its

observance. The Jews of the Egyptian diaspora needed to be re-
minded occasionally of the importance of keeping the festivals.[58] He
may also have wished to acquaint the less well educated Jews with
the content of an important part of the Bible. For the non-Jews he
may have desired to explain both what the holiday was and also why
its historical background made it so eventful for the Jews: a festival
that celebrated and memorialized the liberation of the people.[59]

7. The crossing of the Red Sea (193–242)

The culmination of the Biblical Exodus-narrative comes at the
crossing of the Red Sea. Both the immensity of the spectacle and
the convention of reporting great acts of warfare through messengers
(e.g. *Persae*, *Septem*, *Phoenissae*) prevented Ezekiel from seeking a
direct display of the episode.[1] In this undertaking Ezekiel knew who
his master should be. The influence on this scene of Aeschylus'
Persae was observed by Wieneke (93–4) and more recently by Snell.[2]
I should like to show, more minutely than has been done, how clear
it is that Ezekiel was heavily dependent in this episode on the
Persae. The following examples are not of equal force. Some can be
explained away as coincidence, others are no more than just possible.
But some are cogent and the sheer quantity of the evidence seems
conclusive.

  In both the *Persae* and the *Exagoge* the decisive event is graphi-
cally reported by a member of the defeated nation who has been an
eyewitness.[3] One can only guess to whom the speech is delivered
(Snell (174, 177) conjectures the queen, as in the *Persae*). Certainly
it must be delivered in Egypt. Kuiper's view that it is spoken in
Arabia is a mere aberration motivated by his desire to preserve unity
of place in the play.[4] Both the Biblical event and the Greek battle are
sea-catastrophes for the defeated. Aeschylus vividly describes this
aspect of the battle, with emphasis on the drowned corpses filling the
water (274–9). There are ἀλίτυπα βάρη (945, if the text is right). All
this suits the destruction of the Egyptians at the sea. Of the actual
drowning Ezekiel seems to say little. But it appears almost certain
that the messenger speech(es) could not have ended where Eusebius
(and perhaps Polyhistor) cuts it off. If so, any ensuing comments
would likely have included some such account of the drowning itself,
the corpses, etc.

In both Ezekiel and Aeschylus emphasis is placed on the disparate nature of the forces. Aeschylus enumerates the number of ships on each side in order to present the overwhelming superiority of the Persian forces (337ff), while Ezekiel stresses the impressive organization and the vast number of Egyptians (one million: 202f). In each case, the count is given after an apparent inquiry as to the size of the army (*Exag.* 202; *Per.* 334–6). Both Aeschylus' Persians and Ezekiel's Egyptians are (unduly) confident in their forces (*Pers.* 352; *Exag.* 219⁵). The phrase ὁ πᾶς ἀριθμός from *Pers.* 339 is used by Ezekiel at 202. Divine intervention is marked in both (*Pers.* 345, 347, 454, 514, etc; *Exag.* 220, 225, 235f, 239ff). In both importance is attached to the cycle of day and night. The Egyptians overtake the Jews near sunset and resolve to await the morning (217–19);⁶ in contrast, the Persians, deceived by Themistocles, resolve to await the setting of the sun and then to act so as to forestall the Greeks' escape (362ff). The Greeks sing a hymn to Apollo (393), the Jews cry out to God for help (211–13).

I note several passages which, whether or not they produced concrete echoes in the *Exagoge*, may have contributed to Ezekiel's seeing in the *Persae* a natural model for his play: ἀρωγὴ δ᾽ οὔτις ἀλλήλοις παρῆν (414); cf. παρῆν αὐτοῖς ἀρωγὸς ὁ θεός ... οἷς μὲν γάρ ἐστ᾽ ἀρωγός (235–6; 240). ἀντηλάλαξε (390); cf. the presence of ἀλαλάζω at 211 and 238. Θεὸς πατρῷος (404 and *Exag.* 213). *Persae* 383 and 384 end in λεών and στρατός, *Exag.* 203–4 in λεώ and στρατός. *Persae* 412 ends Περσικοῦ στρατοῦ, *Exag.* 201 ends Αἰγυπτίου στρατοῦ. παρῆν at verse-end at *Persae* 391, 414 and *Exag.* 235. τὸ δεξιόν ... κέρας ... ὁ πᾶς στόλος (399–400); cf. ἐκ δεξιῶν δὲ πάντας ... τὸν πάντα (201–2). παρ᾽ ἀκτάς (303); cf. παρ᾽ ἀκτήν (205) (same position in verse). παραστάται (957); cf. προστάταισι (196). τεταγμένος (381); cf. ἐκτεταγμένων (197). ὁρμῶντες (394); cf. ἀφώρμησεν (193). πόρους (367); cf. πόρος (241). φέγγος ἡλίου (377); cf. φέγγος ὡς πυρός (234).

Several words or phrases in the Red Sea scene may show the influence of other portions of the *Persae*. Cf. the compound εὐάνδρου (203) with πολυάνδρων (533, 899); εἰσκύρω + genitive (231)/ ἐπικύρω + genitive (853); the description of the departing Persian army has some similarities to that of the Egyptian (16ff/193ff); cf. κἄπειθ᾽ ὁ κείνων ἡγεμὼν Μωσῆς (224)/Μῆδος γὰρ ἦν ὁ πρῶτος

ἡγεμὼν στρατοῦ (765); the image of the inexorable wave in
Aeschylus (87ff)/the actual overwhelming wave in Ezekiel (237f).
One may wonder whether Ezekiel was impressed by Aeschylus'
description of the retreat of the Persians to Thrace when the Strymon
miraculously freezes over and some are able thereby to walk across
the river. But the sun rises, the ice melts and the remainder drown
(495ff). Some possible parallels to this section are: the mention of
στρατός and πόρος in the same sentence (241f; cf. 501); the association of heaven with deity (212; cf. 499); God as the author of the
events (239ff; cf. 495f).[7]

If, as I have argued, Ezekiel's interest in the *Persae* stemmed from
his perception that Greek–Persian history could be seen as an analogue to Jewish–Egyptian, then it is not surprising that he would
have taken special interest in Herodotus' account of Greek–Persian
history and the wars of the early fifth century. In what follows I
want to stress not merely the possibility that elements of Ezekiel's
scene are influenced by Herodotus but also that the encounter with
certain aspects of Herodotus' narrative would have had an effect
on Ezekiel in terms of themes and conceptions. Here I think three
sections of the *Histories* were most important: (1) The crossing
of the Hellespont and the ensuing events, including the description
of Xerxes' forces. (2) The events surrounding Thermopylae. (3) The
battle of Salamis. In the crossing of the Hellespont Ezekiel would
have seen on the one hand a fascinating analogue to the crossing of
the Red Sea, the traversing on foot of a body of water by a large
mass of men, on the other an event that in its spirit was antipathetic
to and irreconcilable with the Biblical miracle. For Moses performs
the miracle only with God's help, Xerxes in contrast takes on the
role of divinity and violates the godhead.[8] Moses strikes the sea with
the staff of God, Xerxes has the Hellespont scourged and branded
(7.35). Later, at the outset of their march to Abydos, there is a
sudden eclipse of the sun and day turns into night (7.37). We shall
see shortly that this constitutes a striking similarity to Ezekiel's
narrative. In the *Exagoge* τεράστια occur as a preliminary to the
crossing, in Herodotus two (ill-omened) τέρατα present themselves
to Xerxes after the crossing (7.57). As in Aeschylus but with greater
intensity and emphasis, Xerxes is portrayed, like the Egyptians in
the *Exagoge*, as overflowing with confidence in his (numerical)

superiority (7.101,103). In this section there are a number of verbal parallels which may be significant: [ἀφ]ορμάω of the troops (193; 7.34, 37), ἀλμυρός of the Hellespont (7.35) and of the Red Sea (229), πεζός of the infantry (198; 7.41) and ἵππος in the feminine of the cavalry (195; 7.41). Ezekiel uses διεκδρομή (199), an unusual noun[9] which seems to mean intervals left between the foot soldiers to allow for the passage of chariots, a sense apparently found nowhere else, though the context makes it virtually certain here. But at 7.36 Herodotus reports that in the construction of the bridge over the Hellespont openings were left for ships to sail through in and out of the Pontus. The noun used is διέκπλους (37), the precise maritime equivalent of διεκδρομή.

In the Thermopylae narrative an unexpected and drastic change of weather takes place: a storm arises and many Persian ships and men are destroyed (7.188). The Athenians, Herodotus tells us (7.189), claim that the storm came up in response to Greek prayers to Boreas. In short, a story of sudden (if not miraculous) changes in natural phenomena brought about by the prayers of the oppressed people to the deity and resulting in the drowning of the oppressors. Quite as Ezekiel represents his episode here. Indeed, Herodotus continues (7.192f) and reports that the Greeks then offered prayers of thanks and libations to 'Poseidon the savior.' Ezekiel might have recognized a parallel to the 'song of the sea,' the song of praise and thanksgiving that the Jews offer upon leaving the sea (*Exod.* 15). It is not even beyond possibility that Ezekiel portrayed the Jews singing such a song of thanks (a choral ode?).[10] As for Thermopylae, the Greeks themselves show signs of uncertainty in the face of the numerical odds (7.207) and the Persian scout is amazed at their apparent lack of preparation (7.208). Similarly, Ezekiel's Jews lack confidence, while the Egyptians derive encouragement from the motley collection of men, women, children and animals clearly unsuited for battle. One also recalls that in the battle itself many Persians drown (7.223).

A few possible verbal parallels. ὁρμάω is frequent (e.g. 7.188), ἐγκύρω + genitive (7.208); the pass is ἀτραπός (7.212); troops are τεταγμένοι (7.208). When Ezekiel reports the size of the army he writes, μυριάδες ἦσαν ἑκατόν. In giving the size of various Persian forces Herodotus frequently uses μυριάδες; one group is ἑβδομήκοντα καὶ ἑκατὸν μυριάδες (7.184). Although chariots were evidently not used in Greek warfare in the classical period, Ezekiel's Egyptians have them since they are so represented in the Bible.[11] Perhaps then he took note of the fact that the Persians did employ chariots in their attack on the Greeks (used, as a matter of fact, by the Libyans 7.184, though not exclusively: see 7.86).

At Salamis, the Persians arrive in the evening and decide to wait for the morrow to do battle (8.70). Meanwhile, the Greeks are in a state of fear. This is much the course of events in Ezekiel. Herodotus takes some interest, though not as much as Aeschylus, in the divine aid rendered the Greeks. Thus, a phantom woman appears and spurs the Greeks to action (8.84). Later, a mysterious event leads to the hypothesis that θεῖον τὸ πρῆγμα (8.94). Of course, most of the Persians drown.

One final point. Ezekiel always refers to Pharaoh as βασιλεύς without the article. This may be conditioned by his sense that the Jewish–Egyptian conflict paralleled that between the Greeks and Persians, since the Greeks generally referred to the king of Persia as βασιλεύς without the article.[12]

In sum, I think it likely that these various sections in Herodotus on the Greco-Persian conflict influenced the *Exagoge*. But regardless of the degree to which Herodotean influence concretely shows up in the text of Ezekiel, if one believes that Ezekiel did know Herodotus' *Histories*, then one must recognize the probability that the patterns of history, divine activity, justice and morality that permeate his work would have struck Ezekiel as potentially significant, illuminating and fruitful for his own conception of the Jewish Exodus from Egypt. At the least, it would have made an unconscious impression on the poet who was seeking to be at once Greek and Jewish, with one foot in Greek poetry, literature and history and the other in the Jewish tradition.

At several points Ezekiel appears to diverge from the Biblical account of the happenings at the Red Sea. An examination of these may give us additional insight into his goals and his use of extra-Biblical traditions.[13]

At verse 203 the messenger reports that the sum total of Egyptian troops was one million. Is this merely a large round number to indicate a huge army? Perhaps, but *Jubilees* 48.14 states that all the

Egyptians who pursued the Jews drowned in the sea, one million of them.[14] Is this coincidence? Or was this a traditional number for the Egyptian host?

Other 'innovations' are of more import. Here is the splitting of the Sea (224–8):

> κἄπειθ᾽ ὁ κείνων ἡγεμὼν Μωσῆς, λαβὼν
> ῥάβδον θεοῦ, τῇ δὴ πρὶν Αἰγύπτῳ κακὰ
> σημεῖα καὶ τερ(ά)ατ᾽ ἐξεμήσατο,
> ἔτυψ᾽ Ἐρυθρᾶς νῶτα καὶ ἔσχισεν μέσον
> βι 9ος Θαλάσσης.

Contrast the Septuagint (*Exod.* 14.21):

> ἐξέτεινεν δὲ Μωυσῆς τὴν χεῖρα ἐπὶ τὴν θάλασσαν καὶ ὑπήγαγεν κύριος
> τὴν θάλασσαν ἐν ἀνέμῳ νότῳ βιαίῳ ὅλην τὴν νύκτα καὶ ἐποίησεν τὴν
> θάλασσαν ξηράν, καὶ ἐσχίσθη τὸ ὕδωρ.

Here there is no striking of the sea, indeed no rod at all. Further, instead of Ezekiel's instantaneous division we have a night-long procedure. It is, however, true that in God's earlier instructions Moses is told (*Exod.* 14.16)

> ...καὶ σὺ ἔπαρον τῇ ῥάβδῳ σου καὶ ἔκτεινον τὴν χεῖρά σου ἐπὶ τὴν
> θάλασσαν καὶ ῥῆξον αὐτήν.

Again, there is no striking of the sea but the rod is present. The exact nature of Moses' activity here described is not crystal-clear.[15] The discrepancy between an immediate and a gradual division is readily explained. Ezekiel may have felt that a slow dividing of the waters over many hours was simply not as rhetorically effective as an instantaneous one. Further, his choice to have Moses smite the sea rather than simply raise his hand aloft left him no real alternative. So decisive an action demanded as decisive a reaction. To have Moses strike the sea with grand and rapid gesture and then let the sea spread apart bit by bit would have been intolerable.[16]

So the significant difference between Ezekiel and the Bible becomes the striking of the sea. But the fact is that Josephus, Philo and *LAB* all report the same thing.[17] Indeed, some Midrashic texts also do, in a variety of versions, both implicit and explicit.[18] An index of the prevalence and popularity of this tradition is that it is given as a matter of course by Cedrenus[19] and seems to be the version of the crossing used by the artist of the synagogue at Dura-

Europus.[20] All this is irrefragable evidence that there was a widespread Jewish tradition that Moses struck the sea. Is Ezekiel the first to attest it? Artapanus (*PE* 9.436b) claims that it was a Heliopolitan tradition. To be sure, we do not know whether Artapanus lived before or after Ezekiel, but the fact that he asserts that this version was a community tradition suggests that it was already of some 'antiquity' in his day. Indeed, I would argue that it was a long-standing one, going back to the Biblical period. Isaiah and Zechariah both describe the future salvation of the people as a second Exodus and entry into the promised land. In so doing both make manifest use of themes drawn from the Egyptian Exodus. Isaiah speaks explicitly of the path through water which they will traverse, just as in the Exodus from Egypt (11.16). God 'will raise His hand over the river and strike it into seven streams' (11.15). The entire vision is intended to appear a replica of the Exodus in which Moses did strike the water. Similarly, Zechariah seems to have known a tradition of the smiting of the Red Sea (10.11).[21] As for the origins of this version, one notes both the ambiguity of the Biblical narrative and the stories of the crossing of the Jordan by Elijah and Elisha (*2 Kings* 2.8, 14) who divide the river by striking it (with a mantle). Perhaps the latter tales influenced the development of the 'smiting' of the Red Sea.[22] Thus, it is fair to assume that Ezekiel was drawing on a long-standing tradition. But why did he choose to use it rather than the Biblical version?

The Bible itself reflects a strangely ambivalent attitude toward Moses: on the one hand, great hero, prophet and leader of his people; on the other, a mere man and nothing more. *Deuteronomy* 34.6 records that his burial site was kept secret and known to no man, patently an attempt to prevent the great leader's burial place from becoming a site of devotion and worship. Moses' role in the whole Exodus and in particular in the crossing of the Sea was the object of hesitant caution. In Joshua's narration of the Exodus Moses is given no more standing than is Aaron, 'I sent Moses and Aaron and I smote Egypt' (24.5). The events at the Red Sea are described as follows (24.6–7): 'I brought your fathers out of Egypt and you came to the sea. The Egyptians pursued your fathers with chariots and horsemen to the Red Sea. When they cried unto the Lord, He put darkness between you and the Egyptians and brought the sea on them and covered them.' Everything is God; Moses has no role here whatsoever. Similarly, the summary of world history at *Nehemiah* 9.6ff makes no mention of Moses and in reviewing the Exodus and the crossing refers only to God's role (9.9–11). In the Psalmist's descriptions of the events at the Red Sea Moses is not present; God is the only actor (78.13, 53; 106.9–11). In the latter review of Jewish history Moses' solitary role is to intercede on behalf of the sinning Jews (106.23). At *Ps.* 114.3, 5 the sea (it seems) flees from God (cf. v. 7). At 66.6 we find among God's wonders, 'He turned the sea into dry land. They passed through the water on foot.' At 136.11–15 the Exodus, the cleaving of the sea, the drowning of the Egyptians are all the work of God alone. The only slight deviation from this tendency in the *Psalms* is at 77.17–21, where after a lengthy description of the power and deeds of God the Psalmist concludes, 'You led your people like a flock by the hand of Moses and Aaron.' But even here Moses is no more than an equal of Aaron and both are seen as tools of God. The contrast between their role and that of God as described in the preceding verses is overwhelming.

When *Wisdom* recounts the crossing of the sea (19 7–9) there is only praise of God and no mention of Moses. Nor is there any hint of Moses when *Judith* 5.12f tells of God drying up the sea. In Sirach's review of great personages from Jewish history there is more emphasis on Aaron than on Moses (ch. 45).

In later Rabbinic texts the tension is much more transparent. In several texts the strain is so clear that one almost senses an opposition between Moses and God, as if the emphasis on the powers and achievements of one was antithetic to and a diminution of the glory of the other.[23] Perhaps the most famous example is the exegesis of the verse, 'God took us out of Egypt': 'God did it, no angel, no agent, God alone in all His glory.'[24]

When Ezekiel stresses Moses' role in this episode, not merely by his active presence but by the immediate and indisputable connection between the striking of the sea and its division, we can be sure that he was aligning himself with those who felt that emphasis on Moses' feats was not a lessening of or an insult to the role of God in the Jewish Exodus from Egypt.[25]

Although the conflict over the relative roles of God and Moses in the Exodus and especially in the crossing of the sea was an ancient one, by and large the difference of opinion fell into rather narrow and delimited lines. The Rabbinic texts tend to play down Moses' role at the sea, the Greco-Jewish writers play it up. Those Jews in the Greco-Roman world who chose to write in Greek˙and thereby to establish and maintain lines of communication between themselves and the civilized (if pagan) world about them inevitably felt the need, no matter how devoted to Judaism they were, to produce representations which would, at the least, be comprehensible to the Greeks and, if at all possible, stir feelings of recognition or even empathy among them. Thus, the notion of a particular God for an individual nation would have meant nothing special for them, since the conception was taken for granted by them – but in a way which was totally different from the Jewish one. This was, as it were, a double bind. Stating the idea in its barest form would have no effect on the Greeks; elaborating it in sufficient detail to make its special nuances clear would have alienated them. So the Jewish Hellenists like Ezekiel were compelled to adopt a more anthropocentric position. A great national hero, whether he be a Danaus, a Lycurgus, an Orpheus or an Achilles, made a great deal of sense. For Ezekiel it would have served no purpose to extinguish Moses' part and exclusively glorify God's. It was entirely fitting that ὁ ἡγεμὼν Μωσῆς strike and split the sea.

In sum, Ezekiel did not hesitate to endow Moses with facets of the heroic character when he believed they did not challenge the uniqueness of God's nature. On the other hand, anything that would tend to suggest divine character for Moses he scrupulously avoided. θνητὸν γεγῶτα at 102 is in this respect emphatic. One might usefully contrast Ezekiel's depiction of Moses with the repeated description of Joseph in *Joseph and Asenath* as ὁ υἱὸς τοῦ θεοῦ.[26]

Though one is frankly surprised to see Ezekiel striving for artistic effects, it is hard to avoid such a conclusion at 227–8: ἔτυψ' Ἐρυθρᾶς νῶτα καὶ ἔσχισεν μέσον/βάθος Θαλάσσης. Twice else does he refer to the Red Sea, at 206 and 242: Ἐρυθρᾶς Θαλάσσης, with adjective and noun juxtaposed. At 227–8 not only are the two separated, but at a distance which, I think, cannot be exemplified elsewhere in the *Exagoge*. It is clear that thereby Ezekiel is seeking to represent vividly and concretely the separation of the sea into two segments.

Let us now examine the scene of the crossing as a whole (217–42):

ἐπεὶ δὲ Τιτὰν ἥλιος δυσμαῖς προσῆν,
ἐπέσχομεν, θέλοντες ὄρθριον μάχην,
πεποιθότες λαοῖσι καὶ φρικτοῖς ὅπλοις.
ἔπειτα θείων ἄρχεται τεραστίων
θαυμάστ' ἰδέσθαι. καί τις ἐξαίφνης μέγας
στῦλος νεφώδης ἐστάθη πρὸ γῆς, μέγας,²⁷
παρεμβολῆς ἡμῶν τε καὶ Ἑβραίων μέσος.
κἄπειθ' ὁ κείνων ἡγεμὼν Μωσῆς, λαβὼν
ῥάβδον θεοῦ, τῇ δὴ πρὶν Αἰγύπτῳ κακά
σημεῖα καὶ τερ⟨άΙατ' ἐξεμήσατο,
ἔτυψ' Ἐρυθρᾶς νῶτα καὶ ἔσχισεν μέσον
βάθος Θαλάσσης· οἱ δὲ σύμπαντες σθένει
ὥρουσαν ὠκεῖς ἁλμυρᾶς δι' ἀτραποῦ.
ἡμεῖς δ' ἐπ' αὐτῆς ᾠχόμεσθα συντόμως
κατ' ἴχνος αὐτῶν· νυκτὸς εἰσεκύρσαμεν
βοηδρομοῦντες· ἁρμάτων δ' ἄφνω τροχοί
οὐκ ἐστρέφοντο, δέσμιοι δ' ὡς ἥρμοσαν.
ἀπ' οὐρανοῦ δὲ φέγγος ὡς πυρὸς μέγα
ὤφθη τι ἡμῖν· ὡς μὲν εἰκάζειν, παρῆν
αὐτοῖς ἀρωγὸς ὁ θεός. ὡς δ' ἤδη πέραν
ἦσαν θαλάσσης, κῦμα δ' ἐρροίβδει μέγα
σύνεγγυς ἡμῶν. καί τις ἠλάλαξ' ἰδών·
'φεύγωμεν οἴκοι πρόσθεν Ὑψίστου χέρας·
οἷς μὲν γάρ ἐστ' ἀρωγός, ἡμῖν δ' ἀθλίοις
ὄλεθρον ἔρδει.' καὶ συνεκλύσθη πόρος
Ἐρυθρᾶς Θαλάσσης καὶ στρατὸν διώλεσε.

The precise chronology of events is not clear, mainly because of Ezekiel's vague use of ἔπειτα in 220 and 224. It is evidently almost sunset when the Egyptians decide to set up camp (ἥλιος δυσμαῖς προσῆν, 217)²⁸ and await the morning (218).²⁹ Our understanding of the temporal limits from 220 on is complicated by the fact that Ezekiel turned the Bible's gradual drying up of the sea into an instantaneous act. Thus, that the Bible has a relatively clear sequence (Moses raises his hand – it is evidently evening; the wind blows and dries the sea all night; toward morning the Jews begin to cross and then the Egyptians follow) may not prove as helpful as it otherwise might have been. When Ezekiel writes that the Egyptians encamp near sunset, ἔπειτα miraculous events begin to occur, one assumes ἔπειτα to mean something like, 'shortly thereafter.' The same holds true for ἔπειτα in 224. Then we hear that the Egyptians followed at night (231). This seems internally consistent and reasonable. But there are several difficulties. In *Exodus* it seems that the decisive events in the crossing and drowning take place at or toward morning. While the Hebrew account is not perfectly clear, both for its general vagueness and its phrase אשמרת הבקר (τῇ φυλακῇ τῇ ἑωθινῇ in the Greek), the Septuagint (14.20) explicitly says that the night passed (this is not in the Hebrew). Would Ezekiel have gratuitously violated the Biblical text? Moreover, what does νυκτός mean? If it is a temporal genitive, 'at night,' what is the point of the needless introduction of the time-element here?[30] Without νυκτός one could take ἔπειτα at 220 and 224 as undefined 'later, afterward' (cf. 12, 19) and the text would not stand in contradiction to the Biblical narrative. The key is the proper understanding of νυκτός. If it means, 'at night,' we are left with εἰσεκύρσαμεν βοηδρομοῦντες. εἰσκύρω, according to LSJ which cites this solitary passage, means 'enter.'[31] But there is no reason why εἰσκύρω should mean 'enter.' κύρω (κυρέω) and its compounds tend to mean, 'encounter, meet up with, come in contact with' and to take the genitive or dative case.[32] Above we noted examples of ἐπικύρω and ἐγκύρω with the genitive at *Persae* 853 and Hdt. 7.208. In such wise should we understand εἰσεκύρσαμεν here. Gifford rightly translates, 'we met the darkness of night.' The sense and point of this will become clear when we place it in its context of Biblical exegesis.

Exodus 14.20 contains a perplexing phrase, ויהי הענן והחשך ויאר את הלילה . Here is a typical translation:[33] 'And there was the cloud and the darkness and it lit up the night.' There appears to be some sort of contrast between darkness and light. The Septuagint does not have the vexed phrase. The Targumim translate through explication:[34] 'There was cloud and darkness for the Egyptians, but for Israel there was light all night.' 'The cloud was half light and half darkness. From one side it brought darkness upon the Egyptians, from the other light upon Israel.' 'The cloud was half darkness and half light. It brought darkness on the Egyptians and light on Israel all night.' The Syriac translation has much the same. Thus, the problematic Hebrew text (whatever it may mean; cf. *Joshua* 24.7) produced a tradition that the cloud that came between the two camps cast darkness on the Egyptians while providing light for the Jews. It is possible that the Dura painter has given us this scene.[35] This is, I suspect, behind the statement νυκτὸς εἰσεκύρσαμεν. Ezekiel deliberately avoids defining the time of the passing events. We do not know whether ἔπειτα . . . ἔπειτα refers to the passage of many hours or whether all these events take place shortly after the Egyptians encamp. All we are told is that after the Jews entered the sea the Egyptians followed – and encountered night (this is the first of the series of miraculous but disastrous happenings that now occur to the Egyptians (231-5)). The pagans in the audience would probably take the phrase (regardless how they construed it) as a rather pointless designation of the time. The educated Jews would understand it as a reference to the miraculous darkness God brought upon the Egyptians at the sea, while providing light for the Jews. It is possible that Josephus is making the same point when he writes νὺξ αὐτοὺς ϛοφώδης καὶ σκοτεινὴ κατέλαβε (*AJ* 2.344) of the Egyptians in the sea (unless he means this as a pure metaphor).[36]

The Biblical account of the crossing is, compared to *Exagoge* 232-6, rather straightforward (14.22-5):

> εἰσῆλθον οἱ υἱοὶ Ισραηλ εἰς μέσον τῆς θαλάσσης κατὰ τὸ ξηρόν, καὶ τὸ ὕδωρ αὐτοῖς τεῖχος ἐκ δεξιῶν καὶ τεῖχος ἐξ εὐωνύμων· κατεδίωξαν δὲ οἱ Αἰγύπτιοι καὶ εἰσῆλθον ὀπίσω αὐτῶν, πᾶσα ἡ ἵππος Φαραω καὶ τὰ ἅρματα καὶ οἱ ἀναβάται, εἰς μέσον τῆς θαλάσσης. ἐγενήθη δὲ ἐν τῇ φυλακῇ τῇ ἑωθινῇ καὶ ἐπέβλεψεν κύριος ἐπὶ τὴν παρεμβολὴν τῶν Αἰγυπτίων ἐν στύλῳ πυρὸς καὶ νεφέλης καὶ συνετάραξεν τὴν παρεμβολὴν τῶν Αἰγυπτίων καὶ συνέδησεν τοὺς ἄξονας τῶν ἁρμάτων αὐτῶν καὶ ἤγαγεν αὐτοὺς μετὰ βίας.

It is apparent that Ezekiel is seeking dramatic and rhetorical effects greater than those in the Bible. True as this is, he is quite within the tradition of Jewish elaborations of the Exodus narrative. The Psalmist speaks of נוראות על ים סוף (106.22 = φοβερά), and gives details at 77.17-19. *Wisdom* 19.8 tells of θαυμαστὰ τέρατα. At 232f the wheels of the Egyptian chariots cease to turn and seem to be stuck fast. This may be no more than his elaboration of the Septuagint's συνέδησαν τοὺς ἄξονας (14.25), a text that differs from the Hebrew ('He removed').[37] But Rabbinic elaboration dwells on the same theme, asserting that the ground turned to mud under the chariots and so the wheels stuck.[38]

Light flashes from heaven as if of fire.[39] Presumably, this looks to *Exod.* 14.24 (ἐν στύλῳ πυρὸς). But the expansion is part of a long tradition of heavenly fire at the time of the crossing. This seems indicated already at *Ps.* 77.19 and occasionally develops into a version in which the fire is directed against the Egyptians. Such is the case in Josephus (*AJ* 2.343), the Targumim, and Midrashic texts.[40] Ezekiel's fire is not an active force in the destruction of the Egyptians but a kind of omen of their coming doom. Thus, he does not even say that it is fire; rather, a mysterious light from heaven that looks like fire. Philo reports a divine vision πυρὸς αὐγὴν ἀπαστράπτουσα (*Moses* 2.254), but does not make it a destructive force aimed at the Egyptians. Artapanus (*PE* 9.436c) does not say explicitly that the fire attacked the Egyptians, but it certainly seems implied in ὑπό τε τοῦ πυρός ... πάντας διαφθαρῆναι. In the Dura painting of the Exodus there are strange dots falling from heaven. Goodenough takes them to be Manna, but there is little reason for Manna to be falling at the time of the Exodus. Perhaps we have here the miraculous falling-fire of post-Biblical exegesis.[41]

Exodus continues (14.25–31):

> ... καὶ εἶπαν οἱ Αἰγύπτιοι· φύγωμεν ἀπὸ προσώπου Ἰσραηλ· ὁ γὰρ κύριος πολεμεῖ περὶ αὐτῶν τοὺς Αἰγυπτίους. εἶπεν δὲ κύριος πρὸς Μωυσῆν "Ἔκτεινον τὴν χεῖρά σου ἐπὶ τὴν θάλασσαν, καὶ ἀποκαταστήτω τὸ ὕδωρ καὶ ἐπικαλυψάτω τοὺς Αἰγυπτίους, ἐπί τε τὰ ἄρματα καὶ τοὺς ἀναβάτας. ἐξέτεινεν δὲ Μωυσῆς τὴν χεῖρα ἐπὶ τὴν θάλασσαν, καὶ ἀπεκατέστη τὸ ὕδωρ πρὸς ἡμέραν ἐπὶ χώρας· οἱ δὲ Αἰγύπτιοι ἔφυγον ὑπὸ τὸ ὕδωρ, καὶ ἐξετίναξεν κύριος τοὺς Αἰγυπτίους μέσον τῆς θαλάσσης. καὶ ἐπαναστραφὲν τὸ ὕδωρ ἐκάλυψεν τὰ ἄρματα καὶ τοὺς ἀναβάτας καὶ πᾶσαν τὴν δύναμιν Φαραω τοὺς εἰσπεπορευμένους ὀπίσω αὐτῶν εἰς τὴν θάλασσαν, καὶ οὐ κατελείφθη ἐξ αὐτῶν οὐδὲ εἷς. οἱ δὲ υἱοὶ Ἰσραηλ ἐπορεύθησαν διὰ ξηρᾶς ἐν μέσῳ τῆς θαλάσσης, τὸ δὲ ὕδωρ αὐτοῖς τεῖχος ἐκ δεξιῶν καὶ τεῖχος ἐξ εὐωνύμων. καὶ ἐρρύσατο κύριος τὸν Ἰσραηλ ἐν τῇ ἡμέρᾳ ἐκείνῃ ἐκ χειρὸς τῶν Αἰγυπτίων· καὶ εἶδεν Ἰσραηλ τοὺς Αἰγυπτίους τεθνηκότας παρὰ τὸ χεῖλος τῆς θαλάσσης. εἶδεν δὲ Ἰσραηλ τὴν χεῖρα τὴν μεγάλην, ἃ ἐποίησεν κύριος τοῖς Αἰγυπτίοις· ἐφοβήθη δὲ ὁ λαὸς τὸν κύριον καὶ ἐπίστευσαν τῷ θεῷ καὶ Μωυσῇ τῷ θεράποντι αὐτοῦ.

Ezekiel is not much different (236–42). Moses' passing of the staff over the water is eliminated, probably for economy's sake, and κῦμα suffices for the return of the waters to their normal place.[42] Ezekiel has the Jews reach the other side by the time the waters surge back. The Bible says nothing of this but it seems a perfectly reasonable (perhaps necessary) inference from the text.[43] Ezekiel parallels the Midrashic report that the last Jew left the sea when the last Egyptian entered; then the devastation took place.[44] Josephus, however, may indicate that the Egyptians did not enter the water until the last Jew was safely across (*AJ* 2.340f). At any rate, the prevalence of the tradition that all the Jews were safely across before the Egyptians drowned is effectively used by the Rabbis who declare that this was calculated to keep the Egyptians from thinking that the Jews had also drowned.[45]

As the water surges back an Egyptian soldier cries out in despair (238–41).[46] It is undoubtedly for dramatic effect that Ezekiel's soldier cries out after the surge of water rather than before, as in the Bible. Ezekiel deliberately avoids the Septuagint's traditional rendering of מפני ἀπὸ προσώπου, so as to prevent any misunderstanding by his pagan audience which might construe such a phrase to mean that God (like Zeus, Apollo, etc.) had a face. For χέρας he could claim twofold precedent.[47] On the one hand, Greek commonly used 'hand(s)' in extended metaphorical senses, 'acts, force, etc.' On the other, Biblical accounts of the Exodus often refer to the role of God's 'hand,' e.g. . . . εἶδεν δὲ Ἰσραὴλ τὴν χεῖρα τὴν μεγάλην, ἃ ἐποίησεν κύριος τοῖς Αἰγυπτίοις (*Exod.* 14.31).[48] So too *Wisdom* 19.8 and Midrashic elaborations.[49] Ancient Judaeo-Christian art portrays the presence of God's activity by showing a hand from heaven. Indeed, the Dura painter does this in his representation of the crossing of the Red Sea.

γάρ and τῷδε in 193 indicate that we have been plunged into this scene by Polyhistor *in medias res*. But it is impossible to determine whether many or only a few lines have been left out, or even whether the missing lines were just the opening of this speech or were part of a dialogue between the messenger and his audience. Perhaps all we lack is the report that Pharaoh changed his mind and decided to pursue the Jews. But if we glance at the corresponding section of the *Persae* (249ff), where the messenger enters and first conducts a dialogue with both Atossa and the chorus, describing in both general and particular terms the disaster that has come upon the Persian army, and only then (337ff) launches into a description of the Persian host and an ordered chronological narrative of the martial events, we might well suspect that Ezekiel did much the same here. As for the description of the Egyptian army (193–203),[50] it is hard to tell whether Ezekiel has in mind some genuine battle formation[51] or is merely concocting an *ad hoc* description using pieces of commonplace knowledge (e.g. cavalry at the flanks) and sufficiently adapting it to allow for the use of chariots. The alignment would have looked something like this (A = infantry, B = cavalry, C = chariots):

```
        C   C   C   C
      A   A   A   A   A
          B                   B
     B  B B                 B B
     B  B B                 B B B
     B  B B                 B B B
     B  B                   B B B
```

We then see the Israelite host,[52] lying unarmed in evident disarray by the shore.[53] In a nice touch which I think we can safely assume to be Ezekiel's invention he describes the weary Jews feeding their wives and children.[54] They are ἔμπονοι κόπῳ (208). This must mean 'weary, worn out.' Josephus, in describing the Jews at the Red Sea, uses the participle of κοπ όω, κεκοπωμένοι (*AJ* 2.321). There is no evidence that ἔμπονος ever means anything that will produce a desirable sense here in association with κόπῳ. If emendation be thought expedient, a simple remedy is at hand: read ἔγκοποι κόπῳ. Ezekiel likes adjectives in ἐγκ- (see 77, 252). Further, ἔγκοπος = weary is a Septuagintal word. The jingle is not pleasing, but Ezekiel is not careful about these things; cf. κακούμενον κακῶν (5f), μήτρας μητέρων (174), also 30, 188, 224.[55]

Present too are the flocks and household effects brought out of Egypt (209).[56] The Bible tells us nothing of 'household effects' in the Jews' possession and, unless this be sheer invention by Ezekiel, this may be a good piece of evidence that Ezekiel did not use the Hebrew Bible. ἀποσκευή can mean both 'children' and 'equipment.' The Septuagint uses it in both senses (e.g. 'children' at *Gen.* 43.8, 46.5; *Exod.* 12.37; 'possessions' at *Gen.* 14.12). In *Exodus'* account of the departure the presence of children is referred to several times (e.g. 12.37, 10.10, 24). Each of these passages translates the Hebrew טף (= small children) by ἀποσκευή. Perhaps in recalling these passages Ezekiel carelessly assumed that ἀποσκευή referred to 'household possessions.' We can be sure that he would not have made such an error had he known Hebrew and checked the Greek text against the Hebrew original: טף is unequivocal.[57]

On seeing the pursuing army, the Jews are terrified, cry out, and raise their voices to God[58] (210–12):

αὐτοὶ δ᾽ ἄνοπλοι πάντες εἰς μάχην χέρας
ἰδόντες ἡμᾶς ἠλάλαξαν ἔνδακρυν
†φωνὴν πρὸς αἰθέρα τ᾽ ἐστάθησαν† ἀθρόοι.

As the text may be corrupt, discussion is hard. Scholars have argued, each in his own way, that αἰθέρα and θεόν are not to be taken in apposition, on the grounds that Ezekiel could never have identified God with αἰθήρ.[59] They are probably right, but there is a difference between identification and association. The ancients thought that the Jews believed God was τὸν περιέχοντα τὴν γῆν οὐρανόν[60] and it is a fact that Jewish authors were capable of describing prayer in terms of raising one's hands πρὸς οὐρανόν or εἰς αἰθέρα (*Or. Sib.* 3.591; 4.166),[61] where one senses that the delimiting of God from the αἰθήρ is not clearcut and substantial. One recalls the virtual identification of οὐρανός with God at *Matth.* 21.25 and *Luke* 15.18, 21.[62] In the *Exagoge*, of course, it is the Egyptian who speaks.

In keeping with his 'Tendenz,' Ezekiel leaves out the Jews' chastisement of Moses for having taken them out of Egypt (14.11f). As always, he avoids those incidents which cast the Jews in a bad light, complaining, showing little faith in God and Moses, etc.

This entire passage is not a bad example – if restrained and brief – of pathetic Hellenistic historiography. We might compare it to the description in *2 Maccabees* of Heliodorus' attempt to sack the temple (3.14ff). There too we have the mighty pagan enemy seeking to work its will on the weak Jews, the fear and anxiety of the victims, the cries and prayers to God with hands stretched heavenward, the emphasis on the plight of the women, the miraculous divine apparition which terrifies and defeats the enemy, the enemy overwhelmed by darkness (unless πολλῷ σκότει περιχυθέντα is strictly metaphorical), and the acknowledgement of God's power by the pagans, together with praise of God by the saved Jews (which may well have been found in the remainder of the scene). There are also a few turns of phrase which Ezekiel may have deliberately introduced here as suitable in the mouth of a pagan, e.g. the references to αἰθήρ (212), Τιτὰν ἥλιος (217), and that to God as ὕψιστος.[63]

Finally, this scene may shed light on the relationship between Ezekiel and his successors, Philo and Josephus. On a number of significant points here Philo and Josephus are in agreement with Ezekiel in matters that cannot be attributed to the common use of *Exodus*, e.g. that the Jews are not armed, that Moses strikes the water with his staff, that darkness overcomes the Egyptians. But these are inconclusive, for they may indicate nothing other than that all three were working with the same traditions. But while Philo's version differs from Ezekiel's in distinct ways, Josephus' is so close that one can scarcely doubt that he had read it. Aside from the above-mentioned similarities, one notes the stress on κόπος, the decision to defer the battle till the morrow, the energetic entry into the sea. Moreover, there is one striking comment made by both Philo and Josephus which is hard to comprehend except by assuming that each knew the *Exagoge*. They both conclude their narratives by emphatically asserting that all the Egyptians died and remark that there was not even left a survivor to play the role of messenger for the Egyptians back home. It need not be pointed out how completely gratuitous this remark is, *unless it is meant as polemic.* For Ezekiel had presented a survivor who then served as messenger to the Egyptians. It is hard to see what Philo and Josephus could have had in mind if not to reject insistently and concretely Ezekiel's version. But why would they have been so concerned to do this? I can go no further than to hypothesize that both felt it of serious importance to preserve here the Biblical account to the letter (*Exod.* 14.28: not a single Egyptian survived; so too at *Ps.* 106.11).[64] At the end of his account of the crossing of the Red Sea Josephus stresses that he has found all his information ἐν ταῖς ἱεραῖς βίβλοις (*AJ* 2.347), as if specially to affirm the validity of his version. Since, in fact, his account is certainly not based on the Bible alone, he must mean something like 'authentic Jewish traditions.'[65]

8. The oasis at Elim (243–69)

Shortly after the crossing of the Red Sea the Jews come to Elim. The Bible reports (*Exod.* 15.27):

> Καὶ ἤλθοσαν εἰς Αιλιμ, καὶ ἦσαν ἐκεῖ δώδεκα πηγαὶ ὑδάτων καὶ ἑβδομήκοντα στελέχη φοινίκων· παρενέβαλον δὲ ἐκεῖ παρὰ τὰ ὕδατα.

From the *Exagoge* there is preserved a speech by a messenger, evidently a scout sent to investigate the camping possibilities in the desert. He describes the Oasis of Elim (243–53):

κράτιστε Μωσῆ, πρό⟨σ⟩σχες, οἷον εὕρομεν
τόπον πρὸς αὐτῇ τῇδέ γ' εὐαεῖ νάπῃ.
ἔστω γάρ, ὡς που καὶ σὺ τυγχάνεις ὁρῶν,
ἐκεῖ· τόθεν δὲ φέγγος ἐξέλαμψέ νω
κατ' εὐφρόνης σημεῖον ὡς στῦλος πυρός.
ἐνταῦθα λειμῶν· εὕρομεν κατάσκιον
ὑγράς τε λιβάδας· δαψιλὴς χῶρος βαθύς,
πηγὰς ἀφύσσων δώδεκ' ἐκ μιᾶς πέτρας,
στελέχη δ' ἐρυμνὰ πολλὰ φοινίκων πέλει
ἔγκαρπα, δεκάκις ἑπτά, καὶ περίρρυτος
πέφυκε χλοίη θρέμμασιν χορτάσματα.[1]

The description is abruptly broken off by Polyhistor's remark
(446b), εἶτα ὑποβὰς περὶ τοῦ φανέντος ὀρνέου διεξέρχεται. There
follows a sixteen-line description of a rather unusual bird. This description, I stress, belongs to the same scene, indeed to the same
scout's report, as the account of the Oasis. Frankel[2] and others[3] have
mistakenly held that the description of the bird is part of the report brought by the spies sent to scout the land of Canaan. But if
Polyhistor's statements are to have any value, we must discount this
possibility. He observes before quoting verses 243–53 (445d):

ἐκεῖθεν δὲ εἰς Ἐλεὶμ ἐλθεῖν καὶ εὑρεῖν ἐκεῖ δώδεκα μὲν πηγὰς ὑδάτων,
ἐβδομήκοντα δὲ στελέχη φοινίκων. περὶ τούτων καὶ τοῦ φανέντος
ὀρνέου Ἐξεκιῆλος ἐν τῇ Ἐξαγωγῇ παρεισάγει τινὰ λέγοντα τῷ Μωσεῖ
περὶ μὲν τῶν φοινίκων καὶ τῶν δώδεκα πηγῶν αὕτως·

This can only mean that the scout enters and reports both about the
oasis at Elim and also about the Phoenix. Though of less account,
Polyhistor's εἶτα ὑποβὰς before 254 also suggests, though not in
itself inexorably, that the Phoenix passage belongs to the same
report.[4]

Exodus' account of Elim is sparse and simple: twelve fountains
and seventy palm trees. Ezekiel is faithful to this description and
elaborates it. As so often, we must wonder whether he is exploiting
his own imaginative powers or is following extra-Biblical Jewish
traditions. With the Phoenix the problem is more complicated since
there do not even appear to be any references to the Phoenix in the
Bible,[5] certainly not in the Pentateuch. Several questions face us:
(1) What motivated Ezekiel to introduce the Phoenix in his narrative
of the Exodus and to what purpose? (2) Why did he associate the
Phoenix with Elim? (3) Did he have extra-Biblical Jewish sources as

precedent? (4) What is the relation here to Greek sources on the Phoenix?

Midrashic exegesis stressed the miraculous aspects of the stay at Elim, perhaps in an attempt to make it an experience of the Marah and Refidim type, one wherein the natural character of the site is inhospitable to the wandering Jews, but is miraculously transformed by an act of God into a suitable and refreshing abode. For example, some Midrashic texts assert that Elim was a rather ill-favored spot, with twelve springs of such meager production as to support only seventy trees.[6] Josephus, in greater detail (*AJ* 3.9ff), mentions also the sandy terrain and foul water. The Rabbinic sources above cited add that the meager supplies of fruit and water at Elim miraculously sufficed the whole people, while Josephus has God send quail to feed the people. In contrast, Philo pictures Elim as a magnificent oasis, well wooded and watered (*Moses* 1.188), εὔυδρόν τε καὶ εὔδενδρον . . . πηγαῖς καταρρεόμενον δώδεκα . . . στελέχη νέα φοινίκων εὐερνέστατα, language that is similar to Ezekiel's. One might surmise that Ezekiel is adhering to an Egypto-Jewish interpretation of the Biblical story which was different from (and evidently closer to the Bible than) the Palestinian exegesis preserved in later texts.

Ezekiel has added details to the Biblical narrative. It is a shady meadow, very fertile, and twelve springs flow from one rock. The palms are many[7] and fruitful, water flows round the area, the grass provides food for the animals. There is little here that strikes one as exceptionable, or even notable. Yet, there was a Rabbinic tradition that is in so many respects similar that coincidence seems out of the question. This was the tale of the well that accompanied the Jews through the desert from one place to the next. This well was usually thought of as issuing forth in twelve streams at each camping site (though this is not absolutely clear). The camp would then be surrounded by water; trees and other delights would spring up.[8] A painting at Dura shows some of these motifs and Goodenough has suggested identifying it with Ezekiel's Elim.[9] What may increase the likelihood of a connection between the Rabbis' wandering well and Ezekiel's Elim is that the well is occasionally described as a rock – or as being like a rock (e.g. *Numbers Rabbah* 1.2).

But Ezekiel is also exploiting the motifs of Greek Utopias,[10] both in his general description and in his terminology (περίρρυτος, κατάσκιος, πηγαί, λειμών, δαψιλής).[11] Ezekiel turned the scene of the desert well into a Hellenistic Utopia.[12]

Ezekiel was not the only Hellenistic Jewish writer to describe a 'Jewish' site in the Utopian colors of Hellenistic pagan authors. The author of *Aristeas* gives an idyllic picture of Palestine (112ff), with many points in common with Ezekiel's Elim: numerous trees, abundance (δαψιλής), palms, the sense of enclosure (ἀσφάλεια), the water flowing round (περιρρεῖ). *Aristeas* and Ezekiel are moving within the same Greek genre here.

As Utopias in the Greek world go back to Homer, so those in the Jewish world go back to *Genesis*. But later Jewish sources replaced the simplicity of *Genesis*' Eden-account with elaborate delineation. Even in the Bible we can see this development in the prophet Ezekiel's paradise (28.13ff).[13] But in general the Greek examples tend to be more precise and detailed with respect to the rustic-agricultural phenomena and more concerned to emphasize the sense of separation, enclosure and seclusion. Viewed from this perspective, Ezekiel's account may be set within the Greek genre.

We do not know when Jewish exegesis began to incorporate quasi-Utopian sites into the desert-wanderings of the Jews nor when Elim became one of these. It is conceivable that Ezekiel was the first, but quite unlikely given both the extent of the theme in Rabbinic texts and Ezekiel's general inclination to make use of Jewish extra-Biblical traditions. Philo's description of Elim (*Moses* 1.188f; *Fuga* 183ff) may contain some Utopian elements. It seems evident that at an early stage the sojourn at Elim had been invested with special significance because of the number of palms and springs. The coincidence (if coincidence it be) between the number of trees and springs on the one hand, and the number of tribes and elders of Israel on the other was an obvious starting point for symbolic interpretation at one or another level.[14] Such can be seen in the passages from Philo cited above, and less elaborately in Rabbinic texts.[15] In addition, both Philo and the Rabbis saw in Elim an experience of educational importance, the former considering the place a symbol of the levels of education, the latter using the equation of water = Torah to expound that the Jews began the study of Torah at Elim.[16] Thus, there is little reason to believe that Ezekiel was innovating when he laid stress on the importance and special nature of Elim.

In the *Exagoge* Elim is the first encampment after the crossing of the sea. The Bible has the Jews camp at Marah after their salvation at the Red Sea. But Polyhistor's comments suggest that Ezekiel did not include that episode. He reports that the Jews marched three days, came to Marah where Moses rendered the water sweet and then travelled to Elim where they found the trees and springs, as Ezekiel describes; he then quotes verses 243–53 of the *Exagoge*. Polyhistor's juxtaposition of Marah and Elim, with a citation from Ezekiel on Elim but none on Marah, suggests that Ezekiel simply did not include it. The reason is patent and characteristic. Ezekiel constantly avoids those episodes which place the Jews in a bad light. In Marah the people had railed at Moses when they could find no potable water. Ezekiel skips the unpleasant occurrence.[17] Thus, Elim becomes the first place the Jews reach in their march from the sea and a dramatic and spiritual high point in the play. It will be taken as a sign of divine favor that their first camping place turns out to be a virtual Utopia. Ezekiel may even have intended it as a foreshadowing of the entry into Palestine.[18] For the pagan audience it would have been an incident of moment. In both the themes and language attendant on the description of Elim, they would have recognized one of those far-off Utopias reported by Euhemeros and his ilk and would have taken it as a sign of divine grace (or at least distinguished leadership) that this was the first place the Jews 'stumble' upon in the desert.

Lines 246f have not been sufficiently elucidated: τόθεν δὲ φέγγος ἐξέλαμψέ νω/κατ' εὐφρόνης σημεῖον ὡς στῦλος πυρός. A light flashes out to the scouts, like a pillar of fire. Editors like Snell and Gifford who refuse to emend εὐφρ όνης to εὐφρόνην with Dübner probably still assume the phrase to be temporal. But I do not understand how Dalbert (63) can take the words εὐφρόνης σημεῖον here as predicate.[19] We should, I believe, understand these verses as an allusion to the Biblical pillars of cloud and fire which accompany the Jews through the desert. The cloud accompanies them by day, the fire at night.[20] Thus, we probably have here in the *Exagoge* the discovery by the scouts of the oasis where the people will camp through God's miraculous fire-pillar. The notice of this divine 'guide' will come properly here since this is the first encampment by the Jews in the *Exagoge*.[21] Thus, Ginzberg's suggestion that the scouts find their way to the oasis by following the bird is inadmissible.[22] One further point. What can νιν in 246 mean? Wieneke takes τόθεν as temporal (though this scarcely makes sense and is surely unexpected right after ἐκεῖ) and argues that φέγγος ἐξέλαμψέ νιν means that the light illuminated the valley. But ἐκλάμπω is not used with an external object. Mras emends νιν to νυν, which removes the problem but hardly makes any sense (aside from the fact that Ezekiel nowhere uses enclitic νυν in our 269 lines). What can νυν mean here? Perhaps a better emendation is possible; read νῷν. This dative dual form is common in Greek tragedy. Ezekiel could easily have picked it up from any of the three tragedians.[23] For the construction and phrasing one can compare the startlingly similar expression in Artapanus (*PE* 9.436c) where a fire shines forth to the Egyptians at the Red Sea (αὐτοῖς ἐκλάμψαι). The motif of a pair of messengers or agents is routine in both Greek drama and Biblical texts. Thus, the idea of sending two scouts may well have come to Ezekiel naturally. We may think of Strength and Force at the beginning of the *Prometheus Bound*, the customary pair of Talthybius and Eurybates, Orestes and Pylades, the two angels sent to destroy Sodom, the two spies sent by Joshua to scout the promised land. The last example may have been of particular importance, especially if Elim in the *Exagoge* is a sort of anticipation of Palestine. Ezekiel would not be likely to have adopted the twelve spies sent by Moses, since so large a group merely to find a camping site might have seemed ludicrous, but the two sent by Joshua would have proved a suitable number. The Rabbis, when faced with the bare reference to 'spies' at *Nu.* 21.32, chose to number them at two, in a clear adaptation of the number of Joshua's scouts. Indeed, they identified the two sets of spies as the very same pair, Caleb and Pinechas.[24] It is then reasonable to assume that one of the scouts spoke while the other was a mute. If this emendation be accepted, we have not merely corrected the text of a single verse but expanded our knowledge of the dramaturgy of the *Exagoge*.

We turn to the Phoenix. Though our fragment never identifies it, it is unmistakable that this wondrous bird is the fabulous Phoenix. Eustathius of Antioch, one of our two sources for this passage, does call the bird by this name (*PG* 18.729). More important, comparison with accounts of the Phoenix guarantee the identification. Our text begins with a bit of a puzzle (254): ἕτερον δὲ πρὸς τοῖσδ᾽ εἴδομεν ζῷον ξένον. What does ἕτερον mean? It is sometimes assumed that in the lacuna between 253 and 254 Ezekiel presented another strange creature,[25] a possibility that is reinforced by the existence of a peculiar fragment which has sometimes been attributed to Ezekiel.[26] But were this the case it is unlikely that Polyhistor would have explicitly described the passage as containing accounts of palm trees, fountains and the bird, without mentioning (and quoting) the additional strange creature. We might better assume that the verse means, 'In addition to this ($\pi\rho\grave{o}\varsigma$ $\tau o\~{\iota}\sigma\delta\epsilon$, i.e. the previously described palms and springs; though $\pi\rho\grave{o}\varsigma$ $\tau o\~{\iota}\sigma\delta\epsilon$ might simply = moreover[27]) we saw something else, a strange creature.' This use of $\H{\epsilon}\tau\epsilon\rho o\varsigma$ and more often $\H{\alpha}\lambda\lambda o\varsigma$ is adequately attested.[28] We should assume that the lacuna between 253 and 254 was a short one (as Polyhistor's $\epsilon\~{\iota}\tau\alpha$ $\H{\upsilon}\pi o\beta\grave{\alpha}\varsigma$ also suggests) and whatever it contained it did not, most probably, describe at length any notable or unusual creature.[29]

The only detailed account of the Phoenix (that survives) before the *Exagoge* is Herodotus'. This leaves us with virtually no information from either classical or Jewish sources on the significance of the Phoenix myth before Ezekiel's time.[30] We are thus mainly reliant on later testimony which may or may not reflect earlier traditions.[31] Herodotus (2.73) concentrates his account on the journey of the Phoenix to Heliopolis, carrying the remains of its dead father, an aspect of the myth that appears to have played no role in the *Exagoge*. A mere sentence is devoted to the features of the Phoenix. Neither the regeneration nor the longevity of the bird is mentioned, though the latter is implicit in the fact that the bird needs to bury its father only once in 500 years. The only points of contact between Herodotus and Ezekiel are the multi-colored plumage and the comparison to an eagle.[32] While Ezekiel probably knew the passage on the Phoenix in Herodotus, it is clear that it did not serve him as an important source for information on the bird.

Why did Ezekiel incorporate into a play on the Exodus the appearance of the Phoenix, an appearance which to the best of our knowledge is attested neither in Biblical nor in post-Biblical Jewish sources? It seems clear that by his time two aspects of the Phoenix myth had endowed any appearance of the bird with special significance: first, the fact that the Phoenix was said to appear at only rare intervals, whether 500 years as Herodotus claims or considerably longer (cf., e.g., Tac. *Ann.* 6.28). Thus, his very appearance was an important occasion and was reasonably assumed to mark a moment or an event of great magnitude. As Broek has noted,[33] it became almost traditional for propagandists to claim that the Phoenix had appeared at any event whose significance they wished to proclaim. Second – and perhaps of particular relevance to Ezekiel – the element of regeneration and rebirth associated with the Phoenix may have seemed to the Jewish playwright particularly appropriate for the story of the redemption and birth of the Jewish people out of slavery.[34]

A fascinating and potentially illuminating text is quoted by Bartholomaeus Anglicus (*de propr. rer.* 12.14) in the name of one Alanus.[35] It is one of the few texts that, like Ezekiel, associates the Phoenix with a major episode in Jewish history. We read that upon the dedication of the temple at Heliopolis (i.e. Leontopolis) by Onias in the second century B.C. the Phoenix appeared, alighted on the sacrificial pyre and was consumed. Broek believes that this medieval text must represent a very old tradition. One would be happy to think so, but we cannot determine whether it goes back as far as Ezekiel. If it does, then it would be a striking example of the incorporation of the Phoenix into Jewish history as a signal of some notable event, from approximately the same period as Ezekiel's.[36]

An even more strikingly relevant text has been adduced by Broek (41). A sixth-century Coptic sermon on Mary reports, 'When God brought the children of Israel out of Egypt by the hand of Moses, the phoenix showed itself on the temple of On, the city of the sun.' Unfortunately, the genesis of this is impossible to fix: does it derive directly or indirectly from Ezekiel? Does it come from some other relatively early source? We cannot say.

More than a century ago J. B. Lightfoot keenly observed that Egyptian chronography may be the root of Ezekiel's version.[37] The Egyptian priest Ptolemy Mendesius, whose *terminus ante quem* is the mid-first century A.D. and who may have lived long before, recorded in his Egyptian history that Amosis was king of Egypt at the time of the Exodus (*FGrHist* 611 F19b). Now Tacitus reports, one surmises on good authority, that there was a tradition of the Phoenix' appearance in Egypt in the reigns of Sesosis, Amasis and Ptolemy (*Ann.* 6.28). In other words, there was evidently an Egyptian or Greco-Egyptian tradition that the Phoenix appeared during the reign of Amasis, who was also identified as the king during the

Exodus. It would have been easy enough for Ezekiel – or some other Alexandrian Jew – to make an explicit connection between the two and establish the Phoenix as a sort of divine sign of the momentousness of the Exodus.

In our discussion of the Passover section of the *Exagoge* we noted Ezekiel's change of the Biblical ἀρχὴ μηνῶν to πρῶτος ἐνιαυτῶν. Perhaps he wanted to suggest the technical use of ἐνιαυτός in Stoic-Pythagorean terminology, i.e. to intimate that the divine and miraculous character of the Exodus was a cosmic event of the magnitude of those cataclysmic rebirths of the universe familiar from Greek philosophical schools (cf. Josephus' reference to the μέγας ἐνιαυτός at *AJ* 1.106). If so, Ezekiel's introduction of the Phoenix would fit well. For some ancients held that the life-span of the Phoenix coincided with the *magnus annus*, that is the appearance of the Phoenix marked the beginning of a new *magnus annus*. The Roman Manilius was of this opinion around the year (so it seems) 97 B.C. (Pliny, *NH* 10.3ff; cf. Solinus 33.13).[38] Moreover, the span of 1461 years is given for both the Phoenix cycle (Tac. *Ann.* 6.28) and the *magnus annus* (*FGrHist* 610 F2 = p. 117). The Ethiopians are reported to have used the Phoenix as symbol of the ἐνιαυτός.[39] The Greek *Physiologus* (7) has the Phoenix burn itself 'in the new month, Nisan or Adar, i.e. Phamenoth or Pharmouthi.' Though the text is in dispute (see Broek 131), it is clear that the Phoenix' appearance is being placed in the first month of the year, Nisan, another instance of its symbolic role in the inauguration of an era. Of course, Nisan is probably the month in which Ezekiel sets the Phoenix' appearance in the Exagoge.[40] Jewish sources, which do not seem to connect the Phoenix to any cosmic cycle nor to assert its appearance at significant intervals and events, nevertheless do contain one element which may be relevant. When the Phoenix is rewarded for its piety, it is delegated 'for all generations to be an everlasting witness for Israel' (*Jerahm.* 22.7). So too in a Midrashic text quoted by Jellinek at 6. p. xii: the Phoenix is destined 'To testify to the merit of Israel.' This is, one imagines, the same sort of thing as when God establishes heaven and earth (which are also immortal) as witnesses (*Deut.* 30.19, 31.28, 32.1).[41] The fact that Rabbinical texts emphasize the important role of 'hereditary privilege' in the redemption of the Jews from Egypt is pertinent since Ezekiel may allude to this notion at

104ff. From this perspective, the Phoenix may be intended here as a witness to the merit of Israel and the faithfulness of God.

If then it is possible to understand why Ezekiel chose to present the Phoenix at the Exodus, can we also explain why he associated it with Elim? Here I think there are three main factors which dovetail and a fourth group which is less immediate: (1) The Phoenix is often located in paradisical types of places. Unfortunately, none of our sources antedates Ezekiel, but the tradition may well be older than the extant sources. The most elaborate is Lactantius' *de ave phoenice.* Claudian's is not far behind. Jewish texts about the Phoenix mostly discuss the behavior of the bird in the paradise of Eden. It is, however, not clear whether the Phoenix remains in Eden after the expulsion or not. But the interesting Gnostic text earlier mentioned does place him in paradise.[42]

(2) Hellenistic Utopias were often populated with birds, sometimes rather strange and extraordinary birds.[43] Thus, Euhemeros' Panchaia has an ὀρνέων πλῆθος which, like Ezekiel's Phoenix, sing.[44] Iambulus' island not only has ordinary birds, but also one large and unique bird (εὐμέγεθες ἰδιάζον τῇ φύσει, a description of the sort one commonly finds of the Phoenix) which each member-group of inhabitants maintains for special 'rite de passage' ceremonies. In addition, there is another strange creature which can, so to speak, restore to itself its lost organs through its remarkable blood, a quality which almost approaches the regeneration of the Phoenix (see especially Horapollo 2.57). Thus, one can be sure that at the least Ezekiel was familiar with Hellenistic Utopias in which birds[45] and animals with strange powers resided.

(3) Over three centuries ago S. Bochart, in his learned treatise *Hierozoicon*, suggested that the Greek translation of the Bible was, at least in some measure, responsible for the Phoenix' presence at Elim in the *Exagoge*.[46] He observed that in Greek the Phoenix and the palm tree are called by the same name, φοῖνιξ and pointed out that this noun is used by the Septuagint at *Exod.* 15.27 for the trees at Elim (στελέχη φοινίκων).[47] From this, Bochart argued, Ezekiel took a hint and so introduced the Phoenix to Elim. Though we can be certain that this alone would never have led Ezekiel to inject the Phoenix here, in association with the factors enumerated above this may well have played a part. The objections raised by Hubaux and

Leroy (47) that Ezekiel does not represent the Phoenix in his guise
as bird of the palms nor say anything to suggest such an association
between the bird and the trees, are not cogent. Aside from the fact
that we do not know what followed verse 269, both Ezekiel and his
audience might have been attuned to the association, and the word
φοῖνιξ at 251 could have been enough to call it to mind. At any rate,
the specific item of influence and Ezekiel's use of it need not coin-
cide.

Finally, some unusual aspects of the Biblical and post-Biblical
traditions of the Exodus may bear on Ezekiel's introduction of the
Phoenix in the first days after the crossing of the sea, if not on its
immediate connection to Elim. After leaving Elim, the people
journey to the desert of Sin where, after complaints by the Jews,
God sends quail and manna as food (*Exod.* 16). Josephus telescopes
the episodes and has God send the quail while they are still at Elim
(*AJ* 3.9ff). Hubaux and Leroy (48ff) think that the connection
between the Bible's quail and Ezekiel's Phoenix goes beyond a mere
coincidence of birds at the time of the Exodus. They note ingeni-
ously that the Psalmist compares the quail to the 'sand of the seas'
(*Ps.* 78.27, כחול ימים) and suggest that Ezekiel may have taken חול
in the sense 'Phoenix' and then transformed the quail episode into a
Phoenix story. This is dazzlingly clever, but can scarcely stand up.
The text says חול ימים, the 'chol' of the seas. But the Phoenix has
nothing to do with the sea. Further, it is hard to imagine any reader
understanding this verse as a comparison meaning, 'this bird was
like (another) bird.' Third, what could any reader have supposed
such a comparison ('the quail was like a Phoenix') to mean? Finally,
there is no cogent evidence that Ezekiel knew Hebrew and used the
Hebrew Bible. If there was a Greek version of the *Psalms* in his day,
he would probably have read ἄμμον θαλασσῶν, as we do. However,
a verse from *Wisdom* seems apt and significant in this context,
though I am not certain how to interpret its relevance and importance (19.11): ἐφ᾽ ὑστέρῳ δὲ εἶδον καὶ γένεσιν νέαν ὀρνέων, ὅτε
ἐπιθυμίᾳ προαχθέντες ᾐτήσαντο ἐδέσματα τρυφῆς. This of the Jews
after the plagues. Is it not virtually a description of the scene at
Elim in the *Exagoge*? The people sought delightful foods (which they
evidently received in the paradise of Elim; note that τρυφή is commonly used in the Septuagint for the garden of Eden) and they

beheld a new kind of bird. This is a startling coincidence. Yet, what
is *Wisdom* in fact referring to? The next verse clarifies: εἰς γὰρ παρα-
μυθίαν ἐκ θαλάσσης ἀνέβη αὐτοῖς ὀρτυγομήτρα. The strange birds,
the gourmet delicacies – this is all a reference to the quail. It is hard
to draw any firm conclusions from this, especially since the relative
dates of *Wisdom* and Ezekiel cannot be ascertained with certainty.
Did Ezekiel know *Wisdom*? Might he have taken a clue from *Wisdom*
19.11 to introduce his own peculiar bird here? Or is all this sheer
coincidence?

Another ornithological tradition may have played a role. In
Rabbinical and Hellenistic-Jewish texts Moses is sometimes connected to Phoenix-like birds, i.e. storks or ibises. He is said to have
used them for 'military' purposes when leading the Ethiopian army.[48]
Artapanus, in a slightly different version, reports that Moses founded
a city in Hermopolis and there consecrated the ibis (*PE* 9.432d). Who
knows but whether the Egyptian claim that Moses was originally a
priest at Heliopolis (Jos. *Ap.* 1.250), the home so to speak of the
Phoenix, also played a part?

Ezekiel's description of the Phoenix is brief (we are not sure
whether it has been preserved in its entirety). It is then with some
trepidation that we argue from what he does not say. The Phoenix
was a symbol of the sun (cf. 'Heliopolis'): ἡλίου ἐστὶν ὁ φοῖνιξ
σύμβολον (Horapollo 1.34). Its connection with the temple of the
sun is already present in Herodotus (2.73). The association is frequent in the pseudepigrapha (e.g. *3 Baruch* 6.8; *2 Enoch* 15.1). There
is not a trace of this in the *Exagoge*. Worship of the sun as a deity had
a long history among the Jews (cf. *Deut.* 4.19). The prophet Ezekiel
(8.16) testifies to the sun-worship prevalent in his day.[49] Jews swore
by the sun,[50] and the Helios on synagogue floors may have been an
object of worship. Greco-Jewish magical papyri invoke God and
Helios in virtually the same breath.[51] At Kadesh an altar to a solar
deity has an inscription flanked by palms.[52] The connection between
God and Helios must have been facilitated by the similarity between
the Jewish notion of God who knows and sees everything and the
Greek rhetorical turn-of-phrase 'the all-seeing sun.'[53] The line is hard
to draw. Often the Septuagint refers to God in language that might
recall Helios (e.g. *Esther* 15.2, 16.4; *2 Macc.* 7.35).[54] To this whole
phenomenon one form of reaction can be seen in *Sirach* 43, which

elaborately describes the glory of the sun, only to conclude with a reminder that the sun is, after all, only the handiwork of God and it is God who deserves the praise and reverence. Perhaps Ezekiel leaves out all mention of the sun lest his audience take the appearance of the Phoenix as somehow connected to a solar deity. The omission is the more remarkable when one recalls that Hellenistic utopias sometimes incorporate Helios in perhaps quasi-divine fashion. The river in Panchaia is called ἡλίου ὕδωρ. Iambulus' utopia is evidently called the Island of the Sun and its inhabitants worship the sun.

When Ezekiel ignores the self-regeneration of the Phoenix, this is de-mythologization. Ezekiel wants nothing of the seemingly divine and supernatural aside from God.[55]

With the description of the Phoenix, the fragments from the *Exagoge* in Eusebius come to an end. Editors of the *Exagoge* print the passages on the oasis and the Phoenix as the concluding sections of the play. If detailed reconstructions of the play that see it as a Hellenistic five-act drama with the oasis and the Phoenix as parts of the fifth act are even approximately correct,[56] then we can be fairly certain that not very much could have followed. But if there was anything, what might it have been?[57]

Gutmann (*EJ* 886) proposed a *prima facie* obvious possibility: the revelation and giving of the Law at Sinai. That Polyhistor – or perhaps Eusebius – would leave this out is understandable. The pagan 'anthologist' would probably have had little understanding of or sympathy for such an epiphany. But if perchance he did cite it, Eusebius himself might have preferred not to introduce an episode in which the Jews were recipients of Divine Law in so striking and compelling a fashion. On the other hand, what is the likelihood that Ezekiel would have included such a scene? I think little. If, as I think not really in question, the drama was meant for an audience that included pagans as well as Jews, it seems unlikely that he would have presented this kind of episode. While Greeks were familiar with lawgivers who claimed divine origin for their lawcodes, the spectacular cosmic revelation before the whole people at Sinai would have – at best – not met with understanding and possibly with little sympathy. It is also worth recalling – not least because in his Moses-narrative Philo often seems to follow Ezekiel – that in Book One of his *Moses* Philo completely skips over the revelation at Sinai.

A number of scholars have suggested that the play concludes with the arrival of Raguel and Sepphora to congratulate Moses and the Jews, a scene which would be modelled on *Exod.* 18.1–12.[58] This is a delightful notion and has fine dramatic value, with Raguel entering to take pride in the glory that his son-in-law has attained, glory forecast by him earlier in the play. It is unfortunate that we have no concrete evidence that there was such an episode. The text of Eusebius seems to suggest that Polyhistor, at any rate, did not record any such scene in the *Exagoge*, for Polyhistor appears to have jumped from the Phoenix account almost directly into the settlement of the Jews in Israel. The only material that evidently intervened was a brief gap (note μετὰ βραχέα, 446d) and then an explanation of how the Jews obtained their arms. The introduction of this issue suggests that the brief lacuna in Polyhistor treated the conquest of Canaan by the Jews (though this is not the only possibility; another is the battle against Amalek in *Exod.* 17). This probably excludes the possibility that Polyhistor cited any scene from the *Exagoge* that portrayed the arrival of Raguel and Sepphora.

Trencsényi-Waldapfel has cogently argued (155f) that the arrival at Elim is the end of the play. He sees this as a symbolic precursor of the settlement in Israel. I have argued the latter point at greater length earlier and think it quite plausible, whether or not the play actually ended here. There may, however, be some indications, both within the play and without, that Trencsényi-Waldapfel's view is correct. As I have argued earlier,[59] Ezekiel's phraseology at verses 153–5 and 167–9 seems calculated to leave the non-Jews in the audience with the impression that the fleeing Jews reach their promised land very quickly and consequently to assume that Elim is indeed their goal. If true, this would make the arrival at Elim a very suitable point at which to end the play. For the Jews, as noted above, Elim would be understood as presaging the ultimate arrival in the promised land. One final argument. Goodenough has maintained the centrality of the well-episode in Philo's vision of the *Exodus* (e.g. *Ebr.* 112f), after the departure itself and the crossing of the sea.[60] He notes that in Philo the migrating Jews never do reach the promised land. Goodenough's account here is somewhat exaggerated. Thus, *Moses* 1 refers often and in various ways to the ultimate coming to Israel. That it never takes place is readily explained. Philo is here (and elsewhere) concerned with Moses, who never reaches the promised land. Further, his interest and familiarity is clearly with the Pentateuch, which breaks off before the entrance of the Jews into Israel. Still, Goodenough is right in stressing Philo's emphasis on the well-episode. If we choose to see some similar sense of importance for Ezekiel, then the likelihood that he ended the play at Elim is increased. At all events, in our present state of knowledge no final answer to this question can be attained.

APPENDIX

The metre and prosody of the *Exagoge*

In his metre and prosody Ezekiel's usage is ambiguous. In certain areas he is quite like his fifth-century tragic models, yet in others quite different. Similarly, based on the limited extant fragments of Hellenistic tragedy, we can say that in certain ways he resembles them greatly, in others not at all. Whether in this apparent stratification or conflation of traditions Ezekiel is representative of second-century Alexandrian tragedy or simply a unique phenomenon is something we cannot determine. It will perhaps be easiest to draw a picture of Ezekiel's overall metrical practice by examining various features singly. I have learned much from four studies, those of Wieneke (115-17), Lesky,[1] Snell (*Glotta*) and Strugnell. It is unfortunate that in most cases these four scholars were unable to benefit from the work of the others. Wieneke wrote first and his research was used by the other three. But Lesky's important article of 1953 was evidently not known to Snell and Strugnell, while the latter pair had their articles appear almost simultaneously.

I. *Resolution*: (a) It is commonly held that the Hellenistic tragedians, like other Hellenistic authors of iambic trimeters, adopted the practice of the early iambographers rather than that of the classical tragedians and almost completely avoided resolution. This theory is, of course, based on a very limited number of verses,[2] especially since it does not seem proper to include Lycophron's *Alexandra* as evidence for tragedy. It has, on the other hand, been buttressed by the Gyges-fragment which contains no resolution.[3] Ezekiel, however, clearly follows the usage of the fifth-century tragedians. His verses abound in resolution.[4] Wieneke, using Zielinski's statistics as a basis for comparison,[5] calculated 29% resolution in Ezekiel, which is about the same as in Euripides' *Helen* and *Phoen.* (both 29.4%) and higher than all other Euripidean plays but the three latest: *Or.* 38.6%, *Bacch.* 35.9%, *IA* 38.1%.[6] Strugnell's statistics, using Ceadel as a basis for comparison (including anapests and excluding proper nouns), show a similar relationship. Ezekiel stands at 33.5%, the *Phoen.* at 25.8%, *Helen* 27.5%, *Or.* 39.4%, *Bacch.* 37.6%, *IA* 34.7%. In other words, either set of statistics reveals that Ezekiel uses a great deal of resolution, almost as much as Euripides in his latest plays. It is interesting to note that Ezekiel's percentage also approximates closely that of the fourth-century tragedians as calculated by Ceadel. Ezekiel's 37.5% (Strugnell) or 39.8% (Wieneke, who counts 107 resolutions to Strugnell's 101) is strikingly close to Chaeremon's 40% (early fourth century).[7]

(b) anapests:[8] The high frequency of anapests in the first foot (according to Strugnell 24 out of 101 resolutions, 17 out of 90 without names) differs from Aeschylus, Sophocles and Euripides who usually have about 10%. Again Chaeremon is close with five anapests among his thirty resolutions while the minor late fifth-century tragedians give 26%. Wieneke counted three non-name anapests outside the first foot, one each in the third (226), fourth (135) and fifth (207) feet (135 and 226 being, in addition, split anapests).[9] Strugnell and Snell argue these all corrupt (though Strugnell thinks παρέδωκε at 74 may be correct).[10] At 207 the manuscripts justify reading δίδουν rather than ἐδίδουν and at 226 the manuscripts are defective. Verse 74 yields easily to emendation. But 135 does not lend itself to ready correction. Snell is compelled to posit a lacuna of two half-lines.[11] We cannot then be certain as to whether Ezekiel used anapests outside the first foot. But it will not hurt to remember that both satyr play and comedy allowed non-name anapests in all feet but the last.[12]

(c) dactyls: First foot dactyls account for almost 15% of Ezekiel's resolutions (13 out of 90: Strugnell). This is far higher than Aeschylus, Sophocles (who are usually below 5%) and most of Euripides. But late Euripides approximates this (*Or.* 12%, *Bacch.* 11%, *IA* 14%). The fourth-century fragments do not attest a continuation of this trend, for Ceadel records them at 6%. The first foot split dactyl at 178 τετρὰς ἐπι- is strange, but Snell goes too far in thinking it probably corrupt. There are parallels in late Euripides and of course the usage is common in comedy.[13] Third foot dactyls constitute about 27% of Ezekiel's resolutions (24 out of 90). This is markedly less than Aeschylus (always above 35%) and Sophocles (only once below 30%) but again is in tune with Euripides whose usage of third foot dactyls decreases throughout his career.[14] *Or.* with 29%, *Bacch.* 29% and *IA* 25% are all close to Ezekiel, as again are the minor late-fifth-century tragedians with 23%. Here however Chaeremon is at the Aeschylean and Sophoclean level of 40%.

(d) tribrachs: There is little noteworthy in Ezekiel's use of tri-brachs. They are, as in the classical tragedians, rare in the fifth foot (2 out of 90 instances, which does not differ much from the three tragedians). Euripides tends to be about the same while Aeschylus and Sophocles are a bit higher. In his 18% use of second foot tribrachs, Ezekiel is again closer to Euripides who tends to the mid-teens and a fraction higher in the late plays (*Or.* 18%, *Bacch.* 20%, *IA* 21%), whereas Sophocles and Aeschylus usually show below 10%. In his 11% third foot tribrachs, Ezekiel is close to both Sophocles and Euripides, while Aeschylus is higher. His fourth foot tribrach 8% is somewhat lower than Aeschylus and Euripides, but is fairly conso-nant with other fifth-century tragedy.

Can we draw any conclusions from the statistics on Ezekiel's use of resolution beyond the obvious one that he does not follow the rejection of resolution that (it is generally believed) was adopted by Hellenistic tragedians? Mainly, I suspect, that his usage does not fit readily into any single available category. But on a broad scale it is possible to surmise that he is akin to late Euripides not merely in the frequency of resolution but in some of the specific patterns of resolutions as well.

II. *Porson's Law*: Six violations have been noticed: 62, 131, 163, 174, 233, 240.[15] While this rate of violation does not begin to approach that of comedy, it is far greater than in the classical trage-dians where the law is broken very rarely.[16] Are these six examples all violations? The question is complicated somewhat by the lack of unanimity among scholars in determining what constitutes, strictly speaking, a violation of the law. Three instances are essentially of the same order (62, 131, 240): ἄρχων δ᾽ ἐστὶ γῆς; ἔσται δ᾽ ὥσπερ ἦν; ἡμῖν δ᾽ ἀθλίοις. In all these cases there is elision of δέ at the bridge, after a disyllable. It is generally believed that elision of a polysyllable at the bridge removes any violation of the law.[17] Elided δέ at the bridge does occur occasionally but always, to my knowledge, follow-ing a monosyllable, itself a word-grouping that mitigates the violation (e.g. *Or.* 1035, 1654). I do not know a single example in the tragedians of the elision of δέ at the bridge preceded by a polysyllable as in these cases in the *Exagoge*. Nevertheless, I believe that there is an element of mitigation here. As Sobolevskij has observed with regard to the usage of comic anapests and Porson's Law, postpositive words like αὖ, γάρ, μέν, δέ, etc. are treated like enclitics.[18] This suggests then, rather than a pattern of ἄρχων/δ᾽ ἐστι γῆς, one of ἄρχων-δ᾽ ἐστι γῆς which would effectively remove the pause.[19] Verse 233 is harder to justify: δέσμιοι δ᾽ ὡς ἥρμοσαν. Although monosyllables in the ninth place are indeed a mitigating factor, this seems to be limited to cases where the monosyllable looks ahead to the following word(s) (cf., e.g., *Bacch.* 252, *IT* 501).[20] Here the ὡς clearly goes backward and does not mitigate the violation. The violations at 163 and 174 are quite unambiguous: γυναικὸς λήψεται, μήτρας μητέρων.

III. *Hiatus*: Once we have eliminated all the examples of crasis in the *Exagoge*, we are left with a few cases of hiatus: 158, τῇ πρόσθε νυκτὶ αἵματι; 235, ὤφθη τι ἡμῖν; 252, καὶ ἐπίρρυτος; 255, οὐδέπω ὥρακε. By the standards of fifth-century tragedy each and every one of these is strange. Classical tragedy uses hiatus only after interjections, 'interjectional' vocatives and interrogative τί (no example exists, to my knowledge, after indefinite τι). Wieneke held 252 corrupt, while Snell condemned them all except 235. Certainly 252 readily lends itself to emendation (καὶ περίρρυτος), while 158 is also easily emended.[21] Wieneke, holding only 158, 235 and 255 as hiatus, noticed that all the hiatuses preceded an aspirate and suggested that Ezekiel may not have sensed hiatus here if he pronounced the aspirate like the Hebrew 'consonants' ע and ה which are transliterated in the Septuagint by aspirates. This is quite dubious, for it not only assumes that Ezekiel knew Hebrew (which is by no means certain),[22] but that Hebrew was his first language – or at least an earlier and more familiar language to him than Greek. Further, it makes it hard to comprehend the many cases in Ezekiel where there *is* elision before an aspirate (e.g. 22, 24, 38, 124, 128, 131, 144). It is probably more reasonable to assume that we have another example of Ezekiel's deviance from classical standards and his usage of more comic or vulgar metrical phenomena. As Schmidt has argued, the hiatuses at 158, 235 and 255 can all be 'explained.'[23] That at 158 because of the unelidable short vowel,[24] that at 235 since it can be

paralleled in middle comedy, and that at 255 because the phenomenon of hiatus between two successive identical vowels is not
unusual.[25]

IV. *Short vowels before a mute and a liquid (or nasal)*: (a) within
a single word: The fifth-century tragedians overwhelmingly regard
the syllable as short, 6.5:1 for Aeschylus, 4.5:1 for Sophocles, and
4:1 for Euripides.[26] In contrast Ezekiel is about 1.5:1.[27] It is clear
that even in the fifth century there was a movement toward greater
flexibility and this tendency continued down into the Hellenistic
age.[28] Numerous such words in Ezekiel vary their quantities as need
dictates, e.g. μέχρις, τέκνον, Ἑβραῖος, etc.[29]

(b) Final short vowel 'lengthened' before initial mute + liquid.
The general consensus is that there are very few – and possibly none
at all – examples of this in the fifth-century trimeter.[30] It was, however, the practice of early writers of iambic verse and returned in
the Hellenistic period.[31] There are two examples in the *Exagoge*,
δαίσεσθε κρέα (160) and ἀπέστειλε κριτήν (51).[32]

(c) Syllabic augment 'lengthened' before mute + liquid. A practice
of the early Ionians, this was preserved, but infrequently, in the
fifth-century tragedians. Page counts ten examples, six of them in
Euripides.[33] It occurs in the Gyges papyrus, προέδραμεν, and in a
tragic fragment that Page dates to the fourth century.[34] Ezekiel has
two instances, συνεκλύσθη (241), προσέβλεπε (262).[35]

V. *Medial break*: This is a particularly difficult topic because
metricians differ seriously as to what constitutes a 'medial caesura.'
Thus, some scholars assert that there are barely a half-dozen medial
caesurae in the whole Euripidean corpus, while others believe that
some 2% of Euripides' trimeters show the phenomenon.[36] There
appear to be mid-line breaks in the *Exagoge* at 18, 97(?), 98, 105,
164(?), 184, 193.[37] This rate of occurrence would be in line with
that of all three tragedians, at least according to those who define
medial caesura less narrowly. Aeschylus' major use of medial caesura
appears to be in the *Persae* and *Supplices*. It is a revealing stylistic –
or metrical – feature that Ezekiel frequently follows his (penthe-
mimeral and hephthemimeral) caesurae with καί.

VI. *Elision of middle (passive)* -αι: Middle -αι is very rarely –
many scholars think never – elided in fifth-century tragedy.[38] Snell
counts four examples in the *Exagoge*: 38, 82, 128, 149. As he notes,

ἐξανίσταμ᾽ ἐξ could be prodelision rather than elision. As for 38, Snell is in error: ὑπισχνεῖθ᾽ should be ὑπισχνεῖτο, not ὑπισχνεῖται, as the natural flow of the passage suggests.[39] The remaining two are un-ambiguous: ἔσσεθ᾽ ὥσπερ (128), πείσετ᾽ οὐδέν (149). Once again, the usage is Hellenistic.[40] It is curious – and perhaps not without signifi-cance – that all the five Hellenistic examples I note are future forms.

VII. *Shortening of diphthong before vowel (within a word)*: There are two examples in the *Exagoge*: Χαναναῖαν (1), ἀποσκευή (209). The shortening of αι is not strange (cf. παλαιόν at Eur. *El.* 497, γεραιά at *Hipp.* 170 (lyric)).[41] Εὖ is very strange and not found, to my knowledge, in tragedy or even in comedy. Schmidt has termed the usage vulgar and noticed several examples, in Theocritus (24.71), Hipponax (31 D.), Herondas (9.2) and a few inscriptions.[42]

In his spirited and justified attempt to rescue Ezekiel from the quite undeserved vituperation that has often been launched against him, Snell seems to have gone a bit too far when he claims that Ezekiel's metrical deviations from the classical tragedians lie only in the areas of synaloephe and Porson's Law. His deviations go beyond this and can be seen, at the least, also in his tolerance of hiatus, his 'lengthening' of final short vowel before initial mute + liquid, his elision of middle –αι, and his correction of ευ.[43] On the other hand, if we can take our fragmentary remains of Hellenistic tragedy as representative, he is in his use of resolution completely un-Hellenistic and quite in keeping with fifth-century practice. Of further note is the fact that although Ezekiel tends in most ways to be closest to Euripides of the fifth-century dramatists, there are isolated areas where he is quite unlike Euripides and occasionally rather close to Aeschylus. Can we explain this rampant eclecticism? May we dare to think that Ezekiel might indeed be representative of second-century Alexandrian tragedians? No answer can be given. A tentative hypo-thesis may be offered. Ezekiel was, I think, consciously seeking to imitate the great fifth-century tragedians, most likely because he felt that his serious and ancient theme would be lent a sense of solemn dignity and antiquity by so doing. Many of the subtleties of fifth-century trimeter-metrics were undoubtedly learned and assimi-lated by those living in that period by acute auditory perception and habituation. If, as I suspect, Ezekiel obtained most, though not all, of his familiarity with fifth-century tragedy from reading, this might explain why he failed to pick up certain of the subtle habits and restrictions that were a part of that drama.[44] Resolution, broadly speaking, would not be such a phenomenon, but things like Porson's Law, the tolerance of hiatus, correption and lengthening of vowels, and the precise circumstances under which these kinds of features were and were not permitted might well have been too difficult to pick up without prolonged exposure to classical drama on stage.

NOTES

NOTES TO THE INTRODUCTION

1. The Exagoge

1 See C. Kraus Reggiani's concluding remarks at *Vichiana* 4 (1975) 21.
2 A. Nauck, *Tragicorum Graecorum Fragmenta* (Leipzig 1889[2]) p. xiv.
3 F. Schramm, *Tragicorum Graecorum hellenisticae, quae dicitur, aetatis fragmenta (praeter Ezechielem) eorumque de vita atque poesi testimonia collecta et illustrata* (Münster 1929).
4 Diss. Münster 1931.
5 Volume 1 (Göttingen 1971), no. 128.
6 C. G. Cobet in *Logios Hermes* 1 (1866–7) 457. Further excoriations can be found at G. Bernhardy, *Grundriss der griechischen Litteratur*, vol. 2, pt. 2 (Halle 1880[3]) 76; M. A. Halévy, *Moise dans l'histoire et dans la légende* (Paris 1927) 67–8; Wendland 197; in an anonymous piece at *BAGB* (SC) 5 (1933) 122; L. Herzfeld, *Geschichte des Volkes Jisrael* (Nordhausen 1857) vol. 2, 517; C. Siegfried in *JE* s.v. Hellenism, vol. 6, 339; I. G. Eichhorn, 'De Judaeorum Re Scenica Commentatio', in *Commentationes Soc. Reg. Sc. Gottingensis Recentiores* 2 (1811 = Göttingen 1813) 20; V. Tcherikover, *Eos* 48.3 (1956) 179–80; in an anonymous piece at *Jahrbücher für Philologie* 1831, 2, 450; *RE* (ed. Pauly) 3 (1844) s.v. Ezechiel (by C.F. Bähr) 365; A. Dieterich, *RE* 6, 1701; K. Kuiper, *Mnemosyne* n.s. 28 (1900) 238; G. Karpeles, *Geschichte der jüdischen Literatur*, vol. 1 (Berlin 1920[3]) 183; T. Gataker, *De Novi Instrumenti Stylo Dissertatio* (London 1648) 103; J. Freudenthal, *Hellenistische Studien: Alexander Polyhistor* (Breslau 1875) 39; B. A. Müller, *PhW* 54 (1934) 701. Criticisms like Dieterich's ('Dialogisierung der Geschichtserzählung') may miss the point. In adapting material which suited a narrative form like epic to the genre of tragedy, Ezekiel may be exemplifying a genuine and characteristic Hellenistic phenomenon at work, what W. Kroll has remarked and designated *Kreuzung der Gattungen* (*Studien zum Verständnis der römischen Literatur* (Stuttgart 1924) 202).
7 J. L. Klein, *Geschichte des Drama's*, vol. 2 (Leipzig 1865) 263.
8 G. A. Schumann, 'Vita Mosis', in *Commentationes Theologicae*, edd. E. F. C. Rosenmueller and F. J. V. D. Maurer (Leipzig 1827) vol. 2, 269.
9 B. Snell, *Szenen* 172.
10 B. Z. Wacholder, *EJ* 4.916 (s.v. 'Bible'); S. Sandmel, *The First Christian Century in Judaism and Christianity* (New York 1969) 20.
11 E.g. M. Hadas, *Hellenistic Culture: Fusion and Diffusion* (New York 1959) 131 and 100; H. Hegermann in *Literatur und Religion des Fruhjüdentum* (Würzburg 1973) 170; R. Petsch, *NJbWiss* 1 (1925) 907; A. Kappelmacher, *WS* 44 (1924–5) 81; I. Trencsényi-Waldapfel, *Acta Orientalia* 2 (1952) 150; C. Schneider, *Kulturgeschichte des Hellenismus*, vol. 1 (Munich 1967) 891–2.

12   *Glotta* 44 (1966) 25–32 (see also notes 5 and 9).
13   Oxford 1972, three volumes, see vol. 1, 707f, vol. 2, 987.
14   Vol. 2 (Jerusalem 1963) 9–69.
15   An exception is E. Starobinski-Safran, *MH* 31 (1974) 216–24.
16   Since I conclude below that Ezekiel wrote in Alexandria, I refer to him as Alexandrian throughout. See my discussion in Introduction, sect. 3.
17   See P. Venini, *Dioniso* n.s. 16 (1953) 10ff.
18   On some aspects of historical drama, see O. Ribbeck, *RhM* n.s. 30 (1875) 145–61; D. Bazzell, *Zur Geschichte des historischen Dramas im Altertum* (Zurich 1932), especially 13–24 on the Alexandrian period and 15–16 on Ezekiel (in general quite unilluminating). Norden, in discussing Naevius, observes that his use of idealized history instead of myth in epic and drama may well reflect the influence of contemporary Hellenistic poetry. He cites *inter alios* Ezekiel. See E. Norden, *Römische Literatur* (Leipzig 1923) 11 in A. Gercke and E. Norden, *Einleitung in die Altertumswissenschaft*, vol. 1, pt. 4.
19   See E. L. Hicks, *The Collection of Ancient Greek Inscriptions in the British Museum*, pt. 3 (Oxford 1890) no. 444, pp. 63–5 = *TrGF* 130 T 1.11.
20   I adhere to the general view that this play is from the Hellenistic period.
21   P. 291 of G. Bernhardy's edition (Leipzig 1828). It is not cited by Snell at *TrGF* 172.
22   Christ–Schmid–Stählin 2.1.336 (1920) seem to believe that Nicolaus is the author, but that his 'tragedies' may in reality be romances.
23   Sozomenus, *HE* 5.18.3–4.
24   See W. Fischel in L. Finkelstein (ed.), *The Jews* (1960³) vol. 2, 1166–7.

2. The date of the Exagoge

1   I see no reason to be skeptical about this, but cf. Fraser, vol. 2, 987.
2   In his Latin 'translation' of Eusebius' *PE* G. Trapuzentius wrote extravagantly (Venice 1497): Ezechielus est poeta. universam iudaeorum historiam carmine moreque tragico scripsit. One must also be a shade skeptical when K. Ziegler (*RE* 6A.2, 1972) imagines plays by Ezekiel on contemporary Jewish events from the Maccabean period.
3   For references to scholars who held this view see Philippson 12 and Magnin 199.
4   See Frankel 114, note d. There was a steady increase in the use of Hebrew names among Egyptian Jews from the Ptolemaic to the Roman period (see *CPJ* 1, p. 84). It is strange that L. Zunz, *Namen der Juden* (Leipzig 1837 = *Gesammelte Schriften*, vol. 2, (Berlin 1876) 1–82) does not seem to know Ezekiel as a name in the pre-Christian period. E. R. Goodenough, *By Light Light* (New Haven 1935) 7, n. 3 observes that except for Ezekiel 'every Hellenistic Jewish writer has a Greek name.' This is not true. Consider Artapanus. B. S. J. Isserlin, *JANES* 5 (1973) 193, says that the name Ἐζεκῆλος is one of the names found in *Aristeas* that cannot be matched in the Egyptian-Jewish papyri. This is not quite true. The name is found (with a variation of spelling) at *CPJ* 464, line 24: Ἀζακιελ. As for our poet Ezekiel, Polyhistor and Clemens spell it Ἐζεκιηλος. The prophet's name is spelled Ἰεζεκιηλ (undeclined) in the Septuagint and Ἰεζεκιηλος by Josephus (*AJ* 10.79) and Ἰεζεκιηλ by Eusebius (*PE* 10.503d).

5 F. Delitzsch, *Zur Geschichte der jüdischen Poësie* (Leipzig 1836) 209, n. 1.
6 P. Bayle, *Dictionnaire Historique et Critique*, vol. 2 (Basle 1741[6]) 400 found
   evidence that at least one person believed Ezekiel to be the prophet of the
   same name!
7 For references see Philippson 11 and Magnin 199.
8 P. 11.
9 193-201.
10 See G. Dindorf, *Eusebii Caesariensis Opera*, vol. 1 (Leipzig 1867) xix-xxiv.
   But the question remains: why does Josephus never mention Ezekiel, in particular at *Apion* 1.218 where he lists writers on Jewish matters? In the first
   place, as Frankel observes (114, n. c; cf. Kraus 172, n. 4), Josephus is not
   providing a complete review of literary history. Josephus himself disclaims
   this (1.216). Further, as Freudenthal 171 and 218 has pointed out, Josephus
   tends not to mention Jewish sources other than the Hebrew scriptures.
   Thus, he uses the Septuagint, *1 Macc.*, Philo, but never tells us so. Indeed,
   his only reference to Philo is as leader of the delegation to Caligula (*AJ*
   18.259) (see however the contrasting opinion of Hölscher, *RE* 9, 1964). At
   all events, *Apion* 1.161 suggests that Josephus is going to limit the rest of
   his discussion to Greek, i.e. non-Jewish writers and thus there is no reason
   to expect to find Ezekiel here. This does raise the problem of his inclusion
   of Eupolemus, Philo the elder and Theodotus. Did he not know they were
   Jewish? Did he feign that they were non-Jews (cf. how *Aristeas* pretends
   that the author is an objective non-Jew)? On this issue, see B. Z. Wacholder,
   Eupolemus 1ff and 52ff. Philippson (12f) has suggested that the *Exagoge*
   may have been lost, probably in the library at Alexandria, where Polyhistor
   managed to dig it up. At all events, that Josephus does not mention the
   Exagoge does not mean that he was not familiar with it. Indeed, I believe he
   was well acquainted with it.
11 *OCD*[2] s.v. 'Jewish Greek Literature,' p. 563.
12 See *FGrHist* 3.1, p. 249.
13 For references, see Philippson 10.
14 Bayle (above, n. 6) seems to consider this a real possibility. P. D. Huet,
   Demonstratio Evangelica (Paris 1690[3]) 60 simply notes that some have held
   the position.
15 M. Gaster, *The Samaritans* (London 1925) 143; A. F. Dähne, *Geschichtliche
   Darstellung der jüdisch-alexandrinischen Religions-Philosophie*, vol. 2 (Halle
   1834) 199f, n. 157 (possibly); implied by E. Norden, *Römische Literatur*
   (Leipzig 1923) 11.
16 Snell 171; Kuiper, *Mnemosyne* 274f; Fraser vol. 1, 707f; Wieneke 121.
17 A. Pelletier, *Lettre d'Aristée à Philocrate* (Paris 1962) 237; Denis, *Introduction* 276.
18 A. Lesky, *Hermes* 81 (1953) 3; K. Ziegler, *Der Kleine Pauly* s.v. Ezechiel,
   vol. 2, 486; Dalbert 55.
19 Philippson 11; M. Hengel, *Judentum und Hellenismus* (Tübingen 1973[2]) 200
   and 303, n. 383; M. Hadas, *Hellenistic Culture* (New York 1959) 100;
   Delitzsch (above, n. 5) 28; Gutmann, *EJ* 887; Schürer vol. 3[4], 498 and 502;
   Broyde, *JE* 5.320 s.v. Ezekielus; Christ-Schmid-Stählin 2.1.608; Girardi 15;
   Dieterich, *RE* 6.2, 1701; Ziegler (above, n. 2) 1969; Cancik, (*Artemis*) *Lexikon* 936; A. Lesky, *Geschichte der griechischen Literatur* (Bern 1963[2]) 797;

Kraus 164; Huet (above, n. 14), before Demetrius, who is between Philopator and Lathyrus; Frankel 114; Herzfeld 517; P. Katz, *Philo's Bible* (Cambridge 1950) 48.

20 E. Bickerman, *From Ezra to the Last of the Maccabees* (New York 1972) 80–1.

21 J. L. Klein, *Geschichte des Drama's*, vol. 2 (Leipzig 1865) 262; G. Karpeles, *Geschichte der jüdischen Literatur*, vol. 1 (Berlin 1920³) 183; M. Waxman, *A History of Jewish Literature*, vol. 1 (New York 1930) 100; F. Momigliano, *Nuova Rassegna* 1 (1893) 312.

22 Dindorf (above, n. 10) xxiv; F. Susemihl, *Geschichte der griechischen Litteratur in der Alexandrinerzeit*, vol. 2 (Leipzig 1892) 653.

23 M. Friedländer, *Geschichte der jüdischen Apologetik* (Zurich 1903) by inference from pages 130 and 186.

24 B. A. Müller, *PhW* 54 (1934) 704.

25 L. H. Feldman, *JSS* 22 (1960) 222; N. Walter, *Der Thoraausleger Aristobulos* (Berlin 1964) 42; R. H. Pfeiffer, *History of New Testament Times with an Introduction to the Apocrypha* (New York 1949) 211.

26 J. R. Harris, *The Homeric Centones and the Acts of Pilate* (London 1898) 8.

27 P. Riessler, *Altjüdisches Schrifttum ausserhalb der Bibel* (Augsburg 1928) 1289; J. Ziegler, *LTK* 3.1328 s.v. Ezechiel der Tragiker.

28 Trencsényi-Waldapfel 161f.

29 See below, n. 33.

30 For references, see Philippson 10.

31 M. S. Hurwitz, *EJ* 6.1103.

32 I. Vossius, *De Septuaginta Interpretibus eorumque Tralatione et Chronologia Dissertationes* (Hagae-Comitum 1661) 87.

33 *Apparatus Sacer* (Cologne 1608) vol. 1, p. 562 s.v. 'Ezchiel' (sic).

34 196. See too Philippson 12.

35 Fraser, vol. 1, 707f.

36 Cf. Kraus 169, n. 1.

37 Above, n. 14. See Freudenthal 15 and 38f.

38 For discussion of this question, see the next section.

39 There is some evidence at Clem. *Strom.* 1.21.141 that Demetrius wrote c. 220.

40 Hurwitz (above, n. 31) seems to be following this view.

41 Above, n. 24.

42 I discuss this passim. For concluding remarks on this matter, see Introduction, sect. 4. I assume that Ezekiel wrote in Alexandria which is not guaranteed but highly likely: see my discussion in the next section.

43 There is little question that such could have been incorporated had Ezekiel so desired, either by reference to the future destruction of pagans and paganism or by allusions to past history involving pagans, indeed even involving Javan and his descendants.

44 Though there could have been *Egyptian* anti-Semitism already, especially if the 'anti-Semitic' portions of Manetho are genuinely his. But there is no real indication of polemical rivalry between Jews and Egyptians in that period. On the other hand, there would seem to be present even in the Septuagint calculated Jewish attempts not to lose favor with the Ptolemies. Thus, it evidently avoided translating ארנבת ('hare') at *Lev.* 11.6 and *Deut.* 14.7 (list

of unclean animals) by the common noun λαγώς so as not to offend the Ptolemies who were descendants of Lagos (contrast Aquila who uses λαγωός in both places). See Bab. Tal. *Megilah* 9b; cf. Jer. Tal. *Megilah* 71d (1.10). It is, however, possible that several of the changes listed in the Talmudic passages are meant to counter anti-Semitic propaganda. Certainly the change at *Exod.* 4.6 is so meant. See my discussion in the Commentary, sect. 4.

45 To be sure, Egyptian Jewish literature does not in general give much attention to the Temple in Jerusalem. See J. J. Collins, *The Sibylline Oracles of Egyptian Judaism* (Missoula 1972) 44–53. Jerusalem itself, however, seems to have been a different matter. See J. A. Seeligman in *Judah and Jerusalem* (Jerusalem 1957) 192–208.

46 Cf. *Jubilees* 49.18ff.

47 Josephus regularly, but not invariably, uses 'Εβραῖοι for the Jews of the Biblical period. Thus, note 'Ιουδαῖοι at *AJ* 4.11, 6.26, 30. 'Ιουδαῖοι also at Philo *Moses* 1.34, 2.193.

48 On the term 'Ιουδαῖοι and its implications, see M. Lowe, *NT* 18 (1976) 101–30, especially 102–10.

49 Above, n. 20, p. 73. There are interesting remarks on the notion of 'dual loyalty' at Philo, *Flaccus* 46.

50 Josephus attests that the Greeks of Alexandria did not have any negative feelings to the Jews until the native Egyptians began to stir them up (e.g. *Apion* 1.223, 2.69).

51 A note of qualification should be introduced. The methodology utilized here, that is the attempt to date an author by his attitude toward the general cultural and political ambience of his time, inevitably makes the assumption that the writer can be seen as 'typical,' subject to 'normal' responses to his surroundings, etc. It can in no way take into account potential aberrations of character, personality, beliefs and attitudes. Thus, it must remain far from foolproof, even were we absolutely certain about the external cultural and political environment – and in this case even that certainty is lacking.

52 So recently S. West, *CQ* 68 (1974) 81. H. C. Kee, *SBL Seminar Papers 1976* (Missoula 1976) 190 differs: 'A date after the turn of the eras would be reasonable.' But A. Momigliano, *Alien Wisdom* (Cambridge 1975) 118 puts it in the second or first century B.C.

53 See the brief but valuable words of caution on drawing inferences from the phrase θεὸς ὑψιστος in *Fondation Hardt Entretiens*, vol. 18: *Pseudepigrapha I* (Geneva 1972) 314f.

54 See R. H. Charles, *The Book of Jubilees* (London 1902) 213.

55 R. van den Broek, *The Myth of the Phoenix* (Leiden 1971). See his summary at 393ff.

56 I have ignored the difficult questions of the extent of Hecataeus' treatment and the meaning of Hesiod's fragment. For both see Broek's discussions.

57 The closest seems to be Philo, *Mut. Nom.* 110ff.

58 See especially Jos. *AJ* 13.299f; *Test Levi* 8.15 with Charles' note *ad loc.*; Jer. Tal. *Sotah* 9.24b.

59 For the moment I pass over the questions of Hebraisms, Semiticisms, Septuagintalisms, which are, at all events, not relevant to the problem of dating. See Introduction, sect. 9.

3. The provenance of the Exagoge

1 The following have all expressed this view, in one degree or another: Wieneke 124; Gutmann, *EJ* 887; Broyde, *JE* 5.320; Feldman, *JSS* 22 (1960) 222; F. Delitzsch, *Zur Geschichte der jüdischen Poesie* (Leipzig 1836) 28; Snell 171; Kraus 164; G. Dindorf, *Eusebii Caesariensis Opera*, vol. 1, p. xxiv; P. M. Fraser, *Ptolemaic Alexandria* 707; B. Z. Wacholder, *Eupolemus* 286; M. Hengel, *Judentum und Hellenismus* (Tübingen 1973²) 200; M. Hadas, *Hellenistic Culture* (New York 1959) 100; Dalbert 55; F. Momigliano, *Nuova Rassegna* 1 (1893) 312; Frankel 114 and note d. But he qualifies 'Alexandrian' to mean 'non-Palestinian.' C. F. Bähr s.v. Ezechiel in Pauly's *RE* 3, 365 reports that Ezekiel lived in Alexandria at the court of the Ptolemies!

2 Above, n. 1.

3 One notes, for whatever his testimony may be worth, that Fulgentius, *Myth.* 1.15f seems to indicate a flourishing drama (including tragedy) in first-century Alexandria.

4 That Ezekiel evidently assumes that his audience will recognize the *Egyptian* etymology, Moses from $\mu\tilde{\omega}\upsilon$ = water, further supports an Egyptian location.

5 Somewhat similar arguments have been brought by Charles to support an Egyptian provenance for *2 Enoch*. See W. R. Morfill and R. H. Charles, *The Book of the Secrets of Enoch* (Oxford 1896) p. xvii.

6 See Commentary, sect. 2.

7 Gutman's statement that there is no foundation for the view that Ezekiel was Alexandrian is especially peculiar coming from one who had previously held that view (*EJ* 887).

8 The Alexandrians even described themselves as not living in Egypt: *Alexandria ad Aegyptum*.

9 See Fraser vol. 1, 115f, 214, 232.

10 *Mnemosyne* 278ff. M. Gaster, *The Samaritans* (London 1925) 143 also held this view. He wrote, 'Quippe seems to have proved quite satisfactorily that Ezekiel may have been a Samaritan.' Gaster's 'Quippe' must be a corruption of Kuiper.

11 See F. M. Cross Jr, *HTR* 59 (1966) 208–10; J. D. Purvis, *The Samaritan Pentateuch and the Origin of the Samaritan Sect* (Cambridge, Mass. 1968) 16ff. But cf. R. J. Coggins, *Samaritans and Jews: The Origins of Samaritanism Reconsidered* (Atlanta 1975) 152ff.

12 B. Z. Wacholder, *HUCA* 34 (1963) 87f has shown that pseudo-Eupolemus used both the Hebrew and Greek versions of the Bible.

13 But cf. Wacholder's article (above n. 12) on pseudo-Eupolemus, 83–113, especially the conclusions on 112f.

14 Magnin (201) put the production at Beithar. But this depended on his erroneous view that the play was from the second century A.D. Thus, Wacholder (above, n. 1) 285 is in error when he says that no one in the nineteenth century questioned that Ezekiel was a native of Alexandria. Momigliano (above, n. 1) 314 thought the play intended for production at the Passover celebration in Jerusalem. Hadas (above, n. 1) 100f thinks there is no compelling reason to deny the possibility of Palestinian authorship. Wacholder (above, n. 1) 286 believes the play Alexandrian but thinks Ezekiel's Hebrew name may suggest that he was born in Jerusalem.

15 On the other hand, Kuiper might have argued that the designation of the Jews throughout as Ἑβραῖοι, not Ἰουδαῖοι, might suggest a Samaritan author (cf. Jos. *AJ* 11.340, 344). I argue in the preceding chapter for a different reason. Ἰσραηλῖται might have also been a possibility (rare in the Septuagint, but common in Josephus, e.g. *AJ* 2.202, 204, 205, 215).

16 See J. Macdonald, *The Theology of the Samaritans* (Philadelphia 1964) 147ff.

17 See Cancik, *Artemis Lexikon* 936; Denis, *Introduction* 276; J. H. Charlesworth, *The Pseudepigrapha and Modern Research* (Missoula 1976) 110; T. H. Gaster, *The Interpreter's Dictionary of the Bible* (New York 1962) 4.196.

18 *The Book of the Samaritans* (Jerusalem 1970[2]) 153.

19 This is dubious. See my recent discussion at *GRBS* 22 (1981) 171-2.

20 H. Graetz, *MGWJ* 25 (1876) 340. In his *Geschichte der Juden*, vol. 3 (Leipzig 1905[3]) he seems to waver between certainty and doubt. At 355 he writes, 'der Dichter Ezekielos (Theodektes?)' and at 608 he refers to the 'Vermutung' that Ezekiel is 'wohl identisch mit ... Theodektes.' But at 355 he speaks of *Ezekiel* as being stricken and says that this was assumed to be his punishment.

21 *MGWJ* ibid; *Geschichte* 595.

22 See *CPJ* 1, p. 28.

23 P. de Lagarde, *Onomastica Sacra* (repr. Hildesheim 1966 of second edition 1887) 173.70, 192.87, 46.6.

24 The fact that he prayed to God and changed his plans would hardly make this more reasonable, especially if *Aristeas* is interested in condemning Ezekiel.

25 See *Fond. Hardt. Entretiens* vol. 18: *Pseudepigrapha I* (Geneva 1972) 243.

4. Ezekiel's audience, purpose and religious position

1 E.g. Philippson 14-16; Dalbert 55; O. Weinreich in *Genethliakon W. Schmid* (Stuttgart 1929) 337f; C. R. Holladay in *SBL Seminar Papers 1976* (Missoula 1976) 448; M. A. Halévy, *Moise dans l'histoire et dans la légende* (Paris 1927) 68; F. J. Biet, *Essai Historique et Critique sur l'école Juive d'Alexandrie* (Paris 1854) 163.

2 E.g. W. A. Meeks, *The Prophet-King* (Leiden 1967) 149; M. Hadas, *Hellenistic Culture* (New York 1959) 100; N. Walter, *NBGAW* 1 (1964) 373 and 376. Herzfeld (519) and Schürer vol. 3[4], 502 believe the play intended for a Jewish audience, but leave open the possibility of pagans as well. So too A. Dieterich, *RE* s.v. Ezechiel, 6.2, 1702. V. Tcherikover, *Eos* 48.3 (1956) 179f, in accord with his general view believes the *Exagoge* meant solely for Jews. So too the writer (G.H.A.E.) at *GGA* 1831, 615. M. Hengel, *Fondation Hardt Entretiens*, vol. 18: *Pseudepigrapha I* (Geneva 1972) 306 and *Juden, Griechen und Barbaren* (Stuttgart 1976) 138f holds that Hellenistic-Jewish literature in the main was meant for a Jewish audience, not a pagan one. See too his comments and those of M. Smith on pp. 325f of the *Fond. Hardt* volume.

3 E.g. Kuiper, *Mnemosyne* 280; Kraus 173; Kappelmacher 84; Gutman 69; Trencsényi-Waldapfel 163; Christ-Schmid-Stählin 2.1 608 and n. 2;

J. Geffcken, *NJb* 29 (1912) 602; R. H. Pfeiffer, *History of New Testament Times with an Introduction to the Apocrypha* (New York 1949) 211f; R. Marcus in L. Finkelstein (ed.), *The Jews: Their History, Culture and Religion* (New York 1960³) vol. 2, 1100.

4   See e.g., K. Ziegler s.v. Tragoedia in *RE* 6A.2, 1981. Also, Kuiper, Geffcken, Dalbert, Holladay and Philippson cited above in notes 1 and 3. When Tcherikover (above, n. 2) 179 claims that the *Exagoge* has 'nothing in common with apologetics' he is demonstrably wrong. Nor do I think that Greeks in the audience would have been particularly offended either by Moses' slaying of the Egyptian (by which Ezekiel may have sought to associate Moses with Greek hero-types like Oedipus), or by the plagues inflicted upon the Egyptians (see Introduction, sect. 3).

5   See, e.g. Kuiper, Geffcken and Gutmann (*EJ* 887).

6   Philippson (14), for instance, simply concludes that the play makes changes and additions which amount to profanation of Scripture and consequently could not have been meant for Jews.

7   I have argued at *GRBS* 22 (1981) 167–75 that the *Exagoge* was probably intended for production in a theatre.

8   Ziegler (above, n. 4) 1979f.

9   J. Fürst, *Geschichte der biblischen Literatur und des jüdisch-hellenistischen Schriftthums*, vol. 1 (Leipzig 1867) 349 describes the *Exagoge* 'welche fast ganz der hebräischen Erzählung ... folgt.' D. L. Tiede, *The Charismatic Figure as Miracle Worker* (Missoula 1972) 171 speaks of Ezekiel's 'usual scrupulous attendance to the Biblical text.' In contrast, Kraus (173) observes that it diverges from and profanes the Bible, and J. M. Reese, *Hellenistic Influence on the Book of Wisdom and its Consequences* (Rome 1970) 22 says that Ezekiel 'took great liberties with the Biblical text for dramatic effect.' P. M. Fraser's view, *Ptolemaic Alexandria* vol. 1, 708, is a puzzle. He points to Ezekiel's divergences from the Bible, yet remarks that Ezekiel reveals his own faith in the scriptural narrative by his scrupulosity in the use of it.

10 See M. H. Schroyer, *JBL* 55 (1936) 261–84.

11 See J. M. Allegro, *Discoveries in the Judean Desert of Jordan*, vol. 5 (Oxford 1968) 1–6.

12 B. Z. Wacholder, *HTR* 61 (1968) 457, n. 19 thinks it is a post-Maccabean phenomenon. It is unfortunate that S. Z. Leiman, *The Canonization of Hebrew Scripture: The Talmudic and Midrashic Evidence* (Hamden, Conn. 1976) in his lengthy discussions of the notions of canonicity and inspiration never raises the question of the authority of the narrative sections of the Pentateuch. I do not quite know what to do with Josephus here. On the one hand, he tells us more than once (*AJ* 1.17, 2.347) that he is only reporting the Scriptures, adding or subtracting nothing, which seems to suggest at least awareness of the concept of the authority of Biblical narrative (cf. too *Ap.* 1.37ff). Yet he proceeds to add, subtract, and occasionally change, with some freedom.

13 L. H. Feldman, *JSS* 22 (1960) 226.

14 The *Exagoge* lacks the extreme and narrow religiosity of *Joseph and Asenath*, but we are unable to say where the author of that work would have stood within the religious-social context of his Jewish community.

15 Mishnah *Avodah Zarah* 3.4.
16 Above n. 13, p. 227.
17 But there is equally no solid evidence to support Snell's sweeping evaluation (185): 'Zweifellos war Ezechiel trotz dieser leichten Hellenisierungen ein frommer und gläubiger Jude.'

5. Traditional exegesis in the Exagoge

1 For discussions of Midrash, see, e.g., R. Bloch in *Dictionnaire de la Bible*, sup. vol. 5 (1950) 1263–81; G. Vermes in *The Cambridge History of the Bible*, vol. 1 (Cambridge 1970) 199–231; L. Zunz, *Die gottesdienstlichen Vorträge der Juden historisch entwickelt* (Hebrew ed. revised by H. Albeck, Jerusalem 1974) 163–75.
2 It is possible that Ezekiel's introduction of Chum, the Phoenix and Moses' dream also have roots in the Aggada, but there is no available evidence for this.
3 A few scholars have occasionally noted possible Midrashic parallels, most notably Frankel, Trencsényi-Waldapfel (158–60) and Gutman. The latter rashly concludes that all non-Biblical material in the play was taken by Ezekiel from traditions that circulated among the Jews (66). We should not forget the cautionary remarks (made in a different context) of P. Walters and D. W. Gooding, *The Text of the Septuagint* (Cambridge 1973) 302, n. 13 on the potential for excesses in resorting to 'tradition' in order to explain an inexplicable text or version. But it is incredible that I. Heinemann should have asserted that Ezekiel is influenced neither by the Hellenistic Moses-Romance nor by Rabbinic exegesis (*RE* s.v. Moses, 16.1, 365). This view no doubt accounts for the fact that, as far as I can tell, Heinemann never mentions Ezekiel in his book *Darkhei Haaggadah* (Jerusalem 1970[3]).
4 See R. Gordis, *JBL* 49 (1930) 417–22. For an elaborate attempt to prove the existence of Midrashic exegesis already in Biblical times, see J. Weingreen, *From Bible to Mishna: The Continuity of Tradition* (Manchester 1976).
5 *Hellenism in Jewish Palestine* (New York 1950) 50.
6 Above, n. 1, p. 1278. Cf. too Heinemann, *Darkhei* (above, n. 3) 169ff. The two studies of L. Prijs, *Jüdische Tradition in der Septuaginta* and *Beiträge zur Frage der jüdischen Tradition in der Septuaginta* (both Leiden 1948) are examples of this view carried to an extreme.
7 I avoid getting entangled in the question as to whether there was a translation of some or all of the Pentateuch into Greek even before the Septuagint, as seems attested at *Aristeas* 30 and 314 and Clemens, *Strom.* 1.22.150 (from Aristobulus). Kahle and Bickerman have been major warriors in this scholarly struggle. A. Momigliano's verdict is, 'A pre-Septuagint translation of some sections of the Torah is not altogether incredible' (*Alien Wisdom: The Limits of Hellenization* (Cambridge 1975) 84). If there was such, it might somewhat increase the probability of the development of Alexandrian Jewish Biblical exegesis before the Septuagint. For a brief but valuable discussion of the whole question of the Biblical text, including treatment of the Septuagint and the evidence from Qumran, see S. Talmon in *The Cambridge History of the Bible*, vol. 1 (Cambridge 1970) 159–99.
8 *Studies in Jewish and Christian History*, vol. 1 (Leiden 1976) 143f.

9   *Vorstudien zu der Septuaginta* (Leipzig 1841), *Ueber den Einfluss der palästinischen Exegese auf die alexandrinische Hermeneutik* (Leipzig 1851). Cf. R. Marcus in *Louis Ginzberg Jubilee Volume* (New York 1945) 243.
10 See *JTS* 25 (1974) 1–11; and his essay in J. Schreiner (ed.), *Wort, Lied und Gottesspruch* (Würzburg 1972) 39–48.
11 *Relics of Ancient Exegesis* (Cambridge 1976).
12 P. 107.
13 Heinemann, *Darkhei* (above, n. 3) treats in some detail the question of the relation of Alexandrian to Palestinian Midrash. Some conclusions at 182ff.
14 *The Samaritans* (London 1925) 112–23.
15 See, e.g., S. Jellicoe, *The Septuagint and Modern Study* (Oxford 1968) 56; B.S.J. Isserlin, *JANES* 5 (1973) 191–7; B. Z. Wacholder, *Eupolemus* 276.
16 Freudenthal 65ff.
17 *RE* 9, 1959ff (s.v. Josephus).
18 B. Z. Wacholder, *HTR* 61 (1968) 454 believes that Demetrius is probably a representative of an exegetical and chronographical school. Cf. the remarks of W. Bousset and H. Gressmann, *Die Religion des Judentum im späthellenistischen Zeitalter* (repr. Tübingen 1966) 21.
19 P. 115.
20 See S. Belkin, *Philo and the Oral Law* (Cambridge, Mass. 1940); H. Wolfson, *Philo* (Cambridge, Mass. 1947) vol. 1, 90ff; also E. Stein, *Philo und der Midrasch* (*BZAW* v. 57, 1931); P. Borgen, *Bread from Heaven* (*Novum Testamentum* sup. 10, 1965, passim). But see E. R. Goodenough, *JBL* 59 (1940) 413–19; 67 (1948) 100ff. Recently, R. G. Hamerton-Kelly on Philo's techniques of Midrashic exegesis in *Jews, Greeks and Christians: Essays in Honor of W. D. Davies* (Leiden 1976) 45–56.
21 M. Gaster, *The Asatir* (London 1927) 83 thinks there may have existed 'Greek paraphrastic commentaries' on the Bible.
22 See, e.g., Philo, *Somn.* 2.127, *Apol.* 7.12f, *Moses* 2.215f, *Spec. Leg.* 2.62, *Opif.* 128; *Acts* 13.14ff, *Mark* 1.21.
23 Indeed, K. Kohler (*JE* s.v. *Wisdom* p. 539) has suggested that approximately the last eleven chapters of *Wisdom* (9.18–19.22) appear to be 'part of a Passover Haggadah recited in Egypt [and it] abounds in genuine haggadic passages of an ancient character.' Cf. E. Stein, *MGWJ* 78 (1934) 558–75.
24 *JBL* 67 (1948) 100ff.
25 *JBL* 68 (1949) 115–23.
26 On the legal side we may note that a Passover law was found in the Elephantine archives that (if the reconstruction of the text is correct) had not been known previously before the Mishna, more than half a millennium later. See B. Porten, *Archives from Elephantine* (Berkeley 1968) 133, 313.
27 See B. Z. Wacholder, *HUCA* 34 (1963) 109.
28 M. R. James, *The Biblical Antiquities of Philo*, with Prolegomenon by L. H. Feldman (New York 1971) p. LXVIII.
29 *Scripture and Tradition in Judaism* (Leiden 1961), especially chapters 4 and 5 (pp. 67–126).
30 P. 95.

6. The Exagoge and fifth-century tragedy

1 See, e.g., Kuiper, *Mnemosyne* 264, *RSA* 8 (1904) 75–9; Christ–Schmid–Stählin 2.1.608; Kappelmacher 75, with n. 2; O. Weinreich, *Genethliakon W. Schmid* (Stuttgart 1929) 338. Girardi's view that Ezekiel was completely dependent on the Hellenistic theatre and did not know Euripides at all is extreme (46). As Lesky well observes of Ezekiel (*DLZ* 53 (1932) 2219), the poet 'in der Beherrschung euripideischer Diktion eine gewisse Virtuosität erreicht hat.'

2 *RPh* 59 (1939) 102.

3 171f. See too *Glotta* 32.

4 176ff. This of course had been noted by many before him.

5 *Ptolemaic Alexandria*, vol. 1, 707f. Cf. N. Walter, *NBGAW* 1 (1964) 373. Of course, it is hard to know to what extent Euripides' style was typical of fifth-century tragic style. See P. T. Stevens, *CR* 79 (1965) 270.

6 See my article on Ezekiel and the *Oedipus Coloneus* at *GRBS* 22 (1981) 175–8. Ezekiel was also familiar with Homer, but I am not sure there is reason to believe that Ezekiel's mind was 'saturated with Homeric language and ideas,' as J. R. Harris writes (*The Homeric Centones and the Acts of Pilate* (London 1898) 9).

7 I bring here a number of parallels and possible examples of Aeschylean influence on the *Exagoge* not presented in Commentary, sect. 7. First, a number of parallels between the *Exagoge* and *Persae* (first references to Ezekiel, second to Aeschylus): ἐκπρεπεστάτα (264/184); ἄμωμος (177/185); πυργόω (11/192); στολή (165/192); παρθένος in a strange use (173/613; cf. 249f/613). Compare the line structure of 192 to *Pers.* 350. At verse 207 the syllabic augment is omitted in δίδουν. This ('Homeric') omission is a phenomenon of messenger speeches in tragedy. It occurs most frequently in *Persae* (see Page *ad Medea* 1141). Aside from parallels to the *Persae* we note the following: If τόθεν at 246 is temporal (as Wieneke believes; I am dubious), this is a usage found at *Agam.* 220, but not in Sophocles or Euripides. πικραίνω (141) may occur at *Eum.* 693, but does not occur in Sophocles or Euripides. ἐκλάμπω (99, 246) is found in a fragment from the *Memnon* which speaks of Ethiopia, the Nile and Egypt, all themes of the first act of the *Exagoge* (frg. 300 = Mette 193). Ezekiel affects βασιλεύς without the article, an Aeschylean habit. πλίνθευμα (9) occurs only once elsewhere, in a fragment which Nauck and Mette think may be by Aeschylus (adesp. 269 = Mette 664a). Both Aeschylus and Ezekiel describe an unusual bird at length (frg. 304 = Mette 609a). The three-word trimeter (260) is an Aeschylean characteristic. Change of time and locale is most familiar from the *Eumenides*. Multiple shifts of scene, as in the *Exagoge*, were present in the *Aitnae*.

8 πέφρικα plus a participle meaning 'see' may be one (*Exag.* 126, *Suppl.* 346). There are some possible parallels in the use of caesura; see Wieneke 116.

9 See *Exag.* 60ff. Cf. *PV* 851 and see F. M. Snowden, *Blacks in Antiquity: Ethiopians in the Greco-Roman Experience* (Cambridge, Mass. 1970) 157. Note that Apollodorus (*Bib.* 2.1.5) says that Danaus had seven daughters by an Ethiopian woman.

10 The Greeks in Alexandria considered themselves a sort of 'pocket' Greece and did not even think of themselves as living in Egypt: *Alexandria ad Aegyptum*.

11 E.g. Manetho *apud* Jos. *Ap.* 1.229.
12 See Hecataeus of Abdera *apud* Diod. Sic. 40.3.2. Cf. Manetho *apud* Jos. *Ap.* 1.98ff, 231.
13 *PE* 9.432a (so Artapanus).
14 To try to discuss the influence of Hellenistic tragedy on Ezekiel and his position within that genre would be an exercise in futility, given the nature and quantity of the extant remains.
15 So V. Tcherikover, *Hellenistic Civilization and the Jews* (repr. New York 1970) 387.
16 See especially M. Philonenko, *Joseph et Aséneth* (Leiden 1968) 43-8; also, S. West, *CQ* 68 (1974) 70-81.
17 See H. St John Thackeray, *JTS* 13 (1911) 46-66. The date is uncertain but Thackeray would place it in the first half of the first century B.C. Two poetic sections of the Pentateuch are described by Josephus as being in hexameter verse (*AJ* 2.346; 4.303). Presumably this is merely Josephus speaking in terms understandable to his pagan audience and calculated to appeal to them. But might it also reflect his acquaintance with sections of the Bible that were translated or adapted in Greek verse?
18 Unfortunately, there is no evidence that Ezekiel had Jewish predecessors writing plays on Jewish subjects, in both Greek and Hebrew, as H. M. Kallen, *The Book of Job as a Greek Tragedy* (repr. New York 1959) 23 asserts. Might Ezekiel's assumption of an available audience suggest that there were such predecessors (in Greek)?
19 The tragedies were being edited at the Alexandrian Library. Even in Jerusalem there was (in Herod's day) a library filled with many of the old pagan Greek classics. See B. Z. Wacholder, *Studies in Bibliography and Booklore* 5 (1961) 102-9.
20 Note, e.g., 3.97-113 and consider the reference to Homer at 3.419ff. J. J. Collins, *HTR* 73 (1980) 91-104 has now argued that Theodotus was a Jew.
21 So J. Reider, *The Book of Wisdom* (New York 1957) 26.
22 T. Middendorp, *Die Stellung Jesu ben Siras zwischen Judentum und Hellenismus* (Leiden 1973) 7-34.
23 See M. Hengel, *Judentum und Hellenismus* (Tübingen 1973²) 165f; B. Z. Wacholder, *Eupolemus* 255.
24 H. St John Thackeray's view (*Josephus: The Man and the Historian* (New York 1929) 100-24) that such influence is the result of Josephus' use of well-read assistants does not seem generally persuasive, especially in light of Josephus' own declaration at *AJ* 20.263 that he worked hard to gain knowledge of Greek learning and poetry.
25 *The Third and Fourth Books of Maccabees* (New York 1953) 100f and notes *ad* 12.8 (p. 207) and 13.11 (p. 211); also 96f on the influence of *Bacchae* on 2 *Maccabees*.
26 *Hellenistic Culture* (New York 1959) 130. I wonder whether the Greek *Esther*'s epilogue on the feast of Purim was influenced by the Euripidean technique of etiological epilogues.
27 For a brief discussion of the *Nachleben* of Aeschylus, with particular focus on the Church Fathers, see I. Opelt, *JbAC* 5 (1962) 191-5.
28 It is unfortunate that we cannot tell to what period Quintilian refers when he speaks of later poets at Athens producing *correctae fabulae* of Aeschylus'

plays (10.1.66). Cf. too schol. Aristoph. *Acharn*. 10c on the special treatment accorded to the revivals of Aeschylean tragedy.

29 See E. Turner, *AC* 32 (1963) 120–8.

30 See A. D. Trendall and T. B. L. Webster, *Illustrations of Greek Drama* (London 1971) 41–62.

31 R. A. Pack, *The Greek and Latin Literary Texts from Greco-Roman Egypt* (Ann Arbor 1965²) nos. 31, 35, 39.

32 See D. L. Page, *A New Chapter in the History of Greek Tragedy* (Cambridge 1951) 41, n. 14; 43, n. 22; 44, n. 25.

33 It contains the very rare word ἀθελκτος which does not occur in Sophocles or Euripides but is found at *Suppl.* 1055. See D. L. Page, *Greek Literary Papyri* (London 1942) 172ff, verse 28.

34 O. Ribbeck, *Die römische Tragödie im Zeitalter der Republik* (Leipzig 1875) 686f. Also, W. M. Calder III, *GRBS* 11 (1970) 173–4 argues that Accius' *Philoctetes* was influenced by Aeschylus' *Philoctetes*.

35 See L. Herrmann, *Le Théâtre de Sénèque* (Paris 1924) 305–12.

36 *Repub.* 3.391E. See I. Heinemann, *Philons griechische und jüdische Bildung* (repr. Hildesheim 1973) 339, n. 4.

37 Philo quotes a number of times from Euripides, usually not by name. He quotes Sophocles at *Probus* 19.

38 *PE* 13.667d; Clemens, *Strom.* 5.14.113 = 1025 N^2 = 1126 Pear. The passage at *Strom.* 5.14.113 is misunderstood by Wacholder, *EJ* s.v. Hecataeus of Abdera, 8.237.

39 I relegate to a footnote the view that *Job* was influenced by Aeschylus' (?) *Prometheus Bound*. For references to scholars who have held this view, see Hengel (above, n. 23) 199, with n. 8.

7. The dramatic structure of the Exagoge

1 On the whole question of 'act-division' in fifth-century tragedy, especially Aeschylus, see now O. Taplin, *The Stagecraft of Aeschylus* (Oxford 1977) 49ff and passim (henceforth = Taplin).

2 A. Dieterich s.v. Ezechiel, *RE* 6.2, 1701, claimed six, but did not give details. It is not clear to me why R. J. Tarrant (*HSCP* 82 (1978) 220) refuses to accept a five-act structure for the play.

3 This appears to be Kuiper's view too, though he does not argue it *expressis verbis*. A. Lesky also follows it (*DLZ* 53 (1932) 2220).

4 I argue below that there is no good reason to follow Kappelmacher in placing the Chum-scene after the dream.

5 E.g. Kuiper, *Mnemosyne* 266–70. It is interesting that Kuiper's hypothetical opponent (269) puts forth better arguments than Kuiper himself.

6 For the rapid-fire movement from virtually distinct action to action, one may think of Euripides' *Phoenissae*.

7 Five distinct locations: G. M. Sifakis, *Studies in the History of Hellenistic Drama* (London 1967) 123; Snell 172ff; Trencsényi-Waldapfel 154f; Wieneke (passim); O. Zwierlein, *Die Rezitationsdramen Senecas* (Meisenheim am Glan 1966) 140. Four locations: Gutman, *Beginnings* 147ff. Four or three locations: Lesky (above, n. 3). Three locations: K. Ziegler, s.v. Tragoedia in *RE* 6A.2, 1980; Kappelmacher 81f. One location: Kuiper, *Mnemosyne* 266ff; Gutmann, *EJ* 885; and amazingly Christ–Schmid–Stählin 2.1.608 (1920⁶).

8   C. Kraus Reggiani, *Vichiana* 4 (1975) 16 and 18.
9   On lapses of time in fifth-century tragedy, see Taplin 290–4, 377–9.
10   See the good remarks of P. Venini, *Dioniso* n.s. 16 (1953) 7.
11   It is possible that Euripides' *Stheneboia* is closer to the *Exagoge*. D. L. Page,
     Greek Literary Papyri (London 1942) 127 posits two long time-intervals
     during the course of the play. This is disputed by B. Zühlke, *Philologus* 105
     (1961) 1–15, 198–225, but T. B. L. Webster, *The Tragedies of Euripides*
     (London 1967) 80–4 has returned to the earlier view. It is conceivable that
     Ezekiel got the idea from one of the connected trilogies of the fifth century
     in which time lapsed and location changed between plays. On the other
     hand, Aristotle's remarks at *Poetics* 1456a15ff seem to attest the existence
     of tragedies extending over a long period of time with discrete segments. Cf.
     too 1449b12ff.
12   On 'unity of place' in fifth-century tragedy, see Taplin 103ff, 377f.
13   *POxy* 2257, frg. 1. See T. B. L. Webster, *Greek Theatre Production* (London
     1970[2]) 15f. Recently, Taplin 416–18.
14   Sifakis (above, n. 7) 135.
15   E.g. Herzfeld 517, presumably F. Susemihl, *Geschichte der griechischen Lit-
     teratur in der Alexandrinerzeit*, vol. 2 (Leipzig 1892) 654.
16   Lesky (above, n. 3) 2219f. The argument was already made by Philippson
     16, n. 1. Cf. Kraus 169f.
17   See Wieneke 30.
18   See Kappelmacher 83.
19   See Barrett, *ad Hipp.* 58–71 and 1102–50; J. Diggle, *Euripides: Phaethon*
     (Cambridge 1970) 144, 149; A. F. Garvie, *Aeschylus' Supplices* (Cambridge
     1969) 191ff; A. Pickard-Cambridge, *The Dramatic Festivals of Athens*
     (Oxford 1968[2]) 236f; Taplin 236f; Wilamowitz, *Heracles* 1[2] (1895) 116,
     n. 13. The examples in Seneca (?) seem closer to what Ezekiel may have
     done: see *Agamemnon, Octavia, HO*. See too J. Carrière, *Le Choeur Secon-
     daire dans le Drame Grec* (Paris 1977).
20   Sifakis (above, n. 7) 113ff. See now the additional evidence from *POxy*
     2746.
21   Sifakis 117.
22   See H. D. Jocelyn, *The Tragedies of Ennius* (Cambridge 1967) 18–20, 30f.
23   This was suggested by G. Delling, *HUCA* 45 (1974) 160.
24   See too M. Hadas, *The Third and Fourth Books of Maccabees* (New York
     1953) *ad* 8.29 for a possible underlying conception of a chorus here too.
25   See Pickard-Cambridge (above, n. 19) 239 and n. 2.
26   Some believe all seven, e.g. Trencsényi-Waldapfel 146, Gutman 12f; others
     six (not including Sepphorah), e.g. Sifakis (above, n. 7) 122f.
27   Sifakis seems to suggest that the chorus of Raguel's daughters is present
     throughout the play but the illogic would have been alleviated by their
     being in the orchestra while the actors were on the raised stage. I am not
     certain that this is what he means, as his treatment is unclear (see pp. 124,
     135).
28   A. Lesky, *Hermes* 81 (1953) 9 believes they would have been fillers between
     acts. So too O. P. Taplin, *LCM* 1 (1976) 48.
29   See Lesky (above, n. 3) 2219f; Kappelmacher 83.
30   See, e.g., Ziegler (above, n. 7) 1980; Kappelmacher 76, n. 4; Gutman 12.
     For a valuable discussion of the 'law of five acts,' see W. Beare, *The Roman*

Stage (London 1964³) 196–218, also 340–6. Some of his conclusions are debatable.

31 With rare scholarly exception, e.g. K. Anliker on the *Phaedra*: *Prologe und Akteneinteilung in Senecas Tragödien* (Bern 1959).
32 Thus, the comparison between the *Exagoge* and Menandrean New Comedy made by Taplin (above, n. 28) 49 is much weaker than it initially seems.
33 See Snell 173. For a useful and cautious discussion of the value of deictic pronouns in establishing the presence of a character on the stage, see Taplin 149–51.
34 How Ezekiel handled three days of darkness is hard to tell. He may simply have had a character on stage say that this particular plague has lasted three days.
35 See, e.g., Ziegler (above, n. 7) 1980; Gutman 12.

8. Ezekiel's influence

1 C. G. Cobet, *Logios Hermes* 1 (1866–7) 457 thinks Clemens copied from Polyhistor but offers no argument or evidence. The same holds true for H. B. Swete, *An Introduction to the Old Testament in Greek* (Cambridge 1902) 369, Snell 170, and N. Walter in *Studia Patristica* 7 (1966 = *TU* 92) 315.
2 See Freudenthal 12; Schürer vol. 3⁴, 469; J. R. Harris, *The Homeric Centones and the Acts of Pilate* (London 1898) 8, n. 1. On the problem of Clemens' continuous text of verses 1–31 and 32ff, see Commentary, sect. 1.
3 That survival of an ancient text or author often hangs by so slight a thread is really no surprise. The discovery of the Gyges-papyrus brought to light a play about whose existence we had previously known absolutely nothing.
4 Exactly how and where the Hebrew translation of Moses' dream (see Commentary, sect. 3) fits in is impossible to say. Jellinek gives us no indication whatsoever as to its date. We need not even assume it is the work of a Jew. Further, whoever the translator was, he may have been using Eusebius.
5 See Introduction, sect. 2.
6 I am in disagreement with B. Z. Wacholder, *HTR* 61 (1968) 479, n. 115, 'It is clear that Josephus made no use of his Greco-Jewish predecessors, including Philo of Alexandria, whom he mentioned once.' G. Hölscher, *RE* 9, 1963f s.v. 'Josephus' is also very dubious about Josephus' use of the Greco-Jewish writers. He cites possible examples of the influence of these authors on Josephus, which he then rejects. But he does not bring even a single example from the *Exagoge*, citing only from Demetrius, Artapanus, Theodotus, Eupolemus and Philo!
7 Philo, *Moses* 1.179 has the same polemical comment which I take to be his similar response to the *Exagoge*. The language of Philo and Josephus here is sufficiently different to keep us from thinking of Philonic influence on Josephus.
8 See Commentary, sect. 4.
9 But this seems widespread. Cf. Philo, *Moses* 1.8; *Jubilees* 46; *Jerahmeel* 42; *LAB* 9.
10 See Jacoby, *FGrHist* 273 F 102 and vol. 3.1, p. 269, who believes the quote from Cleodemus-Malchus taken from Polyhistor's *On the Jews*, though he

notes the possibility of its coming from the *Libyca*. Wacholder, *Eupolemus* 54f and Walter (above, n. 1) 316 opt for the *Libyca*.

11   Whether *Apion* 1.216 and 218 reflect use of Polyhistor is hard to tell. There is certainly some commonality of names present.

12   M. Freyhan, *Jahrb. f. jüd. Gesch. u. Lit.* 31 (1938) 56; Wieneke 78 (*ad* 113).

13   Cf., e.g., 135 and *Wis.* 19.10, where σκνῖπα and πλῆθος βατράχων are mentioned hard upon each other. A κλύζω compound of the drowning of the Egyptians at *Exag.* 241 and *Wis.* 10.19. At *Wis.* 16.16 the Egyptians are ἀσεβεῖς, while Ezekiel refers to ὕβρω ἀνθρώπων κακῶν, both in the context of the plagues.

14   In *Genethliakon W. Schmid* (Stuttgart 1929) 340f.

15   J. L. Klein, *Geschichte des Drama's*, vol. 2 (Leipzig 1865) 263.

16   See Commentary, sect. 8.

17   R. van den Broek, *The Myth of the Phoenix* (Leiden 1971) 41 thinks some connection is possible.

18   Snell himself writes on page 170 that the *Exagoge* seems to have had no influence on any poet.

9. Ezekiel's knowledge of Hebrew and the Hebrew Bible

1   J. R. Harris, *The Homeric Centones and the Acts of Pilate* (London 1898) 8, n. 2 makes the additional suggestion that the phrasing of *Exag.* 134 is influenced by the Septuagint of *Gen.* 1.10. This was also noticed by Girardi (55).

2   For the language of verse 6 Philippson sees the influence of *Exod.* 1.13. *Exod.* 6.6 may be more likely.

3   There are, to be sure, some examples where Ezekiel's phraseology matches that of one of the non-Septuagint translations but these are relatively few. Thus, e.g., at 52 Ezekiel writes κτενεῖς, where the Septuagint has ἀνελεῖν but Aquila and Symmachus use ἀποκτείνω; at 140 Ezekiel has λοιμός, as do Aquila and Symmachus, while the Septuagint uses θάνατος; at 232 Ezekiel has τροχοί and Aquila τροχόν, but the Septuagint ἄξονας. All these can readily be explained as alterations of the Septuagintal text by Ezekiel.

4   For a recent statistical study of syntactical criteria of Greek texts translated from Hebrew or Aramaic, with masses of data, see R. A. Martin, *Syntactical Evidence of Semitic Sources in Greek Documents* (Missoula 1974).

5   E. Bickerman, *Studies in Jewish and Christian History*, vol. 1 (Leiden 1976) 143f does argue that in the main the Greek Bible used by the Hellenistic Jewish writers was substantially the same as our Septuagint.

6   F. Momigliano, *La Nuova Rassegna* 1 (1893) 312 suggested that Ezekiel may have used the Hebrew rather than the Greek Bible but offered no argument or evidence.

7   E.g. Gutman 32, Snell 185.

8   See my discussion in the Commentary, sect. 1.

9   One's instinctive reaction – is it really possible that an educated and committed Alexandrian Jew with a deep interest in the Bible did not know Hebrew? – should be resisted. Even Marcus' simple statement, 'there is no reason why an Alexandrian Jew should not have known Hebrew in addition to Greek' (in L. Finkelstein (ed.), *The Jews: Their History, Culture and Religion* (New York 1960³) 1081) may be a bit optimistic. Philo, after all,

is generally believed not to have known Hebrew; see recently D. Rokeah, *JTS* 19 (1968) 70–82. And, as Feldman has well noted (*JSS* 22 (1960) 217f), the evidence of the papyri suggests that between 300 B.C. and A.D. 400 Alexandrian Jews knew neither Hebrew nor Aramaic. The extent of the knowledge of Hebrew in the Hellenistic-Roman period even among Palestinian Jews is a debated issue. See, e.g., J. N. Sevenster, *Do You Know Greek?* (Leiden 1968) 33ff and 61ff. It is generally held, for example, that Josephus often used the Septuagint rather than the Hebrew Bible. See the discussion by H. W. Attridge, *The Interpretation of Biblical History in the Antiquitates Judaicae of Flavius Josephus* (Missoula 1976) 30ff. On the use of Hebrew in the last days of the second temple see too Y. M. Grintz, *Chapters in the History of the Second Temple Times* (Jerusalem 1969) who argues (against the common opinion) that Hebrew was the main living language in Judaea during that period.

10 But one could never tell from Josephus' Greek style that he knew Aramaic or Hebrew, though we must remember that his Greek may owe much to his assistants. A. Thumb, *Die griechische Sprache im Zeitalter des Hellenismus* (Strassburg 1901) 125f, thought that only one Hebraism was present in Josephus, προστίθεσθαι + infinitive. Thackeray (*JTS* 30 (1928–9) 361ff) argues that it is not a Hebraism. On Josephus' knowledge of Greek and related problems, see Sevenster (above n. 9) 65ff, especially 75, n. 2.

11 G. A. Deissmann's classic studies initiated the rejection of the 'Jewish Greek' view. See especially his *Bibelstudien* (Marburg 1895), *Neue Bibelstudien* (Marburg 1897), and his article 'Hellenistisches Griechisch' in the *REfProt. Theol. u. Kirche* 7, pp. 627–39. Further support for this view in the important book by Thumb (above, n. 10), especially pp. 120–32. For general discussions of the subject see, e.g., H. St John Thackeray, *A Grammar of the Old Testament in Greek According to the Septuagint*, vol. 1 (Cambridge 1909) 25–55 and J. Vergote s.v. 'Grec Biblique' in *Dictionnaire de la Bible: Supplément*, vol. 3 (Paris 1938) 1320ff. The foremost authorities disagree on the question. Thus, E. Norden, *Die Antike Kunstprosa* (repr. Darmstadt 1958⁵), vol. 2, Nachträge p. 3, *ad* p. 484 accepts the existence of a Jewish Greek while Bickerman (above, n. 5) 176 rejects it. One notes a distant ancestor of Deissmann's views in the monograph of S. Pfochenius, *Diatribe de Linguae Graecae Novi Testamenti Puritate* (Frankfurt 1689) who tries to argue that the so-called Hebraisms of the New Testament are in fact good Greek. This received well-deserved attack by T. Gataker, *De Novi Instrumenti Stylo Dissertatio* (London 1648; the illogic of the dates of publication is to be explained by accessibility of editions to me).

12 One thinks of another Hellenistic-Jewish Biblical work, *Joseph and Asenath* which contains numerous 'semiticisms' that are, as M. Philonenko, *Joseph et Aséneth* (Leiden 1968) 27–32, has argued, merely reflections of the author's familiarity with the Septuagint.

13 See the attack on Deissmann and Moulton by R. R. Ottley, *A Handbook to the Septuagint* (London 1920) 159–74.

14 *Ptolemaic Alexandria*, vol. 1, 708.

15 *Mnemosyne* 265.

16 *Szenen* 172; *Glotta* 32 with n. 2.

17 A standard discussion and list (if not quite complete) of semiticisms (or

rather suggested semiticisms) in Greek can be found at J. H. Moulton and
W. F. Howard, *A Grammar of New Testament Greek*, vol. 2 (repr. Edinburgh
1960), appendix pp. 411–85. See too the index of Blass–Debrunner (1976[14]),
p. 435 s.v. *Semitismen* and P. Walters and D. W. Gooding, *The Text of the
Septuagint* (Cambridge 1973) 141–96.

18 Wieneke's *index verborum* p. 128 gives twenty examples in the fragments.
Note especially the nominatives at 76, 86, 118, 210 and the somewhat gratuitous oblique cases at 49, 93, 110, 150, 202, 231, 244, 258.

19 To be sure, ellipse of εἶναι as copula is common enough in good Greek, but
Ezekiel's examples go beyond the general types of sentences in which such
ellipse takes place. See, e.g., KG 1.40–2.

20 The Book of *Wisdom* is replete with such sentences. A glance at, e.g., chapter 3, verses 11–15 is revealing.

21 See Blass–Debrunner sect. 468.

22 Gesenius–Kautzsch sect. 111g–h. On the problem in Ezekiel see Strugnell
455f.

23 On οὐρανοί = םימש, see P. Katz, *Philo's Bible* (Cambridge 1950) 6 and 141–6.

24 Ezekiel's transliteration of Hebrew names seems to give us no indication
whether he knew Hebrew or not. In general he follows the Septuagint.
Metrical need determines his prosody and also whether he declines names
that are usually not declined (cf. 105, 116). His choice of Μωσῆς (rather
than the Septuagint's Μωυσῆς) was probably determined by the metre. At
any rate, it seems to have been an accepted spelling of the name Moses at his
time. So too Eupolemus.

25 Pp. 116f. I detail my dissatisfaction with Wieneke's argument in the Appendix.

26 *DLZ* 53 (1932) 2219.

27 A sentiment expressed also by F. Momigliano (above, n. 6) 313.

28 See Denniston, *Particles* 377.

29 See, e.g., Denniston, *Particles* 369, n. 1; KG 2.100; Schwyzer–Debrunner
1.2, p. 406.

30 See Blass–Debrunner sect. 468.

31 Further discussion of this passage in Commentary, sect. 7.

32 See Denniston, *Particles* 385 and KG 2.269f. Translators of the *Exagoge* act
as if οἱ μέν . . . οἱ μέν simply = οἱ μέν . . . οἱ δέ. But this seems hard to believe.

33 *Glotta* 32, n. 2.

34 *Glotta* 30, n. 2.

35 See KG 2.227f and 1.587f. On article for relative in the tragedians see too
Dodds *ad Bacchae* 712.

36 For peculiar uses of the dative one cannot refrain from mentioning Nonnus.
See R. Keydell, *Nonni Panopolitani Dionysiaca* (Berlin 1959) 58* ff.

37 For some examples see E. Mayser, *Grammatik der griechischen Papyri aus
der Ptolemäerzeit* 2.3 (Berlin 1934) 160ff. There is a peculiar use of τε καί
. . . τε . . . καί (cf. *Exag.* 165) at *Acts* 26.20, though it is not an exact parallel.

38 See *CPJ* 1, p. 130 and L. Radermacher, *Neutestamentliche Grammatik*
(Tübingen 1925[2]) 5. Cf. Mayser (above, n. 37) 156.

39 See, e.g., KG 2.244f; cf., e.g., Hdt. 7.1. One cannot ignore here the innumer-
able problems raised by Nonnus' use of τε.

40 The latter, it seems to me, may be the replacement of relative οὖ by article τοῦ, rather than τοῦ = τίνος as Wieneke argues.

41 Girardi gives a long list, worth consulting even if marred by some errors and misrepresentations, of the many syntactical, grammatical and lexical solecisms and peculiarities he detects in the *Exagoge* (48ff). But he does not conclude from this that Greek was not Ezekiel's native tongue nor even that Ezekiel knew Hebrew. To him this is rather evidence that Ezekiel is a semi-barbarous poet whose Greek was corrupted by his Jewish education and familiarity with the Septuagint (p. 19, n. 2 and p. 48). Some of the fiercest attacks against Ezekiel's Greek have been made by C. G. Cobet, in *Logios Hermes* 1 (1866–7) 457–9. But it is a simple truth that unidiomatic style, clumsiness and solecisms very often characterize the language of a native speaker while on the other hand a particularly talented writer may write a fluent, idiomatic and correct style in a second or third language. Conrad, one supposes, is the best example of this.

42 But he is occasionally capable of effective changes in tone and style. Thus, God's speech at 96ff is clearly written in an elevated style. See A. Lesky, *Hermes* 81 (1953) 4.

NOTES TO THE COMMENTARY

1. The prologue

1 All the internal evidence points to this speech being the play's prologue. There is no external evidence with the exception of the comments of Polyhistor discussed below.

2 The *Bacchae* too (including the opening ode) seems fairly close, possessing some common technical elements like geographical movement as well as the story line of a child's birth involving secrecy and plotting. But here too there is little to make us tie it closely to the *Exagoge*. The same may be said of the many similarities to the *Phoenissae*.

3 Stoessl's assumption (*RE* s.v. Prologos, 23.2, 2368) that the Gyges-papyrus represents a portion of a prologue-speech seems overly optimistic. The fact that the extant readable verses are from the second column of the papyrus is not conclusive evidence, but does make it less likely that they come from a prologue. Further, it is easier to account for them within the body of the play than at the beginning. At all events, when Stoessl remarks (and Gutman, 12, agrees) the unmistakable stylistic similarity to the opening of the *Exagoge* one is entitled to ask for some particulars, since – to this reader at least – there seems to be virtually no similarity.

4 See W. J. Verdenius, *Mnemosyne* (ser. 3) 13 (1947) 274f; (ser. 4) 8 (1955) 17; 27 (1974) 173f.

5 Consequently, it may be relevant to observe that δή is commonly used following temporal relative adverbs. See J. D. Denniston, *Greek Particles* (Oxford 1953²) 219–20.

6 See L. Duebner, *NJb* (1921) 373–5; also D. A. Campbell, *Greek Lyric Poetry* (London 1967) 140–1.

7 Though see Broadhead's discussion *ad loc.* But Campbell (*loc. cit.*) has noted speeches in Xenophon and Herodotus opening with δέ.

8   Some explain this away by considering the *Life* an addendum to the *AJ*. But, strictly speaking, ἐμοὶ δέ scarcely seems a suitable join.

9   But some scholars argue that the actual opening is lost.

10 That the non-Jews in the audience would not thus be able to define precisely who Jacob was seems immaterial. The context would make it clear that he is an ancestor of the Jewish people and that is sufficient.

11 Demetrius in *PE* 425d. The *Assumption of Moses* begins by dating the year of Moses' testament from two events, the creation of the world and the departure from Phoenicia (presumably a reference to the descent to Egypt), a 400-year period.

12 I do not mean to imply that the Seder liturgy and Haggadah were already in the second century B.C. fixed in a form nearly identical to that we know today, as some believe. But I do think that S. Stein's skepticism in this matter is much exaggerated (*JJS* 8 (1957) 15).

13 Clemens, *Strom.* 1.23.155–6. To the possible objection that Clemens and Polyhistor are writing for very different audiences and the latter may think it necessary to fill in his audience on this background material, we must respond that sufficient background would already have been provided in his excerpts from Demetrius and Artapanus.

14 Gutman writes as if there were no doubt (30, n. 2 and 34).

15 So too B. A. Müller, *PhW* 54 (1934) 702.

16 For a discussion of this matter and its implications, see Introduction, sect. 2. For the non-Jews in the audience 'Canaan' would have probably been a strange-sounding name for some unknown country. Ezekiel avoids mentioning Palestine by a familiar name.

17 How Snell justifies maintaining the manuscripts' reading κακούμενον at 5 he does not say. δέ (1) makes it virtually certain that a main verb could not have appeared in a verse before line 1. See my further discussion in the Introduction, sect. 9. Dübner's κακούμεθα is easy and provides good sense.

18 Whether Manetho himself held the anti-Semitic views attributed to him by later sources is immaterial for our purposes.

19 T. Reinach, *Flavius Josèphe: Contre Apion* (Paris 1930) 45, n. 1. Some disagree. See J. G. Gager, *Moses in Greco-Roman Paganism* (Nashville 1972) 115, n. 5 with references, though p. 122 (top) does not seem quite consonant with his argument at 115. Cf. the interesting association of Joseph and Serapis at Bab. Tal. *Avodah Zarah* 43a.

20 Freudenthal (156–7) has detected recollections of the Hyksos in Artapanus' versions of Jewish history. A. von Gutschmid's view (*ZDMG* 15 (1861) 5–6) that such are also evident in *Jubilees* 46 seems very doubtful.

21 Cf. Jos. *AJ* 2.232; Philo, *Moses* 1.13, 19–20. As for Moses' significant dream at 68ff, this has nothing to do with him and the *Egyptian* kingship. See my discussion below.

22 In the Passover Haggadic Midrash on the history of the Jews in Egypt Joseph is again conspicuously absent. Finkelstein has argued the same motivation there as I have here for Ezekiel (*HTR* 36 (1943) 26–7).

23 On the text of 12–13 see *AJP* 98 (1977) 415–16.

24 The use of λανθάνειν here and at Jos. *AJ* 2.218 may reflect the influence of Ezekiel. For a discussion of the general question, see Introduction, sect. 8.

25 I have not bothered, here and elsewhere, to specify 'pseudo-' of a work when it was irrelevant for my purposes.

26 In Philo's account the absence of the ark, the change of the Septuagint's
παρὰ τὸν ποταμόν to παρὰ τὰς ὄχθας τοῦ ποταμοῦ and the phrase ἐν τῷ
δασυτάτῳ τῶν ἑλῶν may all again reflect Ezekiel's influence (*Moses* 1.10,
14).

27 Wieneke notes the possible influence of the 'exposure' motif in Greek drama,
wherein the baby is decorated or supplied with tokens to facilitate the
hoped-for later identification. I do not see how, dramatically, this notion
could have served any role in the play (unless to suggest that Jochebed did
hope to get the baby back). Further, κόσμος is not usually the term used for
the recognition-tokens (σύμβολον is), though cf. Men. *Epit.* 28.

28 Again Philo's account is closer to the *Exagoge* than to *Exodus*. He writes
μικρὸν ἄποθεν (*Moses* 1.12). One of the finest instances of the defense of
Jochebed is at *Jubilees* 47.4 where she comes every night to nurse the infant.

29 See Midrash Hagadol *ad Exodus* 2.5; Targum Jon. *ad loc.*; Pirqe deRabbi
Eliezer ch. 48; Bab. Tal. *Sotah* 12b.

30 See G. Vermes in *The Cambridge History of the Bible*, vol. 1 edd. P. R.
Ackroyd and C. F. Evans (Cambridge 1970) 231.

31 This is a neat but simple expansion of the Biblical text, but is chiefly of
interest because Philo may again be following Ezekiel here: προσδραμοῦσαν
(*Moses* 1.16).

32 However, the same elaboration is present at *Sotah* 12b, based on an etymo-
logical play in the Hebrew text of the Bible. Thus, it is conceivable that
Ezekiel's amplification here is borrowed from Palestinian exegesis.

33 *Mnemosyne* 244.

34 Girardi's view (32, followed by Kraus 165–6, n. 4) that τούτοις μεθ' ἕτερα
should be taken as independent of the following and with reference to
Polyhistor, with ἐπιλέγει καὶ περί etc. being a quote from Polyhistor, should
not be rejected out of hand. Kuiper's objection (*RSA* 63–5, n. 1) that τούτοις
should not lack an explicit verb to govern the dative seems justified, but we
should probably read: Eusebius: τούτοις μεθ' ἕτερα ἐπιλέγει; Polyhistor: καὶ
περὶ τούτων ὁ Ἐζεκιῆλος etc. Kuiper himself notes this possibility, but
rejects it on the grounds of the absent name or pronoun. This is not a cogent
objection. The verb ἐπιλέγει is used frequently in these contexts by Eusebius
(410b, 417d, 444a, 457c), but hardly ever by Polyhistor (453a, where however there are textual problems). The type of phrase τούτοις μεθ' ἕτερα
(ἐπιλέγει) is also more characteristic of Eusebius than Polyhistor (e.g. 410b,
421b, 442a, 444a, 445d, 446d, 455c, 457c; Polyhistor at 421d). If this view
is correct, then Clemens' quotation of these verses with no break between
31 and 32 is not necessarily erroneous. If I am right in arguing (see Introduction, sect. 8) that Clemens cited Ezekiel through Polyhistor, then his juxtaposition of verses 31 and 32 would be probably no more than a reasonable
guess on his part.

35 Philo (*Moses* 1.19) has the princess feign pregnancy and then claim that
Moses is her natural son.

36 See Gutman 31. On the whole subject see the discussion in Wacholder,
Eupolemus 71–96.

37 Syncellus (p. 227) states that Moses was trained in all Egyptian education.
A. M. Denis, *Fragmenta* (100) prints this as being from *Jubilees*, but I see no
reason to think this so.

38   μηδένα rather than οὐδένα at 44 is strange. Wieneke's explanation is based
     on the occasional use of μή with οἶδα and ἐπίσταμαι (see KG 2.203), but
     Ezekiel's text has neither of these (rather ἰδών). The relevant construc-
     tion can I think be found at Blass–Debrunner (1976[14]) sect. 430 and L.
     Radermacher, *Neutestamentliche Grammatik* (Tübingen 1925[2]) 210ff. Cf.
     R. Keydell, *Nonni Panopolitani Dionysiaca* (Berlin 1959) vol. 1, p. 79*.
     Although Kuiper's objection (*Mnemosyne* 245) to lines 46–7 seems over-
     exact, Wieneke's explanation cannot be accepted for it would probably re-
     quire a finite verb, not the infinitive. The use of ὥστε + infinitive to indicate
     purpose is not unusual in the Septuagint and New Testament.

39   Editors consistently follow Stephanus in reading ἐν χειρῶν νόμῳ although
     the manuscripts read ἐν χειρῶν νομαῖς. But in fact *Syll.*[3] 700.29 has the
     exact phrase (see Snell's ap. crit.) and *3 Macc.* 1.5 has ἐν χειρονομίαις, suf-
     ficient support for the manuscript tradition here.

40   But at times readers of Ezekiel carelessly take for granted his dedication to
     the Biblical text. Thus, Dalbert (61) speaks of 'dem mishandelten Hebräer'
     and Gutman (32) of the Jew who is struck by his oppressor. But this is
     exactly what Ezekiel does not say.

41   So, at least, it looks on the surface, but it is possible that his tale at *PE* 434a
     of Chanethothes' attempted murder of Moses and subsequent death at the
     latter's hand may be Artapanus' strange adaptation of this episode. This is
     what J. Bergmann, *Jüdische Apologetik im neutestamentlichen Zeitalter*
     (Berlin 1908) 154 seems to think.

42   Midrash Hagadol *ad. Exod.* 2.11; *Divre Hayamim shel Mosheh Rabbenu* in
     A. Jellinek, *Bet ha-Midrasch* (repr. Jerusalem 1967[3]) vol. 2.4; Philo, *Moses*
     1.44.

43   I assume, of course, that our text is fundamentally sound. If indeed some-
     thing is faulty, e.g. a form of τύπτω driven out by Αἰγύπτιον or a lacuna of
     some two lines, then all problems might vanish. I do not believe that the dif-
     ficulty can be completely eliminated by assuming ἐρρυσάμην emphatic
     enough to convey to the reader that the Jew was victim and the Egyptian
     oppressor. Contrast the clear and explicit indication of victim and perse-
     cutor at line 50. Perhaps Ezekiel is portraying Moses here after the model of
     the Greek hero who impetuously rises up to kill, for instance Oedipus (for
     other contacts between Sophocles' Oedipus and Ezekiel's Moses, see my
     recent article at *GRBS* 22 (1981) 175–8).

44   Gifford, vol. 3, pt. 1, 468; Gutman 32; Dalbert 61. So too Dübner (2) 'duos
     viros, maxime quidem nostrae gentis' and Magnin (202), 'tous deux de ma
     nation.'

45   αὐτοὺς συγγενεῖς means that the two are kin to each other and need not
     imply anything as to their connection with Moses.

46   Remarkable support for this hypothesis is present in Kappelmacher's account
     of this scene, for he assumes that the two combatants are Egyptians (70, 76).

47   Josephus too ignores the event (and its antecedents). *Acts* 7, with very dif-
     ferent purpose, chooses this event as an instance of the rebelliousness and
     misbehavior of the Jews (especially verses 25ff and 35).

48   For an account of Midrashic traditions surrounding Moses' birth, see R.
     Bloch in H. Cazelles, *Moïse: L'Homme de l'Alliance* (Paris 1955) 102ff.

49   *Mekhilta deRashbi* (ed. Epstein) p. 6; Targum Jon. *ad Exod.* 2.2; Midrash
     Hagadol *ad Exod.* 2.2.

50 Bab. Tal. *Sotah* 12a. Possibly also in *Mekhilta deRashbi*, ch. 15 (see Epstein p. 100, ap. crit.).

51 See *LAB* 9.15; *Jerahmeel* 44.5; Targ. Jon. *ad Exod.* 2.5. There is a hint of divine impulsion in Philo's account (*Moses* 1.14).

52 Ezekiel had ample precedent in Euripidean tragedy for a character's narrating amazing events surrounding his (or her) birth and infancy. See, e.g., *Helen* 16ff; *Her.* 1263ff.

53 E.g. Gutman (32) and Wieneke (27, n. 1).

54 Throughout I leave aside the possibility, as noted by Frankel, 116, n. g., that Ezekiel's Septuagint text read 70 here. Cf. too Girardi 19; also *BAGB* (SC) 5 (1933) 122–3.

55 *Sepher Hayashar* (pp. 218f) lists 72 descendants of Jacob, then gives the sum as 70 without explicitly saying who has been excluded.

56 One manuscript does read 75 but this is clearly an alteration to make the text consistent with *Gen.* 46 and *Exod.* 1. Philo's discussion of this passage at *Migr. Abr.* 199ff confirms the reading 70.

57 Note that at 176 Ezekiel appears to choose a Deuteronomic version over that of *Exodus*. To be sure, the 'descent' terminology does not guarantee dependence. By the time of the N.T. at least, καταβαίνω is used simply of departure from Jerusalem and sometimes of departure from Palestine. It is also possible that by the time of the N.T. Jacob's move to Egypt was simply known as his 'descent,' since *Acts* 7.14–15 follows the Septuagint in giving 75, yet uses κατέβη. Cf. Philo, *Sacr. Cain.* 48.

58 Cf. Siphre *Deuteronomy* 301 *ad Deut.* 26.5. Again, we cannot be sure that Ezekiel's Passover rite included this text.

59 We should remember that Amram's role is often heightened in post-Biblical versions (e.g. Jos. *AJ*, *LAB*, *Jubilees*).

60 It would be no more sensible to argue that Ezekiel's ὥσπερ τὸν ἐχθὲς ἄνδρα (53) proves no knowledge of the Hebrew text on the grounds that the ἐχθές of the Septuagint is an addition to the Hebrew text. This would be an inconclusive argument since the fact that this *is* the next day (*Exod.* 2.13) makes the addition of 'yesterday' of no significance. (Indeed, *Jubilees* 47.12 also adds it.) At all events, Ezekiel's use of the Septuagint is not at issue.

61 Although Wieneke's emendation is absurd, the text does look in need of improvement. παρ' ἄκρα ποταμοῦ, one imagines, means 'at the river's edge.' But there is no evidence it can mean this. Of emendations offered Stephanus' παρ' ὄχθην would probably be the best, if we could endure the second foot dactyl. Philo writes παρὰ τὰς ὄχθας (*Moses* 1.10).

62 *PhW* 54 (1934) 702–3.

2. Sepphora: meeting and marriage

1 Wieneke notes the remarkable similarity of verse 60 to Soph. frg. 377.1 N^2 = 411.1 Radt. The latter verse is from the *Mysoi*. I observe the coincidence (?) that that play may run along the following lines. Telephus arrives in Mysia as an exile, he defeats a threatening enemy and is rewarded by being given the king's (adopted) daughter.

2 For a recent discussion of 'Ethiopia' in ancient Greek sources see J. W. Gardner, *G & R* 24 (1977) 185–93. I see no reason to seek a precise geo-

198 Notes to pages 86-87

graphical definition here since Ezekiel probably was not concerned with one. 'Libya' may mean no more than Africa; cf. Hdt. 4.42. Consider too that Herodotus has Ethiopians living 'at the extremity of Libya' (3.115).

3   *Mnemosyne* 277.

4   Girardi 16 made essentially the same point. See too his discussion of the whole question, 17–18. Cf. Kuiper (*RSA* 87ff).

5   As for the Jews, one calls to mind, for example, the many geographical errors found in the books of *Judith* and *Tobit* (cf., e.g., *Judith* 2.21ff).

6   See, e.g., Targum Jon. *ad loc.*; Siphre *Numbers* 99 *ad Numbers* 12.1.

7   See, e.g., Targum Jerus. *ad loc.*

8   *AJ* 2.238ff; *Jerahmeel* 45–6. It is not clear whether Artapanus knew some such version too (cf. *PE* 432c ff). On the Moses–Ethiopia romance, with particular attention to Josephus and Artapanus, see T. Rajak in *JJS* 29 (1978) 111–22.

9   Whether Ezekiel also introduced the element of kinship between Moses and Sepphora is impossible to know, but Polyhistor's vague λέγει δὲ περὶ τούτων καὶ Ἐξεκιῆλος (439d) leaves this possibility open. One could readily construct a scene in which Chum protests that Moses is an alien and a foreigner, especially if Ezekiel followed the Bible in having Raguel's daughters refer to Moses as an ἄνθρωπος Αἰγύπτιος (2.19). Thereupon, Moses (or Raguel or Sepphora) could respond that in fact he is kin to Sepphora in a line of descent from Abraham.

10 For some useful comments on this, see E. Ullendorff, *Ethiopia and the Bible* (London 1968) 5ff. One wonders whether the semiticization of Ethiopia through the Arab conquest may have already begun in Ezekiel's time and so rendered it all the easier to place Midian in Ethiopia.

There exist in classical mythology myths (and personages) which are variously set in Ethiopia and the Near East, e.g. Andromeda (cf. Strabo 1.2.35, Apollod. *Bib.* 2.4.3) and Memnon (cf. Paus. 10.31.7, Philostr. *Imag.* 2.7.2). Perhaps the association of Ethiopians and Arabs (and Indians) is indicated at Lucan 9.517–18. On Ethiopians and Indians see J. Y. Nadeau, *CQ* 64 (1970) 339–49.

11 *AJ* 1.239–41. See Gutman 36–7.

12 Josephus also reports that the children of Abraham and Keturah took possession of Troglodytis (*AJ* 1.239), which Thackeray (*ad loc.*) places on the Arabian shore of the Red Sea. But the term Troglodyte (or Trogodyte) is also used of inhabitants of Ethiopia.

13 Cf. Jos. *AJ* 8.165; *Acts* 8.27.

14 See Ptolemy 6.27.7. Artapanus and Philo both have Moses flee to Raguel in Arabia (*PE* 434a; *Moses* 1.47). Cf. Jos. *AJ* 2.257.

15 See Jos. *Ap.* 1.246.

16 See A. Caquot in *Mélanges Marcel Cohen* (The Hague 1970) 219–23.

17 With regard to connections between Raguel-Midian and Ethiopians note that in *Jerahmeel* (46.9) Raguel imprisons Moses in order to please the Cushites. In addition, one of Raguel's other names in Midrashic texts is פוטיאל. Perhaps this name is related to – or at any rate was believed related to – פוט, the name of one of Ham's sons and brother of Cush, a name used, it appears, to designate Libya. One notes the juxtaposition of פוט and כוש in the Bible, e.g. *Jer.* 46.9; *Ezek.* 30.5. The name seems to have been in use in Egyptian also. As a

final point of interest, I call attention to the strange connection made by Tacitus (*Hist.* 5.2) between Jews and Africa. On connections between Jews and Ethiopians in ancient texts, see J. H. Levy, *Studies in Jewish Hellenism* (Jerusalem 1969) 204–8.

18   Wacholder, *EJ* 5.1491 (cf. *Eupolemus* 243; *HTR* 61 (1968) 455, n. 9) asserts that Ezekiel here and elsewhere was influenced by Demetrius. There does not seem to be any evidence for this.

19   Perhaps Ezekiel elaborated the confrontation between Moses and the shepherds and gave Moses a fairly long speech in which he rebuked them. So Philo, who was, as I argue, often influenced by the *Exagoge*.

20   It was long common to give both verses (66–7) to Chum, punctuating after ξένῳ. Thus, for example, Stephanus' edition of the *PE*, Viger's translation *apud* Gaisford's edition of the *PE*, Herzfeld (518), W. N. Stearns, *Fragments from Graeco-Jewish Writers* (Chicago 1908) 111. But this ignores Polyhistor's opening remarks. Further, the introduction here of a direct quote seems unlikely. Philippson (44) says that Morel (whose edition of 1590 I have been unable to obtain) was the first to divide the verses between the two characters. The edition of the *Exagoge* in the *Poetae Graeci Veteres* (Geneva 1614) vol. 1, 1017–22 divides the verses between the two (1018).

21   For a detailed discussion of this scene, with particular emphasis on the identity of Chum, see my article in *Hebrew University Studies in Literature* 9 (1981) 139–46.

22   See my discussion in the Introduction, sect. 7.

23   For further discussion of the relationship of the Danaid trilogy to the *Exagoge*, see Introduction, sect. 6.

24   E.g. *Mekhilta Jethro* 1 p. 190; *Mekhilta deRashbi* p. 128; Targ. Neofiti, Onqelos and probably Targ. Jon. *ad Exod.* 2.16.

25   Trencsényi-Waldapfel (148) also adopts Kappelmacher's view.

26   *Pirqe R. Eliezer* 40.

27   Lesky (*DLZ* 2219–20) rejects Kappelmacher's transposition with some useful remarks. His defense of ξένε at 83 by ξένῳ at 67 may not, however, be as strong as it *prima facie* seems since it is not clear whether the marriage has yet taken place or merely betrothal has. At all events, there is a difference here since Moses is not the addressee as at 83, but rather a removed third person. Regardless, I agree with Lesky that ξένε (83) has no significance for the order of the scenes.

3. Moses' dream

1   For a recent overview of the different possible sources of influence here, see E. Starobinski-Safran, *MH* 31 (1974) 216–24. For a detailed discussion of the dream's relation to mystical and apocalyptic texts, see my article at *ICS* 6 (1981) 272–93.

2   It seems never to have been noticed by students of Ezekiel that there exists a (medieval?) Hebrew translation of this scene, both the dream and Raguel's interpretation. It is printed at Jellinek 5.159–60. It is unfortunate that Jellinek gives us no information as to where he has found the text nor as to its date (see pp. xxxix–xl). With perhaps one exception there do not appear to be significant or illuminating differences between this translation and our

Greek text. Most of the variations can be easily attributed to the translator's occasional tendency to elaborate the original or to his accommodation of the text to Hebrew idiom.

At 68 the manuscripts read κατ' ἄκρας ἵνου θρόνον, which (aside from its lack of meaning) does not fill out a complete verse. Editors since Dübner (p. viii) have supplemented in such a way as to give a reference to Sinai. Snell follows Dübner in reading κατ' ἄκρα Συ⟨αι⟩ου, though Wieneke has observed that there is no evidence for Σῡ- and himself reads Συαϊκοῦ. Our (medieval?) translation of this passage makes no mention of Sinai, but rather has 'on top of a high mountain.' One hesitates to make emendations on this basis. But since the text is corrupt, one can readily imagine an original κατ' ἄκρον αἰπεινοῦ θρόνον.

3   For pertinent observations on the phenomena of dream-vision encounters with a god, see West *ad* Hesiod, *Theogony* 22–34.

4   Ezekiel's emphasis on the great size of the throne (and evidently of the man) is probably significant, but one should recall that in antiquity figures and objects in dreams are frequently described as large. See A. S. Pease, *M. Tulli Ciceronis De Divinatione* (repr. Darmstadt 1963) 165. In Nebukhadnezzar's dream at *Daniel* 4.10ff, a tree reaches to the sky.

5   Perhaps a somewhat closer parallel, in general, than the ones Gutman brings is at *Petirat Mosheh* (Jellinek 1.122).

6   If T. H. Gaster's fascinating interpretation of this *Psalm* is correct (*Myth, Legend, and Custom in the Old Testament* (New York 1969) 773–81), namely that it is in fact the text that spells out a coronation ritual, then the possibility of drawing illumination from it for our passage is even increased.

   Perhaps the (eschatological) visions of *1 Enoch* in which God's 'elect one' evidently sits on His throne are in this tradition (51.3; 61.8; 62.2). For the image compare the ultimate triumph of Adam as described by his sitting 'on the throne of him who hath been his supplanter' (*Vita Adae et Evae* 48.3; *Apoc. Mosis* 39.3).

7   For a vision involving a symbolic change of clothing, see *Zechariah* 3.1ff. There is an interesting but much more complex 'transfer of power' dream including a sceptre at Soph. *Electra* 417ff.

8   See J. C. Greenfield in *Near Eastern Studies in Honor of W. F. Albright*, ed. H. Goedicke (Baltimore 1971) 254–8. Might the sceptre given here to Moses be the alter ego of the rod given him at *Asatir* 9; cf. *Jerahmeel* 46.11?

9   For the transmission of an object to a dreamer in a dream, cf. Judah Maccabee's dream in which the prophet Jeremiah gives him a sword with which (the prophet declares) he will kill his enemies (*2 Macc.* 15.11ff).

10 Is LXX *Esther* 5.1c–e an adaptation of the divine figure on the throne motif? Notice how Esther faints as people in the pseudepigrapha do on approaching *God's* throne.

11 Starobinski-Safran, *MH* 31 (1974) 223–4, argues that Moses' dream alludes to a Messianic age and supports this primarily by Raguel's rather straightforward wish (84) ζώην δ' ὅταν σοι ταῦτα συμβαίνῃ ποτέ. I see no evidence or reason to think this so. In Jewish tradition Moses is not generally thought of as a Messiah, though he is sometimes seen as a paradigm or type for the future Messiah. See G. Vermes 78ff and R. Bloch 149ff in H. Cazelles (et al.), *Moise: l'Homme de l'Alliance* (Paris 1955).

12 Another possible source of influence from *Genesis* is Jacob's dream at 28.12ff. There a ladder reaches from earth to heaven (like the throne in Ezekiel), at its top appears God (like the divine surrogate at the mountain-top in Ezekiel). Immediately after the dream Jacob meets his future wife at the well, whereas in the *Exagoge* it seems that Moses may have met his future wife at the well in a scene closely preceding the dream.

13 See *Divre Hayamim shel Mosheh Rabbenu* (Jellinek 2.3–4); *Sepher Hayashar* pp. 245–7.

14 Is the theme of Moses sitting on a throne related to the phrase $\kappa\alpha\theta\acute{\epsilon}\delta\rho\alpha$ $M\omega\ddot{\upsilon}\sigma\acute{\epsilon}\omega\varsigma$ which occurs at *Matth.* 23.2 and *Pesiqta derav Kahana* 1.7 (Mandelbaum vol. 1, p. 12)? The Samaritan *Death of Moses* (below, n. 18) p. 307 tells of Moses making a throne and sitting on it shortly before his death. Another Samaritan tradition has Moses, after descending from Mount Sinai, sit on a great chair and write what God taught him (*Memar Marqah* 4.6). The *Mekhilta* says (Jethro 2, *ad* 18.14 p. 196) that Moses was like a king sitting on his throne. The *Pesiqta* passage appears to asso-ciate the throne with a golden sceptre and crown.

15 *LAB* 18.5; *Gen. Rab.* 44.12. The latter passage interestingly continues with a statement to the effect that Abraham was a prophet, not an astrologer, an association which seems comparable to the interpretation of the dream pre-sented by Raguel.

16 In general there are some interesting interconnections between post-Biblical Moses and Abraham traditions. See G. H. Box, *The Testament of Abraham* (London 1927) xviif, M. R. James, *The Testament of Abraham* (Cambridge 1892) 64ff, and especially K. Kohler, *JQR* 7 (1895) 581ff.

17 Cf. too *3 Enoch* 46.1ff.

18 See M. Gaster, *The Asatir* (London 1927) 317 and 319.

19 The possible connection to Joseph's dream has been noticed by many scho-lars.

20 At verse 81 R. Renehan, *Studies in Greek Texts* (Göttingen 1976 = *Hypom-nemata* 43) 68–9, would read $\kappa\alpha\grave{\iota}$ $\grave{\iota}\delta o\acute{\upsilon}$ for $\kappa\grave{\alpha}\mu o\tilde{\upsilon}$.

21 See, e.g., Siphre *Numbers* 42; *Numbers Rab.* 11.7 (in a completely military context). Gutman's (46) suggestion that the stars refer to the nation of Israel is best supported by a passage he does not cite, *Yalkut* 888 *ad Ps.* 147.4 which says that the stars are the tribes of Israel.

22 See A. L. Oppenheim, *The Interpretation of Dreams in the Ancient Near East* (Philadelphia 1956) 191.

23 I do not understand what Dalbert means when he says (58) that dream-interpretation of this sort is a Greek phenomenon and does not occur in the Bible until the Book of *Daniel*. The instances in *Genesis* are clear. It is how-ever true that the Bible does not promote the science of dream-interpreta-tion among Jews. See Y. Kaufmann, *History of the Religion of Israel* (Tel Aviv 1963) 1.2, 507–11.

24 So Gifford (vol. 3, 470), Viger (*apud* Gaisford *PE* (1843)), Gutman (149), Wieneke.

25 So Herzfeld (518), Kuiper, *Mnem.* 249, Dalbert (58), Frankel (118), Riessler (339), Philippson (27), Dübner (3), Magnin (204), Kappelmacher (72), Starobinski-Safran (above n. 1, 219 and 222); also the translator at *Poetae Graeci Veteres* (Geneva 1614) vol. 1, 1019.

26 *Gnomon* 9 (1933) 57.
27 Freudenthal (172) certainly goes too far when he says that Ezekiel des-
    cribes Moses as seizing Pharaoh's crown and ascending his throne.
28 Notwithstanding ibn Ezra's comments *ad. Gen.* 36.31 and *Deut.* 33.5.
29 ARN, vers. B, ch. 48. Cf. the slightly but significantly different version
    at Siphre *Numbers* 119 and that at Targ. Jon. *ad Deut.* 34.5. Note too
    Moses' God-bestowed crown at *Tanhuma* (ed. Buber) 51, where Moses
    is also said to have God's sceptre and is referred to as a king (52). In general,
    see W. A. Meeks, *The Prophet-King* (Leiden 1967) passim (see index) and
    especially 176ff and, with reference to the ascension motif, 192–5.
30 See Gutman 44.
31 In general, see Meeks' treatment of the Moses as seer tradition passim (see
    index). See too Bloch (above, n. 11) 138, no. 127 for some references to
    Midrashic texts on Moses as 'prophet.'
32 E.g. Targum Jon. *ad Exod.* 1.15; *Midrash Hagadol ad Exod.* 1.22.
33 *Jerahmeel* 43; *Sepher Hayashar* 239–40. M. Hengel in *Fondation Hardt
    Entretiens* vol. 18: *Pseudepigrapha I* ed. K. von Fritz (Geneva 1972) 243,
    n. 4, has noted some of these as examples of Palestinian dreams but has
    made no attempt to tie them to Ezekiel's narrative.
34 Midrash Wayosha (Eisenstein 1.150). What may also have induced Ezekiel
    to put Raguel in the position of interpreter for Moses is the Biblical portrait
    of him as adviser to Moses (*Exod.* 18.13ff). Josephus expands and elaborates
    this role (*AJ* 3.66–74).
35 Philo *apud* Eus. *PE* 8.355c mentions dreams and visions foretelling the
    Exodus.
36 Suetonius' *Lives of the Caesars* are filled with accounts of omens (including
    dreams) foretelling the rise (and fall) of the various emperors, e.g. *Aug.*
    94–5, *Vesp.* 5. Cf. too Plut. *Sulla* 9.4, *Alex.* 2.2–3.
37 C. R. Holladay in *SBL Seminar Papers 1976* (Missoula 1976) 447–52 has
    argued that Ezekiel's throne is not the kingly throne but the mantic one.
    See my discussion of this view at *ICS* 6 (1981) 287–93.
38 E.g. *Test. Levi* 2.5ff; *Test. Napht.* 5.1ff; *2 Esdras* 3.1ff.
39 Cf. *Midrash Megillat Ester* (Eisenstein 1.54).
40 On the other hand, one remarks the violent polemic of Sirach (34.1ff)
    against the belief in significant dreams, to which we might compare *Jerem.*
    23.25.
41 One notes that the dream of a man, not a woman, is in the Biblical and
    Herodotean traditions, not in that of Greek tragedy. The latter genre almost
    exclusively gives dreams to women. The sole exception in the extant plays
    is at *Rhesus* 780ff.
42 It seems fairly clear that this is the usage at 68–9, though the lacunose con-
    dition of the manuscripts here bars us from certainty.
43 Raguel congratulates Moses (83) immediately after the latter's review of the
    stars, just as Xerxes congratulates himself after his review of his troops
    (7.45). It is curious that Raguel's felicitations include a wish that he live
    long enough to see Moses' success (84) for in Herodotus Xerxes' review is
    followed immediately by a discussion between him and Artabanus on the
    advantages and disadvantages of the short life.
44 Herodotus was well known in the Hellenistic period (and later). His popu-
    larity is attested by the Gyges tragedy and by the interest in his *Histories* on

the part of later critics and editors. See A. Lesky, *Geschichte der griechischen Literatur* (Bern 1963²) 360 and F. Jacoby at *RE* supp. 2, 511ff. For detailed discussion (with many examples) of Herodotean influence on Josephus' *Antiquities*, see S. Ek, *Bulletin de la Société Royale des Lettres de Lund* 1945–46, 27–62 and 213.

45 See U. Wilcken, *Urkunden der Ptolemäerzeit* vol. 1 (Berlin 1927), no. 81, col. II, 5ff (p. 370).

4. The burning bush

1 So Dodds *ad Bacchae* 644. See too Page *ad Medea* 1004.

2 Ezekiel is looking to God's words at *Exod.* 33.18ff.

3 For a general discussion of the question of the *Exagoge's* staging, see my article at *GRBS* 22 (1981) 167–75.

4 Gutmann originally went too far in assuming that the bush was simply not shown (*EJ* 886). He later changed his view (*Beginnings* 149).

5 On the use of suggestion and illusion in these cases, see P. Arnott, *Greek Scenic Conventions in the Fifth Century B.C.* (Oxford 1962) 123ff. Also, O. Taplin, *The Stagecraft of Aeschylus* (Oxford 1977) 34, 273–5. See too E. C. Kopff, *GRBS* 18 (1977) 118f on special effects for fires, with specific reference to the end of Aristophanes' *Nubes*.

6 On the possible presence of a bush in the orchestra in Sophocles' *Ajax*, see Stanford's commentary p. 166. But cf. W. M. Calder III, *CP* 60 (1965) 114–16.

7 A disembodied divine voice is also present at Soph. *OC* 1626ff, but there it is in a messenger's speech.

8 To be sure, this would require that the Greeks identify Ezekiel's God with Zeus, which is by no means certain.

9 Cf. U. von Wilamowitz-Moellendorff, *Aischylos: Interpretationen* (Berlin 1914) 246 and H. J. Mette, *Der verlorene Aischylos* (Berlin 1963) 112. Taplin (above, n. 5) 431–2 has now argued that Zeus did not even appear in the *Psychostasia*.

10 For a discussion of the various views that see here Philonic, mystical or Stoic elements, see my article at *ICS* 6 (1981) 279–93.

11 Cf. too Aeschylus' κτύπον δέδορκα (*Sept.* 103). On the use of such sound/sight 'mixed metaphors' in Greek poetry, see W. B. Stanford, *Greek Metaphor* (Oxford 1936) 47–59.

12 *Mekhilta deRashbi*, p. 154 (Epstein).

13 See too *Decal.* 46–7, *Migr. Abr.* 47.

14 A variant at Neofiti 3.2 also gives מרטיב.

15 E.g. Midrash Hagadol *ad Exod.* 3.2; *Exodus Rabbah* 2.5.

16 Ezekiel's ἕρπε καὶ σήμαινε (109) seems a clear paraphrase of Septuagint *Exod.* 6.6, βάδιζε εἰπόν, an interesting piece of evidence for the poet's use of the Septuagint rather than the Hebrew which reads לכן אמור 'therefore say' (unless, of course, we choose to assume that Ezekiel had a Hebrew text reading, e.g, לך, 'go'). ἀλλά at 109 is a fine instance of the use so described by Denniston (*Particles* 14), 'a transition from arguments for action to a statement of the action required . . . usually occurs near the end of a speech.'

17 See S. E. Loewenstamm, *The Tradition of the Exodus in its Development* (Jerusalem 1972²) 49.

18   Verse 119 is problematic and editors usually follow Stephanus by emending
     ἡμᾶς to ἡμῶν. Snell maintains the transmitted reading nor does it seem im-
     possible to believe that such inconcinnity of construction was not beyond
     Ezekiel (cf. 9ff, 198ff), though Snell's comparison to *Exod.* 4.16 τὰ πρὸς
     τὸν θεόν seems without point since in the Septuagint passage there is no
     sense of direction or communication in the πρός phrase. It might be possible
     that 119 begins a sentence whose continuation has been cut off. Otherwise,
     one could suggest reading λεών for λαβών (cf. 203 and *Exod.* 4.16, πρὸς
     τὸν λαόν), taking it as object of πρός (for the ellipse of the preposition see
     KG 1.549 and L. Edmund's discussion of one aspect of this idiom, *HSCP* 80
     (1976) 42f. The corruption that appears in some manuscripts in the prece-
     ding line, βασιλέων for βασιλέως, may be due to an original λεών in 119. I
     note, however, that the use in this context of λαβών is coincidentally paral-
     leled in the Jerusalem Targum *ad* 4.16, 'You will be for him as one who
     seeks instructions from God.' Finally, one fact that may suggest that the
     corruption is in ἡμᾶς: Ezekiel never refers to God (either with verbs or pro-
     nouns) in the plural.
19   See Loewenstamm's good remarks on this (above, n. 17) 65.
20   Compare the way *Wisdom* avoids mentioning the infidelities of the Jews on
     leaving Egypt. See J. Reider, *The Book of Wisdom* (New York 1957) 137,
     ad 10.15.
21   Similarly, in *Exodus* God says nothing of 'sending Aaron' to Moses. Ezekiel
     introduces into the bush episode later material, for at *Exod.* 4.27 we learn
     that indeed God does *send* Aaron to meet him.
22   See Kuiper, *Mnemosyne* 268 and Gutmann, *EJ* 886.
23   With Stephanus' likely emendation of ἐστι to ἔσται.
24   So Wieneke 72.
25   E.g. Soph. *Ajax* 591ff, *OR* 626ff; Eur. *Hipp.* 352.
26   In the extant corpus only at *PV* 980, though some emend it away.
27   See, e.g., Targ. Jon. *ad Exod.* 2.21, 4.20; *Midrash Hagadol ad Exod.* 4.17;
     Asatir 9.22; *Jerahmeel* 46.11ff.
28   So Apion and earlier Manetho. See Jos. *Ap.* 2.8; 1.233ff.
29   See Helladius *apud* Photius, *Bibl.* 279 (p. 529B Bekker), Ptolemy Chennos
     apud Photius, *Bibl.* 190 (p. 151B Bekker), and Nicarchus *apud* Photius
     Lex. s.v. *Alpha.* συμμεμιαμμένων at Jos. *Ap.* 1.241 may imply that Manetho
     also utilized this tradition. See too *AJ* 3.265ff.
30   An interesting variation on this at Bab. Talm. *Shabbat* 97a.
31   There is no reason to believe that Polyhistor has reversed the order. This
     would be contrary to his custom (as far as we can tell). Further, it is un-
     likely that he would write ὑποβάς τινα ἀμοιβαῖα before 113–15 and then
     come back to these skipped verses without any notice.
32   This is what Philo, *Moses* 1.83 also has, possibly another instance of Ezekiel's
     influence. But at *Quis Heres* 16 he writes ἄλογος. Thus, we should not
     assume, with E. Bickerman, *Studies in Jewish and Christian History*, vol. 1
     (Leiden 1976) 145, that Ezekiel and Philo had a Septuagint text that read
     οὐκ εὔλογος.
33   Cf., e.g., *Ephesians* 6.5–9; *1 Pt.* 2.16; *Acts* 16.17. This concept does not
     occur often in classical Greek texts, but there are a small number of passages
     which may suggest that it was not completely unknown, e.g. Eur. *Ion* 131,

309 (though this is in a sense literally true of Ion's position), *Bacchae* 366. A distinction has to be made between the verbal and nominal notions: one who serves is not necessarily a servant.

34 Nor παῖδες nor οἰκέται.

35 E.g. *Lev.* 25.42, 55: οἰκέται, παῖδες; *Isa.* 41.8–9: παῖς; *Deut.* 32.36: δοῦλοι; also perhaps for Hebrew עם of the Jews at *3 Kings* 8.34, 16.2. The patriarchs and Moses are οἰκέται of God (*Exod.* 32.13; *Deut.* 34.5).

36 Jer. Talm. *Pes.* 5.5 (32c). See too Midrash Tehillim *Ps.* 113 (469–70), *Jerahmeel* 54.6.

37 See, e.g., Jer. Tal. *Kid.* 1–2·(59d); Bab. Tal. *B. Kamma* 116b, *B. Mezia* 10a; *Kid.* 22b.

38 Bab. Tal. *B. Bathra* 10a. *Persae* 242 would have made an impression on Ezekiel with its strikingly different conception: the Greeks are slaves (δοῦλοι) to no one.

39 But at least the association of the Exodus with the Jewish servitude to God seems present at *Lev.* 25.42, 55.

40 Cf. Bab. Tal. *Arakh.* 10b, *Meg.* 14a.

41 Bab. Tal. *Pes.* 117a.

42 See, e.g., *Pes.* 5.7; Tos. *Sukk.* 3.2, Tos. *Pes.* 4.11.

43 Cf. *Pes.* 10.6; Tos. *Pes.* 10.9. Cf. *Matth.* 26.30, *Mark* 14.26.

44 *HUCA* 23, pt. 2 (1950–51) 324.

45 Tos. *Pes.* 10.9.

46 S. Pines in *Studies in Literature Presented to Simon Halkin*, ed. E. Fleischer (Jerusalem 1973) 174–6, 178f, has pointed to an interesting parallel between the Passover Haggadah and *Joseph and Asenath*, though it cannot be determined whether there is direct influence here or, if there is, what direction it has taken.

47 That this was Palestinian exegesis may be suggested by the fact that the Greek translation of *Psalm* 113.1 (as of 135.1) strangely (and, of course, for this reading erroneously) makes 'God' not genitive dependent on 'slaves,' but rather accusative object of 'praise.' (So the Septuagint, Aquila, Symmachus, Theodotion.)

48 One should note that God's declaration at 104–5, ἐγὼ θεὸς σῶν, ὧν λέγεις, γεννητόρων/Ἀβραάμ τε καὶ Ἰσαὰκ καὶ Ἰακώβου τρίτου does not quite jibe with the Bible where (3.6) He says, Ἐγώ εἰμι ὁ Θεὸς τοῦ πατρός σου, θεὸς Ἀβραὰμ καὶ θεὸς Ἰσαὰκ καὶ θεὸς Ἰακώβ stressing first that he is God of Moses' father and then of the ancestral patriarchs. Indeed, Ezekiel's version says precisely what the Samaritan Pentateuch here reads, אבותיך. But I do not think we should make anything of this. This is both abridgement and laying emphasis on what Ezekiel feels is important here, i.e. the role of the patriarchs in the Exodus story (as discussed below). A useful parallel is at *Acts* 7.30ff where the story of the burning bush is narrated and, just as in the *Exagoge*, God declares Ἐγὼ ὁ θεὸς τῶν πατέρων σου, ὁ θεὸς Ἀβραὰμ καὶ Ἰσαὰκ καὶ Ἰακώβ leaving out the relatively insignificant mention of Moses' father. ὧν λέγεις (which Gifford simply ignores in his translation) should be taken, with Gutman, as 'whom you call by the title "patriarchs",' referring to the customary appellation of Abraham, Isaac and Jacob as אבות = πατέρες.

49 Girardi (52) cites the use of δωρέομαι at Aquila, *Ps.* 9.14, 36.26 and Jos. *AJ* 2.212 as support for δώρημα = promise here, but none of the examples seems persuasive.

50 Magnin (204), 'mes dons'; the translator at *REJ* 46 (1903) 61, 'mes bienfaits passés.'
51 Cf. Aesch. *Pers.* 523, *Eum.* 402; Soph. *Tr.* 668.
52 E.g. Eur. *Med.* 634, *Ion* 1428, *Helen* 883, *HF* 612; Aristot. *Eth.* 1.9.2. Further examples from Christian texts in Lampe s.v.
53 E.g. Siphre *Deut.* 96 and 184. Other references in Finkelstein's apparatus *ad* 96.
54 E.g. *Mekhilta Vayehi* ch. 3, pp. 98, 100; *Mekhilta deRashbi* 59; *Mekhilta* p. 62; *Exod. Rab.* 1.36; *Ag. Ber.* 10. It is possible that this is what Josephus too has in mind at *AJ* 2.212, τήν τε εὐσέβειαν αὐτῶν ἔλεγε διὰ μνήμης ἔχεω καὶ τὴν ὑπὲρ αὐτῆς ἀμοιβὴν ἀεὶ παρέξεω, though this would be clearer if αὐτῶν were not so vague.
55 E.g. *Gen.* 12.7–8, 22.13, 28.22, 33.20.
56 The Septuagint uses δῶρα and δόματα of offerings to God: *Nu.* 28.2 (cf. Philo, *Cher.* 84).
57 *Mekhilta* pp. 24–5, 38–9, 100. On the sacrifice of Isaac, cf. *LAB* 32.2.
58 Though contrast Spanier's view (*MGWJ* 81 (1937) 71ff) that it signifies 'who remembers the love that He has shown to the patriarchs.' Even this would be relevant and suitable for Ezekiel, if we take ἐμῶν δωρημάτων in such a sense.
59 See S. Schechter, *JQR* 10 (1898) 656. Cf. K. Kohler, *HUCA* 1 (1924) 394–5.
60 Theodotus, for instance, refers to an (alleged) promise of God to the descendants of Abraham as μῦθος Θεοῖο (*PE* 9.428c).

5. The plagues

1 The introductory remarks of Eusebius and Polyhistor preceding 132 do not enable us to determine whether 132ff belong to the bush-scene at Sinai. Girardi (34–6) thought they might belong to a later separate scene. The fact that the opening verse of this scene (as preserved) ἐν τῆδε ῥάβδῳ πάντα ποιήσεις κακά is clearly Ezekiel's adaptation of the final verse in the Biblical bush-scene (4.17, τὴν ῥάβδον ταύτην . . . λήμψη . . . ἐν ᾗ ποιήσεις . . . τὰ σημεῖα) supports the traditional view that 132ff are Ezekiel's elaboration of the bush-scene.
2 Wieneke's view that αἷμα at 133 is subject is misguided. The fact that πηγαί and συστήματα follow clearly shows that ποτάμιον must be subject and αἷμα internal accusative. Compare for example the Septuagint's translation of חלב ודבש זבת: ῥέουσα γάλα καὶ μέλι. When Philo describes the divine sign of water changed to blood the structure is the same: τὸ ποτάμιον ὕδωρ is subject and αἷμα is predicate (*Moses* 1.81).
3 For detailed discussion of the plague traditions see S. Loewenstamm, *The Tradition of the Exodus in its Development* (Jerusalem 1972²) 25–79.
4 But there may be a similar juxtaposition at *Wisdom* 16.15ff, 17.2ff. Artapanus (if my interpretation is right) submerges the darkness plague beneath the hailstorms.
5 The metrical problems of 135 should not lead us to assume a lacuna, as does Snell. Strugnell suggests an emendation to heal the difficulties (*HTR* 60 (1967) 451, n. 6). When D. F. Sutton writes, 'LSJ⁹ incorrectly reports the accusative . . . as σκνίπας' (at *Exagoge* 135) 'σκνῖπας is guaranteed by the

meter' he himself is wrong (*Glotta* 55 (1977) 212). As the verse stands in our manuscripts σκνίπας is guaranteed by the meter. It is for this reason that Snell posits the lacuna. The emendation ἀναβρυάσεται at 137 is Gifford's, not Gaisford's (as Sutton writes).

6 One might suppose that an erroneous transposition of verses is the problem here and that Ezekiel actually did follow the Pentateuchal order. In support one could refer to the ambiguous οἷς at 136. But Ezekiel is rather careless in his use of pronouns and in general is prone to a certain looseness of expression. Further, to so argue would require shifting the plague of boils to a position between pestilence and hail, but there is no room for such a possibility (cf. 141). On δέ at 137, see Snell, *Glotta* 30, n. 2 and references.

7 Sutton's arguments (*loc. cit.* 210) against Mras' πικράνω are invalid. He fails to realize that this is a subjunctive.

8 *Moses* 1.113ff; Midrash Hagadol *ad Exod.* 9.22.

9 Note also that immediately after announcing the tenth plague God proceeds to give instructions on the laws of the month Nisan (153ff). This is the precise pattern in *Exodus* (11.4ff, 12.1ff).

10 ῥυήσεται at 133 is an exception but I think understandable because of the clear allusion to the use of the rod in 132.

11 Cf. below my discussion of 175ff.

12 Assuming, of course, that חיתם and נפשם are so to be understood.

13 This is a reasonable assumption, though since we are not certain either when Ezekiel lived or when the *Psalms* were first translated into Greek, we cannot be sure; nor, even if there was a Greek *Psalms* in Ezekiel's day, whether this was the same translation now preserved in the Septuagint.

14 So too, by the way, does the Targum. The vagueness of the Greek translation (דבר = θάνατος) would have made it almost impossible to be certain that Septuagint *Psalms* 78.50 indeed refers to the specific plague had it not been for the use of κτῆνη.

15 Midrash Hagadol *ad Exod.* 9.1–3.

16 *Pesiqta Rabbati* 197a seems to imply that דבר killed men too.

17 So too Targumim translate דבר as מותא.

18 I see no reason to believe that *Exod.* 9.14–16 is a rejection of the דבר באדם version. One might even conjecture that it gave rise to it. The text may well mean, as many hold, 'I could have smitten you with pestilence but did not because . . . ' The Septuagint clearly understands the words to mean 'I will send my hand upon you and smite you, etc.' But taking שלחתי as a direct statement of declaration raises a difficult question. How can God say that he will now kill Pharaoh when in fact we know that Pharaoh does not die till the Red Sea (if then)? So the translators made a subtle change which produced πατάξω σε καὶ τὸν λαόν σου θανατώσω, thus removing the element of death from Pharaoh himself and limiting it only to his people. Thus, when Rahlfs prefers θανάτῳ of MS M to the well attested θανατώσω he fails to consider the calculated implications of the revised translation.

19 The Rabbis felt much the same and considered the death of the first-born a דבר, just like the fifth plague: Midrash Hagadol *ad Exod.* 9.1–3.

20 *Ad LAB* 10.1, p. XCIII.

21 Note that Philo compares this plague to λοιμώδεσι νόσοις (*Moses* 1.133), while Ezekiel calls it λοιμός (140).

22 E.g. *1 Clem.* 51.3–5. See A. Hermann, 'Das steinharte Herz,' *JbAC* 4 (1961) 77–107.
23 So Dübner 5; Viger 415; the translator at *Poetae Graeci Veteres* (Geneva 1614) vol. 1, 1020.
24 So Wieneke, Kuiper *Mnem.* 255–6, Gutman 151, Philippson 33, Riessler 342, Magnin 206.
25 Cf. *Exod.* 8.5, 7; 9.26; 10.24.
26 I note, for whatever it may be worth, that the Septuagint evidently never uses πείσομαι from πείϑω, but does from πάσχω.
27 *Leqah Tov ad Exod.* 8.17. It is unclear whether this is related to the texts at *Mekhilta* p. 23, Bab. Talm. *Sotah* 11a; Tosephta *Sotah* ch. 4.12.
28 *Exod. Rab.* 15.10.
29 See too D. L. Tiede, *The Charismatic Figure as Miracle Worker* (Missoula 1972) 171.
30 A point noted only, to my knowledge, by Magnin 'toutes sortes de maux' (205). Cf. the same use of πᾶς (in singular) at 164.
31 Tiede (*op. cit.* above, n. 29) 226ff observes and discusses the fact that in the *Antiquitates* God, not Moses, is in general the miracle worker.
32 *Jerahmeel* 48.1–9 seems to represent the same essential tradition. Moses does not even appear while God is given prominence in the individual plagues.

6. The Passover regulations

1 E.g. Kraus 167f, Trencsényi-Waldapfel 148, 155. Girardi (35) not only believed that 175–92 was a separate speech by God, but that 152–74 was also. The latter view might find support in the introductory remark preceding 152 in MSS ON, if we believe it to be Polyhistor's or Eusebius'.
2 Kraus (ibid.) in particular has emphasized this.
3 At 158 it seems preferable to construe ψαύειν τινί τινος with Wieneke and perhaps consider it another case of the *Persae*'s influence (202), rather than as a lone instance of ψαύειν + accusative as LSJ take it. For the singular cf. σῆμα, not σήματα, in the next verse.
4 Editors follow Stephanus in reading ἐπεξεργαζόμενον rather than ἐπεξεργαζόμενος and this seems right. The words are Eusebius', not Polyhistor's, and he is speaking of Ezekiel. Kuiper's opinion (*Mnemosyne* 257) that the comment is Polyhistor's, referring to God, is unlikely.
5 In discussing the text of 184 Strugnell (449) sets the scene in the following words: 'Moses is giving (to the elders?) prescriptions concerning the Passover.' He does not discuss the matter. To my knowledge he is the only scholar to have seen this speech in this light.
6 This is a device that can be paralleled in Greek epic. At *Il.* 9.260ff Odysseus repeats Agamemnon's earlier instructions (9.121ff).
7 The order of topics is fundamentally the same in A and B: date, sacrifice and blood ceremony, the unleavened bread. The order of A, blood on the posts – Pharaoh will banish you, is reversed in B.
8 It is difficult to conceive what δεινὸς ἄγγελος would have suggested to the Greeks. At any rate, ϑάνατος at 187 would have clarified the matter. Greeks would readily understand a personified ϑάνατος. Consider Euripides'

Alcestis. The construction παρελθεῖν ἀπό appears to be 'Jewish Greek.' See Bauer-Arndt-Gingrich s.v. citing, e.g., *Matth.* 26.39. The Bible speaks of God and τὸν ὀλεθρεύοντα (12.23) as the actors here. No mention is made of any angel (though note *Nu.* 20.16; also the association of angel plus destroyer as at LXX 2 *Kings* 24.16, *1 Chron.* 21.15). It is therefore interesting to observe that Targ. Jon. *ad* 12.13 includes an 'angel of death.' Verses 159 and 187 suggest (in spite of 147 which is too general to infer from) that Ezekiel was a partisan of the view that it was not God himself but rather an angel who passed through Egypt and smote the first-born, a subject of heated debate among the Rabbis. See J. Goldin in *Religions in Antiquity* ed. J. Neusner (Leiden 1968) 412–24; S. Pines in *Studies in Literature Presented to Simon Halkin* ed. E. Fleischer (Jerusalem 1973) 176–8. Ezekiel is strikingly in accord with the view that goes against the literal sense of the Bible and indeed may be our oldest extant source for this position (*Mekhilta* pp. 23, 43; *Jubilees* 49.2; cf. *Exod. Rab.* 17.5).

9   For a discussion of Moses' enhanced role as νομοθέτης in *Aristeas*, see M. Hadas, *Aristeas to Philocrates* (New York 1951) 63, 194. Philo occasionally increases Moses' stature by attributing some (divine) act or remark to him, e.g. *Moses* 1.163f where he makes the choice of route Moses' rather than God's. See too Diod. Sic. 1.94.2 and Longinus 9.9.

10 Frankel 117f; see too Herzfeld 518.

11 Artapanus, on the other hand, has them reach the sea on the third day (*PE* 9.436a).

12 *Pesiqta Hadta apud* Jellinek 6.37 reports that the Jews crossed on the seventh day after setting out, which was the seventh day of Passover.

13 Perhaps the theme of a significant seven-day journey from Egypt with etiological implications is reflected in the scurrilous explanation of the name 'Sabbath' by Apion, which appears to be based on a six-day journey from Egypt to Judaea with rest on the seventh. See Jos. *Ap.* 2.20f, 25; cf. Pomp. Trogus *apud* Justin 36.2.14; Tac. *Hist.* 5.3–4.

14 *Discoveries in the Judaean Desert*, vol. 1 (Oxford 1955) 94.

15 Compare the different but equally non-Biblical etiology of the date of this holiday at *Jub.* 34.18f.

16 The metrical fault at 165 is easily repaired by Snell's τε καὶ στολάς, without needing to read χρυσοῦν τε καὶ ἀργύρειον (Dübner, followed by Wieneke) to bring the text into conformity with the Bible. We are probably dealing here with no more than an 'expansion' on the Biblical text by Ezekiel, but we should at least notice the possibility of another tradition wherein the Jews actually did receive gold and silver on their departure; cf. especially *Psalm* 105.37. If we feel compelled by κόσμον in 164 to emend, Snell (in his *ap. crit.*) and J. Diggle, *GRBS* 14 (1973) 264, n. 62 have offered suggestions.

17 P. 117.

18 Does *Wisdom* 10.17 and 20 represent the same tradition? Note the vocabulary: ἀπέδωκεν . . . μισθόν . . . ἐσκύλευσαν, the first two being the apologetic vocabulary Ezekiel uses here, the last the Septuagint's verb for the spoliation of the Egyptians (12.36). Artapanus (*PE* 436a–b) reports a version in which Pharaoh pursues the Jews in order to retrieve the borrowed property.

19 *Mekhilta* p. 33, Siphre *Deut.* 128, Tos. *Pes.* 10.9.

20 *Midrash Tehillim* 113, pp. 469f.
21 Cf. *1 Cor.* 5.6–8, *Matth.* 16.5ff; *Targum 2* to *Esther* 3.8.
22 Ezekiel writes μείς, the Septuagint μήν. Indeed, the Septuagint (and perhaps Philo too) never uses μείς. I observe, in view of my belief that Herodotus was an important influence on Ezekiel, that μείς is Herodotean (2.82).
23 *Pesiqta deRav Kahana* pp. 100, 210f (Mandelbaum).
24 To be sure, there are hints of such a notion in the Bible. See, e.g, *Exod.* 19.1, 40.17; *Nu.* 1.1, 33.38; *Deut.* 1.3; *1 Kings* 6.1.
25 At 177 Ezekiel uses ἄμωμα for the Septuagint's τέλειον. If one believed that he knew some Hebrew one might suspect that he chose ἄμωμα as an equivalent of α privative plus Hebrew מום ('blemish'). L. Feldman, *Scholarship on Philo and Josephus* (1937–62) (New York 1963[?]) 24 has suggested that the word מום may have even been known to non-Jews and perhaps influenced the development of the meaning of μῶμος. If τέλειος had already taken on any mystical overtones by Ezekiel's time, he may have sought to avoid it on those grounds.
26 Frankel 119, n. k thought Ezekiel's version might reflect the ritual of Onias' temple in Heliopolis. See too H. Graetz, *Geschichte der Juden*, vol. 3 (Leipzig 1905⁵) 608. *2 Chron.* 35.13 seems already to be a reconciliation of the conflicting regulations of *Exod.* 12 and *Deut.* 16. See too the elaborate exegetical translation of *Deut.* 16.2 by Targ. Jon. Cf. too *Mekhilta* p. 13, Siphre *Deut.* 129. I note however a Qumran text in which a regulation of the Pentateuch is supported at the expense of a later adaptation and revision of the law. See J. M. Allegro, *Discoveries in the Judaean Desert of Jordan*, vol. 5 (Oxford 1968) 6–7.
27 Pseudo-Philo and other post-Biblical Jewish texts seem to reflect the strong influence of *Deuteronomy*. See Feldman, *LAB* pp. xxxiii–xxxiv. There is unfortunately no evidence that this section of *Deuteronomy* was part of the Passover scriptural reading in Hellenistic times, as it was later on.
28 On ἴδιος (167), see Blass–Debrunner sect. 286, p. 236.
29 πρωτότευκτα at 172 appears to be a *hapax legomenon*. If πρωτόγονος or πρωτότοκος already had mystical connotations in Ezekiel's time, he may have avoided them for that reason (cf. above, n. 25). –τευκτος compounds are by and large a Hellenistic phenomenon, found in, e.g., Lycophron, Philo, Josephus, Polybius. Interestingly, χρυσότευκτος occurs twice in Aeschylus (*Sept.* 660, frg. 184 N²), one of Ezekiel's favorite literary sources.

παρθένοι (173) is surely strange. What can it mean? It does not mean 'virgin.' It should not mean 'young,' since the law is not delimited by the age of the mother (though one supposes that with animals such will be the case). It appears to mean, 'one who has never before given birth,' though the sense is without parallel (perhaps the usage exemplified at Soph. *Tr.* 1219 is close. See Wilamowitz *ad Heracles* 834 ('mannbare').). In addition, I am not sure if παρθένος is used elsewhere of animals. Could Ezekiel's exotic use of the adjective here have been inspired (as so often) by Aeschylus' *Persae*, which contains probably the oddest use of παρθένος in Greek literature: λιβάσιν ὑδρηλαῖς παρθένου πηγῆς μέτα (613), a verse which Ezekiel may be echoing at 249–50: ὑγράς τε λιβάδας· δαψιλῆς χῶρος βαθύς,/πηγὰς ἀρύσσων δώδεκ' ἐκ μιᾶς πέτρας. Snell is surely right (*Glotta* 32, n. 2) in rejecting Stephanus' ὅσα τ' which Wieneke adopts.

30 It is, however, curious that Wellhausen believed that the sacrifice of first-born animals was the oldest layer of the Pesach ritual: *Prolegomena to the History of Ancient Israel* (repr. Cleveland 1965) 87–9. Cf. J. B. Segal, *The Hebrew Passover* (London 1963) 103f, 181ff.
31 Cf. *Exod.* 34.18–20.
32 Gutman sought to circumvent the difficulty in his translation (151) by turning the participle ϑύοντες (172) into a finite verb.
33 Either Ezekiel took this for granted after his mention of the tenth plague a few lines earlier or he might have commented on the etiology in the following lost lines. For the etiology of first-born sacrifice/tenth plague, see *Exod.* 13.11–15, *Nu.* 3.13.
34 He may have been unwilling to include a regulation that seemed to give the donkey special status, so as to avoid charges of *Eselskult*.
35 Segal (above, n. 30) 23.
36 J. W. McKay, *ZATW* 84 (1972) 435. Others offer much the same, e.g. the anonymous translator at *REJ* 46 (1903) 65, and Dübner (5).
37 Does he take διχομηνίᾳ and νυκτί as temporal datives: in the middle of the month . . . on the preceding night, with the latter qualifying the former? This would be very awkward. It is hard to tell how Gifford construed the Greek, 'in this month, at evening ere the moon's full orb appear, to sacrifice the Passover to God, and strike the side-posts of the door with blood' (472).
38 On the hiatus see Snell, *Glotta* 26, n. 2; V. Schmidt, *Sprachliche Untersuchungen zu Herondas* (Berlin 1968) 75, n. 6.
39 117, n. h.
40 τῆς . . . νυκτός is Kuiper's suggestion (*Mnemosyne* 256) though he did not suspect the text nor did he suggest *reading* the genitive. He merely observed that had Ezekiel wanted to avoid hiatus here he could have done so with τῆς . . . νυκτός.
41 I know no example of πρόσθε plus the dative. If it is adverbial, one would not expect it to mean 'early in the night.' Xenophon, *Cyr.* 7.5.43 has πρόσθεν ἑσπέρας. Temporal πρόσθε seems to have virtually died out by the Hellenistic period (e.g. not found in the Septuagint) and Ezekiel probably knew it through his literary sources. Perhaps this may account for a somewhat peculiar usage on his part.
42 δαίσεσθε κρέα (160) is a Homeric and Herodotean phrase. δαίνυμι does not occur in the Septuagint or Philo. Similarly, πρόπας (161) does not occur in the Septuagint and Philo, but is a common poetic word, often for example in Aeschylus.
43 P. 452, n. 9.
44 Verses 180–3 also present some problems.

> οὕτως φάγεσθε ταῦτα· περιεζωσμένοι
> καὶ κοῖλα ποσσὶν ὑποδέδεσθε καὶ χερί
> βακτηρίαν ἔχοντες. ἐν σπουδῇ τε γάρ
> βασιλεὺς κελεύσει πάντας ἐκβαλεῖν χϑονός·

This is certainly an awkward sentence. It looks like the kind of imbalance one finds in Herodotus (e.g. 1.8; 1.116). But might ὑποδέδεσθε govern, in a kind of zeugma, both κοῖλα ποσσών and χερὶ βακτηρίαν with ἔχοντες merely tacked on? As for ἐν σπουδῇ τε γάρ etc., I do not find τε γάρ particularly difficult (*contra* Strugnell 452, n. 9). See Blass–Debrunner sect. 443, p. 372; KG 2.245; Denniston, *Particles* 536. Unless I misread him, Strugnell does not seem to realize that ἐν σπουδῇ goes with ἐκβαλεῖν.

45   Philippson 35, Segal 24.
46   Even the Bible may have added an explanation of the name in this context (*Exod.* 12.11–12). Cf. too Josephus, *AJ* 2.313:

> ... ὅθεν νῦν ἔτι κατὰ τὸ ἔθος οὕτως θύομεν τὴν ἑορτὴν πάσχα καλοῦντες, σημαίνει δ᾽ ὑπερβάσια, διότι κατ᾽ ἐκείνην τὴν ἡμέραν ὁ θεὸς αὐτῶν ὑπερβὰς Αἰγυπτίοις ἐναπέσκηψε τὴν νόσον.

47   The Passover home-ritual may be relevant. It begins, 'let every man who is hungry come and eat.'
48   451, n. 7.
49   I would not, of course, claim certainty on this score. I note possible exceptions in verbs compounded from καλέω. At Xen. *Symp.* 1.15 ἀντικληθησό-μενος = be invited in return. At Paus. 5.21.18 ἐσκληθήσεσθαι may belong to the 'summon' rather than 'name' rubric. But in both these cases we are not dealing with finite forms of the verb and the use of the future passive participle and infinitive may be because future perfect passive forms were not available. But most relevant is Philo's ἀνακεκλήσεται, 'will be summoned up,' at *Plant.* 26.
50   Kühner–Blass 2.453 give κέκλημαι = heisse. This is a false exclusion, as the examples in n. 51 prove. The same is true of Schwyzer's κέκληται = heisst (2.237).
51   E.g. *Esther* 4.11, 5.12; *Isa.* 48.1. Cf. *Matth.* 22.3; *Rev.* 19.9. Further, the Septuagint translates (or mistranslates) *Exod.* 3.18 and 5.3 so as to give a text, 'God (summons) invites the Jews to the sacrifice,' προσκέκληται ἡμᾶς. Philo follows in this vein, writing that the people were summoned by God, προσκεκλῆσθαι (*Moses* 1.73).
52   For whatever reason, *Jubilees* 49 also ignores the issue of circumcision.
53   E.g. Kappelmacher 84. Cf. Kuiper, *Mnemosyne* 268–9; Dalbert 65. Such tactics would not be unusual. Josephus alters *Aristeas'* account of the genesis of the Septuagint so that it should not be offensive to non-Jews.
54   See, e.g., Jos. *AJ* 12.241; *Ass. Mosis* 8.3; *1 Macc.* 1.12–15; The Edict of Hadrian.
55   It is immaterial whether or not all male Egyptians were routinely circumcised or only certain select ones. What is relevant is that circumcision was widely associated with the Egyptians in antiquity.
56   See, e.g., Diod. Sic. 1.28.3; 1.55.5; cf. Strabo 17.2.5. For a brief but good discussion of the general issue, see J. Bergmann, *Jüdische Apologetik im neutestamentlichen Zeitalter* (Berlin 1908) 102–4.
57   E.g. *CPJ* 139 from the first century B.C.; *CPJ* 467 from the second/third century A.D.
58   Consider, for instance, the opening of *2 Maccabees*.
59   A papyrus fragment from Euripides' *Erechtheus* (C. Austin, *Nova Fragmenta Euripidea in Papyris Reperta* (Berlin 1968) #65, pp. 33ff, especially verses 83ff) shows a number of verbal similarities to this Passover scene in the *Exagoge*. This may be coincidence due to the ritualistic character of both passages. On the other hand, the papyrus itself proves that the play was known in Egypt.

7. The crossing of the Red Sea

1 When Ezekiel here follows the convention of Greek tragedy, we have an example of substantive change (no Egyptian survives in *Exodus*) produced by the dictates of the literary form.

2 Snell thinks it 'nicht unmöglich' that Ezekiel knew the *Persae* (176).

3 Messenger speeches which are eyewitness reports of disasters are fairly common in Greek tragedy, especially in Euripides, e.g. *Hippolytus*, *Phaethon*, and *Helen* where it is virtually a survivor's account of a sea-disaster.

4 *Mnemosyne* 270.

5 Verse 219 seems particularly Biblical: the folly of Man's reliance on and confidence in his own powers in the face of God's supreme control. In these Biblical contexts the Septuagint regularly uses $\pi \acute{\epsilon} \pi o i \vartheta \alpha$, e.g. *Isa.* 36.6, *Jer.* 5.17, *Ps.* 49.7, 146.3.

6 This is without foundation in the Biblical narrative. Gutman's assertion that it is based on a hint at *Exod.* 14.20 is barely tenable (56).

7 It is conceivable that Ezekiel followed Aeschylus even further and had Pharaoh later arrive at the court, lamenting his defeat and acknowledging the might and justice of God. There was a Rabbinic tradition that Pharaoh did survive and then proclaimed the glory of God. (*Pirqe deRabbi Eliezer* 43, *Jerahmeel* 48.12. *Mekhilta* p. 111 simply reports that Pharaoh survived.) But this seems highly unlikely. So bizarre a version would not, most probably, have gone unmentioned by our sources. On the other hand, one can readily believe that Ezekiel's messenger added a few summary lines like *Pers.* 429–32 at some point in the speech.

8 Xerxes calls himself $\delta \epsilon \sigma \pi \acute{o} \tau \eta \varsigma$ (Hdt. 7.35) a title reserved by Ezekiel for God alone.

9 Though not, as Wieneke thinks, found only twice elsewhere. See Lampe for additional examples.

10 Cf. Jos. *AJ* 2.346.

11 See however on the limited use of chariots in the Seleucid army B. Bar-Kochva, *The Seleucid Army: Organization and Tactics in the Great Campaigns* (Cambridge 1976) 83f.

12 See e.g., LSJ and J. E. Powell, *A Lexicon to Herodotus* (Cambridge 1938) s.v. Aeschylus, by the way, almost always avoids the article with $\beta a \sigma i \lambda \epsilon \acute{u} \varsigma$. Cf. Strugnell 452, n. 9.

13 On the crossing of the Red Sea in general, see S. E. Loewenstamm, *The Tradition of the Exodus in its Development* (Jerusalem 1972²) 101ff.

14 Cedrenus, *Hist. Comp.* p. 85 (Bekk.) reports this passage in Greek but leaves out the number of Egyptians. This does not mean his *Jubilees* text lacked the number; rather that he was abridging it.

15 $\dot{\rho} \tilde{\eta} \xi o v$ is a bit ambiguous, as is וּבְקָעֵהוּ in the Hebrew. But both should mean 'split' without any necessary implication, 'strike and thereby split.' Loewenstamm's assertion (above, n. 13, p. 118) that וּבְקָעֵהוּ means (or implies) that Moses struck the water is hard to justify. Parallel passages in the Bible tend to militate against this, e.g. *Zech.* 14.4, *Gen.* 7.11, *1 Ki.* 1.40, *Ps.* 74.15. While smiting is not excluded, neither is it implied.

On the occasion of the first plague (waters transformed to blood) God commands Aaron to raise his hand over the waters (as at the Red Sea) and this is immediately followed by his striking of the water with his staff (7.19f).

But this 'inconsistency' is alleviated or removed by the fact that the smiting has already been foretold at 7.17. I do not think any confusion could have arisen from 17.5, even in the Septuagint translation.

16 For the chronology of the events in 217ff, see below.

17 *AJ* 2.338; *Moses* 1.177; *LAB* 10.5.

18 *Deut. Rab.* p. 40 (ed. Liebermann, 1964[2]); *Aboth deRabbi Natan* vers. A, ch. 33; *Pesiqta Hadta* (Jellinek 6.37).

19 *Hist. Comp.* p. 85 (Bekk.).

20 See the reproduction at E. R. Goodenough, *Jewish Symbols in the Greco-Roman Period* vol. 11 (New York 1964) plate xiv and figure 330. As Prof. Ann Perkins points out to me, the clear flexing of the elbow and knee are indications that this is meant to illustrate the first part of the act of striking.

21 One could argue that such passages were the impetus for the genesis of the 'striking of the sea' version, but this seems much less likely.

22 Many aspects of the sea-crossing in the Midrash which are elaborations of the Pentateuchal narrative seem to me to be quite early, i.e. already in existence in the Biblical period (e.g. in *Isaiah*).

23 See the recently published Targum on the Red Sea crossing: J. Komlosh, *Sinai* 45 (1959) 223–8. The version at *LAB* 10.2, in which Moses hits the sea, God rebukes it and it dries up, may represent an attempt to reconcile the two positions.

24 See Midrash Tannaim *ad Deut.* 26.8; also the Passover Haggadah (Goldschmidt 44f). Note too the striking translation of *Isa.* 63.9 in the Septuagint οὐ πρέσβυς, οὐδὲ ἄγγελος, ἀλλ᾽ αὐτὸς κύριος ἔσωσεν αὐτούς.

25 It is, however, probably significant that Ezekiel designates the rod as ῥάβδος θεοῦ here.

26 On the issue of Moses' 'divinity' in Philo, see E. R. Goodenough, *By Light Light* (New Haven 1935) 223–34 and note especially passages like *QE* 2.29, 40; *Moses* 1.158; *Post.* 28ff; *Sacr.* 8–10. There are occasional hints in Rabbinic texts. See *Deut. Rab.* 11.4 *ad* 33.1.

27 πρὸ γῆς μέγας (222) makes no sense. We should probably adopt some adjective like Kuiper's πυριφλεγής or a shorter one which would allow us to keep μέγας.

28 The 'pagan' phrase Τιτὰν ἥλιος should occasion no surprise nor motivate serious speculation on Ezekiel's beliefs. Even Rabbinical literature contains casual allusions to Greek gods, myths, etc. *Judith* 16.6 refers to υἱοὶ τιτάνων, and Josephus uses 'pagan' exclamations, e.g. νὴ Δία at *Ap.* 1.255 (and perhaps 2.263). One might compare the meaningless use of B.C. by Jews of the twentieth century.

29 So too Jos. *AJ* 2.334.

30 Magnin (207) forces the Greek, 'malgré la nuit.'

31 No other standard lexicon seems to record the word.

32 Dübner realized this, but his resultant translation strains both the Greek and the context: 'nocte in eos incidimus' (6).

33 *The New Oxford Annotated Bible* (New York 1973), with note on p. 85.

34 In the order Onqelos, Jonathan, Neofiti. See too *Mekhilta* pp. 101f, *Mekhilta deRashbi* p. 60, *Midrash Tehillim* 27.1.

35 See C. H. Kraeling, *The Synagogue* (New Haven 1956) 76; Goodenough (above, n. 20) vol. 10.107.

36 So too perhaps Philo, *Moses* 1.176 when he tells of the dark night terrifying the Egyptians.

37 Loewenstamm (above, n. 13) 121, n. 36 believes that the translators of the Bible into Greek read וייאסר as does the Samaritan Pentateuch.
Note postpositive ὡς at 233, as at *Persae* 745.

38 *Mekhilta* pp. 110, 108, 132; *Mekhilta deRashbi* p. 59.

39 For a remarkably similar omen preceding a battle, see Plutarch, *Pompey* 68. Cf. *Bacchae* 1082f.

40 *Mekhilta* p. 95; *Mekhilta deRashbi* p. 55.

41 See Goodenough (above, n. 20) vol. 10, 106f; cf. Kraeling (above, n. 35) 76.

42 κῦμα is a natural addition to the Biblical narrative and one made also by Targ. Jon. *ad* 14.28, גללי ימא.
There is no reason to doubt the δέ *in apodosi* at 237. Wieneke notes a few examples from Homer and tragedy. The use seems most common after temporal dependent clauses, just as here in the *Exagoge*.

43 That verse 28 reports the drowning of the Egyptians and verse 29 the safe passage of the Jews seems to me no more than effective literary technique. The latter verse sums up the experience of the Jews, in stark contrast to that of the Egyptians in 28.

44 *Mekhilta* p. 111. Horowitz-Rabin's choice of האחרון ('the last') is amply supported by the repetition of the exegesis in other Midrashic texts, e.g. *Exod. Rab.* 22.2, *Midrash Tehillim* 18.17, *Yalkut* sect. 237 *ad* 14.26. Cf. however *Mekhilta deRashbi* p. 67.

45 *Mekhilta* p. 113; *Mekhilta deRashbi* p. 69.

46 For a direct quotation within a messenger's speech, Ezekiel had a precedent at *Ajax* 764ff.

47 I am consequently skeptical about seeing any particular theological significance here, as Dalbert does (136).

48 See too *Exod.* 15.12, *Isa.* 63.12, 51.10, *Joshua* 4.24. An interesting Greek parallel occurs at Solon frg. 3.4 D³.

49 *Mekhilta* p. 114, *Mekhilta deRashbi* p. 69, *Deut. Rab.* p. 87 (ed. Liebermann).

50 Wieneke well notes the balance here; eleven lines for the Egyptians (193–203), eleven for the Jews (204–14), more or less!

51 Müller, *PhW* 54 (1934) 704 remarks the similarities between Ezekiel's battle alignment and that in the Ninos romance (frg. BIII Lavagnini) and calls it a thoroughly Hellenistic order (with the introduction of the Biblical chariots in place of elephants). While there do appear to be striking similarities, the condition of the papyrus makes it hard to say how extensive and how significant they are.
φαλαγγικοί at 198 appears to be a *hapax legomenon*. It is not recorded in LSJ, Stephanus–Dindorf, Bauer–Arndt–Gingrich or Lampe. At 201f the manuscripts read (with two words reversed): ἐκ δεξιῶν δὲ πάντας Αἰγυπτίου στρατοῦ./ τὸν πάντα δ' αὐτῶν ἀριθμὸν ἠρόμην ἐγώ {στρατοῦ}. Snell, Wieneke, Gifford and Gutman all retain the text, the latter two translating in (different) ways that violate the Greek, the former two giving no indication how they understand the text. Kappelmacher's paraphrase (73) gives sense, but cannot be got from the Greek: on the left flank 'die Reiterei der Hilfsvölker,' on the right 'die ägyptische.' Dübner (6) translates, 'a dextra autem omnes Aegyptii exercitus milites (*pedites*).' Even if στρατός could be

taken = πεζοί, the sense would be less than desirable (*all* the infantry) since we have already been told of infantrymen in the middle (198). The translation at *REJ* 46 (1903) 69, 'à droite tout le reste de l'armée égyptienne' is sensible, but πάντας does not mean 'tout le reste.' In short, the text seems impossible to me. Stephanus' τινας at least gives sense, though it seems like little more than a weak stopgap. Perhaps for πάντας we should have a word meaning 'the best' *vel sim.*, i.e. some of the cavalry was on the left, but the best was on the right. Ezekiel may have vaguely known that in Greek armies the best troops were generally placed on the right. For ἐξ εὐωνύμων and ἐκ δεξιῶν (phrases apparently not found in Hellenistic and classical texts), see *Exod.* 14.22.

52   The account from 205 on bears some interesting similarities to the messenger speech at *Bacchae* 677ff. Each begins with a picture of exhausted people at rest, ends with the rout (or destruction) of a seemingly more powerful force. Each contains scenes of nurturing, the presence of animals, and miraculous events (θαύματα, θαυμαστά). In each the role of deity is seen in the victory of the weaker. The use of the Bacchants' θύρσος in miraculous ways reminds one of Moses' use of his ῥάβδος. In each case, the speech is the report of a member of the defeated group. There are also a few verbal similarities.

53   Ezekiel is in the tradition of the Septuagint which, in translating חמשים as 'in the fifth generation' (13.18), denies the Jews weapons. So too Philo, Josephus and the source at *PE* 446d (many believe it Demetrius). Midrashic texts (e.g. *Mekhilta* p. 77) and Onqelos understand it to mean 'armed.' The Dura painter (above, n. 20) depicts the Jews at the sea with arms.

I do not see any way of making lines 204ff conform to norms of Greek. οἱ μέν ... οἱ μέν ... αὐτοὶ δέ is very odd (contrast Denniston's description of μέν ... μέν ... δέ at *Particles* 384f). Anyway, what is Ezekiel saying? That some Jews were by the shore and others giving food? Or that the Jews were at the shore (can οἱ μέν tolerate this?), some of whom were providing food? An interesting passage in Hesiod (*WD* 161ff) teems with initially confusing οἱ μέν's, but on second glance they are all intelligible.

54   Gutman (55) and Gifford hold that the men and women are feeding the children. This seems reasonable and natural. I do not, however, think the Greek will bear it. ὁμοῦ τε καί makes it necessary to connect δάμαρσιν with τέκνοισι. Further, δάμαρτες καὶ τέκνα is a regular phrase uniting wives and children as a group dependent on the husband-father. See, e.g., Eur. *HF* 1290,1374; *Tr.* 392. This is somewhat like the Biblical נשים וטף (γυναῖκες καὶ τέκνα [παιδία]).

55   Indeed, the classical tragedians are also indifferent to such jingles. See D. L. Page, *Actors' Interpolations in Greek Tragedy* (Oxford 1934) 124, with special reference to Euripides.

56   Wieneke improves the syntax and lessens difficulties by placing 209 after 206. But I suspect the verbless sentence of 209 is one of Ezekiel's 'Septuagintalisms', the complete sentence with no verb. Cf. here verses 198f.

57   One could argue that he was drawing on *Exod.* 3.22, 11.2, 12.35 where the Jews leave with gold and silver vessels called σκεύη. But σκεῦος is not ἀποσκευή. Ezekiel himself, when he refers to these vessels, uses σκεῦος not ἀποσκευή (164).

58 Remark the repetition of ἀλαλάζω at 211 and 238. At the outset of the confrontation it is the Jews who cry out in despair, at the end the Egyptians. Cf. Jos. *AJ* 2.328.

59 E.g. Kuiper, *Mnemosyne* 260, Wieneke 98f. Snell would add a τε after θεὸν πατρῷον to make the distinction crystal clear (*Glotta* 30f, with 31, n. 4.)

60 Hecataeus of Abdera *apud* Diod. Sic. 40.3.4 (= *FGrHist* 264 F 6); cf. Strabo 16.2.35. Compare Iambulus' description of the inhabitants of the Island of the Sun *apud* Diod. Sic. 2.59.2.

61 Of course the fundamental notion goes back to the Bible. See *1 Kings* 8.54. Agatharchides seems to have conceived of prayer with outstretched hands as characteristic of the Jews (Jos. *Ap.* 1.209). I see no reason to distinguish here between αἰθήρ and οὐρανός. αἰθήρ = οὐρανός is common in Greek poetry.

62 O. Stählin, *Gnomon* 9 (1933) 57 notes the interesting parallel at Clem. Alex. *Ecl. proph.* 10 where θεόν is explicit. There is a curiously similar description in Democritus with reference to certain wise men and their view of the ἀήρ (Diels IIB 30).

63 See Dalbert 56, 64; Trencsényi-Waldapfel 160. To be sure, ὕψιστος is used in Jewish texts, including the LXX, of God. There is (perhaps) a similar rhetorical effect in the passage discussed above (*2 Macc.* 3.31) when the pagan friends of Heliodorus, after his downfall, ask Onias to pray on his behalf to τὸν ὕψιστον.

64 Artapanus too (*PE* 9.436c) makes sure to declare that πάντας perished.

65 See L. H. Feldman in *Religions in Antiquity*, ed. J. Neusner (Leiden 1968) 336ff.

8. The oasis at Elim

1 On κράτιστε as a form of address, which Wieneke believes unparalleled, see Bauer–Arndt–Gingrich s.v. περίρρυτος is Wieneke's convincing emendation of ἐπίρρυτος. Cf. Claudian, *Phoenix* 1, *circumfluus . . . lucus.*

2 P. 115. This is the second of Frankel's two alternative views of this passage, the other being the equally unlikely theory that the Phoenix account does not belong to the *Exagoge* at all.

3 Kappelmacher, seemingly without knowledge of Frankel, argues much the same (81f). Lesky appears to hold the same view (*Hermes* 9).

4 Trencsényi-Waldapfel (151) has also argued against Frankel's view, though he does not utilize what seems to me the most cogent piece of evidence, Polyhistor's testimony. Cf., too, Kraus 168.

5 The only possible instance is *Job* 29.18, on which see most recently M. Dahood, *CBQ* 36 (1974) 85–8.

6 E.g. *Mekhilta* pp. 158f, *Mekhilta deRashbi* p. 105.

7 Ezekiel's πολλά before the precise δεκάκις ἑπτά may be deliberate polemic against those who asserted that seventy was in fact a small number of trees (cf. n. 6).

8 *Tosephta Sukkah* 3.11–13; *Yalkut* sect. 426.

9 E. R. Goodenough, *Jewish Symbols in the Greco-Roman Period*, vol. 10 (1964) 32, n. 25. But in the painting the traditional pastoral landscape (trees, grass, animals, birds) is missing.

10 See Gutman 59f. On Greco-Jewish Utopias, see recently D. Mendels, *HTR* 72 (1979) 207–22.

11 Cf., e.g., *Od.* 4.563ff, Pindar, *O.* 2.68ff, Hdt. 2.138, Soph. *OC* 668ff, Plato, *Critias* 113c9, Dionysius Skytobrachion, Euhemeros, Iambulus (the latter three *apud* Diod. Sic. 3.68f., 5.43ff., 2.55).

12 The genre of Utopia is not always distinct from the motif of the *locus amoenus*. On the latter see G. Schönbeck, *Der locus amoenus von Homer bis Horaz* (Diss. Heidelberg 1962), especially 15–60.

13 *2 Enoch's* paradise, though rather simple, includes the singing of angels (8.3ff; it is a heavenly paradise). Jewish paradises tend to include a 'tree of life.' An interesting paradisical account can be seen in a Qumran Hymn, with streams, trees, fountains, etc. See J. Licht, *The Thanksgiving Scroll* (Jerusalem 1957), Hymn 16, pp. 133ff.

14 Perhaps too because of *Psalm* 92.13 which compares the righteous man to a palm tree (note that *Midrash Tehillim ad loc.* expands this to a comparison of Israel and the palm tree).

15 *Mekhilta* p. 159; Jer. Targ. *ad Exod.* 15.27 and *Nu.* 33.9.

16 *Mekhilta* p. 159.

17 J. Hubaux and M. Leroy, *Le Mythe du Phénix dans les Littératures Grecque et Latine* (Paris 1939) 45 inexplicably imply that Ezekiel had a scene at Marah. So too Trencsényi-Waldapfel 155. No evidence is given nor do I think any could be adduced.

18 See Trencsényi-Waldapfel 155f and my discussion below. The importance of palm trees at Elim may have furthered such an interpretation, since in antiquity Palestine was famous for its date palms. In addition to many references in the Bible and in Rabbinic literature, there are also allusions in pagan texts, e.g. Plut. *Quaest. Conv.* 723c–d; Athen. 14.652a. On the date palm see I. Löw, *Die Flora der Juden*, vol. 2 (Vienna 1924) 306–62, vol. 4 (1934) 537–9.

19 Does he perhaps take εὐφρόνη = εὐφροσύνη?

20 *Exod.* 13.21, *Nu.* 9.15ff. The latter passage seems to indicate that the cloud took on the appearance of fire at night and that the cloud determined the camping places for the wandering people. Cf., too, *Ps.* 105.39 and 78.14. The latter verse is (coincidentally?) followed by a reference to water-spots in the desert. Note too that in Philo (*Moses* 1.166) a cloud guides the people, in daytime shining (ἐκλάμπουσα) like the sun (ἡλιοειδές), at night like fire (φλογοειδές). At *Wisdom* 18.3 God gives them a πυριφλεγῆ στῦλον ὁδηγόν. Ezekiel's ὡς στῦλος πυρός may be related to the Bible's כמראה אש ('like the appearance of fire').

21 The (cloud-) pillar has already played a part at 221f, but it is not till here that it takes on its role as guide for the Jews.

22 *Legends*, vol. 6.16, n. 88. Further, the Phoenix is introduced only after the discovery of Elim.

23 E.g. Aesch. *Cho.* 234; Soph. *OC* 29, 1184, 1670; Eur. *Bacch.* 194, *El.* 105, 232, *Helen* 1038 where it is the last word in the trimeter.

24 *Numbers Rabbah* 16.1; cf. Targ. Jon. *ad Nu.* 21.32.

25 Trencsényi-Waldapfel 158; Gutman 153f.

26 For discussion of this fragment, see my article at *AJP* 102 (1981) 316–20.

27 Cf. Aesch. *PV* 254, Soph. *Ph.* 1339.

28 See KG 1.275; Blass–Debrunner 306.5.
29 The scout reports that they have discovered an amazing creature οἷον οὐδέπω ὡρακέ τις (255). On the hiatus see V. Schmidt, *Sprachliche Untersuchungen zu Herondas* (Berlin 1968) 75, n. 6. This sort of expression was commonly used with regard to creatures and phenomena tied to God in Jewish and semi-Jewish texts. See, e.g., *LAB* 9.8, Philo, *Moses* 1.76, 200, Jos. *AJ* 3.137. A magical papyrus (*PGM* 5.99ff.) has 'Moses' invoke the headless deity, the good Osiris, ὃν οὐδεὶς εἶδε πώποτε (parallel noted by Snell, *Glotta* 26, n. 2; this of course may be quite different from the other examples). A pseudepigraphic fragment from the *Apocalypsis Eliae* (Denis, *Fragmenta* 103) tells us that God has prepared for the faithful ἃ ὀφθαλμὸς οὐκ εἶδεν καὶ οὓς οὐκ ἤκουσεν. See too the texts cited by S. Lieberman, *Greek in Jewish Palestine* (New York 1942) 145, n. 7. But cf. Soph. *Ichn.* 138, τὸν οὐδεὶς πώποτ' ἤκουσεν βροτῶν. Finally, a strange magical text (*PGM* 12) records the incantation, 'I am a palm leaf . . . I am the god whom no one sees . . . I am the holy bird Phoenix' (231). Of course, one might consider Ezekiel's statement Jewish (and anti-Egyptian) polemic: it was for the Jews, not for any Egyptian Pharaoh, that the Phoenix first appeared.
30 Kuiper's far-fetched argument (*Mnemosyne* 275f) that Ezekiel was using a (hypothetical) description of the Phoenix in pseudo-Hecataeus, which is unfortunately repeated by Denis (*Introduction* 276), has justifiably been dismissed by Fraser, vol. 2, 989.
31 In describing at length an unusual bird in a tragedy, Ezekiel once again had a precedent in Aeschylus. See Mette frg. 609a (cf. Pearson Sophocles frg. 581). Another lengthy description of an unusual bird (the Sphinx) was present in Euripides' *Oedipus* (frg. 83 Austin = *POxy* 2459 frg. 1). See too Heliodorus, *Ethiop.* 10.27. The description of the Phoenix at 265 as βασιλεύς . . . ὀρνέων may be influenced by Aeschylus' depiction of the eagle at *Agam.* 113 as οἰωνῶν βασιλεύς. Pliny (*NH* 10.2), Herodotus and Ezekiel all compare the Phoenix to an eagle.
      γαυρόομαι is an appropriate verb for the proud bearing of an animal; cf. Dio Cassius 37.54.2, Heliodorus 3.3. The latter passage, of a horse, also describes the steed's rhythmic gait, τὸ βῆμα κατερρύθμιζεν, which can be compared to Ezekiel's κραιπνὸν βῆμα βαστάζων (269). In comparing the Phoenix to a bull, Ezekiel may have had in mind some Greek text of the sort that underlies Virgil's description at *Georg.* 3.212ff. Is it of any significance that the bull, like the Phoenix, was a sacred Egyptian animal? Finally, the three-word trimeter at 260 is another possible example of Aeschylean influence. The three-word trimeter, though occurring occasionally in Sophocles and Euripides, is present in Aeschylus at a rate of frequency some four or five times higher. Further, about 90% of the three-word trimeters in the three tragedians occur in speeches of over ten lines, which must be the case in Ezekiel also, and they are common in long descriptive passages, as here. On this topic, see W. B. Stanford, *CR* 54 (1940) 8–10; J. Descroix, *Le Trimètre Iambique* (Paris 1931) 75ff.
32 The association of the Phoenix with the eagle might have been facilitated for a Jewish writer by *Psalm* 103.5, 'Your youth is renewed like an eagle's.' Indeed, *Jerahmeel* 22.8 says the Phoenix is revivified like eagles.
33 R. van den Broek, *The Myth of the Phoenix according to Classical and Early Christian Traditions* (Leiden 1971; henceforth 'Broek') 113ff.

34 In the Dura painting of the Exodus there seems to appear a salamander; see C. H. Kraeling, *The Synagogue* (New Haven 1956) 76 (Goodenough (above, n. 9) 107 is skeptical). There are certain similarities between the Phoenix and the salamander, such that at times the two even seem to have been confused (see Broek 207f), mainly in the traditions that each is, in its own way, born out of fire (e.g. *Siphra Shmini* 5–6 (52b), *Exod. Rab.* 15.28, Bab. Talm. *Hulin* 127a, *Hagiga* 27a). Perhaps Philo is referring to the salamander at *QE* 2.28. In other words, the salamander at Dura and the Phoenix in the *Exagoge* may be doublets, each symbolizing the forging and birth of the nation of Israel out of persecution and slavery.

35 I know this text from Broek, to whom and to Hubaux-Leroy I am greatly indebted for material on the Phoenix.

36 Gutman (64) believes that *Assump. Mosis* 1.3 contains a reference to dating by the Phoenix. In fact, the text is so garbled as not to allow for any conclusion as to its sense.

37 *St. Clement of Rome: Two Epistles to the Corinthians* (London 1869) 95f.

38 This tradition must have been an Eastern one since it presents the appearance of the Phoenix in 312, the beginning of the Seleucid calendar.

39 Chaeremon, *FGrHist* 618 F 2. For some connections between the *magnus annus* and the Phoenix, see L. Roberts, *Classical Folia* 32 (1978) 79–89.

40 The Bible is not precise but it appears that Elim is reached toward the end of Nisan.

41 Indeed, a Coptic gnostic text calls the Phoenixes witnesses of the judgment of the fallen angels. See *NH* II 5, 170 (= p. 94).

42 Such is the implication of the text: *NH* II 5, 170 (p. 94).

43 There is, of course, Aristophanes' memorable Cloudcuckooland in the *Birds*.

44 The same is true of Skytobrachion's utopia, filled with lovely singing birds. Kuiper (*Mnemosyne* 276f) notes the connection made between Panchaia and the Phoenix at Pliny, *NH* 10.2 and Solinus 33. But it is hard to draw many conclusions since the connection is slight and not explained or elaborated. It is interesting that Iambulus' Utopia has a 600 year period of importance (Diod. Sic. 2.55), since this is one version of the *magnus annus* (Jos. *AJ* 1.106).

45 *3 Baruch* 10 describes a kind of paradisical plain in the fourth heaven wherein are found a huge crane and many other birds.

46 Leipzig 1796, 814 (first edition London 1663).

47 In addition to the common designation of Phoenix and palm in Greek and Egyptian, I note that Syriac 'תמר' is also used for both the bird and the tree (C. Brockelmann, *Lexicon Syriacum*[2] 828a). The association of the palm with strange bird-like creatures is very ancient, found for example in Assyrian art where palm trees are surrounded by winged, eagle-headed creatures (see E. B. Tylor, *Proc. Soc. Bibl. Arch.* 12 (1890) 383–93). Indeed, the first Temple wall was decorated with alternating palms and cherubim. All this not to mention the Egyptian tradition of the *benu* who resides in the willow tree. Cf. too the *ba* of Osiris (see Griffiths *ad* Plut. *Isis and Osiris* p. 368).

48 *Jerahmeel* 45, *Yalkut* ch. 168, *Divre Hayamim* (Jellinek 2.5–7), Jos. *AJ* 2.10f. In connection with the theme of birds killing snakes, note that there are amulets which seem to show ibises and phoenixes attacking snakes; see Goodenough (above, n. 9), vol. 2 (1953) 242.

49 Compare the enlightening passage at *Mishnah Sukkah* 5.4.
50 See S. Lieberman, *Greek in Jewish Palestine* (New York 1942) 137ff and *Hellenism in Jewish Palestine* (New York 1950) 214f.
51 *PGM* 1.112ff.
52 See Goodenough (above, n. 9) vol. 7 (1958) 114f.
53 Cf. *Ezek.* 8.12. God is often described as He who sees but is not seen (e.g. Jer. Targ. *ad Gen.* 22.14, *Pirqe deRabbi Eliezer* 34, Jer. Talm. *Peia* 21b, Bab. Talm. *Berakhot* 10a). He knows both what is visible and what is hidden (*Maaseh Avraham*, Jellinek 1.26). At *Aristeas* 16 God is πάντων ἐπόπτης. On the other side one notes Greek examples, e.g. *Od.* 11.109, 12.323; Soph. *OC* 869; Aesch. *PV* 91, *Cho.* 985. Cf. *Or. Sib.* 2.177, fr. 1.4, *2 Macc.* 9.5. There may be a conflation of the two notions in Theophrastus *apud* Porphyrius *de abstin.* 2.26 where ὁ πανόπτης could be taken as either God or the sun.
54 On the other hand, it is interesting how completely oblivious to the possibilities Jewish authors could be. Witness the juxtaposition of τὸν μέγιστον θεόν in heaven to the rising of the sun without the slightest sense that some connection might be made by the reader at *3 Macc.* 5.25f.
55 I adduce a verse which seems of clear relevance to the scene in Ezekiel, though I do not know what to make of it and how to tie it in. The Hellenistic poetess Moero told how the baby Zeus was hidden away and nourished by an eagle which fed him nectar drawn from a rock (Athen. 11.491b): νέκταρ δ᾽ ἐκ πέτρης μέγας αἰετὸς αἰὲν ἀφύσσων. In this verse we encounter nearly every crucial word and theme of Ezekiel's Elim–Phoenix episode: the source of nourishment is a (single) rock, the verb is ἀφύσσω, there is an eagle (cf. *Exag.* 256) of large size. It is a tale of divinely ordained (at the least unexpected) nourishment for someone in need and incapable of supplying its (his) own needs. Moreover, in the Moero passage Zeus later rewards the eagle by making it immortal (as, of course, the Phoenix in a sense was).
56 See, e.g., Trencsényi-Waldapfel 154f, Gutman 147–54.
57 There is almost no likelihood that the play treated the long journey to the promised land, as is suggested by M. Patin, *Études sur les Tragiques Grecs*: *Eschyle* 1 (Paris 1890[7]) 159, and F. Momigliano, *Nuova Rassegna* 1 (1893) 312.
58 So Kuiper, *Mnemosyne* 270, followed by Kappelmacher 81f and Wieneke 108f.
59 See Commentary, sect. 6.
60 E. R. Goodenough, *By Light Light* (New Haven 1935) 220–2.

NOTES TO THE APPENDIX

1 *Hermes* 81 (1953) 1–10.
2 See the statistics in E. B. Ceadel, *CQ* 35 (1941) 88f, with footnotes.
3 I assume throughout that the Gyges tragedy is Hellenistic, as most scholars now believe. I have, with several exceptions, avoided referring to *POxy* 2746 since its metrical nature is still subject to dispute. See B. Gentili, *Lo Spettacolo nel Mondo Antico* (Bari 1977) 70ff.
4 For the *Exagoge* I rely mainly on Strugnell's statistics which differ slightly

from Wieneke's. I do not think the differences have any substantial effect on anything I say. Similarly, I use Ceadel's statistics for the tragedians which exclude proper nouns, although Wieneke includes them. I trust that no mis-representations have arisen from this fact.

5   T. Zielinski, 'De Trimetri Euripidei Evolutione,' in his *Tragodumenon Libri Tres* (Cracow 1925) 133–240.

6   Zielinski 141.

7   See C. Collard, *JHS* 90 (1970) 30. But Collard is in error when he calls Chaeremon's 40% a bit higher than late Euripides (35–38%). He fails to realize that Zielinski's statistics do not include first foot anapests which, when counted, raise late Euripides to 43–49%.

8   The foot-by-foot statistics are set out very nicely in comparative charts by Strugnell. For a detailed foot-by-foot breakdown of the use of resolution in Ezekiel and the other minor tragedians, see C. F. Müller's monograph *De Pedibus Solutis in Tragicorum Minorum Trimetris Iambicis* (Kiliae 1879).

9   Wieneke counts 25 first foot anapests for a total of 28. Yet, a few lines earlier he speaks of 30. Perhaps he erroneously counted in the anapests at 165 and 206 which he rightly rejects. Or possibly he includes the third foot anapest at 74 which he prints but does not include in his count of anapests outside the first foot.

10 I record here Müller's conjecture (above, n. 8, p. 74) which seems to have escaped the notice of students and editors of the *Exagoge*: δ' ἐμοί τ' ἔδωκε.

11 Here too I record the unnoticed conjecture of Müller (18) βατράχων τε πλῆθος κἀμβαλῶ σκνῖπας χθονί.

12 Tragedy, of course, uses them also outside the first foot, in the case of names. For a discussion of passages in Aeschylus, Sophocles and Euripides where the manuscripts do give anapests other than in the first foot, see C. F. Müller, *De Pedibus Solutis in Dialogorum Senariis Aeschyli, Sophoclis, Euripidis* (Berlin 1866) 121–5, 129–33, 140–7.

13 E.g. *Bacch.* 285, *Or.* 2. See Müller (above, n. 8) 11 and Dodds *ad Bacch.* 192. See too *POxy* 2746, line 10, *if* this be the beginning of an iambic trimeter.

14 Ezekiel prefers dactyls to tribrachs in the third foot by about 2.5:1 (24:10: Strugnell). The three tragedians usually show a far greater preference. The *Persae* however shows only 2:1.

15 Wieneke called attention to 163 and 174, Snell to these two and 62 and 233, Strugnell to all six.

16 In the following discussion I am speaking of the usage as found in Aeschylus, Sophocles and Euripides.

17 E.g. Soph. *Phil.* 22, *Ajax* 1101; Eur. *Heraclidae* 529; many instances of elided forms of trochaic words, especially forms of ὅδε. See Dodds *ad Bacch.* 246.

18 *Eirene* 2 (1964) 43–56, especially 55.

19 If correct, then I suppose that *Didot Rhesis* 10 (*GLP* 184) καίτα γ' ὦ πάτερ might similarly not violate the canon (*contra* D. L. Page *ad loc*).

20 Porson himself did not remark this qualification. See his 1824 edition of the *Hecuba, Supplementum ad Praefationem* xxxii ff.

21 I have argued in the Commentary, sect. 6 that there are other reasons as well for reading τῆς ... νυκτός at 158.

22 See my discussion in the Introduction, sect. 9.

23 V. Schmidt, *Sprachliche Untersuchungen zu Herondas* (Berlin 1968) 75, n. 6.

24 This is not a completely cogent argument. There may be elision of dative singular ι in tragedy (for a list of possible instances see Jebb's edition of the *Oedipus Coloneus* pp. 289f). At all events, there is in the Hellenistic period, e.g. Lycophron 894, 918. Thus, once we assume that Ezekiel was not following fifth-century practice here, there is no reason to believe that he would have considered νυκτί as unelidable.

25 W. Christ, *Metrik der Griechen und Römer* (Leipzig 1874) 33 cites many examples from Homer, one from Hesiod and one (or two) from Pindar.

26 These are Lesky's statistics (above, n. 1), p. 4.

27 Lesky counts 43:28.

28 See, e.g., frgs. 6 and 9 of Moschion, the Gyges-play.

29 For a full list see Lesky 5.

30 For discussions of the possible examples see Dale *ad Alcestis* 542, Barrett *ad Hipp.* 760, D. L. Page, *A New Chapter in the History of Greek Tragedy* (Cambridge 1951) 43, n. 22. One possibility is at *Persae* 782.

31 E.g. Lycophron 1056, 1250, Gyges papyrus col. ii, 5.

32 Snell follows Dindorf and others in 'emending' to ἀπέστειλεν, but since Ezekiel does it once with ε + κρ, there is no reason to doubt a second instance.

33 Above, n. 30, p. 44, n. 25. Of the three examples in Aeschylus one is at *Persae* 395, a second at *Suppl.* 624.

34 *GLP* 172ff, verse 19. See too *POxy* 2746, lines 11 & 17.

35 Unless one chooses to emend a line that seems quite in order as regards sense, style and context, 164 is a puzzle: σκεύη κόσμον τε πάνθ'. E. Harrison, *CR* 47 (1933) 85 accused Wieneke of not noticing the spondee in the second foot. In fact, Wieneke was fully aware, but thought Ezekiel was considering the first syllable of κόσμον short here (unlike in 16) (p. 116). This would be most strange and I do not know whether even possible. The only near-parallel I know of is Pindar's wavering between ἐσλός and ἐσλός (e.g. short at *Pyth.* 3.66, *Nem.* 4.95, *Ol.* 13.96 (100); long at *Pyth.* 8.73, *Nem.* 2.21). If we feel compelled to emend, Snell (in his *ap. crit.*) and J. Diggle, *GRBS* 14 (1973) 264 n. 62 have offered suggestions.

36 On the former side, see J. Descroix, *Le Trimètre Iambique des Iambographes à la Comédie Nouvelle* (Paris 1931) 262f; T. G. Tucker, *The Choephoroi of Aeschylus* (Cambridge 1901) 259. On the latter, see T. D. Goodell, *CP* 1 (1906) 145–66 and now G. Stephan, *Hermes* 108 (1980) 402–18.

37 On the scansion of 105 see Snell, *Glotta* 28. Strugnell (450, n. 5) differs. On the pattern of 97, see Fraenkel's comments *ad Agam.* 943.

38 Soph. *Tr.* 216 (lyric) and Eur. *IT* 679 are disputed.

39 The form itself is attested, e.g. Thucyd. 1.132, Isocr. 5.63, possibly Hdt. 9.109 (Ionic).

40 Lycoph. 850, 1220, *Didot Rhesis* (tragedy?) *GLP* 188, verse 44.

41 It is fairly frequent in comedy. See J. W. White, *The Verse of Greek Comedy* (London 1912) 367 (sect. 801).

42 See Schmidt (above, n. 23) 23, n. 16; 94, n. 20. Perhaps in ευ the second vowel had already begun to be treated virtually as a consonant. See Schwyzer vol. 1, 197f and R. Browning, *Medieval and Modern Greek* (London 1969) 32.

43 In some usages there may even be what looks like comic practice, e.g. hiatus, violations of Porson's Law, split dactyl.
44 This would be much the same whether he read with his eyes or aloud. Reading aloud to one's self is not the same as hearing a text recited by others, especially by trained readers/actors. On the existence of silent reading in antiquity, a practice that was for very long considered by scholars impossible or abnormal, see B. M. W. Knox, *GRBS* 9 (1968) 421–35.

LIST OF ABBREVIATIONS

(*excluding those given in sections III and IV of the Select Bibliography*)

AC	*L'Antiquité Classique*
AJP	*American Journal of Philology*
BAGB (SC)	*Bulletin de l'Association G. Budé: Supplément Critique*
BZAW	*Zeitschrift für die Alttestamentliche Wissenschaft: Beihefte*
CBQ	*Catholic Biblical Quarterly*
CP	*Classical Philology*
CQ	*Classical Quarterly*
CR	*Classical Review*
DLZ	*Deutsche Literatur-Zeitung*
GGA	*Göttingische Gelehrte Anzeigen*
G & R	*Greece & Rome*
GRBS	*Greek, Roman and Byzantine Studies*
HSCP	*Harvard Studies in Classical Philology*
HTR	*Harvard Theological Review*
HUCA	*Hebrew Union College Annual*
ICS	*Illinois Classical Studies*
JbAC	*Jahrbuch für Antike und Christentum*
JANES	*Journal of the Ancient Near Eastern Society of Columbia University*
Jahrb. f. *jüd. Gesch.*	*Jahrbuch für jüdische Geschichte und Literatur*
JBL	*Journal of Biblical Literature*
JHS	*Journal of Hellenic Studies*
JJS	*Journal of Jewish Studies*
JQR	*Jewish Quarterly Review*
JR	*Journal of Religion*
JSS	*Jewish Social Studies*
JTS	*Journal of Theological Studies*
LCM	*Liverpool Classical Monthly*
LTK	*Lexikon für Theologie und Kirche*
MGWJ	*Monatsschrift für Geschichte und Wissenschaft des Judenthums*
MH	*Museum Helveticum*
NBGAW	*Neue Beiträge zur Geschichte der alten Welt*
NJb	*Neue Jahrbücher für das klassische Altertum*
NJbWiss	*Neue Jahrbücher für Wissenschaft und Jugendbildung*
NT	Novum Testamentum
PhW	*Philologische Wochenschrift*
Proc. Soc. *Bibl. Arch.*	*Proceedings of the Society of Biblical Archaeology*
REfProt. *Theol.*	*Realencyklopädie für protestantische Theologie und Kirche*

REJ	*Revue des Études Juives*
RhM	*Rheinisches Museum*
RPh	*Revue de Philologie*
RSA	*Rivista di Storia Antica*
SBL Seminar	
Papers	*Society of Biblical Literature Seminar Papers*
SCI	*Scripta Classica Israelica*
TU	Texte und Untersuchungen zur Geschichte der altchristlichen Literatur
WS	*Wiener Studien*
ZATW	*Zeitschrift für die alttestamentliche Wissenschaft*
ZDMG	*Zeitschrift der Deutschen Morgenländischen Gesellschaft*

SELECT BIBLIOGRAPHY

I. The following works provide complete texts of the *Exagoge*. I refer to them frequently in abbreviated form (usually by editor's name).

Denis, A. M. *Fragmenta Pseudepigraphorum Quae Supersunt Graeca* (Leiden 1970).
Dübner, F. *Christus Patiens, Ezechieli et Christianorum Poetarum Reliquiae Dramaticae* (Paris 1846).
Kuiper, K. '*De Ezechiele Poeta Iudaeo,' Mnemosyne* n.s. 28 (1900) 237–80.
'Le Poète Juif Ezéchiel,' *REJ* 46 (1903) 48–73.
Philippson, L. M. *Ezechiel des jüdischen Trauerspieldichters Auszug aus Egypten und Philo des aelteren Jerusalem* (Berlin 1830).
Poetae Graeci Veteres (Geneva 1614) vol. 1, 1017–22.
Snell, B. *Tragicorum Graecorum Fragmenta* vol. 1 (Göttingen 1971).
Stearns, W. N. *Fragments from Graeco-Jewish Writers* (Chicago 1908).
Wieneke, J. *Ezechielis Judaei Poetae Alexandrini Fabulae Quae Inscribitur Exagoge Fragmenta* (Diss. Münster 1931).

II. The text of the *Exagoge* is preserved in Eusebius' *Praeparatio Evangelica* (Eusebii Pamphili *Evangelicae Praeparationis* Libri XV) 9.436ff. I often cite the following editions of the *PE* by editor's name alone.

Dindorf, G. (Leipzig 1867).
Gaisford, T. (Oxford 1843), with Latin translation of F. Viger.
Gifford, E. H. (Oxford 1903).
Mras, K. (Berlin 1954 and 1956).
Stephanus, R. (Lutetia 1544).

III. The following works of reference are cited frequently, often by author's name or in some other abbreviated fashion.

Austin, C. *Nova Fragmenta Euripidea in Papyris Reperta* (Berlin 1968).
Blass, F. and Debrunner, A. *Grammatik des neutestamentlichen Griechisch*, rev. by F. Rehkopf (Göttingen 1976[14]).
Corpus Papyrorum Judaicarum, edd. V. A. Tcherikover and A. Fuks, vol. 1 (Cambridge, Mass. 1957), vol. 2 (1960), vol. 3 (with M. Stern, 1964) [= *CPJ*].
Denniston, J. D. *The Greek Particles* (Oxford 1953[2]) [= *Particles*].
Encyclopaedia Judaica (Jerusalem 1972) [= *EJ*].
Ginzberg, L. *The Legends of the Jews* (repr. Philadelphia 1968) [= *Legends*].
Jewish Encyclopaedia (New York 1901–6) [= *JE*].
Kühner, R. and Gerth, B. *Ausführliche Grammatik der griechischen Sprache* (repr. Darmstadt 1966) [= *KG*].
Liddell, H. G., Scott, R. and Jones, H. S. *A Greek-English Lexicon*, ninth ed. with supplement (Oxford 1968) [= LSJ].

Mette, H. J. *Die Fragmenta der Tragödien des Aischylos* (Berlin 1959).
Oxford Classical Dictionary (Oxford 1970[2]) [= *OCD*].
Real-Encyclopädie der classischen Altertumswissenschaft (Stuttgart 1894–)
    [= *RE*].
Schürer, E. *Geschichte des jüdischen Volkes im Zeitalter Jesu Christi*, vol. 3
    (Leipzig 1909[4]).
Schwyzer, E. and Debrunner, A. *Griechische Grammatik*, vol. 2 (Munich 1975[4]).
Tragicorum Graecorum Fragmenta, ed. A. Nauck (Leipzig 1889[2]) [= *TGF*].
Tragicorum Graecorum Fragmenta, vol. 1 ed. B. Snell (Göttingen 1971) [= *TrGF*].

IV. Jewish primary sources in languages other than Greek.

A. *Talmudic literature*

Babylonian Talmud: *Talmud Bavli* (repr. New York 1965).
Jerusalem Talmud: *Talmud Yerushalmi* (Krotoschin edit.; repr. Jerusalem 1969).
Mishna: *Shishah Sidre Mishna*, edd. H. Albeck and H. Yalon (Jerusalem 1952–9).
Tosephta: *Tosephta*, ed. M. S. Zuckermandel (repr. Jerusalem 1963).
    Tosefta, ed. S. Lieberman (New York 1955–   ).

B. *Aramaic translations of the Bible* (Targumim)

Onqelos: A. Sperber, *The Bible in Aramaic*, vol. I: *The Pentateuch According to
    Targum Onkelos* (Leiden 1959).
Jonathan: M. Ginsburger, *Targum Pseudo-Jonathan ben Usiel zum Pentateuch*
    (Berlin 1903).
Jerusalem: M. Ginsburger, *Das Fragmententhargum* (Berlin 1899).
Neofiti: A. Díez Macho, *Neophyti 1*, vol. *II Éxodo* (Madrid 1970).
See too the Biblia Rabbinica volumes for the Pentateuch.

C. *Midrashic texts and collections*

Aboth deRabbi Nathan, ed. S. Schechter (repr. New York 1967) [= ARN].
Asatir, ed. M. Gaster (London 1927).
Eisenstein, J. D. *Ozar Midrashim* (repr. Jerusalem 1969).
Jellinek, A. *Bet haMidrasch* (repr. Jerusalem 1967[3]).
Jerahmeel, The Chronicles of, ed. M. Gaster (London 1899).
Liber Antiquitatum Biblicarum: G. Kisch (ed.), *Pseudo-Philo's Liber
    Antiquitatum Biblicarum* (Notre Dame 1949) [= *LAB*].
    M. R. James, *The Biblical Antiquities of Philo*, with Prolegomenon by L. H.
    Feldman (New York 1971).
Lekach-Tob, ed. S. Buber (Wilna 1884).
Mechilta d'Rabbi Ismael, ed. H. S. Horovitz and I. A. Rabin (Jerusalem 1960[2])
    [= *Mekhilta*].
Mekhilta d'Rabbi Simon b. Jochai, ed. J. N. Epstein and E. Z. Melamed (Jerusalem
    1955) [= *Mekhilta d'Rashbi*].
Midrash Bereshit Rabba, ed. J. Theodor and C. Albeck (Jerusalem 1965[2]).
Midrash Debarim Rabbah, ed. S. Liebermann (Jerusalem 1974[3]).
Midrash Haggadol on the Pentateuch, five volumes (Jerusalem 1946–76).
Midrash Rabbah (Wilna edition; Tel Aviv 1961).
Midrasch Tannaim, ed. D. Hoffmann (Berlin 1909).
Midrasch Tehillim, ed. S. Buber (Wilna 1891).
Pesikta Rabbati, ed. M. Friedmann (Vienna 1880).

Pesikta deRav Kahana, ed. B. Mandelbaum (New York 1962).
Pirqe deRabbi Eliezer (Venice edition; repr. Jerusalem 1973).
Seder Eliahu Rabba and Seder Eliahu Zuta, ed. M. Friedmann (repr. Jerusalem 1960²).
Sepher Hajascher, ed. L. Goldschmidt (Berlin 1923) [= *Sepher Hayashar*].
Siphra d'Be Rab, ed. I. H. Weiss (New York 1946).
Siphre d'Be Rab, ed. H. S. Horovitz (Jerusalem 1966).
Sifre on Deuteronomy, ed. L. Finkelstein (New York 1969).
Tanhuma, ed. E. Zundel (repr. Jerusalem 1972).
Tanhuma, ed. S. Buber (repr. Jerusalem 1964).
Wertheimer, S. A. *Batei Midrashot* (repr. Jerusalem 1968²).
Yalkut Shimoni (repr. Jerusalem 1960).

V. Books, monographs and articles. Those works frequently cited in abbreviated fashion (usually by author's name) are preceded by an asterisk.

Bähr, C. F. in Pauly's *RE* vol. 3 (Stuttgart 1844) 365, s.v. Ezechiel.
Bayle, P. *Dictionnaire Historique et Critique* (Basle 1741⁶).
Bergmann, J. *Jüdische Apologetik im neutestamentlichen Zeitalter* (Berlin 1908).
Bickerman, E. *Studies in Jewish and Christian History*, vol. 1 (Leiden 1976).
Bochart, S. *Hierozoicon* (Leipzig 1796).
Broyde, I. 'Ezekielus,' *JE* 5.320.
Cancik, H. 'Ezechiel,' *Lexikon der alten Welt* (Zürich 1965) 936.
Cazelles, H. (ed.). *Moise: L'Homme de l'Alliance* (Paris 1955).
Cobet, C. G. 'Diorthotika eis ta tou Klementos tou Alexandreos' pt. 3, *Logios Hermes* 1 (1866-7) 425-534.
*Dalbert, P. *Die Theologie der hellenistisch-jüdischen Missionsliteratur unter Ausschluss von Philo und Josephus* (Hamburg 1954).
Delitzsch, F. *Zur Geschichte der jüdischen Poësie* (Leipzig 1836).
*Denis, A. M. *Introduction aux Pseudépigraphes Grecs d'Ancien Testament* (Leiden 1970).
*Dieterich, A. 'Ezechiel,' *RE* 6.2, 1701-2.
Eichhorn, I. G. 'De Judaeorum Re Scenica Commentatio,' *Commentationes Soc. Reg. Sc. Gottingensis recentiores* 2, 1811 (Göttingen 1813).
Feldman, L. H. 'The Orthodoxy of the Jews in Hellenistic Egypt,' *JSS* 22 (1960) 215-37.
 Scholarship on Philo and Josephus (1937-62) (New York 1963?)
  *Prolegomenon to M. R. James, *The Biblical Antiquities of Philo* (New York 1971) [= Feldman, *LAB*].
*Frankel, Z. *Ueber den Einfluss der palästinischen Exegese auf die alexandrinische Hermeneutik* (Leipzig 1851).
*Fraser, P. M. *Ptolemaic Alexandria* (Oxford 1972).
*Freudenthal, J. *Hellenistische Studien: Alexander Polyhistor* (Breslau 1875).
*Freyhan, M. 'Ezechiel der Tragiker,' *Jahrbuch für jüdische Geschichte und Literatur* 31 (1938) 46-83.
Gager, J. G. *Moses in Greco-Roman Paganism* (Nashville 1972).
Gaster, M. *The Samaritans* (London 1925).
*Girardi, G. B. *Di un Dramma Greco-Giudaico nell'Età Alessandrina* (Venice 1902).

Goodenough, E. R. *By Light Light: The Mystic Gospel of Hellenistic Judaism* (New Haven 1935).

Jewish Symbols in the Greco-Roman Period, vol. 5 (New York 1956).

*Gutman, Y. *The Beginnings of Jewish-Hellenistic Literature*, vol. 2 (Jerusalem 1963: Hebrew).

*(= J. Gutmann). 'Ezekielus,' *Encyclopaedia Judaica*, vol. 6 (Berlin 1930) 885-7 [= Gutmann, *EJ*].

Hadas, M. *Hellenistic Culture: Fusion and Diffusion* (New York 1959).

Harris, J. R. *The Homeric Centones and the Acts of Pilate* (London 1898).

Heinemann, I. *Philons griechische und jüdische Bildung* (repr. Hildesheim 1973).

Hengel, M. 'Anonymität, Pseudepigraphie und "literarische Fälschung" in der jüdisch-hellenistischen Literatur,' *Fondation Hardt Entretiens*, vol. 18: *Pseudepigrapha I* (Geneva 1972), 231-308 (with discussion on pp. 309-29).

Juden, Griechen und Barbaren (Stuttgart 1976).

Judentum und Hellenismus (Tübingen 1973[2]).

*Herzfeld, L. *Geschichte des Volkes Jisrael*, vol. 2 (Nordhaufen 1857).

Holladay, C. R. 'The Portrait of Moses in Ezekiel the Tragedian,' *SBL 1976 Seminar Papers* (Missoula 1976) 447-52.

Hubaux, J. and Leroy, M. *Le Mythe du Phénix dans les Littératures Grecque et Latine* (Paris 1939).

Huet, P. D. *Demonstratio Evangelica* (Paris 1690[3]).

Hurwitz, M. S. 'Ezekiel the Poet,' *EJ* 6.1102-3.

Jacobson, H. 'Ezekielos 12-13 (TrGF 128),' *AJP* 98 (1977) 415-16.

'Ezekiel the Tragedian and the Primeval Serpent,' *AJP* 102 (1981) 316-20.

'The Identity and Role of Chum in Ezekiel's *Exagoge*,' *HSL* 9 (1981) 139-46.

'Mysticism and Apocalyptic in Ezekiel's *Exagoge*,' *ICS* 6 (1981) 272-93.

'Two Studies on Ezekiel the Tragedian,' *GRBS* 22 (1981) 167-78.

*Kappelmacher, A. 'Zur Tragödie der hellenistischen Zeit,' *WS* 44 (1924-5) 69-86.

Klein, J. L. *Geschichte des Drama's*, vol. 2 (Leipzig 1865).

*Kraus, C. 'Ezechiele Poeta Tragico,' *RFIC* 96 (1968) 164-75.

(Kraus Reggiani). 'Per una Revisione di Ezechiele Tragico in Chiave Aristotelica,' *Vichiana* 4 (1975) 3-21.

*Kuiper, K. 'Ad Ezechielem Poetam Judaeum Curae Secundae,' *RSA* 8 (1904) 62-94 [= Kuiper, *RSA*].

*'De Ezechiele Poeta Judaeo,' *Mnemosyne* n.s. 28 (1900) 237-80 [= Kuiper, *Mnemosyne*].

*'Le Poète Juif Ezéchiel,' *REJ* 46 (1903) 48-73, 161-77 [= Kuiper, *REJ*].

*Lesky, A. Review of Wieneke, *DLZ* 53 (1932) 2217-21.

'Das hellenistische Gyges-Drama,' *Hermes* 81 (1953) 1-10.

Lieberman, S. *Greek in Jewish Palestine* (New York 1942).

Hellenism in Jewish Palestine (New York 1950).

Loewenstamm, S. E. *The Tradition of the Exodus in its Development* (Jerusalem 1972[2]: Hebrew).

*Magnin, C. Review of Dübner, *Journal des Savants* 1848, 193-208.

Marcus, R. 'Hellenistic Jewish Literature,' in L. Finkelstein (ed.), *The Jews* (New York 1960[3]) 2.1077-1115.

'Jewish and Greek Elements in the Septuagint,' in A. Marx (ed.), *Louis Ginzberg Jubilee Volume* (New York 1945) 227-45.

Momigliano, A. *Alien Wisdom: The Limits of Hellenization* (Cambridge 1975).
Momigliano, F. 'Il Primo Dramma d'Argomento Sacro,' *La Nuova Rassegna* 1 (1893) 309-15.
Müller, B. A. Review of Wieneke, *PhW* 54 (1934) 701-2.
Müller, C. F. *De Pedibus Solutis in Tragicorum Minorum Trimetris Iambicis* (Kiliae 1879).
Page, D. L. *A New Chapter in the History of Greek Tragedy* (Cambridge 1951).
Petsch, R. 'Ein Mosedrama aus hellenistischer Zeit,' *NJbWiss* 1 (1925) 803-7.
*Philippson, L. M. *Ezechiel des jüdischen Trauerspieldichters Auszug aus Egypten und Philo des aelteren Jerusalem* (Berlin 1830).
*Riessler, P. *Altjüdisches Schrifttum ausserhalb der Bibel* (Augsburg 1928).
Schmidt, V. *Sprachliche Untersuchungen zu Herondas* (Berlin 1968).
Schumann, G. A. 'Vita Mosis,' in *Commentationes Theologicae*, edd. Rosenmueller and Maurer (Leipzig 1827) vol. 2, 187-274.
Segal, J. B. *The Hebrew Passover* (London 1963).
*Snell, B. 'Die Jamben in Ezechiels Moses-Drama,' *Glotta* 44 (1966) 25-32 [= Snell, *Glotta*].
Szenen aus griechischen Dramen (Berlin 1971) [= Snell or Snell, *Szenen*].
Stählin, O. Review of Wieneke, *Gnomon* 9 (1933) 56-8.
Starobinski-Safran, E. 'Un Poète Judéo-Hellénistique: Ezéchiel le Tragique,' *MH* 31 (1974) 216-24.
*Strugnell, J. 'Notes on the Text and Metre of Ezekiel the Tragedian's *Exagoge*,' *HTR* 60 (1967) 449-57.
Tcherikover, V. *Hellenistic Civilization and the Jews* (repr. New York 1970).
'Jewish Apologetic Literature Reconsidered,' *Eos* 48.3 (1956) 169-93.
Tiede, D. L. *The Charismatic Figure as Miracle Worker* (Missoula 1972).
*Trencsényi-Waldapfel, I. 'Une Tragédie Grecque à Sujet Biblique,' *Acta Orientalia* 2 (1952) 143-64.
Van den Broek, R. *The Myth of the Phoenix According to Classical and Early Christian Traditions* (Leiden 1971).
Van der Horst, P. W. 'De Joodse toneelschrijver Ezechiël', *Nederlands Theologisch Tijdschrift* 36 (1982) 97-112.
Venini, P. 'Note sulla Tragedia Ellenistica,' *Dioniso* n.s. 16 (1953) 3-26.
Vermes, G. *Scripture and Tradition in Judaism* (Leiden 1961).
*Wacholder, B. Z. *Eupolemus: A Study of Judaeo-Greek Literature* (Cincinnati 1974).
'Pseudo-Eupolemus' Two Greek Fragments on the Life of Abraham,' *HUCA* 34 (1963) 83-113.
Walter, N. *Der Thoraausleger Aristobulos* (Berlin 1964 = TU 86).
'Zur Überlieferung einiger Reste früher jüdisch-hellenistischer Literatur bei Josephus, Clemens und Euseb,' *Studia Patristica* 7 (1966 = TU 92) 314-20.
Walters, P. and Gooding, D. W. *The Text of the Septuagint* (Cambridge 1973).
Weinreich, O. 'Gebet und Wunder,' in *Genethliakon Wilhelm Schmid* (Stuttgart 1929) 169-464.
*Wieneke, J. *Ezechielis Judaei Poetae Alexandrini Fabulae Quae Inscribitur Exagoge Fragmenta* (Diss. Münster 1931).
Wolfson, H. A. *Philo* (Cambridge, Mass. 1947).
*Ziegler, K. 'Tragoedia,' *RE* 6A.2, 1899-2075.
Zwierlein, O. *Die Rezitationsdramen Senecas* (Meisenheim am Glan 1966 = Beiträge zur klassischen Philologie vol. 20).

INDICES

1. INDEX NOMINUM ET RERUM

Cush, 87, 198 n. 17
Cyrenaica, 15
Cyrus, 96

Danaids, 24–5, 88
Danaus, 25, 144, 185 n. 9
Daniel, 92
David, 94
Dead Sea scrolls, 21, 210 n. 26
Dedan, 86–7
deictic pronouns, 189 n. 33
Demetrius, 7, 22, 72, 86–7, 184 n. 18, 189
    n. 6, 194 nn. 11, 13, 199 n. 18, 216 n. 53
Demetrius of Phalerum, 16
Despotes, 124, 213 n. 8
Deuteronomy, 130, 210 n. 27
Dionysius Skytobrachion, 218 n. 11, 220 n.
    44
Dires de Moise, 126
dramatic convention, 29
dreams, 89–97
dual form, 157
Dura painter, 141, 146, 148–9, 154, 216 n.
    53, 220 n. 34
Dymas of Iasos, 4

Egyptians, native, 8, 25, 126, 135
Elephantine, 135, 184 n. 26
Elijah, 142
Elim, 152–66
Elisha, 142
Ennius, 27
2 Enoch, 180 n. 5
Ephren, 87
2 Esdras, 95
Eselskult, 211 n. 34
Ethiopians, 85–7
etiology, 125–6, 131–2, 209 nn. 13, 15, 211
    n. 33
etymology, 69, 77, 89, 101, 180 n. 4, 195
    n. 32, 212 n. 46
Euhemeros, 156, 161, 218 n. 11
Eupolemus, 7, 11, 22–3, 26, 37, 177 n. 10,
    180 nn. 12, 13, 189 n. 6
Euripides, 23–4, 30, 69–70, 88, 99, 136,
    167–9, 171–2, 185 nn. 1, 5, 7, 186 nn.
    25, 26, 187 n. 37, 187 n. 6, 188 n. 11,
    193 n. 2, 197 n. 52, 208 n. 8, 212 n. 59,
    213 n. 3, 216 n. 55, 219 n. 31, 222 nn.
    7, 12, 16
Eurybates, 157
Eusebius (*PE*), 1, 5, 7, 31, 36–7, 77, 97, 105,
    122, 136, 164–5, 189 n. 4, 195 n. 34,
    206 n. 1, 208 n. 1

Ezekiel: believed to be christian, 5; date of,
    5–13; both Greek and Jew, 3, 140; his
    Hebrew name, 5, 15–17, 180 n. 14; his
    influence, 36–9, 104, 151–2, 194 n. 24,
    195 n. 26, 199 n. 19; his Jewish plays, 5;
    provenance of, 13–17
Ezekiel's *Exagoge*: apologetics in, 102–3,
    126–7, 134–5, 151, 156, 182 n. 4; its
    audience, 8, 17–20, 25, 80, 99–100, 111,
    115, 124, 131, 134–5, 144, 147, 156,
    162, 164, 165, 194 nn. 10, 16; chorus in,
    24, 31–3, 88, 139; classical tragedians,
    influence of on, 7, 23–8, 30, 167–73;
    Egyptian reaction to, 13–14; errors in,
    13, 86; evaluations of, 2–3; exegesis of
    the Bible in, 18, 20–3, 41 and passim in
    the Commentary; faithfulness to Biblical
    text, 18–19, 29, 34, 79–80, 98, 101,
    114–16, 134–5, 156; Hebrew and Hebrew
    Bible, use of in, 40–7, 81–5, 128, 150,
    162, 170, 210 n. 25; and Hellenistic
    tragedy, 1, 31, 34, 167–73, 186 n. 14;
    medieval Hebrew translation of, 199 n. 2;
    metre and prosody, 131, 167–73, 192 n.
    24, 206 n. 5, 209 n. 16, 211 nn. 38, 40,
    219 n. 29; polemic against, 38–9, 152,
    189 n. 7; purpose of, 17–20, 134–6, 151,
    156, 219 n. 29; religious position of, 17–
    20; scenery in, 31; Septuagint, use of in,
    40–2, 81–2, 128, 150, 203 n. 16 and
    passim; stagecraft in, 98–9, 105, 112,
    136; structure of, 28–36, 121–4, 165–6
    and passim; style and language of, 12–13,
    23–4, 42–7, 70, 93, 98, 104–5, 115, 123,
    130, 131, 133, 144, 150, 158, 185 nn. 7,
    8, 193 nn. 41, 42, 207 n. 6, 208 n. 3,
    210 n. 29, 211 nn. 41, 44, 215 nn. 42,
    50, 216 nn. 53, 56
Ezekiel, one of the Seventy, 6

first-born sacrifice, 130–1
first-fruits ritual, 71
five-act drama, 28, 33–4, 164, 188 n. 30

Gamaliel, 20
Genesis, 155
Genesis Apocryphon, 18
God on stage, 18, 20
God, voice of, 99–100
Gyges play, 4, 27, 167, 171, 189 n. 3, 193 n.
    3, 202 n. 44, 221 n. 3, 223 nn. 28, 31

Hadrian, Edict of, 212 n. 54
Hallel, 109

2. INDEX LOCORUM

PAGAN TEXTS

APOCRYPHA AND PSEUDEPIGRAPHA

Made in United States
North Haven, CT
20 March 2024

50264069R00161